QUEENS OF NOISE

ALSO BY EVELYN McDONNELL

Mamarama: A Memoir of Sex, Kids, and Rock 'n' Roll

Army of She: Icelandic, Iconoclastic, Irrepressible Björk

Rock She Wrote: Women Write about Rock, Pop, and Rap
(co-editor with Ann Powers)

QUEENS OF NOISE

The Real Story of
THE RUNAWAYS

Evelyn McDonnell

DA CAPO PRESS
A Member of the Perseus Books Group

Printed in the United States of America.

For information, address Da Capo Press, 44 Farnsworth Street, 3rd Floor,
Boston, MA 02210.

Set in 11.5 point Adobe Caslon Pro by Marcovaldo Productions for the
Perseus Books Group

Cataloging-in-Publication data for this book is available from the Library of
Congress.
First Da Capo Press edition 2013
ISBN: 978-0-306-82039-7 (hardcover)
ISBN: 978-0-306-82156-1 (e-book)

Published by Da Capo Press
A Member of the Perseus Books Group
www.dacapopress.com

Da Capo Press books are available at special discounts for bulk purchases in
the U.S. by corporations, institutions, and other organizations. For more
information, please contact the Special Markets Department at the Perseus
Books Group, 2300 Chestnut Street, Suite 200, Philadelphia, PA, 19103, or
call (800) 810-4145, ext. 5000, or e-mail special.markets@perseusbooks.com.

10 9 8 7 6 5 4 3 2 1

For Sandy

Contents

QUEENS OF NOISE

1 Girls + Guitars

It's June 1977. Do you know where your daughters are?

Lita Ford plants her leather boots on the stage of a Japanese TV studio. The eighteen-year-old beauty from working-class Long Beach bends her knees, leans back, swings her long blonde hair behind her as if it were a counter-weight to her electric guitar, and shreds. Her left hand runs up and down the frets with easy assurance, deftly picking notes with the creative dexterity of her guitar heroes, men such as Ritchie Blackmore (Deep Purple), Jimi Hendrix, and Jeff Beck. She's playing hard, rocking leads like no teenage girl has played them before or, arguably, since. Even in a grainy nth-generation bootleg of this 1977 show, her confidence is palpable; her smile perks up the smidgen of baby fat still lingering on her cherubic cheeks. Lovely Lita—with satin short shorts, tight T-shirt, and hard-body Hamer guitar—is hot, and she knows it.

All of them, the five teenage girls from suburban Los Angeles who have banded together as the Runaways, are on fire, performing in front of a live audience that screams their names. Singer Cherie Currie wears her infamous bustier like it's athletic wear. She commands the stage with the cat-like moves of her hero, David Bowie—swinging her mic as if she's ready to take someone out with it when she's not singing in a husky, come-here-go-away voice.

Statuesque bassist Jackie Fox doesn't need her bandmates' platform heels; she's a towering Stevie Nicks in peasant blouse and jeans—saluting the Japanese fans in between coolly plucking the bottom tones that give the Runaways' glam rock its boogie base.

Laying down the chinka-chinka guitar rhythms of the band's dirty rock sound, Joan Jett is already Joan Jett: a cute but dark-eyed tomboy in a custom, red catsuit—gymnast meets race-car driver—and, of course, boots. She has outlined her Cleopatra eyes in dark liner and sings with the sexy bravado of one who was once painfully shy.

Behind them all sits the Runaways' not-so-secret weapon: Sandy West twirls her sticks between her fingers, then hits her drums, hard. Her arms are muscled ropes—West had arms like Tina Turner has legs—and her hair is a blow-dried, feathered, golden California dream. She bangs the sticks together: 1–2–3–4. "It's all right," the Runaways sing in unison.

The Runaways were more than all right. Seeing footage of the band at the height of their career, during their triumphant first (and last) tour of Japan, it's hard to believe they didn't become one of the greatest acts of their time—that we don't speak their names in the same breath as the Ramones, Sex Pistols, Kiss, Aerosmith, and Blondie. They had the whole package: Catchy songs, hard riffs, great looks, distinct personalities, and, of course, novelty appeal. (Look: Girls plus guitars!) They also had something that cannot be manufactured, no matter how cunning your maverick manager is: a spark of explosive creative chemistry, the primal energy that Iggy Pop calls "raw power." The Runaways could play like the boys, but without once pretending they weren't girls. They tapped into the hormonal horniness that made Ronnie Spector shout, Tina Turner shake, and Janis Joplin moan, only they did it while also armed with electric guitars and loud drums. Watch wide-eyed Cherie snap her arms and reach down into her diaphragm. She pulls up notes dripping with guts and blood, the cherry bomb about to blow.

"It was about tapping into all the things teenage girls feel, and that means everything, from the sexual, to just the hanging out, to the introspection—you know, self-esteem issues," says Jett. "Everything teenage girls go through, we wanted to try and touch on."

Two years prior to their Tokyo takeover, none of these adolescent Angelenas knew each other. They lived in disparate parts of a sprawling city, a swinging corner of a post–women's lib/Title IX world. They were latchkey kids—children of B-movie stars, of divorce, of death, of immigrants, of *Creem* magazine, and of rock 'n' roll radio. But they all found salvation in music, and they also shared a refusal to see their genital and genetic makeup as a handicap.

A charismatic but eccentric music producer and songwriter—the legendary/infamous Kim Fowley—helped to bring them together in the

Babylon bohemian bacchanal of Hollywood studios, clubs, and rehearsal spaces. They became the first all-girl, all-teenage rock band to sign a major-label deal, release five albums, get tons of press (some ecstatic, some misogynist), and tour the world. They explicitly saw themselves as the female answer to Led Zeppelin, the Beatles, and the Rolling Stones. The Fabulous Five (as Fowley called them) worked their butts off to make it. Along the way they endured perhaps unprecedented levels of abuse, a fair amount of it self-inflicted.

Japan is where it all came together—the dream of becoming rock 'n' roll stars. As in a scene in a Beatles movie, screaming fans greeted the Runaways at the airport, followed them around Tokyo, mobbed their limos, ripped their hair out, treated them like, well, rock stars. They appeared on TV shows, stayed in luxury hotels, were wined and dined. You can see the Runaways' own amazed recognition of their triumph in the grainy vintage videos, in the looks they shoot one another across the stage, in the comfortable exuberance of their playing, in the surefire answers they give to the questions asked by the show's hosts. No one had done this before: crossed the globe to show how girls can play together, a teen team hustling music driven by sexual desire and rebellion. Towering above their hosts in their boots and satin, they are the wild things of which they sing, icons of female sexual autonomy—even when a camera rudely zooms in on Currie's crotch and only slowly discovers her face.

And Japan is where it all came apart—the nightmare of being a band on the road, of being young girls in show business, of drugs and sexploitation and egos and insecurity and shitty teenage girl behavior and even shittier grown-up men. Mobs, soft-core porn spreads, a broken bass, a broken glass, and broken hearts rent the Runaways. They left Japan bigger than ever but in pieces—one member, driven to a state of panic and self-injury, gone, one about to leave.

"It's the paradox of you get what you want, but then it may not quite be what some people wanted or what they thought it would be," recalls Jett. "I think some of the girls were literally frightened at the intensity of it; the intensity of the thousands of kids up against the car rocking the car wasn't funny anymore. Then they were terrified of really getting hurt, where I was like, nah, it's just surreal, we're not going to get hurt.

"It was the best of times; it was big and we were really famous there. But it led one girl to leave, and it led the other to believe that she didn't need the band and she could go on without us."

The story of the Runaways is a story of bravery, passion, friendship, talent, and adventure. They were undoubtedly pioneers: not the first all-girl rock band, but the first to play the kind of hard, aggressive, libidinal music that had long been staked out by men, from Elvis Presley's "Jailhouse Rock" to the Beatles' "Helter Skelter" to Black Sabbath to the Sex Pistols. You can see the power of their revolt against gender norms—the thrill of their refusal to be good girls—in that rare TV footage.

"Most of the time, we had a blast," recalls Jackie Fox. "We were getting to play loud, in-your-face music, getting to dress in whatever you want…We were dating rock stars…And mostly we were playing in front of live audiences that were really receptive to us, people who came because they wanted to see us…We were these ordinary girls doing this extraordinary thing."

The Runaways' story is also one of betrayal, abuse, cowardice, and collapse. More than three decades after their four years together, the members still remain bitterly divided, split into shifting alliances and cliques—unable to come together even for the 2006 burial of one of their founding members, Sandy West.

"When you're sixteen, seventeen, eighteen years old, this is what you dream of: to get away from junior college, community college, from being some idiot's mother or some troll's wife, and you get to go out there and rock and roll, and so it's kind of fun. And then after a while it turns into your demise. And maybe girls that age shouldn't be out there on the high wire without a net," says Kim Fowley, the Runaways producer, manager, director, and mastermind—but evidently, not their safety net.

Telling the Runaways' story is not easy. Strong personalities have completely different takes on the facts of the events, let alone their importance and impact. Fowley is a master myth-maker, and the band members all learned from their would-be puppeteer. Through the cloud of more than three decades (made hazier for many by narcotic use), it's hard to tell what stories really happened and what stories are just good stories, or terrible stories.

Getting most people to talk was the easy part of writing *Queens of Noise*. Perhaps because no one wants to grant five teenage girls their own autonomy, everyone—producers, fans, friends, competitors—wants to claim responsibility for the Runaways' success. (Few accept responsibility for their failure.) The hard part was getting people to stop talking. Even those who were bit players and bystanders felt deeply connected to this pop cultural era and wanted to relive it, whether or not they could remember it. Fowley is the king of these monologists: When the original Mayor of the Sunset Strip (self-appointed) calls you, expect to be on the phone for three hours. One hour of that conversation will be brilliant, colorful, to-die-for quotes ("I saw girls that came back like people from war. They looked like we raped and pillaged. We kicked serious ass. We bombed men. We tore down doors and blew out the walls. We inciner-ated. We set fire. We devastated. We scorched. We bulldozed. We can-nibalized. We cannon-balled. We stormed and tore open and blew apart pretensions. And there they were. They weren't ready for the debutante dance."). The other two hours, he'll say those same things over and over, in escalating scatological metaphors.

The Runaways' story is not exactly what you think, if you've seen Flo-ria Sigismondi's pulsing feature film *The Runaways* or Victory Tischler-Blue's gripping documentary *Edgeplay*, or read Cherie Currie's revealing memoir *Neon Angel*. All of those capture vivid pieces of the puzzle that makes people still obsess over a band that enjoyed only fleeting success during its time. But each film and book omits or neglects key members.

After talking to almost all of the principal players in the Runaways' saga, I've tried to assemble a cohesive narrative out of Rashomon per-spectives. I've backed up stories with physical documentation and sought multiple eyewitness confirmations of information that seems dubious or controversial. Sometimes, I've let a good story remain a good story, even if I couldn't confirm its connection to reality. I've tried not to engage in any of the mud-slinging that sadly seems inevitable when these survi-vors of the '70s start remembering some of the most volatile but vulner-able years of their lives.

There are many skeletons in the Runaways' closets. For the sake of the historical record and cultural understanding, some of these decom-posing bodies seemed well past due for exposure, and I respectfully bring them out to the sunlight. I have also tried to protect the legitimate right to privacy of living individuals and the families of the deceased.

Contrary to what one might think, the Runaways were not innocent victims of an evil Svengali. That widespread narrative denies the women agency in their own life-story and simplistically demonizes Fowley, a complex figure ("I'm a bad guy who does nice things") without whom there would have been no Runaways. Nor is the Runaways story some clichéd Behind the Music rockudrama of drug-fueled triumph, tragedy, and resurrection. For one, there has been no resurrection. Secondly, drugs are also another pat demon of rock biographies. Sure there was a lot of cocaine, pot, Quaaludes, alcohol, and crystal meth, and at least one life was destroyed by addiction. But chemicals and their uses and abuses are just one thread in this multilayered tale.

Queens of Noise is a cautionary tale of what can happen to girls on the cusp of womanhood who dare to put themselves in exciting but dangerous positions. It's a testimonial to the inspiration and insecurity of the trailblazer. It's a period piece about the music industry in the 1970s, the lingering machinations of the old-fashioned Hollywood star system, the decadence and decay of the Sunset Strip. The Runaways' glam rock inspired both the dawn of punk and the reign of hair metal; the band is simultaneously a link between the New York Dolls and X, and Led Zeppelin and Mötley Crüe. *Queens* is a fable of individuals trying to make sense of a country of changing norms, of girls raised to believe they could do what boys do, who then crashed into the wall of sexual harassment and discrimination. It's a parable of prodigal daughters leaving broken homes as well as happy homes, to carve out new ways of being, of playing, of creating. And it's a story of how chemicals can distort individuals' ability to cope and lead to crime, violence, disease, and death.

The Runaways were queens, yes, but of noise, of dissonance and disturbance, of not an inability but a prepunk unwillingness to harmonize. They had minimal commercial success in the United States but phenomenally, thanks to the blazing solo careers of Jett and Ford and the devotion of Runaways fans, the group's impact has continued to grow. They opened the doors for the Go-Go's, the Bangles (featuring early Runaway Michael Steele), L7, Lunachicks, Garbage, the Donnas, Girl in a Coma, and Care Bears on Fire. Their records were a direct inspiration on the Riot Grrrls who would lead third-wave feminism's "revolution girl style" in the early 1990s. "When you hear something like that on a record, I feel like a lot of people are trained to think a full-grown man is doing that," Kathleen Hanna, former singer of Bikini Kill and Le Tigre, says of Lita Ford. "To be able to conceptualize that it's not a full-grown man, it's actually a teenage girl doing it—it changes what is possible for yourself as a girl, as a woman."

In 2010 the Runaways reached a new generation of actors, musicians, and fans when teen screen queens Kristen Stewart and Dakota Fanning starred in *The Runaways* movie. Miley Cyrus (aka Hannah Montana) has called Joan Jett one of her greatest inspirations; they performed together on Oprah Winfrey's TV show in 2010. "I still watch these videos and go, 'These girls can't be fifteen,'" says Stella Maeve, the actress who played West in *The Runaways*. "It blows my mind."

Men love the Runaways, too. Led Zeppelin singer Robert Plant wore a Runaways T-shirt to the Fabulous Five's debut Hollywood gigs at the Starwood. Legendary DJ Rodney Bingenheimer followed and pushed the band so avidly, he was practically a sixth Runaway. Seminal L.A. punk band the Germs asked Jett to produce their first and only studio album. "They certainly were pioneers," says Bun E. Carlos, drummer of Cheap Trick, a band the Runaways took under their wings. "They were good players. It was fun to watch them play, fun to watch the crowd: all the guys with their tongues hanging out."

"What's inside a girl?" gothic punk band the Cramps once asked. The screams of young women have been a driving force of rock 'n' roll since Big Mama Thornton first howled at a hound dog and Elvis shook his hips, through the Shangri-La's pop dramas and the Beatles' debut on *Ed Sullivan*, on up until groupies made the Sunset Strip a playboy pleasure dome. The Runaways knew exactly what it was like to be a teenage girl, and instead of being with the band, they decided to be the band.

The complete story of the four years they spent together creating musical history has never been told. The most telling testament to the importance of the Runaways is the diverse, fascinating trajectories of their lives since. Jett and Ford were top-selling rock stars of the 1980s. Currie turned to acting, writing, and—with a wink and a nod to Wendy O. Williams—chainsaw art. Fox went to Harvard Law School with Barack Obama and became an entertainment attorney. Vicki Blue (Fox's replacement) makes films, videos, and photographs.

Some thirty-five years after she rocked the schoolgirls of Japan, Lita Ford faced perhaps the biggest challenge of her life: a tumultuous divorce. For inspiration, she looked back on the band of her youth. "I started thinking about the Runaways days, and I started thinking about running crazy and running wild, living on the edge," Ford says. "I was living in style."

Only Sandy West didn't survive the Runaways' painful breakup. Although she was one of the strongest musicians in the group, she never found another successful outlet for her music. She battled serious addiction problems and became involved in serious crimes—including, perhaps, a notorious Hollywood murder. She was diagnosed with lung cancer while in prison on drug charges and died at a hospice in 2006, surrounded by her family.

Adolescence is a complicated, deep, formative time in anyone's life. With no role models and questionable guidance, five strangers gave up the normal routines of their teen years—high school, family, prom dates, etc.—to achieve what no girls had achieved before. "Gave up" is the wrong phrase: They escaped those conventions—they ran away.

2 California Girls

On a summer day in 1975, Joan Larkin picked up her Sears Silvertone guitar and boarded a bus in Canoga Park, a Los Angeles suburb in the northern part of the San Fernando Valley. The girl with the Suzi Quatro haircut was sixteen but didn't have a driver's license. Her destination: Huntington Beach, in the heart of what architecture critic Reyner Banham once dubbed Surfurbia, on the opposite end of the Southland sprawl. In mass transit–challenged L.A., there were no trains, high speed or otherwise, to help Larkin reach her destination. So it took four buses and a few hours to voyage the more than sixty miles. Through the windows Larkin could watch the various terrains of the city that was her relatively new home: the famous Hollywood hills, downtown's skyscrapers, the concrete-grid valley that Banham called the Plains of Id, the Golden Coast of Orange County. Joan didn't mind the time and hassle; she was on a mission to make musical history.

The troubadour finally arrived at the town known by some as Surf City USA. A teenager with a golden mane, piercing blue eyes, and impressive biceps greeted her at the bus stop. In notes she wrote before her death, Sandy Pesavento remembered the first time she met Joan Larkin: "There was this girl standing there with a dirty blonde shag haircut and big, mirrored sunglasses holding a guitar case."

Sandy and Joan had never met before, only talked on the phone, after Hollywood hustler Kim Fowley connected them. Joan was ten months older than Sandy but shy and inexperienced. Sandy talked boisterously— with her hands, a true Italian—and already had a band. They both loved sports and rock 'n' roll. They clicked.

"When we met, I don't know, I can't explain it—when you meet somebody that you connect with on such a level," Larkin says. "She was so friendly and outgoing. She was like me: She was a tomboy, she loved sports, she was a rough-houser. We hit it off right away."

Pesavento also immediately sensed a kindred spirit.

"In some ways, personality-wise that is, Joan and I were like night and day," Sandy wrote years later. "She wouldn't say something in twenty words if she could say it in ten... I think I was different for Joan, with me being so West Coast/surf's up and she being so East Coast with her tuff accent and leather jacket.

"Then in other ways she and I were on the same page. She loved playing sports and having fun, and we both had a healthy sense of competition. We were also both really serious about playing music and played our instruments with total commitment. Most importantly, we shared a lot of the same ideals about being in a rock band. When it was time to play, we wanted to go out there and kick everyone's ass. Like a rock 'n' roll football team."

Joan and Sandy went straight to business. The two strangers ascended to the above-garage rec room in the two-story home where the seven-sistered Pesavento–Williams family lived. Sandy's red Pearl drum set held court. Like Joan's silver-flecked Silvertone, the kit sparkled—the girls were literally glitter rockers. Larkin plugged her guitar into a Marshall amp that Pesavento had borrowed from the band she played in, Witchcraft. Sandy was used to playing with others; Joan had only ever played at home, alone. They liked a lot of the same music—particularly English rock bands—but they didn't know how to play many of the same songs. They jammed on simple chord progressions, classic rock 'n' roll stuff, Chuck Berry and Rolling Stone riffs. They settled into "All Shook Up," the Elvis Presley tune—but they played Suzi Quatro's version.

"I couldn't believe how she played," Larkin says. "She was such a solid, strong, powerful, really good drummer. I don't even want to say for being sixteen, for being anything. She would sit there and play Zeppelin stuff, John Bonham stuff, note for note. Some of those songs are really intense—the double kick drums, the toms. She had this shit down and it was powerful.....We locked in right away."

"Lock in" is musician's lingo, meaning to find a shared groove—to play in time and in sync. Sandy used the same phrase to describe that first rehearsal with Joan. "From the very beginning, she had perfect rhythm," she wrote. "We both looked over at each other and we just locked in."

Joan was never to become a Yngwie Malmsteen–style lead guitarist, someone who could tear off runs of notes in prowess-flexing solos. That became Lita Ford's job. Larkin just wanted to help keep the beat, in the manner of John Lennon or Keith Richards. Sandy, on the other hand, had a bit of the metal show-off in her. They complemented each other perfectly, creating a backbeat backbone. "We didn't have a particular music thing we bonded over; we just bonded over the straight, pure thing of rhythm guitar and drums locking up," Larkin says.

Here they were: Two teenaged tomboys from opposite ends of Los Angeles, jamming. It must have been an incredible feeling, a moment of enlightenment. "We had the hugest smiles on our faces, and I think it dawned on us how awesome this was, two chicks just rocking out together," Sandy said.

So they called Kim.

Kim Fowley was a L.A. music-scene fixture, a notoriously weird character with an impressive two-decade history as a writer, producer, publicist, manager, and singer/spieler of random hits and misses. Larkin and Pesavento had met Fowley separately; he had put them in touch with each other with the hope, shared by all of them, that they could form the zygote[1] of an all-girl rock band. He would be their manager, producer, songwriter, "director" (as he dubbed himself on the Runaways' first album), and "pimp" (also his own term). They would be, in the parlance of the old-school Hollywood into which Fowley—the son of actors—was born, "talent."

On that summer day one year before the United States turned 200 years old, in that Huntington Beach house bursting with girl energy, Sandy and Joan played rock and roll into the handset of a phone. On the other end of the line, in his "Dog Palace" just off the Sunset Strip, Kim smiled. Then he passed the phone to the music journalist he happened to be having lunch with, a man who had worked with John Lennon and Led Zeppelin and written for *Rolling Stone* and *Billboard*.

"Kim said, 'Have a listen to this and tell me what you think,'" Ritchie Yorke remembers. "I said, 'You know, sounds pretty good to me.'"

Thus, in a rec room—that most '70s suburban of locales, a space set aside for the leisure-time hedonisms of youth—a milestone in musical and women's history was laid.

"That's really how the Runaways were formed," says Larkin. "It wasn't Kim saying, 'I have this vision, let me go out and find girls to do this.' It was we who brought this idea to him and he said, 'Sounds great; let's try to do this together.'"

Within a month the Runaways would play their first gig; in six they would be signed to a multi-album major-label deal; in one year they would be touring the States; in a little over a year, they would make it to Europe.

And in four years they would be over. The two founding members' lives after the Runaways split bitterly would head in opposite directions. Joan Jett, as she dubbed herself shortly after that first rehearsal—the girl who learned how to play guitar with the accomplished Sandy West behind her—became a top-10 rock icon with such hits as "I Love Rock 'n' Roll" and "Bad Reputation." Sandy—the teenage John Bonham, the golden-haired surfer with the heart of gold—never succeeded commercially in her subsequent musical efforts and never got over the Runaways. She hit (rock) bottom, performing brutal acts of violence as an enforcer for a drug dealer, before dying of cancer.

And yet together, Jett and West provided the bedrock on which the Runaways was built—the bass-drum heart and the rhythm-guitar and songwriting soul. They were girls from opposite ends of Exopolis—as author and professor Edward W. Soja put it—who recognized in each other rebel souls.

"We definitely felt like there was an us and a them," Jett says. "And it was really distinct. You almost reveled in that. Yeah, we reveled in the fact that we're different and we're going to show you. And it's not bad. We're just playing music."

"I turned to Joan and we both almost cried at the Hollywood premiere of *The Runaways* movie when I reminded her that years before, in 1975, Sandy and I and Joan had seen two movies, *A Clockwork Orange* and *Rollerball*, which became the cinematic bookends of the Runaways' total attitude," Fowley says. "I said, 'Let's take the rock 'n' roll attitude of *Clockwork Orange*…and then let's take the sporting team, the athleticism, of *Rollerball*, and put them in guitars instead of sporting instruments, and that's what this band should be.' I said to Joan at *The Runaways* premiere, 'If the other three girls would have been like you and Sandy, the band would still be together. We would have had the female Rolling Stones/Beatles.'"

In 1972 President Richard Nixon signed a bill that said girls must be allowed to do what boys do. Title IX declared, "No person in the United States shall, on the basis of sex, be excluded from participation in, be denied the benefits of, or be subjected to discrimination under any educational program or activity receiving Federal financial assistance." The law was one of the most direct and profoundly affecting results of the women's liberation movement of the 1960s. Title IX made concrete the search for gender equality espoused by such second-wave feminists as Betty Friedan, Angela Davis, and Gloria Steinem. It took the fight against the institutionalism of sexism right into the American heartland and childhood, making it illegal for public schools to deny the same athletic opportunities provided for boys to girls. A whole generation of tomboys and girl-jocks found themselves newly empowered. According to the Women's Sports Foundation, in 1972, 294,015 girls competed in high schools; in 2012, the number had risen to 3,173,549. "Because of 37 words, millions of dream have become reality," *Sports Illustrated* writer Kelli Anderson wrote in 2012.[2]

Some girls had to fight for their right to scrimmage, or to drum, on their own. Two years before the federal mandate for equity, fourth-grader Sandy Pesavento decided she wanted to play drums in the school band. Her parents supported her having musical ambitions, but they hoped their youngest daughter would play violin, so she could complete a string quartet with her three sisters, Ellen (violin), Lori (viola), and Teri (cello). The athletic Sandy lasted about two weeks with a bow. She wanted sticks.

Sandy's school told her girls couldn't play drums. She begged to differ. "She said, 'You know what: I can be the first girl drummer in Prisk Elementary School,'" her mother, Jeri Williams, says. "That's how it began."

Sandra Sue Pesavento was born July 10, 1959, in Long Beach, the last of four daughters in a tight-knit, middle-class Italian-American family. Father Gene worked for a gas company, mother Jeri held various jobs, including dental assistant and chiropractor assistant, along with her domestic duties. Like many residents who had been lured by warm weather, cheap housing, and abundant jobs to the city nicknamed "Iowa by the Sea," the couple had migrated from the Midwest, in their case, Indiana.[3] The Pesaventos settled in Los Altos, a neighborhood of ranch houses not far from the 405. Eisenhower was president, and Johnny Horton's version of the country song "The Battle of New Orleans" was number one. From the oil refineries to the aerospace industry to Hollywood, Southern California glistened with prosperity; in a few years, the Beach Boys would be singing about good vibrations and desire for California girls.

The doted-on baby of the family, Sandy was an extremely active and generally happy child. Maybe because he realized he was never going to have a son, Gene bonded with his youngest, fixing cars and playing ball together. "They were close. She related to him and he related to her," says Teri Miranti, the second oldest daughter.

Sandy became a tomboy, despite childhood bouts of ill health. That challenge to do whatever the guys did was both Sandy's lifelong drive and part of her downfall. She played tennis and basketball, swam competitively, ran track, surfed, water-skied, and rode horses. "She was incredibly energetic, hysterical, very funny, athletic," says Lori, the third daughter.

Sandy's physical power and strong personality made her "a force to be reckoned with," says Ellen, the oldest sister. Lori recalled Sandy begging Gene for a raise in their allowance. Their father was strict: "Do you think money grows on trees?" he answered. But Sandy was not someone who took no for an answer. One day Gene responded to her entreaties by taking her outside. There, tied to a tree, dangled two dollar bills.

Sandy was not stupid, but she struggled in school. Lori attributes her difficulties to conditions with which she was diagnosed decades later: "Early on she had a lot of challenges with academic performances primarily because she had a lot of learning disabilities...later on in life we learned that she had ADHD. She had challenges that were around things like mood disorders, bipolar disorders."

Drumming provided a natural outlet for an athletic, active child in a musical family. At first Sandy played a snare loaned to her by her grandfather. She played it so loud, she was relegated to the garage. At nine, Ellen gave Sandy her first very own drum. "It was by far the greatest present that I had ever received (no offense to whoever got me the G.I. Joe)," Sandy wrote. "Before I was ten years old, I was trying to teach myself the drums, playing guitar and piano and listening to everything from rock to classical music."

Forget the string quartet: Sandy wanted to form a band with her sisters. Both her mother and the school fought her quest to play drums in the school band. "People thought/think that if you're female that you can't play a certain instrument or a certain kind of music," Sandy recalled. "It's crazy. The other boys in that class were the same age as I was and no one was having a meeting about whether or not it was 'appropri-ate' for them to learn to play the drums. Why was it inappropriate, be-cause I was a girl? What is so different about a girl's hands, holding sticks and hitting drums to a beat, from any other kid? It's idiotic."

Sandy won. She played the school's drums and eventually got a set of her own. She played in the orchestra, stage band, and marching band, and fought to be not just the first girl drummer but to hold the first seat in the orchestra. When the family moved to Huntington Beach, the movers promptly set up the kit in the bonus room over the garage. Sandy began bashing, and Jeri worried what the neighbors would think.

West had almost no distaff role models in her chosen instrument. There had been only two significant female drummers in rock and pop music up to that point: Maureen Tucker of the Velvet Underground and Karen Car-penter. West was as different from those musicians—Tucker at once prim-itive and artsy, Carpenter a subtle pop player best known for her sad, beautiful singing voice—as they were from each other. Hard rock drum-mers such as Led Zeppelin's John Bonham and Queen's Roger Taylor were her heroes. Sandy poured her athleticism into pounding those skins.

By that point, tragedy had shattered the Pesaventos' suburban idyll. On January 25, 1971, Gene Pesavento died suddenly of a massive heart attack while at home. Sandy, eleven, had just returned from school. "It was very traumatic for my family," recollects Lori. "It was off the Richter scale."

Sandy was particularly devastated. She carried a letter from her fa-ther with her until the end of her life.[4]

"When I first met her she talked a lot about her dad, how much she missed him," says Pam Apostolou, who befriended West in 1980. "Los-ing her dad was really really hard on her. Her dad got her."

Perhaps the death deepened her connection to her mother, a relation-ship that those who knew her say was the most important in her life. When Sandy's family and friends circle the wagons around the painful details of West's life—which almost everyone does, even those who don't know Jeri—they say they want to protect her mother from any more suffering. Before Sandy died, Jeri made a scrapbook for her, of old photos, newspaper clippings, lyrics, telegrams, etc. There's a page devoted to pictures of Sandy hugging her short, sweet mom. "We were close," Jeri simply says.

In 1972 Jeri married Dick Williams, a former colleague of Gene, whose wife had also recently died—and who had three daughters, in-cluding a Sandy. Thus Sandy earned the unfortunate family nickname

"Sandy Pee" (Pesavento) as opposed to "Sandy Wee" (Williams). Jeri and Dick each adopted the other's kids. There's a picture of all seven girls on Christmas wearing long skirts in a kaleidoscopic array of colors and patterns; if you look closely, you can see that Sandy had her jeans on underneath. The new, blended family moved into a larger house in Huntington Beach, to a place where they could start over on equal ground, not surrounded by memories of lost loved ones. Some of the daughters were in college or lived elsewhere. Still, the Huntington house held five girls, three cats, and two dogs, all trying to navigate their deep hurt, massive change, puberty, and each other's spaces. Sandy connected with the sportiness of the Williamses: Dick introduced her to her lifelong love of water skiing, and new sister Cheryl shared a horse and a bedroom with Sandy. But the dislocation, coming so soon after Gene's death, was traumatic. "Blended families aren't easy," Teri says.

"We were struggling at first, getting to know each other," recalls Jeri. "To see the love that's transferred through all that, it's wonderful."

Sandy was outgoing, fun, easy to get along with, popular enough to be elected governor of her class in seventh grade. But Lori says her transition into puberty was rocky. "She was very androgynous. She was one of those girls who didn't develop very early. In early adolescence, people used to make fun of her. They used to call her a boy. That upset her."

Around this time, Lori and Sandy were realizing they had something in common: They both liked girls. During her lifetime Sandy also had boyfriends, but her primary relationships were with women. "She and I were very open with each other," Lori says. "She was very clear with me about her orientation. I don't sense she ever really struggled with it."

Sandy also, years later, came out to her parents, and they accepted her. "We can't say okay, they're not our daughters anymore just because they have a different lifestyle," Jeri says. "I don't agree with it. It's not what I wished for them. But on the other hand, they're still wonderful daughters."

Music and sports were Sandy's outlets and her ways of gaining acceptance. Ellen introduced her youngest sister to the Beatles and Bob Dylan and taught her to play guitar. By the mid-'70s Sandy was listening to hard rock and playing in local bands. She was the only female in Witchcraft and Stillborn.

"Sandy early on was pretty determined that she wanted to play rock music," Lori says. "It was a way for her to translate the grief."

By sixteen Pesavento had turned into the kind of suntanned blue-eyed beauty of Beach Boys songs. She had a long, blonde Farrah Fawcett 'do—a sunny mane that she liked to flick back over her shoulder and out of her eyes. By the time Joan Larkin showed up at her door, Sandy was already an incredible sight behind those Pearls, her long hair and sinewy arms flying.

"She would smash those cymbals," Joan says. "It was very rhythmic and percussive. She kept right on time."

"Sandy showed that you don't have to be just hot or pretty and you don't have to just be tough," says Torry Castellano, former drummer for the all-girl 1990s band the Donnas, one of the many musicians who cite West as an influence. "You can be both. A lot of times people want to put women in the music industry in a box. She did what she wanted to do."

"She was a phenomenal natural drummer," Lori says. "I don't think the boys in the business ever even saw that coming."

Joan Larkin also played outside the box. Like Sandy, her parents raised her without gender limitations. She played sports. She dreamt of being an astronaut, archaeologist, astronomer, actor, or doctor ("until I realized I'd have to cut people and see blood and dig around in them"). She heard Led Zeppelin and she wanted a guitar. "A girl can do what she wants to do and that's what I'm going to do," Joan Jett sang in "Bad Reputation," her 1981 anthem.

Joan Marie Larkin was born September 22, 1958, in Penn Wynne, a suburb of Philadelphia, the first of three children. She played sports, rode horses, went to the Smithsonian with her dad, swam, bowled, and played clarinet ("I wasn't passionate about it"). "I look at my childhood as being fairly normal, very loving, and not really out of the ordinary from what I saw with a lot of the people around me," she says. "It was very suburban, and we spent a lot of time from sunup to sunset out in the street with our friends and playing."

Like Sandy, Joan identified as a girl who could play like a boy. "I've always been a real tomboy, since I was a little kid," Jett says. "I've always kicked boys' asses in a lot of things: games, tug of war, dodge ball. I'm good at all of it."

By the early '70s, fueled by the women's lib movement, tomboyism was enjoying a wave of respectability. The term dates to the sixteenth century, when it first described a rude boy, and then a "bold or immodest woman" and then "a girl who behaves like a spirited or boisterous boy; a wild romping girl."[5] From Jo of *Little Women* to Scout of *To Kill a Mockingbird* to Pippi Longstocking to Katherine Hepburn to Kristy McNichol to Chrissie Hynde to MC Lyte to Lisbeth Salander, there's a noble tradition of great women, fictional and real, who avoided girlie-girl activities—who played sports, wore pants, shot guns, climbed trees, threw balls, spat, swore, and never demurred. Around the time the Runaways were forming their sense of gender identity, movies such as *Paper Moon* and *Alice Doesn't Live Here Anymore* presented boyish girls as charming and clever. The 1980 movies *Foxes* (featuring Cherie Currie), *Little Darlings*, and *Times Square* (about girls in a punk band) showed women interacting in ways that were almost unprecedented in American cinema. At least two of those films were undoubtedly influenced by the Runaways. "These movies made girlhood interesting and exciting and even sexy," writes Judith Halberstam in *Female Masculinity*, her landmark 1998 history of tribades, butches, and bull dykes. "They also, of course, tended to imagine girlhood as tomboyhood."[6]

"It's gender fuck," Jett says. "It's the androgyny. You strap on; you're being a girl but you're being a boy."

Being a tomboy didn't make it hard for Joan to fit in, but the Larkins' frequent moves, apparently necessitated by her father's job selling insurance, did. "It was hard to make deep friendships early on," she recalls. She describes the five pubescent years she spent in Maryland as the most stable period of her childhood. To this day, she's a Baltimore Orioles fan.

Music was not Joan's first passion. She wanted to be an actress. Then she saw Liza Minnelli in *Cabaret*, Bob Fosse's 1972 movie about nightlife in the Weimar Republic just before World War II. Minnelli plays Sally Bowles, a skinny dancer with short black hair and a derby—a sexy androgyne. Jett embraced Bowles's version of femininity—not delicate or voluptuous, but active and strong. "Cabaret and the decadence and puberty and all that stuff was hitting at once," Joan recalls.

Artists such as Minnelli, David Bowie, the New York Dolls, and Suzi Quatro, who challenged gendered constraints by blurring the lines between what it meant to look and act like a man or woman, were her heroes. Years later she would incorporate the Replacements song "Androgynous" as a staple of her live set, singing this love song about "something meets Boy, and something meets Girl / They both look the same / they're overjoyed in this world / Same build, revolution / Unisex, evolution / Tomorrow who's gonna fuss." By then Joan herself had become a gender-bending icon for a new generation of misfits and rebel girls.

Larkin's "ordinary" life began to detonate with her maturing hormones. While being a tomboy is generally accepted for girls, as teens, tomboys are expected to become women. "We could say that tomboyism is tolerated as long as the child remains prepubescent; as soon as puberty begins, however, the full force of gender conformity descends on the girl," writes Halberstam.[7]

Jett, like other women who would fuel the late-'70s punk movement, found a road out of such restrictions in rock 'n' roll. She listened to Elvis Presley, the Beatles, the Rolling Stones, Led Zeppelin, and Sweet. She particularly liked the English rock stars—the guys with the long locks and tight pants, the artists whose dandyesque take on fashion and art had been dubbed glam because its lurking vulgarity kept it shy of being glamorous.

"You hear a song like 'All Right Now' by Free or 'Bang a Gong' by T. Rex, and I'm thinking, I want to make those sounds," she says.

At thirteen, Joan begged her parents for a guitar. To her surprise, she got one for Christmas. Her first ax was a Silvertone from Sears, a solid-body electric guitar with trademark "lipstick-tube pickups"—so named because the guitar's inventor, Nathan Daniel, originally built the tiny mics out of chrome, tubular lipstick cases. Silvertones were cheap, starter guitars with amps built into their carrying cases, glitter sprinkled into their bodies, and white formica sides. Jimi Hendrix, Bob Dylan, Jack White, and Beck have all played Silvertones.

Joan's first lessons were hilariously caricatured in *The Runaways* movie. She went to an acoustic guitar teacher with her electric Silvertone. "As a teenager, you want to do everything now. Right now," Joan recalls. "As I reflect, I realize I had to learn the basics. You can't just walk in and learn how to play a song, necessarily. I walked in and said, 'Teach me how to play rock 'n' roll.'"

The poor teacher tried to instruct Joan to strum "On Top of Old Smokey," as corny a folk tune as there is. Larkin quit after her first lesson.

"I went and bought one of those learn-how-to-play-guitar-by-yourself books, and I sat in my room, and I learned basic chords—you know, an E, an A, a D, a G, a C—and tried to learn how to play to my records, whatever it was at the time, whatever singles were around," Joan says.

"Black Sabbath was good, because they had big fat chords that were really slow."

Rock stars ruled the earth in the 1970s—or at least suburban America. Thousands, if not hundreds of thousands, of thirteen-year-olds wanted to be like Keith Richards, or Pete Townshend, or Ritchie Blackmore, and were begging their parents for guitars. That's why Sears made them affordably available to average consumers and why music stores stocked chord books. But just as Sandy had no real female drummer role models, Larkin's guitar heroes were mostly men. Joni Mitchell was a genius at guitar, vocals, and songwriting, but she, Joan Baez, and Carole King all played soft rock, folk rock, and jazz-inflected pop. Joan liked her music loud, sexy, driving—hard rock, glam, garage, punk. Cultural norms were not keeping pace with the fight for political and economic equality. Despite Title IX, junior high girls in American schools were still getting tracked into studying home economics—sewing and cooking. Metaphorically, Joan wanted to take shop.

People told the young woman who had been raised to believe she could do anything that she couldn't play electric guitar. Joan knew that "couldn't" didn't mean "can't"; it meant they weren't supposed to. Holding a solid piece of wood at crotch level while running your hand up and down its neck wasn't proper, ladylike, feminine, "good."

"Being told that girls can't play rock and roll—I mean even as a kid, it was so illogical to me," she says. "It's like, what do you mean, that they can't master the instruments? I'm in school with girls playing cello and violin and Beethoven and Bach. You don't mean they can't master the instrument; what you mean is they're not allowed, socially—it's a societal thing. You're not allowed to play rock and roll, because rock and roll means they're covering *Sticky Fingers*; rock and roll means 'Whole Lotta Love.' You go listen to these songs again and realize how dirty they sound, how much sex is dripping from that. I wanted to do that, and that kind of stuff is very threatening."

If good girls couldn't play electric guitar, then Joan Larkin was going to be very bad.

When Joan was fourteen and entering tenth grade, her family moved again, this time clear across the country, to L.A. California was exciting, glamorous—all those movie stars and rock stars that Joan had read about in magazines like *Creem*. But it was also a place of disconnection and danger. Joan Jett the icon was born in L.A., but Joan Larkin the person ultimately lived there less than a decade of her life.

First, the family settled in the Valley suburb of West Covina. Then they relocated again to Canoga Park. By that time, Joan's home life was falling apart.

"My father left the house," she says. "My parents were going through a divorce. It was traumatic for my brother and sister, but it allowed me to get the fuck out, because I think if my father was home it would have been harder for me to get out and go to Hollywood."

Larkin attended West Covina High and then Taft High School in Woodland Hills. Increasingly, though, she was getting her education in Hollywood clubs and record stores. The shy teen was starting to realize that she wasn't like the other kids at school—she wasn't boy crazy, she didn't envy the cheerleaders, she didn't have a crush on David Cassidy. Joan began honing her identity through infatuation with and imitation of musicians and albums.

"I was a big Bowie fan, and the *Diamond Dogs* album really got me through those last years of high school," she says. "I remember the kids yelling at me, 'cause I was probably the only kid dressed like a glitter kid, a glam kid. I probably had bell-bottoms and platform shoes with glitter on them that I put on myself, a T-shirt that I probably wrote 'Hollywood' in glitter—that kind of stuff.... I guess I really stood out, but I didn't think I was that freaky looking compared to some of the kids that I'd see in Hollywood. A lot of kids at school would howl, 'Aaaawooo, Diamond Dogs!' You know, really lame harassment. But you know it didn't bother me; it gave me more resolve. It was like, okay, I'm getting under their skin. I must be doing something right."

Joan Larkin began her reinvention as Joan Jett. She was creating a costume, a persona, a hard shell to compensate for her shyness, cover the pain of her dissolving family life, and embrace her difference by making strange beautiful. Soon, she had donned the black leather jacket and bad-girl stance of a female bassist who came from Detroit but had made it big in England: Suzi Quatro.

"People thought I was really mean because of the way I looked: leather jacket, and the heavy makeup," Joan says. "People were scared to death of me. I think I'm pretty nice and easy to get along with, as long as you're not a jerk to me."

When Quatro came to town in the spring of 1975, Joan staked out her hotel, the Hyatt House, aka the Riot House, a site of infamous rock 'n' roll parties and debauchery.

"I got back from sound check and I saw this little girl, in my haircut and my leather jacket, sitting in the lobby," remembers Quatro. "Toby Mamis, my press agent, told me she was a huge fan. I saw her in lobbies waiting for me every time I played in L.A. Sometimes it was a little too much though, I must admit. She was obsessed with me for a while, which I am sure she would be the first to admit. But again, always cute."

Sixteen-year-old Joan Larkin was a shy but determined waif, adrift from her family and searching for a new home. At the Hyatt, she made a friend who would eventually serve a stint as her manager.

"You're sort of aware who's in a hotel lobby when you're walking through, and there was a girl who looked like a young Suzi: jeans, black top, sunglasses, shag haircut," Mamis says. "Then we walked back again; she's still sitting there. 'Suzi, I think she's stalking you.' Literally, about 10:30 or 11 that night, she's still sitting there."

Mamis walked over to Larkin. He recalls the conversation from his first meeting with Joan:

"You should just go home; Suzi's asleep," Mamis said.

"I can't go home," Joan replied.

"What do you mean, you can't go home?"

"I told my mother I was staying at a friend's house. Besides, the last bus left."

"Well, you can't sit here all night."

"So what am I going to do?"

"No ulterior motives: You're going to sleep on the floor in my room."

And thus, like many a teenage girl in Los Angeles in 1975, Joan Larkin spent a night in a Riot House hotel room. She had a male friend with her, just in case Mamis did have ulterior motives. And already, her love of Quatro was inspiring a new dream.

"Suzi Quatro was a huge thing to me, cause I never had seen a woman play rock 'n' roll," Joan says. "To see her with her bass, just like screaming, really inspired me. I thought, well, if she can do it, I can do it, and if I can do it, then there's got to be other girls out there that are thinking about doing this."

3 The Roads to Ruin

The Runaways peddled California dreaming (and scheming). The California dream was a specific iteration of the American dream, and Fowley and his dream team did their best to conflate the two. Prior to the Runaways, after all, he had produced the music for *American Graffiti*, George Lucas's ode to '50s teenagers, cars, and rock 'n' roll, which was set in the Central Valley city of Modesto. On such songs as "Cherry Bomb," "Is It Day or Night?," the over-the-top operetta "Dead End Justice," "Hollywood," and of course, "California Paradise" (in which Currie hisses, "California—you're so nice" with sibilant sarcasm), the erstwhile Gene Vincent producer carried on these themes of sex, juvenile delinquency, and music—fast women in fast cars with loud radios. A writer in the British fanzine *Bump 'N' Grind* described the theme as "the saga of California—'It's Paradise'. You know the format—non-stop all-night partying, skipping school and getting stoned, and other very naughty things like that. Y'know, I'm seriously thinking of going to live in California."[1]

To understand the Runaways, you have to understand Los Angeles in the 1970s—and visa versa. The story of five girls, from five different neighborhoods, whose paths converged in the teen clubs, rock bars, recording studios, and rehearsal spaces of Hollywood, provides a clear window into that epochal time and place. The Runaways' sexploitation/liberation bridged the heterogeneous topography and aesthetic, social, and ethical contradictions of one of the world's most loved and hated cities. The adolescent guitar-slingers also blew up a few bridges.

"Being in L.A. in the mid '70s was all about Santa Ana winds, Benedict Canyon, tanned skin, and Malibu," says Vicki Blue, one of the Runaways' several bass players. "It was driving down Santa Monica Boulevard then turning north on Doheny before it got to be Beverly Hills, and making the loop back down to Sunset. It was about Chemin de Fer pants, fitting into them, size twenty-six, extra long legs, with platform boots."

But the Runaways' L.A. wasn't the groovy, bohemian Laurel Canyon hangout of Joni Mitchell and Crosby, Stills, and Nash. Nor was it the apocalypse-soon noir bummer of the Germs, X, and Black Flag, of punk clubs Madam Wong's and the Masque. The Sunset Strip of the mid-'70s was a good trip going bad. The Runaways, as they sang, were "Neon Angels," in the City of Angels. But they were also on "the roads to ruin."

Around the time Sandy was fighting to play drums in her grade-school band, two critics had a heated public debate about the Angeleno aesthetic. One point upon which Reyner Banham and Peter Plagens agreed was that theirs was a storied divide. "Los Angeles has supported an extensive and responsible literature of explication, and an equally extensive literature of well-informed abuse," the British Banham wrote in his 1971 book *Los Angeles: The Architecture of Four Ecologies*.[2] "Los Angeles is thus a city of extremes and it provokes either adoration or contempt," wrote artist and critic Plagens in *Artforum* magazine in 1972. "San Franciscans, New Yorkers, and Colorado hippies look down their hand-tailored, granola-filled noses at this brown-aired basin of vulgarity. Continentals, Okies, Londoners, Arkies, and visiting artists to the contrary warm their dispossessed souls on our sandy bosom."[3]

English architecture scholar Banham was one of the adorers. In *Four Ecologies*, he praised the very qualities of a modern, mobile metropolis that other critics derided: the freeway system, the "dingbat" apartment buildings, the neon signs. He was perhaps the most learned and erudite—yet still quite cheeky—in a long line of what scholar Mike Davis has called the Boosters: the writers, politicians, poets, filmmakers, and songwriters who sold the sunny southern California lifestyle to the world as an endless summer of oranges, snow-capped mountains, date shakes, and beach blanket bingo. "California Paradise," indeed. Banham even based a BBC documentary on the popular *Four Ecologies*, so appealing was his description of independent, self-determined, open lifestyles to Brits fed up with town councils, privet hedges, and planning ordinances. The city, said the professor in the aptly titled *Reyner Banham Loves Los Angeles*, "makes nonsense of history and breaks all the rules. I love the place with a passion that goes beyond sense and reason."[4]

But Banham's book blithely ignored key recent events and longstanding economic and political exploitation. The City of Angels had become the city of the Watts riots and Charles Manson. Unlike the outsider Banham, Plagens was an American who had spent two thirds of his then-thirty-one years living in L.A. when he wrote his response to Banham's boosterism. In "The Ecology of Evil," published by *Artforum* (then a L.A.-based publication) in December 1972, he blasted the academic for glossing over the real social and environmental problems of a city wracked by decades of robust but almost unrestrained development. Mostly, the artist and critic bemoaned L.A.'s "spiritual disease." "L.A. is an elusive place: all flesh and no soul, all buildings and no architecture, all property and no land, all electricity and no light, all billboards and nothing to say, all ideas and no principles," he wrote.[5]

Plagens, who not long thereafter decamped for New York, was a theorist for what Davis has identified as the other pole of Los Angeles literature, oppositional to Boosterism: Sunshine Noir (think: Nathaniel West's classic downer novel *The Day of the Locust* or Davis's own 1990 landmark study of the region, *City of Quartz*). A previous generation of European intellectuals had been morally and aesthetically appalled by their stay in Los Angeles during World War II, seeing nothing less than the decline of Western Civilization in American consumerism. (Filmmaker Penelope Spheeris would also see this connection when she examined the L.A. punk scene in her 1981 film *The Decline of Western Civilization*.) Theodor Adorno, Max Horkheimer, and other snobs of the Frankfurt School based much of their critique of mass culture as a form of passive brainwashing on their years spent cowering in the Pacific ('cause things were going so well in Europe.) Later, the postmodernists and semioticians joined in on the L.A.-bashing. French theorist Jean Baudrillard and Italian writer Umberto Eco attacked Southern California as the home of "hyperreality."

This is the contested landscape—Banham's "Surfurbia" versus Plagens's "spangled pothole"; Beach Boys Boosterism versus Frank Zappa Sunshine Noir—in which the Runaways formed. Their brief but notorious career confirmed Banham's "Autopian" visions and Plagens's "Pit" falls. They also showed that in the city of reinvention, anything's possible.

Or as native Californian Joan Didion—who has analyzed her home state with more intelligence and empathy than perhaps any other journalist and novelist—has written: "...California is a place in which a boom mentality and a sense of Chekhovian loss meet in uneasy suspension, in which the mind is troubled by some buried but ineradicable suspicion that things had better work here, because here, beneath that immense bleached sky, is where we run out of continent."[6]

Banham divided 1970s LA into "four ecologies." The Runaways' origins can be situated in the Plains of Id, Surfurbia, the Foothills, and Autopia.

In the anti-Eden of Los Angeles's lowlands, Kari Krome is the Runaways' Eve. She's the first lady who inspired Fowley to seek a female Rolling Stones; her poems about adolescent existentialism got the self-styled Animal Man thinking about the need for girls' voices (as opposed to just girls' bodies) in rock 'n' roll. The Scotch-Irish-Cherokee-Italian welfare child really did live the down-and-out, teenage misfit life that Fowley and Jett wrote about (she was Neal Cassady, they were Jack Kerouac). Krome's the one who actually was fourteen when the Runaways started (press accounts often exaggerated the Runaways' youthfulness). She's the only one who, at sixteen, lived up to the name and ran away.

"I came from a relatively poor background; I grew up on welfare," she says. "I got exposed to a lot growing up. I was an outsider kid. I'd sit in my room and read books and draw. My parents had high hopes I was going to be an artist growing up. Once I discovered rock 'n' roll, all that went out the window."

Krome (she does not want her birth name revealed) was born in the planned post–World War II suburb of Lakewood, the Levittown of California—home to the 1990s adolescent sex bullies the Spur Posse. "Naively, you could say that Lakewood was the American dream made affordable for a generation of industrial workers who in the preceding generation could never aspire to that kind of ownership," Donald J. Waldie, author of the 1996 Lakewood remembrance *Holy Land: A Suburban Memoir*, told Joan Didion. "... They worked for Hughes, they worked for Douglas, they worked at the naval station and shipyard in Long Beach. They worked, in other words, at all the places that exemplified the bright future that California was supposed to be."[7]

Krome's future was quickly not so bright. Her family moved frequently around the bleak south-central neighborhoods of L.A. She describes Bell Gardens, Compton, Downey, and North Long Beach as "a cultural wasteland.... I [was] looking at these horrible, really depressed environments with no gardens....I did not fit in culturally. I was a real lonely kid."

Banham gave the sprawling flatlands that are the cross-hatched, stucco soul of the city and its suburbs, from San Fernando to San Gabriel to Compton to Orange County, a more prosaic name: "the Plains of Id." But even he was hard pressed to find a positive spin on this "endless plain endlessly gridded with endless streets, peppered endlessly with ticky-tacky houses clustered in indistinguishable neighbourhoods, slashed across by endless freeways that have destroyed any community spirit that may once have existed, and so on...endlessly."[8] Imagine growing up there.

Plagens had his own term for this area: the Pit, parts of which, such as Watts, he described as a "horizontal, open-air prison." In the early '70s, shows such as *The Beverly Hillbillies* and *The Brady Bunch* beamed images of glamorous, successful SoCal living into American homes. But in the real city, L.A.'s plains were filling with grim boxlike housing and barbed-wire fences, urban cells that confined but couldn't contain kids like Krome.

Unlike Kari, Sandy West did live a Brady Bunch existence. By her teens she was residing, like the TV characters, in a conjoined family. Huntington Beach is the banner city of what Banham called "Surfurbia." The English scholar described the beaches as the most enviable aspect of Los Angeles, which he dubbed "the greatest City-on-the-Shore in the world."[9] By the 1960s, surf music and movies were replacing Hollywood glamour as the defining culture of Southern California. The surfer epitomized the healthy outdoors lifestyle that lured immigrants even as smog began obscuring the landscape. With his/her barefoot stance, the surfer was also an icon of independence, mobility, adventure, and alternative lifestyles. "The culture of the beach is in many ways a symbolic rejection of the values of the consumer society," Banham wrote, "a place where a man needs to own only what he stands up in—usually a pair of frayed shorts and sunglasses."[10]

With her long blonde hair and deep tan, West certainly looked the part of the fun-loving, free-spirited athletic youth; that was her image in the Runaways, "the California golden girl, the female Dennis Wilson" as Fowley said, referring to the drummer for the Beach Boys. Even Sandy's name evoked the granular firmament of Surfurbia. West did surf, but an accident scared her off the boards. It was Jackie Fox who had once earned the nickname Malibu Barbie for her wave-riding skills, before she took up the bass. As they became vampiric club-crawling proto-punks, the Runaways kept one foot on the Santa Monica boardwalk. To the Germans, Swedes, and Japanese who were devoted, slavering fans, much of the Runaways' appeal was that they were California girls, even if they were not quite as sweet as the ones the Beach Boys sang about. "The Runaways are Californian perfection," burbled an Australian writer. "Beautifully browned, their teeth glow with white health."[11] In one early Richard Creamer photo shoot for *Creem*, the Runaways frolicked in the waves in bikinis and wetsuits, hoisting surfboards like banners.

"...the higher the ground, the higher the income," Banham wrote, describing the class base of the area he dubbed the Foothills.[12] This generalization was not entirely accurate. In fact, as Plagens pointed out, the well-to-do had almost entirely taken over the supposedly democratic beaches by 1972. The only Runaway with a serious trust fund, Victory Tischler-Blue (aka Vicki Blue), grew up in affluent Newport Beach—Surfurbia central.

Still, it's undoubtedly true that if they didn't settle on the shore as they gained wealth, Angelenos climbed out of the plains and up into the Foothills. Beginning with early movie stars Douglas Fairbanks and Mary Pickford, Los Angeles royalty made Beverly Hills and the Hollywood Hills the quintessential sites of the American mansion on the hill. Later, the rock stars gentrified the canyons—Laurel, Topanga, Tujunga, Benedict. The upwardly mobile—literally—middle class followed the local nobility up the Foothills. Runaways singer Cherie Currie's mom was a wannabe star who raised her family in Encino, on the San Fernando side of the Hollywood Hills. Fox also came from the Valley side of the Foothills, the middle-class enclave of Woodland Hills. Jett lived just to the north in Canoga Park. For the lords and ladies of the Foothills and canyons, trekking to the Sunset Strip (which runs along the foot of the Hollywood Hills) or the Sugar Shack (the teen club tucked into a North Hollywood strip mall) was a short ride in Mom's car, or maybe even your own car.

All of the Runaways—the Valley girls, the surfurbians, the plains-dwellers—were residents of Banham's final ecology: "Autopia." Autopia is the freeway system that binds Los Angeles more than any natural geographical feature. To learn to speak like a native Angeleno, Banham learned to drive. Without the highways tying Huntington Beach to Long Beach to the Valley to Hollywood, there would have been no Runaways.

There are other names, besides Autopia, for urban areas that are shaped not like wheels, with concentric rings of suburbs spreading out from a central downtown, but more like blobs or amoebas, with multiple nuclei. Scholars and planners talk of the Exurbs, Edge Cities, and Metroplexes that characterize America, where, after all, cities were not originally built around castle centers. In his *Neuromancer* science fiction series, William Gibson calls an XXL urban area the Sprawl. In his influential 1996 postmodern tome *Thirdspace*, UCLA professor Edward W. Soja hones in on the "Exopolis" of Orange County, the conservative region south of Los Angeles County that was largely manufactured by developers in the mid-twentieth century and has served as an oasis of white flight. "These are not only exo-cities, orbiting outside; they are ex-cities as well, no longer what the city used to be," Soja wrote.[13] He called the OC "the generative utopia, a make-believe paradise that successfully makes you believe in make-believing, the most irresistibly California-looking of all the Californias, the most like the movies and TV 'situation comedies,' the most like the promised American Dream."[14]

The Runaways' far-flung homes exemplified the distinctive, centripetal geography of Los Angeles, one of the most sprawling cities in the world, a metropolis that is essentially a web of suburbs. Los Angeles has a downtown but it's never really had a center. The city's political and economic bases have long been spread out, from Pasadena to Santa Monica, Burbank to San Pedro; downtown WASP old money against West Side Jewish new money.

Sprawl spawned the Runaways. They were refugees from the make-believe paradise, like five points on a star—that never meet in the middle. None of the members went to high school together, or played in the same local clubs, or had any idea that one another existed, until each came across Kim Fowley in Hollywood. They didn't form in their parents' basement or garage. This inorganic origin undermined their credibility from day one. They were seen as a manufactured band, put together by an impresario as a commercial novelty, the female Monkees (and later, the role model for the Sex Pistols and Spice Girls).

On the other hand, sympathetic observers understood that, in a sense, the Runaways' origins made them the ultimate rock band: alienated adolescent Americans whose shared roots were rootlessness. Lisa Fancher, herself a teenage Valley girl, celebrated their differences in a 1976 article for *Who Put the Bomp* (which later became *Bomp)*, one of the first ever profiles of the band. "The predominantly white middle class suburbs were bound to have an outgrowth of teen troublemakers like the Runaways," she wrote with formidable sociological understanding for a high school student. "These aren't jaded Hollywood girls; they come from the sprawling bedroom valleys of Orange County, spreading out to the beach, and they built their popularity in the growing circuit of small teen clubs in these suburbs, where discos never infiltrated. Their roots are just as real as Bob Marley's only theirs are TV, driving around, and going to Hollywood on weekends because it's the only thing to do after five days of school and partying."[15]

They came from different neighborhoods, but the Runaways had similar back stories. They were white and predominantly from middle class families; they by no means represented all of ethnically diverse Los Angeles. Their families had come to California looking for the usual goods: stardom, an aerospace job, sunshine, change. They came like the pioneers, gold miners, and missionaries had come before them. "It was the true California spirit that found expression through him, the spirit of the West, unwilling to occupy itself with details, refusing to wait, to be patient, to achieve by legitimate plodding; the miner's instinct of wealth acquired in a single night prevailed, in spite of all," wrote Frank Norris in the epic Golden State novel *The Octopus.* The muckraker was describing the railroad, but he could have been writing about the star system also being birthed in California.

Ford was born in England to an English father and Italian mother and immigrated to the States when she was two. Joan moved with her parents from the East Coast when she was a young teen. Fox's Jewish parents moved from New York and plugged into the swinging '60s Cali lifestyle. Raised by supportive families in an era shaped by the push for equal rights, each member had remarkable confidence and ambition even before they signed a major-label deal. Joan wanted to be an astronaut or president. Vicki Blue was sure she would someday win an Oscar. Sandy knew they would be rock 'n' roll stars. These were women with options in life but who wanted adventure.

"I got rescued," Jett told a reporter in 1976. "If I hadn't joined, I probably would have gone to college, gotten a Ph.D., and be bored stiff. I'm sure I would have had a fine life at UCLA, but I dreaded it. I was working in a cheese store in the Valley."

Also typical of 1970s California, the Runaways were children of divorce and remarriages—quintessential latchkey kids of Frankenstein families. Fowley came up with the band's name as jailbait shtick; only Krome would eventually run away from her troubled family. But for all of the girls, while home was not necessarily broken, it was a confining territory that they were not hesitant to leave behind. Rock 'n' roll was a way out of the suburbs, the plains, the Valley, the Foothills. A band was a new kind of family.

"We're grown up in places like Orange County and the San Fernando Valley, really boring suburbs," Joan Jett told a reporter. "We had nothing to do, rock 'n' roll is the only escape." [16]

The fact that these five strangers were thrown so quickly together, signed to a major label within months of meeting, and sent touring the States and Europe within the year, did make their cohesion, personally and musically, a challenge. In short, it was a real pain to get them together for rehearsal. They were teenagers, after all, from middle and working class families, who didn't have their own cars. With their record advance, Sandy made Fowley buy her a truck so she could haul her drums. She would pick up Lita in Long Beach. A roadie would drive through the Valley to get Joan, Jackie, and Cherie. They converged on their infamous trailer rehearsal space on Cahuenga and Barham, or at SIR studios. The Runaways found themselves in Hollywood, which is nothing like coming from Liverpool, or Rockaway Beach, or Athens, Georgia. And some of them lost themselves there.

4 Hollywood

The first step was a fib. Sandy Pesavento told her parents she was going to Disneyland. On a summer day in 1975, she and friends from Edison High School got in a car in Huntington Beach. Like the proverbial pilgrims headed to Mecca, or mascaraed moths to the flame, Pesavento and her rock 'n' roll–loving voyagers rolled north through the golden exurbs, past Anaheim, leaving the steel simulacrum of the Matterhorn and the rest of the cheerful, scripted family fun park in the rear-view mirror, a craggy vestige of more innocent times. With the radio blasting—or maybe some Deep Purple, or T Rex, or Suzi Quatro on the eight-track player—they headed for the heart of a Saturday night. Pesavento's odyssey on the evening that would change her life took her not to Walt Disney's nostalgic, romanticized Main Street USA. They drove past the skyscrapers of Downtown and the seedy tourist trap of Hollywood Boulevard with its sidewalk stars. Pesavento turned West off the 101 and followed the last rays of the sun to probably the most notorious byway in rock 'n' roll: the Sunset Strip.

Ponder the name: Sunset Strip. The two words encapsulate the binary views—the polar opposites—that have long cast Los Angeles as the expanding, yet empty, city.

Sunset	Strip
location of vivid beauty	segment of unadorned utility
romantic longings	undress
natural phenomenon	commercial mall
the end	the piece

To reach the Strip, Sandy (probably) had to travel west from the Hollywood Freeway on Sunset Boulevard, the glamorous thoroughfare that, since Billy Wilder named his 1950 movie about a doomed screen siren after it, has become synonymous with Tinseltown—the fabled Boulevard of Broken Dreams.[1] After three miles, when directionless Hollywood becomes roiling West Hollywood, and before it turns into bourgeois Beverly Hills, lies a neon cluster fuck of nightclubs, billboards, liquor shops, hotels, and corner stores. In 2013 the Strip exists mostly as a postcard playset, buildings marked on star maps sold to sightseers and gawked at from double-decker tour buses. But in 1975, the Sunset Strip was glitter heaven.

Brad Elterman used to drive into West Hollywood from the posh San Fernando Valley community of Sherman Oaks. He was a young man whose camera gave him entrée to the clubs where teenaged girls necked on the dance floor and to the poolside parties of swingers and celebrities. He remembers driving to the Strip through the Hollywood Hills. "There was a wonderful view," he says. "Coming from Sherman Oaks Drive over Benedict Canyon, you'd get to Sunset, make a left, and head to the Strip. I felt like I'd entered a different civilization. The kids were cool, the fashion—it was nothing like I'd ever seen before."

A photograph from the era captures the commercial sprawl then: Pictures the size of eighteen-wheelers stagger like dominoes atop one or two-story buildings, boldly advertising new albums by Mott the Hoople and David Bowie, MainMan (Bowie's management team), and something called "Jamie '08." A skyscraper looms in the background, like a modernist monolith or a glass boner, a middle finger extended against the relentless horizontal bop of Los Angeles. Motorcycles, VW bugs, and even a city bus[2] motor past a venue called Filthy McNasty's (which later became Johnny Depp's Viper Room). The marquee of the Classic Cat Club simply pronounces "Bottomless."

The Sunset Strip has been the Sodom and Gomorrah of Babylon since Prohibition times, when it was an unincorporated ribbon of Los Angeles, meaning the usual rules didn't apply—it was a no man's land, a last outpost of the Wild Wild West. Speakeasies, gamblers, gangsters, loan sharks, and movie stars all took up shop between Highland and Doheny. John Lautner's architectural landmark the Googie Shop and the famous Schwab's Drugstore offered cheap eats. No one stopped the billboards from rising. James Dean and his beatnik friends hung out there. Then came the L.A. rockers, the Beach Boys, the Doors, the Mamas and the Papas, Frank Zappa, etc., with the English rock stars close behind them, and the groupies hot on their heels.

In a sense, Los Angeles was the harbinger of the sophisticated late twentieth century city that urban scholar Richard Florida has celebrated, its economy shaped by the "Creative Class." "Hollywood brought to Los Angeles an unprecedented, an unrepeatable population of genius, neurosis, skill, charlatanry, beauty, vice, talent, and plain old eccentricity, and it brought that population in little over two decades, not the long centuries that most metropolitan cities have required to accumulate a cultured and leisured class," Banham wrote.[3]

By the late '60s the Strip was crawling with rock stars, wannabes, starfuckers, and freaks. "On a Friday or Saturday night it could take as long as four hours to navigate the mile and a half from Beverly Hills city line to Schwab's. The sidewalks were jam-packed with girls in boots and bellbottoms, and with boys in tunics and white Levi's," Barney Hoskyns wrote in *Waiting for the Sun*.[4]

Musicians crossed oceans and continents to hang out in L.A.'s famous hotels (the Hyatt, the Sunset Marquis, the Beverly Hills Hilton, the Tropicana), record in state-of-the-art studios, do business in the multinational labels' headquarters, get wasted in clubs, recover in the sun, and of course, enjoy the scantily clad nubile beauties for which Southern California was world famous, first the pinup girls, then the surfers, then the go-go dancers (birthed at the Whisky a Go Go), then the groupies. Sexual liberation had fostered sexual experimentation and was about, as the Runaways epitomized, to head full-circle back to sexual exploitation. Girls still in the first flushes of hormonal change were escaping out their windows, hitchhiking up from Long Beach, telling their parents they were going to Disneyland—all those awakening latchkey libidos inexorably drawn to the mythic phallic appeal of the rock star. You can almost see them crawling out of the suburbs, like the nymphets on the cover of Led Zeppelin's *Houses of the Holy*.

"I was able to sneak out my second story window and with friends we could literally walk down to the Strip, which we did," remembers Darcy Diamond, a rock fan who went to Hollywood High and wrote for the *Los Angeles Herald Examiner*. "It was an innocent time, before creeps and weirdos and child molesters, and we were already rocker chicks. It was not unusual to be able to sneak into clubs and have some older dude say, 'Do you want to go fuck Michael Bloomfield?' The guy would be some kind of pimp. And we'd go, 'Excuse me.' 'He's at Chateau Marmont.' And being good girls, it was like, 'Yeah right.'"

Kim Fowley has a quintessentially colorful explanation for the Strip's inexorable appeal. "Underneath the Sunset Strip, between Doheny and Laurel Canyon, are magnets in the sewer, and the magnets are attached to women's vaginas, uterus, g-spots, clit," says the Runaways' evil genius. "It pulls them into the Sunset Strip! It's the magnets underneath the sewers that cause the best-looking women for over a hundred years now to all show up there and have this pagan type of response."

Whatever the source, the pull of Hollywood went far beyond the lure of stardom, of fame and her handmaiden fortune. The rock 'n' roll crowd flocked to the Sunset Strip not just to get discovered sitting at the counter at Schwab's (as actress Lana Turner allegedly was) or dancing at the Starwood rock club on Santa Monica Boulevard (where Rodney Bingenheimer met Jackie Fox, then introduced her to Fowley). In the 1970s, Hollywood, especially West Hollywood, was also Bohemia. It was a Mecca where oddballs and outsiders, gays and lesbians, trannies and bull daggers, could find acceptance and community. Like Greenwich Village, or the Castro, or South Beach, it was a refuge from the suburbs, family, and all the little boxes on the hillside. In the Autopian city defined by houses separated by yards and hedges and connected by the mobile, solitary cubicles called cars, the Strip was a relic from traditional urban areas—a walkable neighborhood. For someone like Fowley, whose post-polio syndrome prevented him from driving, it was a neighborhood where you could get everything you needed on foot. You could reinvent yourself in Hollywood: Joan Larkin could be Joan Jett, Sandra Pesavento could be Sandy West.

For a girl like Kari Krome, a lifelong tomboy who was already experimenting with the androgynous glam styles she saw in such magazines as *Rock Scene,* clubs like Rodney's English Disco were havens not just from conformity and conservatism, but also poverty and abuse. While her mom was out trying to pay the bills by dancing at clubs, the lyricist would hitchhike to Hollywood to be with other social and sexual misfits. "It was safe," she says. "There were guys running around like [DJ and groupie] Chuck E. Starr. He was practically the mascot of the place. Despite all the hormones jumping off, guys like him were sexually non-threatening because they were gay. They made it a safer place to be. It sent a message that it was okay to be gay or bi, and that they wouldn't hit on us. Rodney's was gay/bi, a smattering of creepy swinger couples, groupies, and glitter babies, and musicians and sexual predators. There were people jumping off on whatever. But it was also extremely sleazy. There were fifteen- and sixteen-year-olds that were extremely jaded. Like mother and daughter groupie teams."

Rodney's English Disco was owned by ultimate scenester Rodney Bingenheimer, a sort of glorified, glorious groupie who parlayed his eternal nightlife presence into attachments to Cher and David Bowie and eventual real power as a tastemaking DJ, one of the best in the world. His strange journey to the inner circles of Hollywood was captured in the 2003 biopic *The Mayor of the Sunset Strip*. "He could almost have been created specifically as the personification of the Hollywood music business scene," London journalist Chris Salewicz wrote in 1976. "Understand Rodney, and you're halfway—quarterway?—to understanding the wacked-out nuttiness of Hollywood rock 'n' roll."[5]

The Disco was styled (badly) like an English pub, and had nothing to do with disco, except for a shared '70s vibe. Fresh from a visit to the U.K. with Bowie, where he was turned on by the hard but melodic sounds filling the dance floors, Bingenheimer was one of the first American club promoters to program glam and early punk rock.

"Everyone was dancing to the coolest music around: Bowie, T. Rex, Quatro, Slade, Mott the Hoople, the Sweet, New York Dolls, Alice Cooper, Barry Blue," recalls Rodney. "Everybody had stopped hitchhiking in 1969, after Charles Manson. For my club, hitchhiking came back."

While still living in Maryland, Joan had read in music magazines about Rodney's. She arrived in Los Angeles not long before the club shut down, but in time to become a semi-regular. Her mom would drop her off. "That music, and that sort of combination of glam and intensity—it was decadent," Joan says. "It was very attractive."

Current and future celebrities—McKenzie Phillips, Keith Moon, Led Zeppelin, Pamela des Barres, Bianca Jagger, Angela Bowie, Lance Loud, Patti Smith, Elton John—danced alongside kids who had hitchhiked in from the Valley and South Bay. Girls tied scarves criss-cross their chests. Guys donned velvet coats and platform boots. Men could dress like dandies, and women like pimps. Krome recalled her outfit one night: "I had on cream-white, flared cords, a brown lapel, and wallabies.

And a white denim jacket, with rhinestones on it. And a striped T-shirt."

"You could be completely INDIVIDUAL, do ANYTHING, and people would never put you down," Joan described Rodney's to *NME* writer Julie Burchill in 1977.[6]

The Hollywood scene in general "was empowering," Jett says. "I felt I could be what I wanted to be there. I wasn't quite sure what I wanted to be yet, but I knew I wanted to play music at this point. It had gone from acting into wanting to play guitar, and figuring I'm in Hollywood, if I want to play guitar there's got to be other girls that want to do the same thing. So that was really a sense of freedom, all these other kids that I guess most people would term freaks, misfits, stuff like that—which to me they were just kids who were dressing different."

Glam helped birth the punk scene. "Glam appealed to me on at least two different levels," says Alicia Velasquez, who, as the singer Alice Bag, would push the fashion and musical buttons of the Hollywood scene. "The first and most obvious is that it showed you an impossibly posh and polished version of a rough and raunchy rock medium. Glam added a theatrical dimension to rock music that made it visually pleasing. The second reason it appealed to me is because there was also a certain androgyny to it. When I first stumbled onto glam, I read an interview with David Bowie where he talked about being bisexual. The concept appealed to me, and it seemed that most glam rockers cultivated an ambiguous sexuality that drew in both genders. As a teenager who was just discovering my sexuality, the idea of bisexuality just doubled my options!"

Rodney's was also one of the first rock clubs where the DJs were the stars. Only a couple musical acts ever performed there. Most infamous was the night Iggy Pop sliced his chest to ribbons in his opera "Murder of a Virgin," a sort of deformance-art statement about the Hollywood music industry in general and Rodney's in particular.

"The walls were mirrored," Pop recalls Rodney's. "That was very important there. You would want to go and go stand by the mirror and pretend to dance and check yourself out. Everybody would do that for long periods....Rodney's was like a hobby for a sick person; it wasn't like a business or anything. There was no good reason for that place to exist. There were lots of bad reasons for it to exist. And it was kind of great. The way it looked was exactly like the most low-rent, bad-neighborhood, trailer-park-adjacent or hillbilly neighborhood bar. There was strip-mall siding, beige wood siding, that was very cheap and ubiquitous. It had unlit gold lettering in old script: 'English Disco.' I realized how ridiculous that was. I'm not sure everyone did who attended."

Pop may ridicule Rodney's, but he had been drawn to L.A. from first Ann Arbor, then New York, by the city's primeval, fertile ooze. "I often find myself getting something really good done in a place when there's what was a vibrant economically viable city, and all of a sudden it isn't," he says. "Opportunities arise, because down go the rents, down go the supervision levels, and all that stuff."

At a cinema near Rodney's, Pop and gal pal Sable Starr saw *A Clockwork Orange*. Perhaps it was the same cinema where Fowley, Jett, and West took in a double bill of *Orange* and *Rollerball*. Iggy remembers the violence in *Clockwork Orange* seeming familiar, not shocking—a sign of the protopunk times. "Part of that delinquency, a lot of it was anger," Pop says. "Everything was more loosey goosey and cheap, not quite so tied up."

One night, a body lay on the pavement outside Rodney's. Jett remembers being awed as nightcrawlers nonchalantly stepped over what she told interviewers was a dead person. "Rock 'n' roll!" she thought. (Thirty-something years later, Jett admits that this might be a moment of Runaways mythology—that if there was a body, she doesn't know if it was dead or alive. It could have been Iggy Pop.)

Sleaze seemed to come with the sense of freedom and release, not to mention with the Quaaludes and Mandrax. These barbiturates, which were sold over the counter until 1973, and then still widely available by prescription or illegal distribution until the early 1980s, set the laid-back, loose, euphoric, horny vibe of the '70s rock scene. Methaqualone slows your heart rate but rouses your sex drive. It makes you feel like doing things you wouldn't normally do—for better or worse.

"I knew people who knew people who would go to doctors and get a huge jar of them and sell them to people for fifty cents or a dollar," recalls Mike Hain, who was a young fan hanging out on the Strip. "They lasted for a few hours. To me it felt like you were really, really drunk. Everybody is your best friend. You get kind of numb. If you knew someone took a Quaalude, you'd get laid."

Groupies gobbled 'Ludes and Mandrax. Middle-aged men fed them to teenage girls.

"Rodney liked young girls, and his club was full of them," Angela Bowie told Marc Spitz and Brendan Mullen. "Visiting rock stars off the leash from their wives in England would go to the English Disco to look for young girls under the auspices of arranging record promotion with Rodney."[7]

"People were having orgies and three-ways," remembers Genevieve Broome, who failed a Runaways audition, then joined a band called Backstage Pass. "There were a lot of drugs and a lot of sex, and then all these groupies. There were so many things you could get lost in."

For most revelers of the Strip, the polymorphous perversity and chemical experimentation didn't seem dangerous—sex and drugs and rock 'n' roll, baby. "It was a wide open, free wheeling, and wonderful time for a bunch of kids who basically had been picked on all the time by everyone around them," recalls Nicole Panter, a frequent club-goer who eventually managed the Germs.

"It was the '70s in L.A.; it was drugs and sex," says Hernando Courtright, a flamboyant figure whose father owned the Beverly Hilton and who became a sort of Boy Friday for the Runaways. "Everyone was having fun. It was Quaaludes, pre-AIDS and herpes. Rock 'n' roll was a fun thing to be in at that time. It was still the Wild Wild West. There were all kinds of characters, some good and some not so good."

"We're living in a time that's very neo-puritanical," says DD Faye, who was a critic for the influential South Bay music fanzine *Back Door Man*. "It just wasn't like that then."

It's hard, from the advantage of the twenty-first century, with our panic over pederasts and molesters, our consciousness of addiction, our post-AIDS restrictions and Rapture-driven chastity chic, and our general fear of human touch and sensory indulgence, to realize just how permissive pockets of American culture became in the 1970s. And by pockets I mean Los Angeles. California epitomized the swinging lifestyle. From the 1920s through the 1960s, approximately half a million people flooded the state every decade, many of them leaving their quaint Midwestern Protestant values back in the small towns they left behind. If you weren't divorcing your wife—the parents of Currie, Fox, and Jett all split shortly before the Runaways formed—you were swapping her with your neighbor's.

"My parents were transplants from New York," Fox says. "They got married really young, and it was the swinging Sixties. They were exploring that whole vibe. They had gay friends, they had friends that were obviously alcoholics, friends who were married to an actor. They were urban bohemians."

Even before she joined the Runaways, Fox remembers taking the bus to Hollywood, with her parents' permission, and spending all night roaming the streets with her high school friends. Strangers would pull up in cars and hand the girls Quaaludes. (Fox says she quickly discovered she didn't like drugs.) "We were latchkey kids with young, permissive parents," the bassist says. "We grew up quickly."

Some kids grew up too quickly—if they were lucky enough to survive at all. Hollywood and West Hollywood may have offered a respite from broken homes and strict parents, but they were not necessarily safe spaces. Quaaludes loosened you up; they also made you vulnerable. Just ask Denise Lisa.

Lisa lived in the San Fernando Valley town of Van Nuys. She ran away from home when she was sixteen in part because sexually, she didn't fit in. "My father was an asshole," she recalls. "He tried to beat the tomboy out of me. I left home because of him mainly, and I was struggling with my sexuality."

Bravely, especially for the mid '70s, Lisa came out while she was in high school. "My girlfriend and I would get kicked out of school dances for dancing together," she says.

She found a sort of acceptance in the squalid Hollywood apartment owned by Kim Fowley. Kim didn't mind if she was gay or bisexual. "Kim was all for anything that had to do with sex and anything he could watch or participate in," she says.

For someone fleeing an abusive, oppressive upbringing, the rock scene was a permissive playground for experimentation, exploration, and expression. Participants were encouraged to shuck off their Puritan past and pursue desires, to revel in pleasure. The Strip could be a particularly liberating environment for women, gays, lesbians, and transgendered people. Being a groupie may not have been a feminist ideal, but it was a way for females and queers to gain entrée to the powerful world of rock 'n' roll, as Pamela des Barres's excellent memoir *I'm with the Band* documented.

"Back then it was anything went," Lisa says. "At parties everybody was sleeping with everybody in front of everybody. I don't recall any judgment in the music industry."

Before he became one of the city's top club DJs, Chuck E. Starr was a self-identified groupie during the era of Elton John and T. Rex. "A male groupie is a lot different than a female groupie," he says. "Basically with a male groupie, you were doing it in the presence of a toilet in a men's room backstage somewhere."

Lisa says she, too, was a groupie for a time. One night, she learned firsthand how predators can turn a sexually permissive environment into a sexually violent one. A passing stranger caught her, literally, with her pants down behind Rodney's—she had to pee and couldn't wait in the line to get into the club. He raped her. Men, of course, pee in alleys all the time—Title IX had not reversed the double standards of street life. It was the second time Denise had been raped; a neighbor assaulted her when she was twelve. "My drinking and drugging got me into situations that left me vulnerable," she says. "That incident, because of my own experience, I felt like I couldn't do anything. I just shut down emotionally."

Lisa's story is an extreme, cautionary tale of the risks of freedom. (With a happy ending: She left L.A. and is now a successful realtor.) It raises a question that eventually, to varying degrees, all the girls who passed through the Runaways, and Kim Fowley's house, and the Hollywood rock 'n' roll scene in general, must have asked themselves: Had they exchanged restriction and repression for exploitation and abuse? Had they leapt out of the frying pan and into the fire?

At the corner of Doheny, in the middle of the elbow where Sunset begins to angle south, to slip downward, before straightening out again for the rich folks, sits the Rainbow Bar & Grill. In 2012 the two-storied venue's flyer- and graffiti-covered walls testify to the joint's legacy. In 1975, everyone who was anyone—who wanted to be part of the rock 'n' roll scene that had eclipsed the casting couch as the stagepost to glamour—knew that the Rainbow was where you went to be an outsider who was an insider. You didn't even have to step through the door. You just had to hang out in the parking lot.

"Sandy knew that the Rainbow parking lot was where a lot of bands went after their show to eat food and meet girls," says Jett. "When the place closed, everyone would hang out and talk. The parking lot was full of people talking. Led Zeppelin. Big bands. Sandy must have known

Kim was there a lot. Maybe she just knew it was a place rock stars and producers hung out."

In the parking lot of the Rainbow, especially after the bars (the Whisky, and Rodney's, and the Starwood) closed and there was nowhere else to go, and you were staying out all night because your parents thought you were sleeping over at your friend's house after your wild rides at Disneyland, you might see Jimmy Page. You might lock eyes with a girl in a shag haircut, share some Quaaludes, and make out. And you might meet a crazy six-foot-four character in a peach suit who promises to make you a rock 'n' roll star.

Kim Fowley was the original Mayor of the Sunset Strip. Rodney Bingenheimer became famous for the sobriquet, but even in his biopic *The Mayor of the Sunset Strip*, the infamous DJ and scenemaker admits he inherited the title from Fowley when Kim skipped town for Europe in the late 1960s. Of course, you can never quite get rid of Kim Fowley, and by 1975, the notorious (at least in his own mind) songwriter, producer, performer, huckster, and hustler was back on his old turf. He didn't have to give himself the fake mayoral honorific in order to get into clubs anymore, because by then, everyone knew who Kim Fowley was. Everyone, including Sandy. Fowley had been making records for almost two decades. He could have afforded a house in the hills, or in the canyons, but the former foster child and polio survivor was a man of the streets. He lived and breathed the Sunset Strip.

"I'm emotionally immature!" Fowley says. "And I'd rather stand out with my artists who didn't have a fake ID or any ID. These kids had no money, they were living at home, they'd get rides, quarters, dollars and nickels to pay for gas in their mom's car, leave home, stand around because they couldn't get into real clubs, and wait for a party."

Accounts of what happened that midsummer, mid-seventies night vary. Fowley says Sandy was standing with her male friends, "weekend warriors." He approached Sandy, told her she looked like she was a musician, asked her, was she?

"There's Sandy standing there looking like Dennis Wilson's sister," Fowley says. "She was with a bunch of guys in a musician's stance, one of those, 'Hi, I bet everybody here should know I'm a musician.' Like Billy the Kid coming to town ready to have a gunfight."

Lori Pesavento says her younger sister went to the Strip knowing full well who Fowley was; in fact, she had seen his ad seeking girl musicians in *Bomp*, and was there in part on a musical mission. "Sandy had been playing with these boys," says Lori. "It was okay, but she hated being the only girl in the band."

Sandy also hated being the only musician in a crowd of provocative young women. "It was weird, I felt like a groupie standing out there," she wrote in notes for her memoir. "I didn't want to be a groupie; I wanted to be in the group."

Fowley says he approached West; she has said she went up to him. However it exactly went down, the producer quickly established that she was a drummer, and she found out that he was looking for players for an all-girl band. He already had one, a shy guitarist. Kim Fowley gave Sandy Pesavento Joan Larkin's number.

The Runaways formed with the exuberant optimism of Banhamesque boosterism. Fowley told them they would be the next Kiss, the female Rolling Stones, and the girls believed him. But all too quickly they found themselves sucked into a Sunshine Noir nightmare, a tale of drugs, abortion, assault, and violence so twisted that even Plagens could probably not have predicted it.

It wasn't just the Runaways that slipped into a bad trip; it was the times. The Strip was changing. In fact, the decline had begun before the Runaways even had a chance. Rodney's closed in 1974. The Whisky stopped booking bands for a couple years (changing their policy in time to become one of the Runaways' favorite venues). Music historian Hoskyns writes, "By 1974, rock 'n' roll Los Angeles had reached its moral nadir." Bowie, who lived in the Hollywood Hills at the time, told Hoskyns, "There was something horrible permeating the air in L.A. in those days. Maybe it was the stench of Manson and the Sharon Tate murders."[8]

Phast Phreddie Patterson, who ran the magazine *Back Door Man* and DJ'ed at the Starwood, said by the end of the decade, the Rainbow—aka Fowley's office, where Kim met Sandy—was a sick joke. "The guys had long hair, velour shirts with wide lapels and bell bottoms. The girls all seemed to be blonde and wear halter tops, spike heels and pouts. An even bigger spectacle happened in the parking lot after two in the morning when the bar closed and these sad people made final, desperate attempts to con some sweet young thing or anybody with an English accent (often simulated) to go home with them. The Rainbow was a watering hole for old wave rockers. Perhaps a better location would have been next to the La Brea Tar Pits," he wrote in October 1996.[9]

As the '70s slipped into old age, the music on the strip got harder: Punk bands like the Germs and Black Flag, metal acts such as Mötley Crüe and Guns N Roses, took over. The drugs got harder, too. "What killed that era was the drugs," says Chuck E. Starr. "When crystal meth happened, that was what killed everything."

It was the end of California's Golden Era. The ugly conservatism of the Midwestern émigrés raised its head with the anti-tax Proposition 19, which broke the back of what had been one of the world's greatest public school systems. Five decades of population growth slowed precipitously in the 1970s. The very air stank.

One thing Banham and Plagens agreed on in the early 1970s was the importance of Los Angeles as a model not just for the U.S., but for the world. Banham's blithe boosterism bothered the L.A. critic so intensely precisely because the stakes were so high, and, as a longtime resident, Plagens was so invested in them. "Los Angeles is the harbinger of America's future—if we can save the children of Los Angeles, we can save anybody, everybody," his *Artforum* article argued. He thought little of the "seedy stucco 'Strip' with juice-sucking neon and carny pitchmen," and one has to wonder if he knew of Fowley. "… Los Angeles produces the greatest per capita crop of creeps in the Western world," he wrote. "Realtors, *record producers* [emphasis added], agents, interior decorators…" the list went on.

Strangely, in their respective rave/rant, Banham and Plagens each devote little space to Hollywood. Except for its residential neighborhoods in the Foothills, the most famous part of Los Angeles doesn't fit anywhere in the four ecologies. It's as if Hollywood is so other, so mythic, so blazingly bright in the global marquee, so surreal, such a site of dreams, that it's not an actual geographic location. Maybe that's one of the reasons the Runaways never truly made it, outside of Japan and a few other countries. Hollywood is where you went to, not where you came from. To be a Hollywood band was like being spiders from Mars, or being from a soundstage, or being from nowhere. It was the most elusive part of Plagens's "elusive place: all flesh and no soul, all buildings and no architecture, all property and no land, all electricity and no light, all billboards and nothing to say, all ideas and no principles."

5 Legendary Prick

Central to the story of the Runaways lies the fruitful but tortured relationship between a thirty-something genius with a Mommy complex and his teenage protégés, many of them working out their own Daddy issues. Kim Fowley did not manufacture the five musicians who became the Runaways, but he did create the concept, find the talent, cowrite many songs, and manage, produce, promote, and finance the band. He also insulted, alienated, exploited, and, finally, lost them.

Kim Fowley was an abandoned child of Hollywood, who became the original mascaraed Mayor of the Sunset Strip, who, in his sunset days, still trolled the Strip looking for young blood—a dirty old man with a gigantic musical history. There would have been no Runaways without Fowley's inspiration and perspiration, and the manager/producer/songwriter/"pimp" (his own word) also helped destroy his creation. His three-year affair with the band he assembled and named is perhaps the most infamous "Svengali" relationship in rock history. His own decades-long career never recovered from the tarring he received once his crew mutinied and denounced him. If he didn't literally fuck any member of the band—he denies such accusations—he did figuratively. Opinions about Fowley split volatilely, among the Runaways and everyone else who knows the semi-legend: People either love the guy or hate him. He's charismatic and repulsive, brilliant and demented, a visionary and a scumdog. He has carefully cultivated his own bad-guy persona—the working title of his unpublished memoir is *Legendary Prick*. (Kick Books published a first volume of Fowley's autobiography, *Lord of Garbage*, in 2012.) Loud, freakish, vulgar, vulnerable, and just plain weird, Fowley has long served as the fall guy in the story of the Runaways' fall. It's a role he has cultivated; this son of Hollywood actors knows that the villain is more interesting than the hero.

But Fowley is also the guy who supported and promoted the Runaways—who didn't want to just fuck teenage girls, like so many of the men who hung around the Strip, but who wanted to see them raging on stage. Kim Fowley is an appalling character. The appall is part of his appeal.

"I'm everybody's worst nightmare and somebody's wet dream," he says. "I'm a horrible human being with a heart of gold, or a piece of shit in a bag of diamonds. I'm a bad guy who does nice things, as opposed to a nice guy who does bad things."

To understand Kim Fowley is to understand Hollywood at its crassest level, but also to glean how stages and studios can function as platforms for the reinvention of a forgotten boy. The man, like the band he helped form, was spawned by a town whose primary industry lures men and women with promises of fame and fortune, often at the expense of family and relationships; where artistic expression flowers alongside—in spite of, and sometimes because of—aggressive capitalism. The lovechild of low-level actors is a company man who was hustling records and sex by the time he was a teenager.

Fowley was shaped—malformed (literally)—by his environment, but he is also a true original. His *Bleak House* upbringing made him a showbiz Fagin; like any Dickens villain, he may yet be capable of redemption.

Kim Vincent Fowley was born July 21, 1939, at St. Vincent's Hospital in Los Angeles. (At times the self-mythologizer has told people he was born in the Philippines; his birth certificate states otherwise. Perhaps overreaching in his search for a metaphor, he also says this is the day Hitler invaded Poland; in fact, that occurred September 1, 1939.) His twenty-eight-year-old father, Daniel Vincent Fowley, aka Douglas Fowley, had already played in a string of minor movies when he had his first child. The actor continued to have a successful if unremarkable film and TV career until 1982, performing most notably alongside Gene Kelly in *Singin' in the Rain* and with a recurring role in the TV series *The Life and Legend of Wyatt Earp*. The elder Fowley played cowboys and bad guys, in the company of such heavyweight talents as Charlie Chan, Clark Gable, Spencer Tracy, and Lassie. He also continued to marry, have kids, divorce, and repeat.

Kim's twenty-one-year-old mother, Shelby Payne, was also an actor, under contract to Warner Brothers, albeit in bit parts that always went uncredited. The young beauty hit her career high-water mark playing a cigarette girl in the 1946 Humphrey Bogart movie *The Big Sleep*. Fowley has called his father a B-movie actor and his mother a F-minus movie actor.[1] He has also speculated that he might be the love child of Howard Hughes.

"I had a goddess mom," he says. "I had a fuckable mother. I had a Dorothy Lamour mother who was an asshole, and my father was a jerk, and I'm the fucking psych child in makeup sometimes."

While Kim was still a baby, his father was drafted into the navy. His mother put him in foster care during the war years. As a toddler, he learned how to fight to survive. "It was twenty-seven kids in a one-bed-room house in Culver City, which was a very Charles Dickens type of situation, with fighting for food, fighting for privacy, fighting for bath-tubs," he says.

In true Hollywood fashion, the marriage of Douglas and Shelby only lasted a few years. Fowley does not wax sentimental about his childhood nor his parents. "My father was an opium addict and my mother was a lesbian, and I had a different insight into Hollywood," he says. "Dad said she was a lesbian; maybe she was a Catholic girl who didn't like him. Her second husband killed himself; she married him possibly for his money. The marriage ended, then he committed suicide. Father had eight wives. … I have some issues, and the issues come from not having parents."

After the war, he drifted between his mom's house in Beverly Hills and his dad's house in various L.A. neighborhoods. To put it mildly, Fowley did not develop a strong sense of family.

"I was bounced back and forth like a ping pong ball between those households, which were always changing," he says.

Stints with his mother acquainted the young Kim Fowley with Hol-lywood's dubious casting-couch tradition. She would take the boy with her on trips to the studio to get her check, to pick up her war ration card, or to buy lingerie. "The guy would start to pull his cock out, and I would start crying and screaming on cue, and then the guy would get confused and he'd give my mother a check and her gasoline ration card and her nylons, and she'd wink and go," he recalls. "I used to come home [one day a week] for cock-block, and then she'd put me back in the foster home. So I knew what it was like to be a woman in show business."

In 1946, Kim was stricken with paralytic polio. He was infected again in 1957, with the non-paralytic variety. The virus caused residual nerve damage in his extremities. Fowley walks with a cane and can't perform such basic functions as typing and driving. The disability combined with his height—he measures almost 6 foot 5—gives him his arresting, freakish appearance. Then Kim piles on kabuki makeup and peach pimp suits.

"I can do what nobody can and I can't do what everyone can," he says.

Kim says his dual experiences with polio, along with parental neglect, made him a survivor and a fighter.

"The illness has always been the foundation of my battling with people," he says. "I was overcompensating as the cripple, as the handicapped, as the extremely exaggerated tall crippled person, a foster-home child, an abandoned child, a neglected child, a child of divorce, etc. So throw your bricks and your bottles and your bombs at me, and I'm still standing because I've been left for dead since day one."

Kim also claims to be a genius, with an IQ measuring 164. Certainly, he's a man with a great deal of knowledge on a variety of subjects and a mordant wit. Journalist Darcy Diamond calls him an idiot savant. Fowley has a needling intelligence combined with a strange emotional affect. If you rise to his challenge of wits, he will grace you with invitations to his myriad hustles. If you fail, he will be merciless in his cruelty. As he himself says, "Part of me is funny, if you have high self-esteem. If you have low self-esteem, I'm a threat."

Payne married again, to musical arranger William Friml, the scion of American musical royalty. William's father, Rudolf Friml, composed operettas and played concert piano; he was one of the charter members of the American Society for Composers, Authors, and Publishers, the music-industry's first performing-rights organization. Kim says his stepfather had no interest in this strange boy who had suddenly shown up at their doorstep—Payne may have forgotten to mention to her second husband that she was a mom. But Friml did leave a lasting impact on the adolescent. Fowley's parents showed him the film industry; he received his first music-biz lesson by listening through the walls as his stepfather worked with musicians to craft hits and careers. It was an education not in musical inspiration, talent development, and the frisson of collaboration, but in shrewd packaging and manipulation—the worst mass-culture nightmare of Theodor Adorno and the Frankfurt school.

"The client would come in and these guys would figure out ways around their inabilities to sing and play and perform, and at the end of it they had a package and would make thousands of dollars a week," he recalls. "That's when I learned how to record attitude and arrange attitude, as opposed to actually having musical talent. The Runaways, for example, as a group were not great. They had strengths and weaknesses individually, and I was always aware of what they couldn't do musically, and I would hide that from the audience, and then I would play on the things they could do...I learned at a young age that not everybody who walks in the doors is Caruso or somebody who's going to be Al Jolson and stop the show every night. Some of these people don't deserve to be on a stage, they don't deserve to be on an album cover, but they have pretty faces, or they can dance, or they can do something else, and then suddenly, it becomes product....

"It was never a matter of art for me, it was never a matter of fun. It was just like, 'Oh, this is what you do.' Just like if you were a kid and your dad worked in coal mines, you say, 'Well, Dad digs, someday I'll go down and check it out.' Show business was the family business for me."

Fowley went to University High School, along with Nancy Sinatra, the surf duo Jan and Dean, actors James Brolin and Ryan O'Neal, and future Beach Boy Bruce Johnson. While still in ninth grade, he began taking classes at UCLA as part of a program for gifted students. But teenage kicks landed him in hot water. Fowley was the head of the Pagans of West L.A., a car club and "rich-boy nuisance brigade." In twelfth grade, he was caught selling alcohol. He says he was given the choice of jail or the military; he chose the National Guard.

Thanks to his juvenile delinquency, University High mailed Fowley his diploma but did not allow him to walk during graduation. Along with being a weekend warrior, Fowley took classes at a few colleges. But true to Frank Norris's gold-miner California spirit, the rebel without a cause decided to pursue quicker roads to riches than higher education. He had found his calling.

While he sometimes paints himself as a soulless hustler, in fact, Kim was genuinely inspired by 1950s R&B and doo-wop, by the sounds coming from L.A.'s black neighborhoods. True to the Velvet Underground song that the Runaways would later cover, Kim's life was saved by rock 'n' roll.

"Imagine hearing Bo Diddley on marijuana in the tenth grade," he told *Goldmine* magazine.[2] The gifted but crippled teenager wanted to be a "white Negro—to live in Hollywood and wear silk suits and do doo-wop music."

Fowley fought with his father over his future. Around this time, he showed up at one of the homes he had lived in during his itinerant childhood, during the brief time his father was married to its matriarch, Joy McAllister. Her son Dan remembers meeting his half-brother for the first time. He felt in awe of his accomplished sibling, with his bravado talk about doo-wop bands and record labels. He also remembers being told Fowley was being shipped out to military school, because his father didn't know what to do with him. "He just came to reconnect," says Dan McAllister. "He was this young boy who didn't have any place to go."

Kim became independent at a young age. He says while his dad was out of town he stole his car, TV, and a picture of Douglas playing piano ("because I knew I'd never see him again"), and drove to Hollywood. "I ceased to deal with them as soon as I had a number-one record," he says of his parents. "I became my own mother and father at an early age."

And what a number one it was. Fowley arrived in Hollywood on February 3, 1959—the day the music, in the form of Buddy Holly, the Big Bopper, and Ritchie Valens, died. "I figured the torch was being passed to me," Kim says.

Ambitious and knowledgeable, the teenaged Weekend Warrior presented himself to various studios, songwriters, producers, and artists. He worked for film producer Martin Melcher, Doris Day's husband, and Alan Freed, the DJ and record promoter who coined the phrase rock 'n' roll, as an unpaid assistant. For a time he lived in a gas station at Argyle and Sunset, because it was next to American Recording studio and he wanted to be near the action. (At seventy-two, Fowley still chose to live in a ramshackle apartment in Hollywood rather than a fancy house in the hills. He was also still working in a plain studio just a dozen blocks from his old petrol domicile.) In exchange for letting him use the station's bathroom, songwriter Dallas Frazier gave Fowley a novelty doo-wop song about a comic-strip caveman. Kim promptly paid some musicians $92 to record the track. He and singer Gary Paxton (an old schoolmate of Fowley's who was the Flip of the duo Skip and Flip) dubbed themselves the Hollywood Argyles, and "Alley Oop"—with its inimitable nonsense-syllable tag line, "Alley Oop, oop, oop, oop oop"—became a number-one song in 1960.

Meanwhile, the young Fowley had other hustles on besides the records business, he says. A psychiatrist hired him to provide sexual services to middle-aged women with physical disabilities. "I specialized in burn victims and cripples, disfigured women," he says. "I had a captive audience. I was the surrogate, the sexual surrogate. That's how I learned how to fuck."

It's hard to verify Fowley's gigolo experience or his other claims to early crime: "I was a burglar, I sold weapons, I also did SAT for people, term papers for people, college entrance tests... All my Beverly Hills show business education was balanced by being a professional teenage prostitute and criminal.... I had quite an interesting time growing up."

What is verifiable is Fowley's prodigious musical career. For the next fifteen years, until his name become indelibly linked with the Runaways, he was involved in various capacities—songwriter, producer, publicist, manager—with a potpourri of almost random acts. He had a knack for novelty numbers, helping deliver "Nut Rocker," a boogie woogie version of "Nutcracker Suite," and the inimitable Rivingtons songs "Papa-Oom-Mow-Mow" and "The Bird's the Word." He produced "Popsicles and Icicles" with girl group the Murmaids and coowned the label on which it was released. He recorded with Frank Zappa, cowrote for folk rockers the Byrds, and produced garage rockers the Seeds, the Soft Machine, and rockabilly legend Gene Vincent. He went to England and did publicity and MC duty for English pop star PJ Proby, witnessing Beatlemania and the Rolling Stones firsthand. He was the West Coast publicity man for the Yardbirds and was the announcer for John Lennon's Rock and Roll Revival festival (he got laid a lot thanks to that credit, he says). He recorded Jonathan Richman's Modern Lovers and wrote songs for Kiss, Van Halen, and Alice Cooper. He also made records under his own name, such as *Animal God of the Streets*: strange and psychedelic spoken word albums that showed the strong influence of the Beat writers.

"I have a great sympathy for Kim," says Iggy Pop. "I was always into him. I was always interested in song forms that communicate lyrics by speaking: talking blues, talking cowboy songs."

Kim's resume is impressive. He has worked with artists in classical, folk, pop, punk, and rock. In a sense, he's a virtuoso of the low-rent trash-pop aesthetic that writer Lenny Kaye celebrated in the seminal 1972 garage-rock anthology *Nuggets*, one of the sonic bibles of punk. Fowley modeled himself after brilliant, weird producer Phil Spector and shrewd but overbearing Elvis Presley manager Colonel Tom Parker. Mostly, he's the American equivalent of Malcolm McLaren, the dapper but abrasive London fashion impresario who managed (or mismanaged, or mangled) the New York Dolls, Sex Pistols, and Bow Wow Wow.

Fowley claims to have had a charting song every year since 1960. But despite its volume, Fowley's portfolio is incoherent, random, inconclusive—a testament to valuing quantity over quality. "He must have had twenty misses for every hit, if not thirty or forty," says Cliff Burnstein, who did early record promotion for the Runaways, then became one of the top managers in the music business. "His hits came out of a more freewheeling era of pop, which had changed radically by the '70s."

Fowley never found his star act, or signature sound—or if he found them, he failed to recognize or deliver on their promise, to register his Caruso or Jolson. Perhaps, his stepfather-trained disbelief in talent deafened him to potential stars in front of his ears. Loud, vulgar, and fond of obscenities, Kim may also have been his own worst enemy, alienating himself from professionals who preferred to keep their ugliness on the inside and dismissed this barbarian.

After all, the act for which Fowley remains most known to this day— the Runaways—was a commercial failure. "'Kim Fowley has the Midas touch,'" says Nickey Beat, of the Fowley-created band Venus and the Razorblades, in Alice Bag's memoir *Violence Girl*. (Beat and Bag were boyfriend and girlfriend.) "'Only it's the Midas touch in reverse. Instead of everything he touches turning into gold, everything he touches turns to shit.'"[3]

Fowley may have had his foot in his mouth, but he also had his ear to the ground. In the early 1970s, Manhattan band the New York Dolls created sonic and stylistic blueprints for glam and punk. Wearing tattered semi-drag and singing about trash and personality crises in bruised, brash tones over Johnny Thunders's splattering guitars, the group's five members never had commercial success. But—like the Velvet Underground and the Modern Lovers—the Dolls had a huge influence on generations of bands to come. Jett tells a formative coming-of-age story about swiping a beer from singer David Johansen during a Dolls concert—a sort of involuntary passing of the baton. Malcolm McLaren applied all his lessons learned by failing to capitalize on the Dolls into creating the sensation of the Sex Pistols.

In 1974 Fowley recognized the Dolls' androgynous appeal and decided Los Angeles needed its own idols of raunch and roll. So he assembled the Hollywood Stars: five male, long-haired rockers, including sometime Flaming Groovie Terry Rae and future Runaways songwriter Mark Anthony. "They were the male Runaways before the Runaways," their creator says. "I crossed the New York Dolls and the Raspberries."

At the time, the singer-songwriters of the Foothills—i.e. Jackson Browne, the Eagles, Linda Ronstadt, Carole King, etc.—dominated the California music scene. Manufacturing a glam band was a way to counteract the troubadour tradition and put power back in the hands of producers and publishers, of hustlers like Kim. The Stars, along with such bands as the Stooges and Imperial Dogs, evinced a prepunk reaction against the hippie sensibility. Fowley was animal god of the streets, not the hills. "For Fowley, the enemies of rock 'n' roll lived up in the canyons," notes John Scanlan in his book on Van Halen.[4]

But again Kim's quest for superstardom was thwarted: The Hollywood Stars broke up in the studio and Columbia never released their album. Fowley went on to sell three Stars songs to bigger acts: Bachman-Turner Overdrive ("Down the Line"), Kiss ("King of the Nighttime World"), and Alice Cooper ("Escape"). Although the Hollywood Stars were Kim's idea, he wound up neither managing nor producing them. Stung by their failure, he was probably reluctant to ever relinquish that control again.

By then, Fowley had another idea: Why not put together an all-girl band? (Perhaps after battling the egos of the Stars, he thought a group of teenage girls would be more pliable. If so, that hope was to prove fatally misplaced.) There were already such all-female groups as Isis and Fanny, but Fowley wanted something younger and sexier. Nor did he want a vocal group; he wanted girls with guitars.

"I thought up a Darwinian evolutionary metaphor in a rock 'n' roll sense," he says. "You would go from Elvis Presley doing female moves with his hips with the striptease pit type drummer, all the way to the high voice of Robert Plant, into the New York Dolls, into David Bowie, into all the glitter and glam guys, and all of a sudden, you turn the page and there's a woman on the page with a vagina and a guitar looking you right in the eye. It was inevitable that evolutionary wise, women would pick up the obnoxious rock 'n' roll pitchfork and ram it up the ass of the world."

In the summer of 1974, Fowley placed an ad in his friend Greg Shaw's magazine *Who Put the Bomp*, one of a handful of music rags that were helping to document and define the growing LA music scene. The spot announced a contest hosted by *Bomp* and Kim ("renowned maker of stars"). "Wanted: Four Girls," read the balloon-lettered banner across the top. "JOB: to play pop music / PURPOSE: to find the female Beatles, Stones, Who, Shangri-las of the '70s!"

In the center of the ad was a recognizable picture of the Beatles in black leather holding their instruments, with famous women's heads cut and pasted over the bodies. George Harrison sports Suzi Quatro's noggin, Annette Funicello holds a bass, Brigitte Bardot plays drums. The ad copy is surprisingly clean, articulate, even feminist-minded. "We're looking for girls who will take up where Suzi Quatro and Fanny leave off, the kind of girls who always dreamed they were in a Phil Spector group, girls with the desire and ability to carve out a place for women in '70s rock as significant as that they held in the '60s. Girls who can bring hysteria, magic, beauty and teen authority to a stage. Girls with youth, energy, dedication, wildness, discipline, dedication and style."

Note the repetition of "dedication." Fowley wasn't fooling around. Free of sexual allusions, the ad shows that Kim was looking for more of an innocent, bubblegum outfit than he would assemble with the Runaways. With stars encircling exclamations of "stardom!", "hit records!", "fame!", and "$$$!", the layout has an old-fashioned, *Star Search* quality. The ad repeatedly refers to an older era of pop, when Phil Spector and the Beatles sold teenage rebellion. The copy sagely points out that despite Carole King, Joni Mitchell, and Fanny, '70s female rockers didn't have the same power as the girl groups had. Maybe, the ad also revealed that Fowley was still mired in the past.

Silly, funny, and clever, the Fowley/*Bomp* ad got no replies. At least, not right away.

Controversy clings to Kim Fowley like shit on a cowboy boot. To many people, he's an idiosyncratic visionary whose verbose vulgarity punctured the smug, bucolic image of Los Angeles's rock scene as a Laurel Canyon haven for hippies. Musicians including Mötley Crüe's Nikki Sixx and the Germs' Don Bolles were drawn to Los Angeles in part because of Fowley's voluble eruptions and swinging image in the music press.

"He and Captain Beefheart made L.A. seem like Mecca," says Bolles. "I thought that guy was a genius."

Fowley can have a strange charisma and charm. He waxes flip and flamboyant, then suddenly turns unexpectedly empathic and emotional. In the rock scene of the '70s, he knew everyone who was everyone, and anyone who wasn't anyone wanted to hang with Fowley to become someone. He drew smart, creative people to him, like moths to the flame. "Kim was hilarious, funny, knew everything," recalls Rodney Bingenheimer. "He could read you the telephone book and make you laugh. He would make up songs and ideas on the spot."

True to his "white Negro" aspirations, Fowley could lay down a rap full of wry observations and scatological metaphors. His favorite word was dog. "Dog cunt," "sex dog," just "dog." He called girls' boyfriends "failure cocks." To this day, he speaks a sort of Tourette's jive that's a crucial link in the lineage from the Beats to Jack Bruce to Tom Waits to Wildman Fisher to David Lee Roth to Perry Farrell. Kim is rude by reflex.

The king of quotes, Fowley has always known how to play the media—even when he won't let journalists off the phone. Lisa Fancher, the teenage scribe for *Bomp*, recalls him calling her in the middle of the night at her suburban family home, not noticing when she had fallen asleep at the kitchen table. "I like him a lot though; he's a really smart guy," she says.

DD Faye wrote reviews for *Back Door Man*, a music magazine based in the South Bay. "I thought he had a good heart, and said [things] to shock people," she says. "You know he had polio growing up, and I imagined that had to be hard for him. I always had compassion for him. He can't help but say the wrong thing. ... I like Kim because he invents his life as he goes along. He was like then as he's living now."

Iggy Pop, for one, sees a somewhat tragic human behind Fowley's belligerent dandy pose. Around the time the Stooges were disbanding and the Runaways were forming, Pop and Fowley considered collaborating. It was a wild time in Pop's life (to put it mildly); he barely remembers living in L.A. But he recalls Fowley as a more compassionate figure than the brilliant but deranged exploiter played by Michael Shannon in *The Runaways*.

"Kim's more vulnerable than that person," Pop says. "He just looked like you could just dis him and he'd die. He looked physically frail. And he looked a lot like Boris Karloff's Frankenstein. He was the kind of guy, if you were into something like comics, and he was too, he'd be your friend over that for forty-seven years and always be decent to you. But not a nice person, not a human being oriented person. When he talks to you, he stays on point. He's always trying to think of some project."

Kari Krome remembers being initially seduced by those late-night phone calls and Fowley's sympathetic ear. "Kim started calling my house," she says. "He would call and call and call … He talks forever and it's all about his fucking ego. He was picking my brain: What do you think of this, what do you think of that? About music, about what was going on in the street. Being a lonely kid, I liked the attention. He was someone who was not talking down to me, telling me to change my shirt because it was cut too short. We would just sit and we'd talk. Which is what I like.

"But then later, I figured out what he was doing. By then I was already signed to him. The pressure just became really intense. He was really a dick, because I didn't want to fuck him."

While some women speak warmly of Fowley, his haters are mostly women. Their stories take on a shared narrative: Fowley became their friend, their confidant, their supporter, their backer, their manager/publisher/producer. Then he began to pressure them sexually. If they refused, he became angry and abusive.

"I was a kid," says Krome. "It broke my heart. I was devastated. I didn't know how to handle that. I didn't know how to play a game like that."

There's no denying that Kim Fowley was looking for, well, something—love? Sex? A slave? A dominatrix? In June 1975, about a year after his *Bomp* ad, Fowley placed another ad, this time in *Back Door Man*, under his pseudonym Lance Romance. He was seeking not a band, but a girlfriend. First, he stipulated that she must be at least eighteen or legally emancipated. Then, he described the girl of his dreams, in language that eerily presaged his descriptions of soon-to-be Runaways singer Cherie Currie: "I demand a blonde, blue-eyed Sex-dog; a modern Brigitte Bardot with no sagged-out tits or stretch marks. Brown hair with brown eyes tolerated only if it is massively titted with biker mama vibes.

"Surf stink is most appealing.

"If you enter my world of broken dreams you receive free rent, clothes and medical benefits. I've always liked girls with open minds or brilliant girls with rotten minds…."

Fowley has long surrounded himself with young, beautiful, interesting, and sometimes damaged women. In the mid-'70s various females lived in his West Hollywood duplex, including, for stints, Joan Jett and Lita Ford. The squalid apartment was a place of Bohemian revelry, but it was also a bustling office—for Fowley, play is work.

"He always had these young girls surrounding him," says Danielle Faye, who was very briefly a Runaway and later played in the Fowley-assembled Runaways replicates Venus and the Razorblades. "I don't know if they were gullible or if it was something that he would do for attention, but he would hold onto them, and they would like faint. 'See how much power I have over these girls.' His apartment was sparse and crappy and there were a stream of young girls that came in and out."

Genny Schorr (now known as Genevieve Broome) tried out for the Runaways and later became a member of Backstage Pass, an all-girl band. She was a victim of one of Fowley's vulgar power trips at a Rhino Records party; Kim, mistaking her for one of her friends, loudly proclaimed her bisexuality. "He was into humiliating people, no matter what it cost or how it affected other people," she says. "He was into making a scene."

Broome also remembers his predilection for fair-haired women. "He used to talk about blonde pussy all the time," she recalls. "That's what he wanted."

One resident of Fowley's "world of broken dreams" when the Runaways formed was Denise Lisa, the queer sixteen-year-old rape victim who had fled her physically abusive father in Van Nuys. She cleaned and cooked for Fowley and took some of the first Runaways photos. She became good friends with the band and, she says, lover to both Joan and Sandy. She also says she had sex with Fowley.

"I think I did sleep with Kim, before the Runaways," she says. "I think I was high. He asked me for a ride home. I remember taking a shower because I was disgusted that I did that. I think I felt like I was expected to sleep with everybody because that's what they wanted from me. During that time I just sexualized everything."

Kim has never made any pretense of being a gentleman. "The reason I'm in the record business is to fuck young cunt, you know," he told the *International Times* in 1972.[5]

"In the '70s, on a combination of beer and Quaaludes, you could take on a roomful of lesbians and tear them apart," he wrote in 1999. "The favorite sport then was squatting on a table and fucking as hard as you could when the beer and 'ludes hit, and then you would fall to the floor and roll around and come that way. That was the orgasm of choice in the '70s for me. You'd be surprised how many girls wanted to do this."[6]

Fowley didn't harass every woman in his circle. He himself admits he picked on people with soft spots: "I'm like a shark; I'll smell the blood." Women who were damaged from past abuses or had low self-esteem were most vulnerable to his venality. Even to women he didn't harass, his proclivities were apparent. "Kim Fowley seemed creepy to me," says writer and performer Nicole Panter. "He seemed like something risen from the grave, ghostly, you know, and the idea of him and these young women was creepy, and, of course, the intimation was that he was fucking one or all of them."

"For him, it was all about the victim thing, just damaged kind of Hollywood girls," says Fancher. "He was always all about underage girls. Rodney's was—all that crew was all about that stuff."

At the very least, Fowley represented an old-school model of the Svengali as a lecherous older man. But this old Hollywood hustler was running up against Title IX-empowered girls. "I don't have respect for people who prey on others," says Alice Bag. "It seems to me that Kim thinks of people as resources to be exploited."

"He's a dog," says Lisa. "He's a gross man. He was inappropriate, especially with teenagers."

"I couldn't figure out why he was being so mean," says Krome. "And when you think about it, a grown man of his age, being so mean because you didn't get to fuck someone—so you're going to pull that on a child? A child?! Pick on someone your own size."

Kim Fowley has a penis problem. He has trouble controlling his dick, literally. Polio left him with nerve damage in his extremities. When he serviced crippled women as a teenaged sex surrogate, he had to work around his own disability and find creative ways to bring them pleasure.

"Kim Fowley is an incomplete man," says Kim Fowley, who likes to speak of himself in the third person. "Parts of my body don't work, and in my reproductive area and my digestive area, I have obstructions. It means I can't function as a traditional male."

Fowley's confession of virility issues doesn't mean that he wasn't a womanizer, that he didn't harass girls half his age. In fact, it provides a psychological motive for his behavior: Kim may have been overcompensating. Polio didn't kill his sex drive or desires. It didn't make him a nice guy.

But penile dysfunction complicates the story—his is not the hammer of the gods. With his makeup and pink suits, Kim has long confounded gender binaries. He remembers explaining his sympathies to the Runaways: "I'm suffering because I'm a feminine man, you know: I wear lipstick and nail polish and all that dog shit," he recalls telling the band. "I understand what it's like to be a feminine man, and you know what it's like to be masculine women. I get it."

It's no surprise that in later years, Fowley found a place in the fetish community. "Funnily enough, I was accused of being gay more than I was accused of being a womanizer," he points out. "Decide: Am I gay or am I a womanizer?"

Nonetheless, one would think that the man who served as a child cock-blocker for his starlet mother—who claims to therefore understand what it's like to be a woman in entertainment—would have treated all the women around him with respect and care.

In 1970s Hollywood, lots of middle-aged men were sleeping with girls half, or even a third, of their age. It was all the rage. Fowley friend Jimmy Page traded twenty-one-year-old Pamela Ann Miller (who later became Pamela Des Barres, after marrying another English rock star and Sunset Strip fixture, Michael Des Barres) for fourteen-year-old Lori Mattix. In 1977, director Roman Polanski got busted for having sex with a thirteen-year-old.

As Denise Lisa says, it was just assumed she would make her body freely available. That's what girls who hung out on the Strip did. Until the Runaways came along.

Chuck E. Starr doesn't believe stories about Fowley being a predator. "Kim was a good guy," he says. "Kim never seemed like somebody who was going to do something to a person that didn't want it done. There's a big question mark when you hear some of these girls. Kim attacked you or you attacked Kim? You wanted to be a star; Kim was the road to the stars. Who attacked who? I never saw Kim do anything with any of those kids…And I think that Kim was more talk than anything else. I mean, those days, you could say you wanted to screw a fourteen-year-old. Today, you say that, you're going to jail."

If nature and nurture combined to make Fowley a freak, then a freak he was going to be. He was fortunate to flourish in an era when the band

Funkadelic encouraged people to "let your freak flag fly." "Le freak, c'est Chic," disco band Chic sang in 1978. But even in a laissez-faire age, the same carnal acts committed by a guitar god or a Hollywood rainmaker would not necessarily be tolerated when committed by an Ichabod Crane figure dressed as a giant peach.

As Fowley says, "I'm a convenient target because I'm theatrical and creepy and weird."

Daniel Vincent McAllister is eleven years younger than his half-brother. He got their father's first and middle names but he never met the man until shortly before Douglas Fowley's death. Dan McAllister, as the Treasurer and Tax Collector for San Diego County signs his name, also has nothing positive to say about the actor he describes as "a [sperm] donor: He was too much of a big deal in his own head to reach out to his biological children," says McAllister.

The Treasurer was raised by his educator mother and a stepfather who adopted him. He has immense sympathy for the sibling who never had such familial resources.

"I understand that it had a lasting impact on him to not have had any of those influences on his life," he says of Kim. "I think he's doing well despite that. He has been able to promote and push himself to the levels of success he's attained, in spite of all that. In a way he's proved that people can overcome that."

After that one late '50s visit to San Diego, Fowley didn't see Dan McAllister again until 1980, when a journalist arranged a meeting. The two men with shared genes but different lives became friends. Then one day, Kim called Dan.

"Would you like to meet your father?" he asked.

"I already know my father," McAllister answered, referring to the man who had cared for him since he was a toddler.

"No, your real father," Kim said.

Douglas Fowley was in his eighties, living in Temecula with his eighth wife, a former flight attendant. The half-brothers visited him together. He was largely bed-bound and not very lucid. McAllister is not sure he even understood what was happening. He kept breaking into the voices of various characters he had portrayed—ever the actor, never the father. Douglas Fowley died not long after meeting Dan McAllister for the first time.

McAllister still looks up to the big brother who first impressed him with his rock 'n' roll spiel. "He's a pretty straight shooter, and the more you talk with him the more you get to know him, the more you appreciate him and the more you understand his dry sense of humor, his cynical and sardonic sense. He's got a way about him," the tax man says.

"For all that's said, there's a guy with a heart of gold. He truly is a good person. He's a thinker, he's an analytical guy, he has some interesting perspective on things. He just keeps his guard on a lot. I think once people break down that barrier and get through, there is a kind, wonderful, good person there who really does reach out and deserves some respect and attention for all he's accomplished."

6 Yesterday's Kids

As the zero response to Fowley's *Bomp* ad showed, few girls were picking up electric guitars and drumsticks in the mid-'70s. In fact rock 'n' roll was becoming more masculinized than in the Aquarian age of Janis Joplin, Grace Slick, the Supremes, and the Shangri-La's—although the typical rock male sang in a sort of semi-drag: in a high voice, bedecked in flowing hair, beads, and even eyeliner. It was okay for a guy to vamp like a girl, but not for a girl to rock like a guy. Finding four female musicians who could agree musically and get along personally was a fool's errand. Add requirements regarding age, looks, and style—it's no wonder Kim Fowley shelved the girl-band idea after the *Bomp* bomb. The female bands who had tried to make it—Goldie and the Gingerbreads, Isis, Fanny, Birtha—had little commercial or critical success. The music industry was ready for pop stars jauntily singing, "I am woman, hear me roar" (as Australian Helen Reddy did in her 1973 hit)—but it wasn't so ready for roaring women.

Then one day in the summer of 1975, Rodney Bingenheimer introduced Kari Krome to Kim Fowley.

Krome was just twelve or thirteen when she started hanging out at Rodney's English Disco and other Hollywood clubs. As a tomboy outsider in the Plains of Id, she had sought refuge in jazz records and rock magazines, which she perused at a favorite newsstand. *Rock Scene* and *Creem* offered glimpses of a lifestyle seemingly light years away but in fact, available just up the 110. The androgyny of such artists as the New York Dolls and Lou Reed turned the pubescent on. Kari began threading her way through Autopia, hitchhiking to Hollywood or bumming rides with friends like Danny Woods, a flamboyant Oscar Wilde to her butch George Sand.

Krome wrote poetry and lyrics, songs with titles like "Switchblade Music" and "Yesterday's Kids." "I'd always written poetry," she says. "I wanted to play the drums in junior high, and they wouldn't let me, because they thought it wasn't appropriate for a girl to play drums. So they stuck me on flute. And I hated it. So I didn't learn to read and write music. What I would do is I devised my own way of writing songs and musical notation. I made do with what I had. And I would write lyrics. I just figured it out in my head. I wrote songs and I drew sketches of my dream band."

Writing, art, and music offered Kari escape from difficult and sometimes abusive circumstances. Her father didn't accept or understand her; "he thinks I should go right back in the closet or be shot." Krome was mostly raised by her mother and stepfather. Her mom danced in clubs and knew such performers as the Coasters and Ike and Tina Turner. They were too poor to buy a guitar. "I didn't have the money," Krome says. "I had a pen, I could do that."

Her literary and visual creations became vessels for feelings of deprivation and alienation. She would make "tree spirits" by tying objects to branches and hanging them in the yard. "I found a portal and I went through it. I constructed my own world. That was my creative side. And I felt better when I did that."

Like any adolescent songwriter, Krome wrote love songs. But she also tapped into feelings of social disgust and discord that were typical of the earliest stirrings of punk—the same nascent fury Pop sensed when he saw *A Clockwork Orange*. "A lot of it was really being angry, and being pissed off, and wanting out, wanting to get away," says Krome. "There has to be something better."

In a 1975 issue of *Back Door Man*, Phast Phreddie Patterson described Krome as being "like an alcoholic Emily Dickinson inspired by Lou Reed and Chuck Berry on a suburban gutter/bubblegum level."[1]

Krome became a regular of the rock dives and gay bars of Hollywood. Her good looks, sartorial savvy, and young age quickly won her friends and admirers, including Rodney. Bingenheimer introduced her to Fowley at a birthday party for Alice Cooper at the Palladium, announcing Kari as a songwriter. Everyone laughed.

"So I let it rip," Krome remembers. "I started dropping lines. They stopped laughing."

Imagine the scene: a table full of men in their thirties, late twenties at the youngest. Bernie Taupin, Elton John's songwriting partner, may have been there (accounts vary). These were powerful rainmakers who would still be in their prime in most industries, but in pop music, their continued reign was dependent on the fickle tastes of youths half their age, from suburbs far from the Sunset nightlife. Up walks this striking boyish girl speaking intimate insights from the front lines of adolescence. Lust turns to wonder turns to envy.

The tableau brings to mind the first chapter of George Du Maurier's smash 1894 novel *Trilby*, in which the heroine of the title enters a Parisian garret full of artists and musicians and stuns them with her precocious beauty: "She bore herself with easy, unembarrassed grace, like a person whose nerves and muscles are well in tune, whose spirits are high, who has lived much in the atmosphere of French studios, and feels at home in it ... one felt instinctively that it was a real pity she wasn't a boy, she would have made such a jolly one."[2]

Most of the men in Du Maurier's roman a clef instantly covet the young, androgynous artist's model as a lover and muse. But one man sees Trilby as a potential star in her own right (even though she proceeds to prove she can't carry a tune). The manager and mesmerist Svengali will make Trilby a star, and destroy her.

At the Palladium, Kim embraced Kari as "the teenage Bernie Taupin. She had a notebook full of lyrics," Fowley recalls. "I said, 'wow, these are great.'"

"I remember Kim saying, 'I've got this fourteen-year-old writer and she is REAL jailbait,'" says Danielle Faye. "That was a real appeal to him."

For her fourteenth birthday on August 1, 1975, Fowley signed Krome to a publishing deal and brought her to BMI, the organization for songwriters. She says she urged Fowley to find female musicians to perform her songs. Perhaps, after the failure of the *Bomp* ad, he figured the search was futile. "I was telling him, 'I want to start an all-girl band. How come there's no female New York Dolls? How come there's no girl Stones?' I was just so relentless that he acquiesced to it. He said, 'Okay, see if you can find someone.'"

Los Angeles has long been infamous for its poor mass transit system. And yet at least twice, buses played a crucial role in the Runaways saga. After all, teenagers who are stuck in the suburbs and need to get to where the action is, who don't have cars or driver's licenses, ride buses. Joan rode four of them to rehearse with Sandy. She was riding one again the day Kari first saw her. The two glitter babies eyed each other.

"She looked like Suzi Quatro," Krome says. "She had a guitar and everything. She sat in the front, and I sat in the back. And we just stared at each other."

They saw each other again at Rodney's. They had mutual friends, such as Randy Kaye, an outgoing gay youth who would become a much-loved music-industry figure. Kari says Joan began writing her letters, saying she had heard about her publishing deal, that she played guitar. They hung out, spending the weekends at each other's houses.

"I asked Kari, 'Do you want to form a band?'" Jett recalls. "I thought she played. She said she only writes lyrics. 'Talk to my publisher, Kim Fowley.'"

The sixteen-year-old Joan Larkin did not resemble the rock star Joan Jett. She had frosted hair and was, in her own words, "really painfully shy." She possessed the drive and determination to be in a band, but not the blazing gumption to be the singer or lead guitarist. Fowley remembers the first time they met, on Kari's birthday. "Joan was very shy, very moody on a James Dean level," he says. "Looking at her burger, face down. I said, 'Hey Joan, are you God? Are you great? Are you ready to take over the world?'"

For her part, Joan remembers Kim being "very intimidating at first, but really, I became great friends with him and still consider myself a good friend of his to this day. And I think he had a great mind, and is very creative and really thinks outside the box. He was another guy that people called a freak, and I think we just kind of fit in. Even though we were all different kinds of freaks in our own right."

Larkin was naïve about what it took to be a musician. Fowley asked if she had a demo tape—a cassette showcasing her songs and playing, a standard sampler for aspiring musicians and bands.

"I didn't even know what a demo tape was," Jett remembers. "I had never heard the term. I was sure I made the worst impression you could make."

Joan instead went home and played for Kim over the phone. He remembers her strumming her brother's ukulele; she says it was a guitar. She played along to a Quatro record. He says he recognized her talent immediately.

"She was John Lennon," Fowley says. "She was Keith Richards. She had amazing time. Joan Jett plays in time like either one of those guys do."

After a year of no movement on Kim's idea of an all-girl band, things suddenly started happening at lightning speed. Kim says it was the same day that he auditioned Joan over the phone that he met Sandy in the Rainbow parking lot. Within the week—the band's start has historically been dated as August 5—they were jamming in Pesavento's rec room.

Fowley waxes poetic about the importance of Ritchie Yorke's stamp of approval, as he heard those young girls playing "All Shook Up" over the phone wires from Huntington Beach. "That was the turning point because at a certain point…you always have these dreamers in a dirty room somewhere with no money, and they really feel great. They are entitled to participate in the rock 'n' roll dream, and it's only a matter of time until somebody says, 'Yes,' which is the best word that any human being can hear when he is creative. When somebody will say, 'Yes, let's try,' or, 'Yes, it works,' it's just a matter of time."

Sandy and Joan were not on the same page right away. "I was immediately aware of the differences between the two of them," Krome says. "Joan came from a very Gary Glitter, Suzi Quatro, verse-chorus-boom-boom-bridge, which is really an extension of old song lyrics, bubblegum '50s rock 'n' roll. And Sandy was from a different, more jam-oriented [place.]…I was excited. But my first thing was, how is this going to work?"

"Sandy was a genius drummer who was already in her high school band," Fowley says. "She was very advanced for her age. She played like a thirty-year-old man. She was a very gifted player and already had her own musical identity, but she didn't look down at Joan, and Joan made tremendous growth spurts as a player because she had a great drummer."

The hard-hitting, outgoing Pesavento drew out the soft-spoken, tentative Larkin. Joan credits the younger musician with helping her hone her chops and confidence. "She helped me grow as a rhythm guitar player," she says. "Sandy has a lot to do with the player I became. It's not just guitar influences and the style you listen to; it's also the way you learn how to play and sing with a drummer."

West and Jett instantly became friends and musical collaborators. They spent the days they were not in school at each other's houses. "Joan and I became inseparable," West wrote later. "I was still in Witchcraft, but I started spending every weekend together with Joan, writing and working on songs…The days were filled with practicing, jamming and writing. (Okay, there may have been some sunbathing and heavy drinking in there, too.) We became great friends and I loved hanging out with her. We used to love to go and watch the roller derby whenever we had a chance.… We were young, wild and on an adventure for sure."

When they weren't at each other's houses or at the derby, they were at Kim's, learning how to write songs, looking for new members, doing business. "It was like having a small rock 'n' roll band camp every weekend," Sandy wrote. "Kim's apartment was like band headquarters. We would make phone calls, we would sing songs, place our ads, listen to old records to remake. We spent hours and hours with Kim working on songs and ideas. He would throw ideas at us and get our teenage feedback."

One day, Joan handed Sandy a piece of notebook paper. On it were the lyrics for the first song she'd ever written.

"You Drive Me Wild" is a slow-boiling, sultry blues rave-up about sexual obsession. The lyrics are elemental and elementary: rhymes of "fire" with "desire." There's a doo-wop "do-oo-oo" chorus hook that allowed the girls to show off their harmonic skills, in the band's first-ever demo recording. The song grinds at a sultry pace but with sizable heat. The lyrics reflect Joan's desire to write like a rock star, not a bubblegum singer: "You make me tremble, you make me shake/ Pleasing each other, rocking till daybreak"—not bad for sweet sixteen. Sandy told people that Joan wrote it about her.

A drummer, a rhythm guitarist, a lyricist: They had half a band. But they needed a singer, a bassist, a lead guitarist, maybe even a keyboardist. Fowley put the word out near and far. He ran classified ads in local papers and *Rolling Stone*. He put his friends—Rodney, the writers at *Bomp* and *Back Door Man*—on alert.

They were clear from the start that they only wanted other female players. An aggressive, all-girl, teenage band was the concept; it was a gimmick, and a revolution. In Krome, Larkin, and Pesavento, Kim found three women who didn't just grasp his vision: They made it deeper, grittier, sexier, more real.

"Because it hadn't been done," says Jett. "There's historians who come out and say, 'Well this band did exist before you.' And I'd say you're right, but they didn't do what we do. I'm talking about playing sweaty, crotch-grabbing rock 'n' roll the way the boys do, the way when you see the *Sticky Fingers* album cover and you think Rolling Stones/sex, or you hear 'Whole Lotta Love' and you see Robert Plant with his shirt open holding the mic down there. Go listen to that fuckin' single and listen how right at the beginning, he goes, 'Huh.' It's so dirty, and that's what we wanted to do. We wanted to speak to those things that girls go through. Girls go through puberty, girls want to have sex, girls want to do all these things that boys do, but they aren't allowed because of society's rules about their roles."

The narrow focus of the search made it harder. One musician futilely flew in from Ohio. Another—a tall, intelligent Valley girl named Jacqueline Fuchs—tried out on guitar but got voted down. Some players didn't cut it; others were freaked out by Fowley. Some of the musicians were so bad, Kim started to prescreen prospects with the help of ex-Stooge Ron Asheton.

"It's really hard finding girl players," Krome recalls. "It's like a wasteland out there. It's barren."

"One person literally lasted one rehearsal," Joan recalls. "We were trying to find the pieces that worked, the people that connected, that wanted to do it, because with me and Sandy, it was so natural and immediate."

Despite the hurdles, it didn't take long at all to find the first solid prospect, a woman with an auburn mane, low singing voice, and solid bass skills. Sue Thomas was a few years older than the other girls. She worked at a record store and was another resident of the Exopolis of Orange County. Sandy picked her up, and they drove to Hollywood to meet with Kim and Joan.

"She was older than us; maybe eighteen or nineteen, very nice, very quiet and kind of ... strange I guess, for lack of a better word," Sandy wrote. "She had a deep voice, but she was intelligent and she could play the bass pretty well, even though she didn't seem like a real rocker type."

At the first rehearsal, Kim had the trio sing the 10cc song "I'm Not in Love," a pretty but complicated pop song—"it's tricky," he says. They nailed it.

"Suddenly we had a really good singer," Fowley says. "The harmonies got good immediately. She was a really good bass player. She rocked it with Sandy, and then Joan was a good rhythm player, and as a trio they were really good. Now it's time for the hype to start."

The first step: reinvention. Fowley says he thought of calling the new bass player Micki Steele: an androgynous, hard, metal name (perhaps to counterbalance Thomas's penchant for prog rockers Gentle Giant). Together, he and Sandy came up with West, because her blonde looks so epitomized the California surfer. Joan came up with her own last name. It was alliterative, spelled wrong, implied speed, and matched her new hair color: jet black.

The individuals had been rechristened. Now the group needed a name. They rejected Venus and the Razorblades early on; Fowley would go on to use that moniker with another group, when the Runaways got unruly. On a research mission to find "teenage dog shit," Kim went to shops that sold old paperbacks and movie posters. Digging through memorabilia, he found a poster with a "picture of girls in silhouettes running down the street in a Gothic city. It said something about teenage runaways. I saw if you cover the word teenage and call the band the Runaways, it's a tribute to all the girls who were juvenile delinquents who didn't have guitars and didn't have an outlet, and so they would be a monument to all the teenage girls. It would be like naming a band Rebels Without a Cause."

Fowley brought the poster to the band (in other accounts of the Runaways' genesis, the namesake was a French porno magazine). He put his hand over "teenage" and announced "The Runaways."

"They all cheered and screamed, 'yeah!'" he remembers.

The name was a pose, of course; none of the girls, except Krome, had ever really run away from home. "I thought about it quite a bit and tried it once, but I never got past the corner store," Jett once said.[3] But "the Runaways" implied rebellion, youth, and a break from the past. Plus, it was subtly female—most runaways were young women and gay men escaping repressive households. And so the Runaways were born.

Fowley did not waste a second—after all, in September Joan turned seventeen. He could only work the teen angle so long. The band quickly began rehearsing and writing material. Kim brought the group two songs he had penned with Hollywood Star Mark Anthony, "Thunder" and "American Nights": simple but catchy rock anthems. They pored through the voluminous record collection of Greg Shaw, publisher of *Bomp* magazine and owner of Bomp records, to select a couple choice '60s classics:

the Troggs' "Wild Thing" and the Velvet Underground's "Rock 'n' Roll." These tasty but somewhat obvious covers would stay in the band's repertoire for years.

And then there were the songs they were creating, four teenage girls (including Krome) given license and instruction to vent and steam. After "You Drive Me Wild," Joan composed "California Paradise" and "Secrets" with West, Krome, and Fowley. Steele, West, and Fowley penned "Born To Be Bad." These were guitar-driven midtempo rockers about themes that were to become quintessentially Runawaysesque: youth, sex, California, rebellion, parental discord, naughtiness, summer, partying, rock 'n' roll.

"It was amazing really how well all of our personalities worked together because really, we all were such different individuals," West wrote. "When we were writing songs, we basically would write what we knew. Most of the time that meant that the songs being written were about teenage subjects, or rather I should say from a teenage point of view. Obviously, I mean, we were teenagers. What were we supposed to write about; castles and dragons and shit? (No offense, Dio.)"

Writing songs together was fun and productive, but Fowley rehearsed the girls hard. He may have hated his stepfather but he became Friml, a grim exploiter rather than a nurturing soul. His stint in the national guard taught him how to be a drill sergeant. He demanded discipline of his young charges. This was not unheard of in rock history—James Brown behaved like an authoritarian taskmaster to his group as well. "Rock 'n' roll band camp" became "rock 'n' roll boot camp," West wrote.

"Unfortunately, Kim came to most of the rehearsals, which I hated because when it came to artistic thinking, he did NOT have any," she said. "He wasn't musical and we needed that brain time alone. This may sound strange, but even though Kim is in the music business, he's not really a musical person. He's an idea man. He doesn't play an instrument, he doesn't compose music; he just comes up with words and concepts."

West recalled a typical Fowley tirade: "'I guess staying up late every night and taking pills and smoking grass is more important than learning these fucking songs right? I guess hanging out and listening to the Stooges and the Dolls is more important than getting this fucking song down! Right? Maybe you dog cunts would rather go back to your boring old lives with mommy and daddy. Maybe you don't have what it takes to play this piece of dog shit!'"

The most infamous Fowley training technique became the "heckler's drills." Presuming that the Runaways would get attacked verbally and even physically by their audiences, he taught them how to field insults and objects. Friends would come to rehearsals and throw garbage, wood, and cans at the band as they played. In *The Runaways* movie, even dog shit is tossed—this seems to have been artistic license on Sigismondi's part, although Sandy said someone once threw mayonnaise. Maybe, Kim was just coming up with a creative way to bully the girls—or maybe he was genuinely toughening them up, grooming wolverines rather than wallflowers.

"These girls were taught to attack an audience," Fowley says. "You attack them and you play rock 'n' roll, and you scare the shit out of them."

"Most of the time Joan and I just laughed, but Kim was serious," Sandy wrote. "He wanted us to be able to take a brick and still keep playing. He said that by the time he was done with us we would be able to beat the shit out of the crowd with our instruments if the stage was ever charged."

Sigismondi's movie depicts the drills taking place in an old travel trailer. The Runaways did rehearse in a trailer, but it was larger and less trashy than the cinematic version, more like a portable container office—and they didn't use it until later in their career. The drills took place in a rehearsal room the Runaways used on San Vicente and Santa Monica, above a Rexall's drug store.

Back Door Man writer DD Faye and editor Phast Phreddie Patterson visited early Runaways rehearsals. Patterson remembers the environment as professional. "Kim, as you know, is a weird cat, and speaks in his own language," he says. "At this early stage, I really don't think he was abusive … He may have urged them to play with more enthusiasm or something; that would be it."

Patterson described those rehearsals in a Runaways history he wrote for *Back Door Man* in 1977: "Once Kim asked them to do a song for us the way they'd do it live. This meant that they'd put on a show—chord after power chord; Sandy kept a solid beat, often twirling her sticks like batons; and Micki sang and danced, her voice dripping with innocence and sensuality, her movements nearly perfect. They were actually very exciting like that."[4]

Other Fowley friends visited, including Asheton and a talent scout named Denny Rosencrantz, who worked for Mercury Records. Bingenheimer hung around so much West said he was "an honorary Runaway."

Everyone said the Runaways were onto something—but they needed more.

At first, the Runaways thought Steele would just be the singer. So they kept looking for a bassist. Patterson told Fowley about a nineteen-year-old from the South Bay, DD's sister. Danielle Faye's brother had taught her to play guitar when she was growing up; a friend showed her the bass. She joined the seminal L.A. glam band Atomic Kid in 1974 and stayed with them as they transitioned into the Zippers. But she almost became a Runaway.

Faye drove to Sandy's house to audition. "I remember [the Captain and Tenille song] 'Love Will Keep Us Together' was on the radio," Faye recalls. "I got to her place, a typical southern California, cool house. Everybody was really friendly and nice. Sandy's mom came in and offered refreshments. We were just hanging around talking. We were getting to know each other."

Then Kim walked in. "I was like, well, okay," Faye says. "No one had warned me; no, not at all."

The band was so new they didn't even have songs of their own. So they covered "Wild Thing." "It sounded really good," Faye says. "Kim was like, 'That's it; this is my band. We're taking over the world!' I remember thinking, 'Okay, it's not going to be our band; it's going to be his band.' That was the first thing that rubbed me the wrong way."

Danielle liked Joan, Sandy, and Micki. "Sandy was a great drummer," she says. "She was a very warm, friendly person. She was really enthusiastic, every time I ever saw her. Joan was really sweet, seemed very shy, soft spoken. She actually seemed like a very sensitive person—like I said, quiet, a person of few words. She got her point across though…Micki was more, like, friendly, more of a hippie thing going on—not hippie, but less of a rocker chick thing. We were kind of focused on each other. It was hard to ignore Kim, but we were talking and getting along.

"When I was driving away, my head was spinning," Danielle continues. "I wasn't sure what I was getting into. I had met them more organically. With Kim, everything felt like a runaway train, and I was thinking, 'Do I want to jump on this train?'"

The idea of an all-girl group intrigued Faye. "The concept of it then seemed really cool. It was before Cherie; we were more real rockers. There wasn't this hint of a weird personality thing going on. Everybody was still very cool."

But Danielle was already in a band that had original songs and gigs in L.A. Complicating matters, her boyfriend was also in Atomic Kid. It took her several days to decide not to join the Runaways. By then, Fowley was already making plans for the completed group. He has said that she didn't join because of her boyfriend. Faye says that mostly, she didn't join because she had a bird in the hand—and because the birds in the bush were controlled by Kim.

"Later, when things started taking off, of course I couldn't not have regrets," admits Danielle. The Zippers didn't make it, but the Runaways signed a major-label deal and toured the country and Europe. A couple years later, Faye got over her dislike of Fowley enough to join Venus and the Razorblades. She didn't want to miss out twice on the chance of stardom.

Genny Schorr (later known as Genevieve Broome) was seventeen when she tried out as lead guitarist for the Runaways. She didn't know how to play lead, but she had memorized a solo from Lou Reed's "Rock 'n' Roll Animal." The girls said nothing to her at the audition. Fowley told her she needed to lose weight. She didn't get the job.

The *Back Door Man* crew felt responsible for Danielle letting Kim down. Her sister DD heard about a teenager who played guitar in a hard rock band at parties around the port cities of Long Beach and San Pedro. "After much imploring, DD convinced her to at least try out for the Runaways," recalls Patterson. "I drove out to her place in Long Beach, near the Long Beach airport, and picked her and her amplifier up and drove her to Hollywood to meet Kim and the girls. She had a large amplifier that just barely fit in the back of my Gremlin."

"They called me and said, 'We need a bass player,'" Lita Ford recalls. "I said, 'I don't play bass, I play guitar,' and then they said we need one of those, too."

Lita tried out at the rehearsal space on the corner of San Vicente and Santa Monica. Initially, she played the bass, fitting right into "American Nights." But it wasn't until Jett left the room on a cigarette break, and West and Ford began talking about their love of hard rock, that the guitarist began to get hooked. "I walked in and Sandy and I hit it off right away," Ford says. "She was a powerhouse drummer. She looked great behind the drums."

"We were both more in-your-face hard rockers than into the Hollywood glitter and glam thing," West remembered. "Not that we didn't like it, but we were from Long Beach, which was definitely a heavy metal town. … It turned out we had both played in hard rock bands where we were the only female members."

Lita put down the bass and plugged in her Gibson SG.

"I started playing the old Deep Purple song 'Highway Star,' an oldie but a goodie," she recalls. "She knew the song and I couldn't believe it. The entire song. We just jammed it out. As soon as we did that, we were like, 'I love you.' We came from the same place musically. She liked the heavier stuff."

"We jammed out on that song, and by the time it was done, we were having a musical love affair," West remembered. "There had only been one other experience where I felt how I did when I jammed with Lita. That was when Joan and I played together the first time."

7 Secrets

Lita Rossana Ford is a first-generation European immigrant who brought a rare skill among females (lead guitar playing), a heavy metal sensibility, killer curves, and a no-nonsense temper to the Runaways.

Ford's backstory reads like a plot from a Michael Ondaatje or Ernest Hemingway novel. Her English father, Harry Lenard Ford, was a soldier in World War II. Out of one thousand troops in his platoon, only nine survived. At Anzio Beach, in Italy, a stick grenade took out two of his fingers and half his face. "He was left with the metal salute," Ford says, putting up her pointer and pinky fingers.

Lita's mother, Isabella, was a candy-striper at the hospital unit where the wounded warrior was taken. He fell in love with her thick Italian voice. They got married in England, and Ford was born on September 19, 1958. By all accounts, Ford's parents were extremely cool and supportive of their only child. "My parents were my biggest fans," she says.[1]

"They loved their daughter; that's who Lita is," says Vicki Blue. "They instilled this confidence in her. It was a strong family unit. Maybe because they came from Europe, the three of them here in America forged a togetherness."

Raised on the beaches of Italy, Isabella hated cold, rainy England. The family moved to the States when Lita was four, first to Massachusetts, then Texas, and finally Long Beach, where her mother at last felt at home. Her dad was a creative jack of all trades: a photographer who wound up doing well in real estate. "He did whatever he wanted," Lita says.

Ford was eleven when she asked, and received, her first guitar: a Spanish acoustic with nylon strings. "I wasn't happy with it," she recalls.

"I wanted something a little tougher, meaner sounding." Another acoustic with steel strings still wasn't mean enough. By then, Lita was thirteen, and her cousin had taken her to her first rock concert: Black Sabbath at Long Beach Arena.

"I walked into that place, looked at that band on stage, and my whole life flashed before me," she says. "I knew exactly what I wanted to do." (After the Runaways, Ford had a top-10 duet with Sabbath singer Ozzy Osbourne, was managed by his wife Sharon, and was engaged to the band's guitarist, Tony Iommi.)

Ford saved up enough money from a nursing job to buy a used Gibson SG. She took lessons for two weeks, but "the guy that was teaching me was so boring," she says. "He was trying to teach me Creedence Clearwater Revival; I was always into Black Sabbath and Hendrix. I taught myself."

Lita would plug her SG into her father's reel-to-reel tape recorder, slap on the echo, and "I swear I sounded just like Sabbath." She skipped school and played along to records on her parents' turntable, learning riffs. She blithely ignored the fact that all of her icons were men and paid no attention to anyone who said that girls couldn't be heavy metal lead guitarists.

"I didn't hear them," she says. "It went in one ear and out the other. I didn't understand why they couldn't. I didn't get it."

People would come over and watch the beautiful, buxom blonde shred heavy riffs. "I used to think, 'What's the big deal? I don't get it. Why can't everyone do this?' I had a gift from God; I didn't recognize it at the time."

Ford's parents gave their daughter freedom and respect. "I never really hid anything from them," Lita says. "Whenever I did anything with friends it was always at my house and it was always under their roof. I didn't have to leave home to hang out with friends; I always had their approval."

When she did go to high school, Ford attended Long Beach Polytechnic, which she notes was famous for rioting with Compton High. She was a tough cookie with a notorious Italian temper. Shortly before she joined the Runaways, she got in a fight with other girls that left her with a broken nose. She walked away not letting them know she was hurt.

Ford complemented West's serious chops, adding heft to the group's playing. Joan remembers having to really learn to play power chords to catch up to the pair's skills. "Lita could play guitar like a motherfucker," she says. "She could really move up and down that guitar neck like I've never seen."

She also looked the part. Ford, like West, was a California blonde beauty, but with a more voluptuous body than her tomboy bandmates. She accented her assets by wearing tight T-shirts and short shorts. "She was Ann Margret, a Sophia Loren," says Fowley.

The Runaways could leap to a whole different level of musical legitimacy with Lita's leads. But, there were issues. Ford wasn't comfortable with the simplicity of the band's songs. "Lita was afraid that her friends in Long Beach (a notable stronghold for heavy metal and stompdown boogie!!!!—Aerosmith, ZZ Top, Blue Oyster Cult, and Black Sabbath find their most loyal fans at the Long Beach Arena) would laugh at her if they heard her play 'this shit,'" wrote Patterson.[2]

Furthermore, the easily affronted Ford didn't like Fowley. "Kim was a piece of work and still is," she says. "I wasn't quite sure what to make of the whole situation, so I packed up and left."

Ford was in the band three days when she called it quits. Patterson happened to be there "that day that Lita and Kim could take no more of each other." Back Ford's amp and guitar went in his Gremlin, and he drove the first casualty of Fowley's foul behavior home.

But Kim wasn't the only problem. There was another reason Lita left, an aspect of the girls themselves that freaked the guitar hero out.

"I had never been around people like the Runaways," she says. "They were gay and I wasn't. It was wild to me. My parents had never explained to me that people are gay. When I met them, I was like, 'You like girls, but you're a girl.' I didn't figure it out, I didn't like it, and I didn't want to be around it."

In fifty-three years, Joan Jett has never publicly said, "I'm gay," or "I'm bi," or "I like to fuck females" or "I like to tie girls up and make them beg." In many ways, she's an old-school entertainment figure who prefers to keep private matters private. She doesn't want to alienate any possible fans by removing herself as a potential object of desire. Plus, she hates labels.

"She's not a poster girl for anything," says Toby Mamis. "She's a poster girl for rock 'n' roll, and that's it. That's her message."

On the other hand, Jett has never denied rumors and even public accounts of her sexual orientation. (A 1997 *Rolling Stone* article and the 2011 Jett biography *Bad Reputation* both called her a lesbian.) She has also played numerous gay pride events, sang songs about bisexuality and S/M, and sported classic leather fetish attire. On the famous episode of *Ellen* where Ellen DeGeneres's character realizes she is a lesbian, Jett welcomes her to the club by handing her a congratulatory toaster oven. In *The Runaways* movie, which Jett executive produced, there's a steamy scene where Jett and Currie make out to the Stooges' "I Just Wanna Be Your Dog." She's also seen with a male figure at another point in the movie.

Jett puts it this way: "I'm not discussing personally who I'm doing anything with. As far as addressing sexuality, I'm singing to everyone and always have been since the Runaways. I think I'm being pretty blatant. I think anybody who wants to know who I am, all they've got to do is listen to my music."

In 2010, she told this author she had no problem with the depiction of her relationship with Currie in the movie (though she was not necessarily so happy with the attention paid to one scene). "I'm comfortable with it," she says. "Look, all kids experiment, all kids have those feelings, and so I think it's kind of ridiculous not to give any sort of attention to it."

Was she comfortable being called bisexual or lesbian? "They've always said those kinds of things anyway, to a degree. Anyone who wants to know who I am can just read my lyrics. I've always written about who I am. Look, in the Runaways I learned at a very young age, because I could see the look in the writers' eyes when they would ask me questions about the Runaways and our offstage antics, and I could see the way they asked the questions that if I answered this stuff, that was all they were ever going to write about. It was one of those gut instinct things that doesn't have to be taught ... If you want to go there, that's what they're going to focus on. But that's not what I want people to focus on—I want people to focus on the music. And if they want to know who I am, I write about who I am in the lyrics, so don't be lazy, read the lyrics, and figure it out for yourself. I sing to everyone; that's the bottom line."

West also did not care to be pinned to an identity and apparently had relationships with men, although she primarily dated women. DJ Chuck

Starr, for one, claims to have spent an enchanted evening with Sandy in the summer of '76.

"Sandy and I looked like two innocent surfer kids from Malibu," he says. "Our skin was golden brown, we had blonde hair, and something clicked one night. We ended up going to the motel down the street from the Sugar Shack and spent the night together. It was so magical.... I remember she looked in my eyes, I looked in her eyes, and I was like, 'If it weren't for the Runaways....'"

During the Runaways time, the members may have been singing about "Secrets," but they never behaved in a secretive fashion. It wasn't discussed in the press, but everyone around them assumed they were gay. Joan lived with a beautiful woman named Lisa Curland, who Fowley nicknamed Devil Worship Lisa because she was into the occult. Joan and Lisa's relationship, and their fights, were legendary. Sandy was frequently seen with Linda Spheeris, the sister of filmmaker Penelope Spheeris.

It was a time when people weren't so much trying on identities as trying to explode—or exploit—them, particularly in the world of glam rock. Male artists such as David Bowie, Elton John, Freddie Mercury, and Lou Reed openly proclaimed homo- or bisexuality, made their allegiances obvious to anyone with half a brain, or flirted with queer iconography. Suzi Quatro married her guitarist, Len Tucker, but dressed like a butch top, in biker leather.

"Being homosexual, or at least seeming homosexual, was the new way to be black in rock 'n' roll," writes Robert Duncan. "To seem homosexual was the new way to be different, cool, special, a romantic outlaw (and in this case, truly a romantic outlaw)."[3]

Starr remembers he had a T-shirt that read, "1776 Bicentennial. 1976 Bisexual." (In 2012, graffiti of that analogy still adorned the wall of the pizza shop that stands where teen disco the Sugar Shack used to be.)

"It was a very free time," Starr says. "Gays were totally accepted. There were gay marches. I mean, the thought of sleeping with the same person twice disgusted you. Who would do such a thing? All these girls were sleeping with each other, but all these guys were sleeping with each other. Everybody was sleeping with everybody."

However, the closet door was not open as wide for females as it was for males. Denise Lisa says she used to say she was bisexual because it was more acceptable than being a lesbian.

"I slept with a lot of men to get the lesbian out of me," she says. "In the rock scene you didn't see a lot of lesbians, and if they were they would identify as bisexual; it was cool to be bisexual."

In a male-dominated environment, which the L.A. rock scene was (despite, or perhaps because of, the omnipresence of groupies), it was okay for women to sleep with other women—in fact, it was a turn-on. But it was not okay for women to completely reject men. That was rebellion, a threat to power, an assertion of an all-female space. If you were a woman making hard-rock music, being out might cost you most of your audience. At least, that was the fear.

There's a long history of Hollywood icons who have kept their sexual preferences secret, who have remained inside what Vito Russo has called "the Celluloid Closet." The personal price of harboring such secrets can be deadly: shame, hypocrisy, rage. Many public figures lead double lives, hiding their true loves behind compliant "beards"; perhaps this is why West was publicized as having dated Kiss member Paul Stanley. Anxiety over having to deny a part of yourself can lead to depression. Many closeted gays wind up with drug or alcohol problems. Some kill themselves.

It would be a decade after the Runaways broke up that the AIDS epidemic began to reveal the fatal cost of denying and stigmatizing public identity. It took several more years before such musicians as k.d. lang, Melissa Etheridge, the Indigo Girls, and Bob Mould would publicly declare their homosexuality.

Sexual orientation does not seem to have been an acknowledged issue during the Runaways' career. Folks didn't ask and didn't tell. It was an open time of post-Stonewall bohemian bacchanal. No one was telling anyone to get out of anyone else's pants. Yet clearly, as Ford's initial reaction to the group shows, homophobia—whether latent or blatant—was a factor in the Runaways' development. Fans have criticized Ford for admitting her prejudices, but her candor trumps denial.

Without prying into members' personal lives or focusing exclusively on this one aspect of their beings, it's necessary for the historical record to acknowledge that some members of the Runaways were leading active lesbian lives—this was part of who the Runaways were, and what happened to them. Along with the sexism that swamped their ambitions were undoubtedly currents of lesbophobia. Their ability to soldier on despite such prejudices should be a source of pride to gay, lesbian, bisexual, and transgendered people. Not all of the members of the Runaways slept with other women. But their story should be an honored chapter in queer cultural history.

Besides, romances between the band's members clearly played a role in group dynamics. Kari Krome says that Jett was "pretty much" her first girlfriend. She spent the weekends at Joan's house in Canoga Park. In retrospect, she wonders if she was being used. "Now that I think about it, I think she just did it because she wanted to meet a publisher and get into music."

Certainly, it was not a lasting relationship. Kari admits that her behavior helped push Joan away.

"I started drinking around this time," she says. "I just started feeling really weird, mainly from Kim. For me, my coping mechanism is I retreat. And Kim, his personality as a way to deal with that was to push even harder. Joan was not happy with my drinking."

Then Sandy entered the picture. Krome claims that Fowley pushed Jett and West together as a way to shut her out. The two horny teenagers probably didn't need prodding.

"I remember during the weekend, we were at Kim's, and he had this split-level place, and I heard Sandy and Joan doing it," Kari recalls. "We were literally in the same room but I was in the rumpus room below. And that's the weekend that Kim was being really awful to me. I didn't know how to cope with it, I didn't know how to cope with him, I didn't know how to cope with my girlfriend now sleeping with someone else. I didn't know how to cope with having my heart broken for the first time."

The troubled entanglements may have fueled the Runaways' creativity. Kari says Kim told her that Joan wrote the song "Blackmail," a raging flip-off to an unfaithful lover, about her. "You'll wish you were never born," Jett jabs on the Runaways' first album. "I'll make you pay for the love that you tore."

The revolving beds could also all be in good fun. Guys were sleeping with everyone; why couldn't girls? Denise Lisa says she had sex with both Joan and Sandy. One time, her mom caught her and West at her house. They were in a water bed (sign of the times) and couldn't beat a hasty retreat, floundering in the soft mattress. Another time, they were at a party at Kim's, and Joan was "pretty fucked up." Joan went to lie down, Denise followed her, and they started fooling around. Sandy came in and kicked Denise out. When Joan and Sandy came out of the room a while later, Joan grabbed Denise again, and back in the bedroom they went.

Having lost both Faye and Ford, the Runaways decided to plunge on for now as a three-piece. They had already recorded one of those Joan Jett mystery objects, a demo. Taped by Fowley on a reel-to-reel, those tracks were years later released—against the wishes of Steele—as the album *Born to Be Bad.*

On September 3 they recorded a second demo. Gold Star was a storied Hollywood studio where Phil Spector created his famed Wall of Sound and the Beach Boys recorded "Good Vibrations." Fowley remembers engineer and coowner Stan Ross enlightening him about the different physicality of women playing: "When women play there is a difference, he said. Their fingers are different holding guitars and basses and drumsticks and pounding on pianos. He didn't mention vagina-penis differences; he mentioned the wrists and fingers."

The five tracks recorded at Gold Star Studios, with few of the benefits of autotune-style trickery that enables the pop stars of the twenty-first century, sound bare bones but surprisingly full and accomplished. Already the band was honing its chops. Steele talk-sings the comic, hippie-bashing "Yesterday's Kids," laying down a funky, John Entwistle–worthy bass line to underline the chorus. The Krome-Fowley composition offers a 1970s sequel to the Who's "My Generation," albeit with more pomp than stuttering snarl. "We're the new heroes," Steele exclaims in the break. There's nothing Fowley likes better than a good generational anthem.

The three do a Shangri-La's style routine on "Secrets," a song that efficaciously captures the "double life" of teen girls—especially girls engaged in unapproved sexual liaisons. West does a neat fill at the end, because she can. A great staccato guitar riff opens "Thunder," which even incorporates stormy sound effects—no cheese was too thick for Kim.

Cowbell drives "Rock'n'Roll." The three teens make Lou Reed's song about a woman's radio epiphany a self declaration, changing the location of the stations from New York to L.A. Steele talk-sings the verse but gets inventive in the chorus, building up to playful trills and flips—she was probably the best singer and bassist the Runaways ever had. Jett is more than proficient covering both lead and rhythm. The pace drags a bit on "You Drive Me Wild," but sex still oozes out of the "oo"s. The songs all clock in around two or three minutes—radio-friendly pop songs with heavy rocker riffs. All hail the new queens of bubble glam.

Later, Jett, West, and Steele recorded ten tracks at Cherokee studios, with John Locke from Spirit on keyboards and Mark Andes of Jo Jo Gunne on bass—"so we knew what it would sound like with five people," says Fowley. Along with the same tracks from the Gold Star recording, the demo includes a couple songs that otherwise never made it to record: the rather silly garage rocker "Who Do You Voodoo" and the wishful "I'm a Star." "Born to Be Bad" is glacial and salacious; Steele camps up the spoken rap then wails the chorus, Jett and West echoing and egging her on. "American Nights" debuts as one of the band's best anthems. Already, the Runaways were sounding confident and accomplished, outgrowing their elemental material.

The Runaways were ready for their live debut. But Fowley wanted it to be something small, insider, (almost) secret, renegade. A launch off the beaten Hollywood path would both give the girls space for failure and, if they succeeded, grant them suburban underground cachet. But where could three teenage girls unleash their three-chord sex and rock 'n' roll anthems on an easily swayed, intimate, inebriated gathering?

Where else but a South Bay house party?

Something weird was happening in the Plains of Id in the early Seventies. In the working-class, bedroom communities of Torrance, Carson, Lomita, and San Pedro—south of Hollywood but north of Orange County—kids were rejecting the hippie dreams of their parents and older siblings and the dimwittedness of Top 40 pop. They were looking for music that reflected the failed dregs of bad trips—the curdling of the counterculture into subcultures. They found their grail in such national acts as the Stooges, Patti Smith, the New York Dolls, and the Velvet Underground, as well as in their own backyards, where such bands as the Imperial Dogs, Atomic Kid, and the Berlin Brats were playing.

Imperial Dogs epitomized this prepunk aesthetic. At a 1974 concert at California State University at Long Beach, singer Don Waller did his best to out-Iggy Mr. Pop. "Eight million people in fucking America bought *Tapestry*, we're going to kill 'em all," he ranted, referencing Carole King's seminal folk-pop album—singer-songwriter solid gold. Then he launched into the band's signature song, the proto-grunge "This Ain't No Summer of Love."

The South Bay was twenty miles and a lifestyle away from Laurel Canyon and the other Foothills stomping grounds of King and her soft-voiced cronies. This was the new Ground Zero. "...the hippies had creatively peaked in 1969. What was left five years later was residue, smeared all over a moribund popular culture," wrote intrepid punk historian Jon Savage in an article on the prepunk era in the September 2011 issue of *Mojo* magazine. Savage focuses on the Dogs' concert as illustrating "the dilemma faced during the early '70s ... in white rock the '60s still held sway. In America, the Number 1 albums of November 1974 were by CSNY, Carole King, John Lennon, and the Rolling Stones. If you were ten years younger, you were still waiting for something of your own to happen. What would a true '70s rock music sound like? How could you make an impact in a youth culture that had the consistency of mushy Granola?"[4]

Krome expressed this generational gap in "Yesterday's Kids": "Yesterday's kids better step aside, yesterday's kids with their horrible lies." The Runaways would sing about it again in "Little Sister": "It's too late for the kids in love, we're the kids in hate." Punk rock would soon blow this breach wide open. In 1974, *Back Door Man* was one of the first publications to sound the knells of change.

Fred Patterson—aka Phast Phreddie—founded *BDM* "out of boredom and a desire to become part of a scene," he says. "The decision to start *BDM* was HEAVILY influenced by Patti Smith, who we saw perform at the Whisky a Go Go in November 1974 ... My friends were all smart and into music, so I asked them to write."

Among those friends were DD Faye and her then-boyfriend Waller. *BDM* covered Pop, Smith, and Kim Fowley, as well as the South Bay music scene. Its aesthetic was sub-alternative press, pre-fanzine—a knowing, but knowingly stupid, *Creem*. They were impolite and borderline reactionary, "mostly sexist and subtly racist," as Faye admits. Named after a Willie Dixon song (made famous by the Doors), the magazine both venerated rock's blues roots and was resolutely not nostalgic. "One foot in the past, one foot in the future: That's how revolution happens," says Waller.

"We sold well," says Faye. "The people who bought it were vocal and active fans. We were very well loved and appreciated by people who bought our magazine. People who hated us were so politically correct."

The Runaways found a nurturing first home in the *BDM* community. It was Faye who brought the band Lita Ford. And when the Runaways needed a place to play, Patterson offered his parents' house in Torrance on a Friday, when the folks were out of town.

The flyer for the first Runaways show offends graphic-design taste. It's a typewritten, mimeographed, ugly thing—all blocks of purposely misspelled text in Courier font with one crudely drawn map showing Patterson's house nestled in the infamous curve of the 405. "HEY KIDS, I'm gonna have a party and yer all invited. It'll be this friday, aug. 12 [this is wrong; the actual gig was September 12] at around 8pm or so. It's for the debut performance of the RUNAWAYS—an all-teen-girl-hard-rock-power-trio put together by none other than Kim Fowley. Should be lots of fun."

At the bottom of the 8 1/2-by-11-inch piece of paper is a warning: "Please cool it on the dope, though. We'll have enough trouble with the fuzz with the loud music and all, ya know. Don't wanna make things worse. I'm sure most of you have been busted before. Most of us have." Then a final handwritten admonition: "Be there or be square!"

House parties featuring live music launched the careers of many California bands in the 1970s. Around the same time the Runaways debuted in the down-scale South Bay, four guys named Van Halen were making a name for themselves by staging spectacles around the historic garden city of Pasadena. In these pre-Internet days, a fanzine like *BDM* had impressive pulling power. Although Phreddie's party was by invite only, a couple hundred people showed up. They apparently hadn't read the flyer through to the end. "Everyone was drunk or high," Waller remembers. "It was pretty wild, bizarre to do something like that. Everything was word of mouth."

"The party was out of hand," Patterson says. "More people were there than could accommodate them. The noise was REALLY loud. Everyone got drunk and eventually went home. Kim Fowley dubbed it a great success. My parents were bummed when they realized that someone broke into their bedroom and some stuff was stolen."

The house at 3726 W. 171 Street was a typical two-story suburban affair. The Runaways played in one corner of a sunken living room. A purported bootleg from that evening says they played twelve songs, including "Born To Be Bad," "Yesterday's Kids," "Wild Thing," "Let's Party Tonight," "All Right Now," and "Rock 'n' Roll." No one remembers the evening particularly well, not surprisingly, but the Runaways made their point. "No one expected them to play symphonies," Patterson says. "I was into simple, loud rock 'n' roll, and that's what they did."

Contrary to the scene in *The Runaways* movie, no one pelted the band with anything, nor did the cops show up. (Both of those things might have happened at later gigs.)

Mike Hain was fifteen and a fan of Kim Fowley when he discovered *Back Door Man*. He and a friend felt mild culture shock after the drive to Torrance from Hollywood. "Everyone is wearing black leather and black jeans, and we're going, 'I feel so out of place; they all look like tough bikers,'" he recalls. "But everyone was really nice."

From that first gig on, Hain loved the Runaways. "We thought they were really great. Of course we were fifteen going, 'Oh, my God, there's girls our own age who are really cute playing rock 'n' roll.' I didn't know girls could drum like that and sing and rock. That evening changed my life because it really got me into music and going to see local bands and getting into the scene."

8 Blood and Guts

Ex-cop Elmer Valentine opened the Whisky a Go Go on Sunset Boulevard in 1963. Based on a Parisian disco of the same name, the club sprang to instant fame when Lou Adler recorded a 1964 top-selling Johnny Rivers album there. Women danced in cages suspended from the ceiling; voila the birth of the go-go girl. The Doors, Sam and Dave, the Stooges, the New York Dolls, Aerosmith, Quatro, and countless other acts graced its fabled stage. On a November weekend in 1974, New York punk poetess Patti Smith played with Lenny Kaye on guitar and Richard Sohl on piano. Those shows changed the L.A. rock scene, inspiring, for one, the birth of *Back Door Man*.

"As you entered the club, you were greeted by the dapper doorman, Jimmy (probably an ex-cop also), who would stamp your hand 'no booze for yous' if you could not produce sufficient legal age ID," Patterson wrote in 1996. "Inside the dark room, customers were treated to recorded music via a pretty good DJ (Chuck E Starr, for one; sometimes Rodney the B) and movies projected onto the walls (a B Western depicting California state governor Reagan losing a gun draw always drew applause) as they sat at the red tuck'n'roll booths downstairs or on the benches in the balcony waiting for the show to start."[1]

The Whisky became the Runaways' home. They played their first club gig there and returned often for extended engagements. Fowley hosted a "New Wave" showcase at the Whisky in 1977. His assistant, Michelle Myers, became the booking agent. Jett and Curland lived across the street, in an apartment where everyone partied before and after shows at the Whisky.

After Phreddie's, the Runaways played numerous house parties around Orange County and the South Bay. On September 27, 1975, they opened for the Ratz at the Hilltop Theatre in Tujunga, where they were billed as "heavy metal schoolgirls." But their September 28 and 29 shows at the Whisky marked their Hollywood debut, an industry show-case on the heart of the Strip. The poster for the first Whisky show lists the Stars as headlining, but in fact, this revamp of the Hollywood Stars opened for the newby Runaways. The room was full of friends and family, as well as music-biz pals of Fowley's.

"Truthfully, I think a lot of people had heard about us and they came to see if the girls could really play," West wrote. "Word of mouth traveled fast in those days…I thought about how long I had been dreaming of this very moment over and over. I had fantasized about playing on a world famous stage. A stage where my heroes, my idols, had played. Now I was getting ready to do the same thing. It seemed like forever. Then suddenly, before I knew it, I was clicking my sticks off and shouting over the crowd '1, 2, 3, 4'—click click click."

The Sunday afternoon show began with low expectations. "The Sunset Strip was all sunny & smoggy and everydayish," DD Faye wrote in a *Back Door Man* column that December, the band's first press. "There was no sign that this day could be anything but average. Pleasant at best. Maybe even a dud.

"When we walked into the Whisky, it was murky and black. It might as well have been the middle of the night, and, to be sure, in a short while I actually thought it was. People were dancing, drinking and drunk. There were all these suits & satin dresses. There was the usual squalid Qualuuded crowd of sleaze, and there seemed no end to the tight se-quined T-shirts & rhinestone jeans."[2]

Between bands, MC Fowley got the crowd riled up. Waller, aka Doc Savage, took to the stage and mooned the audience. Another girl flashed her crotch. And then the Runaways played.

"They put on a sterling performance," Faye wrote in the column. In a separate review in the same issue, she said, "Their sound is all rhythm & raunch, in the style of T. Rex or Mott the Hoople, sticking mostly to classic three chord riffs. They have a lot of prime material, some being the stuff hit singles are made of…Micki Steele, who sings most of the tunes and plays bass, proves that The Lips still have their place in Rock 'n' Roll.

The long lean lead singer is endowed with a mouth fit for Jagger himself and a mane of red hair that easily rivals Steve Tyler's lush stuff.

"Joan plays a destroy rhythm guitar while Sandy West kicks absolute ass on drums."[3]

A bootleg recording captured that first club gig. The Runaways opened with the two Mark Anthony songs, "Thunder" and "American Nights." When you have only three players on stage, each has to hold down her part—and then some. You also have to be incredibly tight. The Runaways succeeded on all counts. By the third song "California Paradise," they were positively bristling, the sluggishness of their demos a thing of the past. Micki lead the band with cocky and sometimes corny repartee and her commanding voice. The secret of Jett's guitar parts wasn't their complexity, but their rhythmic charge. Sandy hit hard— "absolute ass" indeed. The Runaways would always be best as a live band, from their first Whisky show to their Cow Palace swan song.

They dedicated a new song, "Voodoo," to Devil Worship (Lisa Curland).

During a hilarious hippie-baiting intro to "Yesterday's Kids," Steele talked about "outdated people trying to pick up on people like me," and a heckler pointedly shouted, "Kim Fowley!" The fast-paced "Rock Rock Rock" featured a drum-solo frenzy; Faye singled out the tune as a favorite, but alas, the band never recorded this proto-punk raveup. They unveiled "Blackmail," with Jett singing lead. "This song reflects our lives," Steele said, introducing the rather overwrought and overdetermined "Born To Be Bad." Jett lay down a decent blues lead while also rapping about having seen *Rollerball*. The rap was lame enough that Waller took her aside and taught her another one, lifted from John Lee Hooker's "Boogie Chillen," for future shows.

To take advantage of the Whisky's elevated dance floor, and perhaps to pad out their set list, the band hosted a raucous dancing contest during the first show. Waller/Savage competed, as did Devil Worship. One "Hawaiian blonde" took off her hat, and then her skirt, and then, "writhing & pumping, in a soporific strip tease [as Faye wrote]," removed her hair. Phast Phreddie won first prize by donning the wig and goosing his G-stringed competitor. "There's one man with balls here," a Runaway (it's hard to tell in the rough recording which one) says of Patterson. "No one out-dances Phreddie," Faye warned.

By their second Hollywood gig, the Runaways were already stars. "… it was total chaos up in the dressing rooms. The Runaways were the hot item, and everyone was there to get a piece of the action," Faye wrote. Perhaps, the teens of the 1970s were finally going to be making their own music. For Faye, the weekend was transformative: "SOMETHING HAPPENED," she wrote, starting her column with all capital letters. "I knew it for sure, because at two in the morning we were having a race who could run from the Whisky a Go Go down to the car first, and it was all adrenalin overload. Something had finally happened was all it was."

Faye's two articles were the Runaways' first-ever press. The raves marked an auspicious debut. Barely one month old, the Runaways had conquered one of the Strip's most fabled clubs, with an established act opening for them. It was the kind of break only someone as connected as Fowley could enable.

One person was impressed enough by the publicity surrounding the gig that she had a change of heart.

"I thought about it," Lita Ford says. "I sat there and thought, 'They're not bothering me; they're cool; there's nothing wrong with them except for their sexual preference.' Two weeks later, I thought, I want to go back. And they called me."

"Lita, we can't find anybody who can play guitar like you can," they begged. "Please come back."

"Yes, I'm coming," Lita answered.

"I threw my amp in the back of my car and drove back and gave everybody a hug," Ford remembers

Ford added crunch and muscle to the Runaways musically and psychologically. Slowly, Fowley was being outnumbered. "When Lita came back into the band, we were much tighter," Sandy remembered. "We banded together like soldiers in combat. Our attitudes had become much more in your face in a 'don't fuck with us because we'll kick your ass' kind of way. Translation: BACK OFF, KIM. We had become a gang."

Two weeks later, the Runaways were back at the Whisky, with Ford on guitar; this time, the Ratz opened for them. It was the last gig the band would play in Hollywood for three months, as Fowley sent them gigging around the 'burbs. When they returned, it would be with yet another lineup.

Ford had learned to live with Fowley. "Kim is eccentric; he's easy to be taken the wrong way," she says. "He was only trying to create rock stars. He was trying to create a group of girls that knew what they were doing. He had a really fucked-up way of going about it. The girls in the band took it the wrong way. I understood him."

But Kim was getting to Micki. He honed in on her as he had Krome, and as with Kari, Fowley's machinations undermined the bass player mentally and emotionally.

"[E]arly on this thing started with Kim, this sordid personal angle," Steele told Ben Edmonds of *Mojo* magazine. "He was enamoured of me in a way that I found very uncomfortable. I'd been raised in a sheltered manner … and wasn't savvy enough to know I could say, 'C'mon Kim, fuck off.' … my performance went down the tubes. I—I started going kind of nuts from it."[4]

"Micki had told me that she was thinking about quitting because she couldn't deal with Kim's weirdness," West wrote. "His behavior toward her was abusive. She didn't care for his filthy mouth or when he would come on to her. When Kim would say inappropriate things or yell at us during a rehearsal, Micki never stood up to him, whereas Joan and I would just tell him to fuck off.… She was a nice girl who always seemed uncomfortable. I think at the time it seemed to me that she really lacked that personality that you need to survive in a band situation."

Whether it was because she was rebuffing his advances, or because she annoyed him, Fowley likewise complained about Steele. He told the other girls that she wasn't rock 'n' roll enough. She was two years older than they were, throwing off the jailbait marketing angle. She didn't fit in and was bringing the group down, he said.

"She always had these migraine headaches. After a gig she would sit in the kitchen and look down on the ground and would put a bummer on the rest of the girls," Fowley recalls.

"What's wrong?" Kim asked Micki (according to him).

"This isn't Gentle Giant!" he said she said. "This isn't tasteful. We're singing to guys who jack off and girls who fist fuck, and there's all this rock 'n' roll shit, and it's fun, and it's interesting, but I'm older than Joan and Sandy, and I want more. This music has to go somewhere. I can't keep doing this stuff."

Jett remembers Micki being distressed. "The vibe was that she didn't like the songs," she says. "She seemed very unhappy after shows, almost to the point of tears, like the shows are depressing. She just didn't seem to be at all on the same page. And it wasn't 'cause she wasn't a nice girl or a talented person; she was a great singer, a really good musician. We were younger than she was—maybe we were just too young for her.

"Part of it had to do with the stage shows as well. We were a little bit boring, and we needed to be a little bit more exciting. I was having trouble enough being petrified. Sandy was great. I needed to come out of my shell to the degree that Sandy was out of her shell, and Micki was pretty much in her shell as well."

The four-piece played its last show October 31 at a theater in Laguna Beach. The band let Fowley do the dirty work of firing Steele. He called Micki up one November day. This is his version of the conversation:

"Micki, sorry to disturb you, but do you know why I'm calling you or can you guess?"

"You're firing me because you found somebody their age."

"How do you feel about it?"

"It's best for your project and their project that they get somebody their age because I have other concepts and other things I want to do and I feel restricted by what the Runaways are being turned into. I wish you the best of luck."

"I wish you the best of luck."

Steele has said the termination took place rather differently. According to the bassist, Fowley did not let the young woman down easily.

"When Kim finally got rid of me, he was out for blood," Steele told Edmonds. "He'd realized I wasn't into it, and I guess he resented my inability to simply tell him to knock it off. But I was just too intimidated. When he pulled the plug he went a little over the top. He said, 'You have no megalo, you have no magic. This is the only chance you'll ever have to be a rock star and you've blown it.' Perhaps my musical thing didn't lend itself to his slutty jailbait design, but the way Kim treated me made me depressed for a long time. Then I got angry, and I decided I was gonna show him."[5]

Show him she did. Rechristened Michael Steele, the bassist joined another all-girl band in the early '80s. With such hits as "Walk Like an Egyptian" and "Manic Monday," the Bangles sold far more records than the Runaways ever did.

There are original Runaways fans—including their very first reviewer—who believe the band died with Steele, that with her they were a true musical group and without her, they became a gimmick.

"I started to lose interest when Lita joined, and I definitely lost interest when Micki left," says DD Faye. "I wanted it to be a female Aerosmith.... Then they became a Kim Fowley manufactured idea of some kind of pop band that would give him a lot of money. I just wasn't interested in it anymore.... They weren't puppets with Joan and Micki. The original lineup was a real rock band."

As a writer for *Bomp*, Lisa Fancher was around the Runaways when they were still a glint in Kim's eye. She, too, was disappointed when Steele was canned. "I didn't see any reason to replace her because she wasn't difficult, she wasn't a bitch. I totally believe that they wanted a blonde chick who would wear a corset, and I don't think Micki would have ever done anything like that.... The way Micki was let go, it was extremely unkind how much it traumatized her. I think it probably took her a while to bounce back from that."

Fowley himself has a soft spot for the first Runaways power trio: "The real Runaways, pre Cherie, pre Lita, pre Jackie, were covered in blood and guts."

9 Cherry Bomb

Oh how quickly the girl-powered football team was becoming a glint in The Man's eyes. Denny Rosencrantz worked Artists and Repertoire for Mercury Records. A&R men—and all too frequently in the history of recorded music, they have been men—are labels' talent scouts, the employees who find Artists and the songs they will sing (the Repertoire). The term itself had become somewhat anachronistic, as in the singer-songwriter 1970s, most rock artists provided their own repertoire. Denny was the West Coast guy for Chicago-based Mercury. He was one of the many industry friends whom Kim invited to early Runaways rehearsals and shows.

The Mercury man attended at least one of the Whisky shows, probably the gig with Ford. So did an even more fabled records man: Arista founder Clive Davis, who had worked with Janis Joplin and would go on to helm the careers of numerous stars, many of them female, including Whitney Houston and Kelly Clarkson. It was a heady crowd for a baby band, but then that was the point of Hollywood gigs—to catch a break with the ever-present bigwigs.

After the show, Davis stood up and said: "Kim Fowley, I have the ultimate female rock artist, Patti Smith. Why should I sign these girls?"

Rosencrantz begged to differ. In a loud voice—to make sure the competitor heard?—he proclaimed: "Clive is wrong. You don't have the lineup yet. You're close. You've got the ingredients of a hit band and you've got songs. Get one or two more members and I'll sign it when it's ready, no demo necessary."[1]

The idea of an all-girl rock band appealed to Rosencrantz. In fact, according to Runaways lore, he had received a prophesy about the distaff future of music from no less a personage than Jimi Hendrix. The rock legend and the A&R guy had attended high school together, and shortly before Hendrix died, Rosencrantz went to see his old friend perform in Phoenix. After the show, they were looking at the sky when Jimi said, "Denny, someday girls with guitars are going to play rock 'n' roll, and they're going to be just like spacemen, they're going to be like aliens when they show up in the rock 'n' roll climate—whenever they show up, no one is going to know what it is. If you're ever in promotion in the music business and an all-girl band comes along, remember this moment."

The advice of the greatest guitarist in rock history—a man who had boldly transgressed racial barriers himself—was not to be taken lightly, even if Hendrix did imagine an all-girl band as some kind of far-out science fiction scenario. But apparently, Rosencrantz wasn't completely ready to let the cosmos determine his paycheck. After the Whisky gig, he told Fowley the first foursome wasn't good enough. He also said—again, according to lore—that what the band needed was a couple more good-looking women, preferably blondes, up front.

"Micki says that Kim made advances toward her," says Phast Phreddie. "I do not doubt this. Kim says that Denny Rosencrantz…wanted a blonde lead singer, and that led to Micki leaving the band. I am sure that elements of both stories have merit."

"One of the problems Denny had was that the band were not attractive enough. So Kim got two girls who were more attractive and feminine," says Jackie Fox, one of those two girls.

Toby Mamis, who eventually took over the Runaways management from Fowley, blames the quest for blondes on institutionalized sexism, rather than Kim's own quirks or the audience's baser instincts. In other words, the horny A&R men and sleazy radio promoters wanted hot chicks. "I remember when they added Cherie to the mix and it was a little weird," says the man who was Quatro's publicist at the time. "You really felt they were more marketable with someone who was visibly a sex kitten. Maybe not to the demographic audience, but to the industry, he needed to sell them in order to get a record deal.…That's the way it is: Blonde bombshells get deals; talented brunette, skinny little tomboyish songwriters don't."

After all, even if Steele wasn't working out, Joan was already beginning to write songs and sing leads. Eventually, she would lead the Runaways on perhaps their best studio album. "I honestly never believed they ever needed another singer," says Mamis, who had become Jett's friend since that night she crashed in his hotel room. "She never expressed being upset, but she was always wary: 'Is this really necessary?' When they got the record deal, she accepted that it had worked. Joan is nothing if not pragmatic."

Whatever he has told others, for this book, Fowley did not assign responsibility for the change in direction to a corporate lackey. Instead, Kim blamed literature. He had read a book, *Blondes in the Cinema*, that explained historically, scientifically, and mythically the Pavlovian response audiences have to fair-haired ladies. "It talked about how blonde women conduct light in a photo and movie scene, so I realized I needed to have my Brigitte Bardot up in front of these girls—Mick Jagger and Brigitte Bardot at the same time in front of these tomboys and volcanic girls," he says. "So I figured, Joan, let's go find a blonde bombshell who's your age. Where would we go?"

Ironically, with the powerhouse lineup of Steele, Jett, and Ford, the Runaways had three front women who would enjoy, in their subsequent careers, more fame and acclaim than they ever knew under Fowley's thumb. On the other hand, Steele's replacement on vocals, Cherie Currie, has never had a similarly successful musical career. Besides, the Runaways already had two beautiful blondes, Sandy and Lita. Micki actually added more pigment variety to the group than Currie. She certainly had superior musical experience and ability. But she wasn't compliant with Fowley's jailbait, cock-tease fantasy of what the Runaways should be.

"She wasn't a sex symbol," he admits. "She wasn't terribly interested in the content."

Ironically, Currie would fight back against Fowley with more innate diva ferociousness than Steele ever did, and cause Kim no end of headaches.

So where would they go to find this blonde bombshell? Rodney's, with its teen groupies and glitter babies, would have been perfect, but it had closed. Instead, there was a new club in North Hollywood, for teens—and their admirers. Fowley and Bingenheimer were regulars at the Sugar Shack. Set in a strip mall with Bavarian-style wood and stucco architecture, where gay club the Outer Limits used to be, the Sugar Shack was like a jailbait petri dish. It was an easy drive up Laurel Canyon for the Hollywood crowd and a short commute for all those Valley girls and guys.

The kids came to the Sugar Shack to dance. DJ Chuck E. Starr had stirred a minor revolt at Rodney's by spinning disco and funk records alongside the usual English rock deities. He was one of the defining tastemakers of the L.A. glam, new wave, and disco scenes, ultimately becoming the king of the dance floor at mega club the Odyssey and confidante to the Go-Go's and Billy Idol. But he made his first big mark as the DJ at the Sugar Shack. His secret was to mix a rock set into the dance grooves: the song "Time Warp" or "Sweet Transvestite" from *The Rocky Horror Show*, some Bowie, "Cherry Bomb." "The Shack provided the greatest soundtrack to a childhood that you could ever imagine," Currie wrote in her book *Neon Angel*.[2]

Cherie was fifteen years old and a Sugar Shack regular on the autumn night that Joan and Kim went hunting for a front woman. The story goes that they discovered her there that evening, but in reality, he must have seen her before. After all, she'd already caught Bingenheimer's eye at the English Disco a year earlier.

"I will never forget the first time I saw [Cherie's twin] Marie and Cherie walk in," Starr says. "Rodney just stood there, and his mouth hit the floor. You couldn't tell them apart. They were the most perfectly beautiful specimens of a fourteen-year-old girl you've ever seen in your life."

Cherie Ann Currie was born November 30, 1959, at Cedars of Lebanon Hospital in L.A. Her thirty-six-year-old mother, Marie Harmon, had been an actor; she appeared in numerous B-movies, including such Westerns as *El Paso Kid* and *Gunsmoke*. With Cherie's forty-one-year-old father, Don Currie, she opened and ran a dress shop, Dona-Rie. Cherie's identical twin, Marie, was born shortly before her. They have an older half-sister, Sandie, who's also an actor, and a younger brother, Donnie. They grew up in Encino, an upper-middle-class San Fernando suburb, in a nice house with a pool. The twins shared a bedroom and were extremely close. But by the time they were teenagers, their different personalities had emerged: Marie was the calm, quieter, level-headed sister; Cherie was the wild child.

Money, comfort, and showbiz surroundings didn't protect Currie from a troubled childhood. In *Neon Angel*, a memoir first released in

1989 as a young-adult book written with Neal Shusterman, then rewritten with Tony O'Neill and republished in 2010, the singer writes extensively about her father's eventually fatal alcoholism and her parents' divorce. She also describes being raped by Marie's ex-boyfriend. A beautiful girl whose world had come crashing down around her just as she entered the crucible of adolescence, Currie became depressed and angry.

She escaped into music. "I wanted the music to make this terrible, empty feeling go away," she wrote. "When I concentrated on the music hard enough, the fear and the loneliness disappeared."[3] She became obsessed with glam icon David Bowie, adopting his shag haircut and, as a Runaway, his lithe moves on stage. She also experimented with bisexuality. In somewhat typically histrionic fashion, she writes in *Neon Angel* about the shocking night when, at age fifteen, she first kissed a girl. Actually, proving herself light years ahead of twenty-first-century Valley Girl and sartorial button-pusher Katy Perry, Currie and her friend did more than kiss.

In retrospect, Currie says she was just seeing what it was like to sleep with women: "I'm definitely not gay," she proclaims. "Back then in the mid-seventies, that was just what happened. At that time, David Bowie and Elton John—everybody was coming out. We experimented together; we had fun. We loved each other."

Currie became a rebel rebel. One day, she showed up at Mulholland Junior High with her hair dyed red, white, and blue. At night, she and her sister would tell their mom they were going babysitting, when, in reality, they were heading to Rodney's, or the Sugar Shack, or a Bowie concert. As if the sight of two identical beautiful blonde teens weren't enough, Marie and Cherie carefully calculated their outfits to attract maximum notice. For five months, Cherie provided eye candy in silver boots and satin pants behind Dick Clark, dancing on the TV show *American Bandstand*.[4]

The twins were prime attractions at the Shack. West remembered "their big blue eyes and slim willowy bods. They were stunning!"

Visually, they were hard to tell apart, but behaviorally, Marie and Cherie were very different people. "Cherie was wild," Starr says. "Cherie would bounce off the walls."

For decades, the legend of the Runaways has held that Fowley and Jett discovered Currie at the Sugar Shack. This is the version they tell interviewers; this is the version in Currie's book *Neon Angel*; this is the version enshrined in celluloid in *The Runaways* movie. But in an April 1976 interview with a Bay Area reporter, Peter Cowan, given before the hype machine was in full swing, Cherie offered a very different, much more plausible narrative of her introduction to the band and its manager: "'When I saw the group as a trio at the Whisky, I hyped myself to Kim Fowley and he accepted me.'"[5]

The story of the starlet discovered outside the mechanisms of the usual showbiz machinery—a lunch counter, a club, a YouTube video—is a favorite Hollywood myth. In fact, the Runaways apparently told the classic version of this myth to *People* magazine in 1976, saying that Currie met Jett at Schwab's drugstore.[6] The story of a wannabe pleading for attention from an established power broker, on the other hand, is a common dismal reality. Perhaps the truth of the Runaways lies somewhere in between these poles of plausibility: Fowley and Currie probably knew each other before that infamous Sugar Shack night. But maybe, with Steele's role in jeopardy, the timing was finally right. Or maybe it was the lighting that was just so, and Fowley, who had been looking for his own Brigitte Bardot for more than a year, finally glimpsed her in the tiny but tough shag-haired blonde walking by him. Even the story of Kim's initial approach has multiple tellings. In some, he came up to Marie first, and she directed him to her sister. In the most common version, the six-foot-four man in orange stopped Cherie and asked her if she was a musician or a singer.

In *Neon Angel*, the Encino girl says she didn't know who Fowley was, that she was taken aback by the "tangerine-Lurch." Since Fowley was still at that point probably more famous than the Runaways, this ignorance seems unlikely. In Currie's version, Kim introduced her to Jett. Cherie did know who Joan was; the Runaways were already the envy of teenage Angelenas. The Bowie look-alike put on her best cocky attitude.

"Yeah, I sing," Cherie said.

In her autobiography, Currie says she had only ever sung publicly with her dad and sister at a Kiwanis club. (In '76, she told Cowan that she had been singing since she was two, and that she and Marie had an act that they performed on TV shows.) She had recently won first prize performing Bowie at a school talent show, but she had been lip-syncing. She had never taken vocal lessons, sung in the school or church choir, or been in a band. But Cherie Currie did have balls.

She also had a generous spirit. According to Fowley, Cherie then said, "What about my sister?" (This exchange does not occur in *Neon Angel* or *The Runaways* movie.)

"For one second, I said to myself, Oh my god, twin Brigitte Bardots," Fowley recalls. "And then I said, No, that's not part of the formula."

It's hard to believe that Kim quickly passed over this ultimate porn-fantasy opportunity. He says that he sensed that it was Cherie who had what they needed, and Cherie alone. "If it was a sister act, it wouldn't work, it wouldn't be the female Rolling Stones," he says. "You need the rock 'n' roll bitch in there ... So then I said something to Cherie which probably changed her life and she did not write about: She had been a twin of somebody up to that point, and then I said, No, we're only interested in one girl, not two. So for the first time in Cherie's life, somebody was noting that she was different from an identical twin."

If Fowley's right, and that encounter encouraged Cherie to own rather than share the spotlight, it was a moment he would come to regret.

"Come to this address, and you'll audition for the Runaways," Fowley told Currie. "Learn a Suzi Quatro song."

Cherie Currie's audition for the Runaways is perhaps the most heavily mythologized moment in the band's history. The same people have told multiple versions of it over the years. All the legends incorporate elements of embarrassing naiveté, spur-of-the-moment creativity, and artistic breakthrough. Almost certainly, the tryout marked the detonation of "Cherry Bomb."

Jett, West, Ford, Krome, and Fowley were all there. The tryout did not take place in the infamous trailer but in the garage of a house where Kim was living. Steele had not yet been fired. Currie had learned only one Quatro song; "Fever" was the sole track Suzi had recorded that the rest of the Runaways did not know. "Fever" was in fact a cover, of the Peggy Lee tune, and it was too slow for the band of rockers. There was a moment of panic, as the girls tried to figure out what else to play. According to West, Cherie suggested a Barry Manilow song, "which needless to say, went over like a lead balloon."

For all her wild style, Currie was at heart a pop fan.

The preferred mythology is that Jett and Fowley wrote "Cherry Bomb" on the spot for Cherie's audition. This is probably an exaggeration. Kim says that he wrote the Runaways' signature song the night before the tryout, expressly for Currie to sing. Krome says that part of the song is based on lyrics she had already written. Momentary Runaways bassist Peggy Foster remembers the tune being "knocked out" in the studio later. On the Runaways' debut album, "Cherry Bomb" is credited to Jett and Fowley. Clearly—with its firecracker title playing off Cherie's name, naughtily referencing the slang for hymen, and teasing the arrival of the blonde bombshell—"Cherry Bomb" was tailor-made for Cherie Currie.

As Fowley puts it: "'Cherry Bomb' was named after a firecracker hot bitch who would be up there singing about her own animalism."

Kim handed Cherie the scribbled lyrics. Then, in his inimitable manic giraffe style, he began singing the melody for her—not meanly, as depicted in *The Runaways*, but like a "comedian clown." It was a dance the girls would come to know all too well, the disabled giant's flapping version of Mick Jagger's rooster strut.

Currie was a girl who sang to her reflection in a mirror, who created a commotion on the dance floor—but who had no actual band experience. Nonetheless, she grabbed the lyrics from the dancing clown and gripped the mic.

"Hello Daddy, hello Mom," she sneered, singing for the first time the tune that would, decades later, remain the Runaways' signature song. She stuttered the song's chorus, like David Bowie singing "Changes": "I'm your ch-ch-ch-ch-cherry bomb!"

"She immediately delivered the fucking thing," Fowley says. "'Hello daddy, I'm your wild girl,' and looked right at your cock, at your balls, at your mouth while she sings—looks at every guy in the room, looks at Joan, breathes fire, heats up the room. There it is, the million-dollar thing."

The band took a vote and the vote had to be unanimous. Though Ford was still skeptical after the "Fever"/Manilow fiasco, the Runaways agreed: Micki was out, Cherie was in.

A few months later, Chuck E. Starr remembered hearing "Cherry Bomb" for the first time, then playing the grooves out of it all summer at the Sugar Shack: "What we were experiencing was Cherie Currie's beautiful breasts saving rock 'n' roll."

10 The Fabulous Five

In Rob Reiner's 1984 mock-rock-documentary *This Is Spinal Tap*, drummers are doomed. The band Spinal Tap goes through skin pounders like Joan Jett goes through guitar picks. Players disappear for various random, unlikely reasons, including, repeatedly, spontaneous combustion.

Minus the combustion bit, Spinal Tap's running gag has factual precedent. The Beatles went through multiple drummers before landing Ringo Starr. For the Runaways, the weak link was the bassist. The group changed bass players four times in as many years. No one ever suddenly blew up—but there were lots of fireworks. (As a kind of inside joke, Vicki Blue—Runaways bassist from summer 1977 to fall 1978—makes a cameo appearance in *Spinal Tap*.)

Currie could take Steele's place on vocals but not on bass. In semi-desperation, Fowley contacted the Musician's Union, Local 47. They gave him the name and number of a nineteen-year-old who lived in North Hollywood. "It took two of us to replace Micki," Peggy Foster says.

Foster had already played bass and guitar in a few bands when Kim called. She was experienced and tough: She had moved around the country, and even to Peru, with her mother and her mother's various husbands. They always wound up in L.A. Two stepbrothers gave Foster her first guitar.

"When they found out I was playing in a band with boys, they said, 'Peggy, don't ever let the boys push you around,'" she says. "So I never have ... I knew as a girl in the business you had to schlep your own gear and be as tough as the boys... You had to be a little bit tomboy to play rock music in the '70s because there weren't that many girls doing it."

Fowley and his panel of male musicians, including Steppenwolf member Mars Bonfire, screened Foster before bringing her to the girls. Apparently, the band accepted her without much of an audition. There was one problem: Kim didn't like her hair. She had a long, blonde mane, like Ford's; Fowley thought they looked too "Mill Valley." He convinced her to cut it off and get a perm. "I sobbed as it hit the floor," Foster says. "I came to rehearsal the next day with this kinky hair, and I hated it. I was crying."

Foster's first gig with the Runaways was on the rooftop of a house party in Manhattan Beach. Like a scene in the Beatles movie *Let It Be*, the surrounding alleys quickly filled with kids, and the cops came. Jett insisted the band play on. "We went down there and played music for a bunch of happy-go-lucky, beer-drinking beach guys, and it was kind of fun," Peggy says.

Foster fit musically, particularly with Lita and Sandy; she liked "really hard, ass-kicking rock." The rhythm section connected. "She hit the drums really hard," Foster remembers. "She hit the drums as hard as any boy I knew. I liked that because I was not going to play with some girl who dinked around. Sandy played like an animal."

But relationships between other band members were strained. Practices were dysfunctional, wracked by personal drama—lots of shouting, crying, tantrums. "Rehearsals were hard because we were young and stupid, young and naïve, and we were messed-up kids," she says. "Most of us came from broken homes and we had issues, and when Kim gave us free rein to be mean, bad, and nasty, we loved it. We wanted to be mean, bad, and nasty … We had a lot of anger and we also didn't know how to get along with other people."

Fowley, whom Foster calls "the most eccentric person in Hollywood," fueled the discord. He pitted the members against each other, playing divide and conquer to maintain control. "Kim was too busy driving us apart for us to be friends," she says. "He was setting us up to compete with each other."

Foster's stint in the Runaways lasted less than a month. According to some accounts, Currie and Foster banged heads over who was going to sing the song "Me N' You," a Runaways tune that never made it to vinyl. In the meantime, Peggy was in other groups, with all-male members, who seemed to be able to work without emotional havoc. Foster says she left the Runaways "because of all the crying at rehearsals... I just couldn't tough it out with Kim and the eccentricity and the crying and all the drama."

Jett told a rather different tale in 1977. "She was some idiot twenty-two-year-old asshole, who came in with the attitude 'I am a musician, you are shit,'" Joan told *Bump N Grind* fanzine. "We kept her for, what, about a week....We didn't like her from the start—she was never really an official member, I guess. We were just trying her out and we dumped her."[1]

"You'll never play in Hollywood again, I'll ruin you." That's what Fowley said to Foster, according to the bassist. In fact, she has had a long career as a studio and performing musician. "Sometimes, I wish I had stayed with the Runaways," Peggy says, "because some of the bad things that happened to the girls wouldn't have happened, because they were afraid of him, and I wasn't."

It was December; Cherie had been in the band maybe a month, and the Runaways had already spit out one bassist. If they could find the right girl, Rosencrantz would sign them to Mercury. They had found a woman who could play well—and who therefore had enough options that she didn't need to put up with Fowley's shit. Maybe looking the part was the prime objective, and playing the parts could be learned.

Back in the early audition days, shortly after Ford briefly left the band, another long-haired beauty tried out for guitarist. Jackie Fuchs was tall, super-smart, softly sexy, and into Creedence Clearwater Revival. Like Cherie and Joan, she was a Valley Girl whose home life was being sundered by divorce and who found refuge in records. But it was clear from the moment she stepped into the rehearsal room that Fuchs wasn't cut from the same hard-rocking cloth as the original Runaways.

"I went in with my tiny little amp and my guitar I was used to playing the Eagles on," Fuchs remembers. "I walk in and there's Joan with a Marshall stack and fuzz pedal...Already, I wasn't on the same page as they were. I didn't like them, they didn't really like me."

At that first tryout, Jackie was able to find common ground with Joan and Sandy (for some reason, Micki wasn't there) in the song "Strutter," by one of her favorite groups, the pop-metal band Kiss. Fuchs could play, she was no dope, and she was cute. But sonically, coming on the heels of Ford's brief initial stint, she had some big boots to fill. The Runaways passed on Fuchs as a guitarist.

Three months later, they were willing to give her a second shot, on bass this time.

Jacqueline Louise Fuchs was born at Cedars of Lebanon Hospital (the same hospital as Currie) on December 20, 1959. Her parents, Ronnie and David, were young, in their early twenties. They had emigrated from New York and quickly adapted to the California lifestyle, becoming urban bohemians in the Jewish San Fernando Valley enclave of Woodland Hills. Jackie's mom would do strange, artsy things, like glue shag carpeting to the fridge. David was an engineer; Ronnie became a nurse. Jackie had a younger sister and lots of pets. Her parents nurtured her creativity.

"I like rules and playing by the rules, but I don't like conformity," she says.

Jackie was a precocious, gifted child—a genius even; Fowley says her IQ is even higher than his. She learned algebra in fifth grade, memorized Coleridge's epic poem "The Rime of the Ancient Mariner" in seventh. By the time she went to El Camino High, a decent suburban school, she was bored—"it was too slow for me."

"This is the thing about me that's kind of different: I was interested in everything and wanted to do everything and felt kind of constrained because I came from this family of very bright people, a family in which almost everyone was a lawyer," she says. "As far back as I can remember, they told me I was supposed to grow up and discover the cure for cancer. So there is this burden that I think almost everyone who grew up in that era from a middle class Jewish family grew up with, knowing we were supposed to be doctors or lawyers."

Fuchs was tall and lanky (she grew to be five-foot-nine), not built for gymnastics but adept at basketball and surfing. At one point, her time on the waves earned her the nickname Malibu Barbie. She wasn't a tomboy, but she wasn't a sissy girl either. She was a bit of an overachiever, with disparate accomplishments ranging from being a quarter finalist in the Miss Teen USA pageant in L.A. to joining the student council. "I did grow up with this thing that whatever the boys do—not masculine stuff, but whatever the boys do that's fun, that's cool—I want to do," she says. "So when I was a surfer, there weren't very many girls that did it. I liked being one of the first. And it was the same with the rock world. I was going to be one of the first."

Because their parents were young, and liked to enjoy the California good vibrations—and because it was the age of latchkey kids, not helicopter parents—the Fuchs sisters did lots of things on their own. Jackie remembers being dropped off at age ten at her first concert, the Carpenters. Her parents liked music—Tom Jones and Engelbert Humperdink. Her mom forced her to learn piano, which she hated, but from which she learned to read music (a rare skill for a Runaway). Jackie got her first acoustic guitar around nine, her first electric a few years later. Her rock-star fantasies were fueled by one band in particular—four guys from New York who took glam makeup to a comic-book extreme.

"The moment that really opened up the possibility of being a musician was the day that one of my rock 'n' roll listening buddies came to school and held up this album cover and said, 'Have you ever heard of these guys?,'" she recalls. "It was Kiss's first album. Back then, to see that for the first time, was scary, theatrical.... As soon as I discovered Kiss, there was something about their sound that absolutely captivated me... The other thing was, I listened to them and went, 'I can do that.'... That's part of why I love them so much, is because it was as much about the stage show as it was about the music."

Music also provoked a bit of a feminist awakening—although Fuchs and her friends would never have called it that; they were too hip and rebellious for the bra-burning women's libber media stereotype. She was a fan of Fanny, the all-girl band who were labelmates with Kiss. "They had this big groupie hair, platform shoes, and crazy clothes," she says. "I saw that and said, 'I want to do that. See, girls can do it.' They had a song, 'Butter Boy,' that KLOS would play in the middle of the night. It was a song that summed up every bit of women's liberation, in a sense of sexual revolution, we can do what the boys do. I was very much into gender equality, which I would never have qualified as feminism. Why can't I do what the boys do? That is so much what that era was about."

She and her friends formed a few bands; she was always the only girl. Sometimes they would wear Kiss makeup. She started hitchhiking into Hollywood with friends, including future Knack drummer Bruce Geary and L.A. punk icons Helen Killer and Trudie Arguelies. They'd go to the Rainbow, the Starwood, or the Whisky, maybe hang out all night in the Rainbow parking lot, then take the morning bus home.

One night when she was dancing at the Starwood, Rodney Bingenheimer approached. He had seen this tall drink of water with the soft brown eyes around the club scene; like Cherie, Jackie was one of those girls you noticed. She favored a Stevie Nicks look: tube tops, long skirts, shawls, platform shoes that emphasized her height. She towered above the Napoleonic DJ.

"Do you play an instrument?" Rodney asked.

"Yeah, I play the guitar," Jackie answered.

"How old are you?"

"Fifteen," Fuchs answered, with a "what are you going to do about it" attitude. She didn't know what Bingenheimer wanted, if her youth was going to count for or against her.

"Come meet Kim Fowley; he's putting together an all-girl band."

It was the 1970s; everything happened NOW. You didn't have your secretary call their secretary to make an appointment; you didn't send an iCal invite. At that very moment, Fuchs and her friends got into Rodney's huge, golden-brown car. Traffic had not yet become L.A.'s albatross—you could still get from one end of Hollywood to another easily, the endless summer breeze making you feel fine. In minutes, Jackie entered, for the first time, the infamous Fowley lair.

"The first thing you get hit with in Kim's apartment was this peculiar smell," Jackie says. "The next thing you know was the floor was completely covered with loose change and pieces of paper. His dresser counter had all these Rx bottles on it. Toto, we're not in Kansas anymore."

Fowley took one look at Jackie: Her fuzzy brown hair, her length, her smile. Immediately, he started casting her as the girl next door, the feminine Runaway, the approachable one. The two hit it off; they were both tall, smart, and prone to ailments. Jackie rolled with Kim's weirdness.

"Kim always liked me," Jackie says. "He was a weirdo, but I was hanging out in Hollywood. My parents had friends who were alcoholics, and actors, and gays. He didn't faze me; he was just another California weirdo. Maybe a little weirder than most."

After Jackie failed the first audition, Kim kept her number. In the meantime, showing an attitude the producer probably admired, Fuchs started forming her own all-girl band. Then one day, Fowley called and asked if she played bass.

She didn't. But in true Currie spirit, Jackie wasn't going to let that stop her from becoming a Runaway—not when she could borrow a friend's Gibson Ripper.

Using only the lower four strings of a guitar, basses are generally easier to play than six-stringed instruments. You can get away with only putting one finger on a single string, instead of having to make chords. You can even get away with only having to move that finger once every measure, and lay down a rudimentary bottom. Most guitarists can pick up the bass. But playing the bass well takes time and practice. A strong sense of rhythm becomes paramount. You have to do more with less, not always an easy job. As Jackie admits, she did not immediately take to the instrument change: "I didn't understand the concept of bass as a rhythm instrument." But even if she didn't quite have a feel for the thing, the girl who could memorize Coleridge could quickly learn ten songs.

Fuchs's second audition marks the entrance of Bud's into the Runaways story. Jackie took a bunch of buses to the band's new rehearsal space, a semi-permanent trailer parked on Cahuenga in North Hollywood, which was known as Bud's. Depicted in *The Runaways* movie as an out-of-place RV—literally, a piece of trailer trash—Bud's was in fact the kind of mobile unit that's commonly used for added space at schools, film shoots, and hospitals. Bud's was roomy, clean enough, and a good place to make a lot of noise.

Polymath novice Fuchs played. This time, whether they had been converted or were just desperate, the same judges who had vetoed her on guitar approved her on the instrument she was just beginning to learn. Ever the diplomat, Fowley took the vote right in front of her: West, yes; Jett, yes; Currie, yes; Ford, no.

The vote needed to be unanimous. That was Fowley's rule. Sympathetic to the plight of a newcomer, and eager to land that deal, Cherie persuaded Lita to let Jackie in. Ford acquiesced—on a contingency basis. If they could get a record deal with Jackie, she could stay.

It took just one rehearsal to convince Rosencrantz he had his group. "First time I saw them they were a power trio and I didn't quite like them," he told *Cashbox* magazine in 1976. "Whatever they were trying to do, they couldn't quite pull it off. But when they added the lead singer and the bass player and made it into a regular band, I fell in love with them."[2]

So Jackie became the fifth Runaway.

Of course, the new bassist needed a name. Fuchs was great if you mispronounced it, but "Fucks" wouldn't play in Peoria. A common Americanization of the German Fuchs, "Fox" was a no-brainer. It rhymed, it was hip '70s lingo, and it described the band's sexy new member. Jackie was, in the words of Jimi Hendrix, one "foxy lady." (A few years later, Adrian Lyne named his feature film about teenage girls adrift in suburban Los Angeles *Foxes*; it starred Cherie Currie.)

Jackie Fox completed the Runaways. Her eighteen-month stint provided them their maximum period of stability, which is to say that of the five women who played bass in the Runaways, she lasted the longest. It wasn't, as she admits, because she was the best bassist in the world. Fox complemented the complex mix of characters in an ensemble culled from L.A.'s sprawling 'hoods.

"The real thing that happened with the addition of Cherie and me is that the very strong personalities that made up the band were suddenly in balance," Fox says. "The chemistry worked. It wasn't because suddenly I was the greatest bass player; I was adequate.... There was this pentagram; each of us had two people in the band, not the same, that we got along with the best, then someone further away. So for me it was Cherie and Lita on one side, next to Cherie was Joan, between Joan and Lita was Sandy. Lita and Joan had nothing really in common except the desire to be in a band. Lita and Sandy like hard rock. Lita and I were the only completely straight girls. We had overlapping taste in clothes; we'd go try on clothes and check out guys together. Cherie and I were the two nice ones in the band; we were the ones into helping other people."

At last, Fowley had his lineup. He called them, in deference to the Beatles, the Fabulous Five. They were not his dream team—he found some of them lacking in rock 'n' roll spirit, he would say later. But, as if they were a comic book or TV show, he could assign them all characters.

"They came partially developed," Kim says. "It took the vision of Kim Fowley to recognize it and capture it. Joan came fully formed and so did Sandy in rock 'n' roll terms. Lita Ford came fully formed in a heavy metal way. Jackie came fully formed as the subversive girl next door that could coexist with bad girls. And Cherie Currie came fully formed as a blonde bombshell. So blonde bombshell; girl next door; heavy metal anger volcano on two legs; Joan Jett was John Lennon, Keith Richards, and Natalie Wood with some Suzi Quatro; and Sandy was Dennis Wilson. We had a chemistry. I call them the Fabulous Five, the ones who made 'Cherry Bomb,' that era of the Runaways. Those were the ones who had the best stage show. They were the magical ones. The ones before, the ones after—no. But that particular version of the band—yes."

11 Signed, Sealed, and Delivered

Mercury Records was headquartered in Chicago. The steel and glass Max Factor building across from Grauman's Chinese Theater housed the label's L.A. offices. The famous Hollywood stars—not Fowley's previous ill-fated group, but the five-pointed plagues celebrating Tinseltown's finest or at least most famous talent—dotted the sidewalks below, on both sides of Hollywood Boulevard. It was "not the hottest building in town," says Ralph Peer, who worked in the Peer Music publishing offices at the same address, but it was conveniently located at glamour and tourism central. Undoubtedly, as they inked their deal and posed for photographers commemorating the moment, the members of the Runaways fantasized about the day that the hordes would parade over their names in the Hollywood Walk of Fame. Three decades later, they were still waiting.

Denny Rosencrantz agreed to sign the Fabulous Five to Mercury based on seeing them at a single rehearsal. They did not record a demo tape; they did not play live. It was early December, maybe the twelfth or thirteenth, around four months since West and Jett had first jammed together and just a week or two after Jackie joined. This would be a vertiginous launch speed for a group of known, experienced musicians, let alone for five neophyte strangers. Usually a band must develop a track record and build an audience before going major—play college ball before going pro. The Runaways were gigging like crazy, sure; Fowley says they played sixty-eight shows before their official January 21, 1976, Hollywood debut at the Starwood. The fact they got a five-figure major-label deal so quickly is testament to the whirlwind power of Fowley's hyper hype machine. Besides, they were under temporal pressure: Kim and

Denny knew the clock was ticking. They were banking on the band's youth as a selling point, and the girls were not getting any younger. In fact, two of them had turned seventeen in those four months. Jett and Ford were practically adults!

Signing contracts with five minors who barely knew each other should have been like trying to herd cats with fountain pens. Parents were legally required to cosign. Tutors and chaperones were supposed to be hired. But again, perhaps thanks to Fowley's skills selling snake oil, the girls and their families all agreed to share a lawyer. A friend of West's parents, Phil Putnam, specialized in family, not entertainment, law. The nervous parents chose familiarity over expertise—a costly misjudgment. Fowley's lawyer was Walter Hurst, a Hollywood character almost as colorful as his client, who died of cancer in 1991.

"There are a lot of people in the Runaways' lives that I could be angry at, and if I could really be angry at one, it's this guy that was our lawyer, who was a friend of Sandy's mother, and not an entertainment attorney," says Fox, who, after leaving the Runaways, went to Harvard Law School and became an entertainment lawyer. "When we went in to meet him, the guy was there in cowboy hat and cowboy boots and unbelievably arrogant."

Perhaps Putnam was suited up for the Wild West of rock 'n' roll contracts. Certainly, the documents they were about to sign were no suit-and-tie affair.

Even before Fowley inked the Runaways, he had had to convince the girls' parents that their daughters were in good hands. This was easier with some families than with others. Currie's dad didn't trust this strange man who couldn't drive and talked incessantly. Neither did West's mom and stepfather, when Kim came to see them at their Huntington Beach house early in the Runaways' career.

"When he walked in the door, I was not happy," recalls Jeri Williams. "He wasn't good news."

"He kept talking and not saying anything," says Dick Williams.

Fowley piled on the charm, the compliments, and the pressure. He promised that the girls would get their high school diplomas; they would be safe; he would set up a trust fund for them; they would have a chaperone and tutors on the road; they would get a recording contract; and he would provide a thorough accounting of all monies earned. Most of the girls did get GEDs or diplomas. On one tour to Europe, Ronnie Fuchs chaperoned. And Kim landed the Runaways a major-label record deal. The rest of the promises were as good as the paper they weren't written on.

Whatever their misgivings, the parents didn't have much choice. As Sandy wrote in her memoirs, if they hadn't agreed, "then I really would be a runaway, because there was no way I was not going to be in this band." ·

Fox concurs that these were five willful girls during a time when some youth had a strong say over their own lives.

"It was an era and a place where parents were kind of afraid to tell their kids no," she says. "We wanted to do this and we were pretty headstrong. None of us came from strict authoritarian households; it was a kind of hippie era. My parents wanted to be cool; they wanted to shake off the whole '50s New York thing, so they were being very permissive. Telling me no would not have been a good thing to do, because either we would have done it anyway, or we would have punished them and said, 'Fuck you.'"

"The girls were so anxious," Jeri Williams says. "They were ready to jump in and sign right now … He promised chaperones. He promised tutoring for the girls when they were on the road. Those were promises made that never happened."

Tales of naïve, eager artists willing to sign on a dotted line to exchange their rights/future/skills/soul for fame/fortune/escape/change fill the annals of commercial music. The heroine of *Trilby* gives all her agency to the mesmerist Svengali. Robert Johnson reportedly sold his soul to the devil.

"Contracts back in the day—and probably to some degree today—are taken in favor of the people doing the signing as opposed to the artist desperate for a break," says Toby Mamis. "They take advantage of artists' desperation to get a break and get a record deal and be in the business."

Most exploited artists don't have the familial and financial resources that were available to the Runaways. But the girls would have gladly traded a nice house in the 'burbs for the squalor of a Sunset rental—in fact, they did. What could a parent do, but hope for the best?

"It was her whole life," says Jeri Williams. "That was her dream. What were you going to do? … It was awfully early for it to happen, but she was happy doing it, that's for sure."

The Runaways actually signed two contracts. The first, dated December 29, 1975, and signed by the five members and five parents, was a partnership agreement with Fowley. It includes a recording agreement, merchandising rights, and a songwriting and publishing agreement. This contract allowed Fowley to act as the Runaways' agent in signing them to a label. On February 4, 1976, the girls and their guardians signed a second contract, with Phonogram, the parent company of Mercury. This two-tier relationship "wasn't an uncommon structure in those days," says Fox.

The partnership deal is fascinating, hilarious, disturbing, prophetic, ingenious, and pure Fowley. Replete with broad music-history assertions, parental psychology, egotistical claims, and etiquette dictums, the contract reads as much like a Fowley monologue as a legal document. It's hard to believe any attorney acquiesced to it, no matter what their experience with entertainment law or choice of haberdashery.

An overbearing, paternalistic, and pedantic tone drives much of the agreement. Fowley looked at his charges as a group of unruly teenybopper puppets who needed instruction and control, rather than an autonomous rock band whose affairs he was managing. In the third paragraph, he states that he conceived the Runaways as a female answer to the Jackson 5 and Osmond Brothers, two bubblegum-pop family-based groups that enjoyed wide popularity in the early '70s, in part because they had Saturday-morning cartoons based on them. This is a very different comparison to the ones he would make later to the press, when he would peddle the Runaways as competitors to the Rolling Stones or Led Zeppelin. In Paragraph R, Kim retains the right to determine which members will play at any particular session and on any song. (This clause would haunt the bassists.)

The contract also expressly separates the group from their parents. "One of the essentials to a teenage child working happily within a group is proper parental attitude," says Paragraph E. "A child torn between her group activities and her parents is in trouble. No such torn child is wanted in the group by the group or by KIM FOWLEY. KIM FOWLEY hereby requests any child who believes she will not receive cheerful and willing home cooperation to not enter into this contract."

Writing the name of a party in a contract in all capital letters is standard legal prose. Still, it's hard not to read passages like this and hear the imperious way in which Fowley often speaks of himself in the third person. Perhaps, he developed this style of speech from his regular legal wranglings.

In some places, Fowley appears to be trying to reason with the group. In a series of paragraphs pondering what happens if the members get unhappy and want to leave, he asks them to consider rhetorical questions that appeal to their senses of guilt and responsibility: "How would she be affected if she left the group voluntarily or involuntarily, and how would she be affected if another artist left the group voluntarily or involuntarily."

In other places, the tone becomes comic, as Fowley pleads with a group that was already clearly having troubles behaving civilly: "FOWLEY hereby informs and advises each member of the artist group that FOWLEY does not want to suffer because the members can't do their jobs or can't get along," reads Paragraph T.

You can also see Kim struggling to prevent increasingly emancipated teenage girls from getting themselves, and him, into trouble. In Paragraph U, perhaps the most jaw-dropping section of a unique document, he threatens each member with expulsion if she commits "an offense involving moral turpitude…or conducts herself, publicly or privately (if the private behavior becomes known to the public), in any manner which offends against decency or morality, or causes a public scandal."

Fowley may have been trying to protect himself from being accused of corrupting minors. But the paragraph has a chilling tone if you consider the fact that, by sleeping with members of the same sex—or indeed, by having sex at all as minors—the girls could have been accused of acts of "moral turpitude" by some keepers of morals and of the law. Was Paragraph U, intentionally or not, a way of threatening the girls and keeping them in the closet?

The first part of this partnership contract between Fowley and the band—labeled the "Recording Agreement"—ends by laying down specific rules whose violation could get a member terminated: if they were arrested for drinking or drug use, or any felony; if they were convicted for the same; if they let themselves be "photographed in any partially or wholly nude or obscene manner"; and if they missed or were late to meetings and rehearsals. The document includes a fine schedule: $50 for lateness or for "failure to follow instructions given by producer as to means of transportation to and from a rehearsal for recording or a recording session"; $100 for talking about group business to anyone outside the group or management; $200 for "indulgence" in drugs or alcohol during rehearsals or recording.

Fowley apparently never enforced the fine system. Or, as Fox jokes, maybe that's why the girls rarely, if ever, got money from him.

Kim did not invent the idea of financial punishments for wayward band members. The wannabe "white Negro" possibly modeled the contract after the Godfather of Soul: James Brown fined members of his group for infractions including tardiness, missed cues, unshined shoes, and wrinkled suits.[1]

If the contract's restrictive language was meant to intimidate the band, it seemed to have little effect, given how grossly most of the rules were violated. "It was like a joke contract," Jett says. "Do you think I ever listened to that shit, really? I mean I didn't even know I wasn't supposed to do that. I didn't really pay attention to the business, I just really wanted to be in a band... Maybe he had to do that, like a wink-wink nod-nod, you better put that in there cause these girls are under age.... If somebody was going to get in trouble, if there was something illegal going on, you know on a sexual level that you'd get busted for, I don't know that they'd be busting us; they'd be busting him. So maybe it's all just protection for his own self, 'cause we didn't really have those kind of discussions about well, you can do this, but you can't do that. It was just, we're going to play rock 'n' roll. It certainly wasn't about keeping things under wrap."

Rhetorical flourishes and odd clauses aside, the most important aspect of the agreement between "the businessman, producer, publisher" (according to Paragraph B) and the Runaways is that it is a naked power grab by the former. The substantive parts of the contract follow the strange partnership prequel. In a more traditionally worded Artist–Recording Company Agreement and Songwriting Contract appendix, Fowley claims all rights to the name the Runaways (he filed for the trademark in December 1976), all rights to merchandising, all rights to songwriting, and ownership of their recording masters. He does agree to compensate the band for these rights, albeit after expenses are recouped and at low royalty rates (five percent the first year, rising half a percent each subsequent option period). It's the kind of contract artists sign when they are young, hungry, and foolish.

The contract with Mercury was more straightforward. For the fee of $30,000 per album and an initial term of sixteen months, Mercury bought the exclusive worldwide right to release all Runaways masters (i.e., recordings). There was also a signing bonus of $15,000 (an advance against royalties), paid to the PRODUCER (Fowley) over three payments: immediately, upon commencement of recording, and upon completion of the first album.

"The Runaways and Mercury were like the New York Dolls and Mercury," says Fowley. "They were the only game in town. It was a pretty bone dry deal."

For these not insubstantial but not amazing sums (considering they were to be divided among five artists and Fowley), the Runaways were to work their asses off. The contract required them to deliver one album and, if that debut sold 50,000 copies, a second album during the first term (sixteen months). For each year that Mercury picked up the four-year renewal option, the band was to deliver two albums (for $35,000 per LP the first and second option years, $40,000 the third and fourth). For each album, the "ARTISTS" had to tour the U.S. at least twice for six weeks each time. It was a grueling workload for teenagers who were also supposed to be getting their GEDs or diplomas.

"There's a reason so many bands in the '70s started using drugs," says Fox. "It was a tremendous amount of pressure and no downtime."

The contract likewise placed a heavy burden on Fowley. He was now legally obligated to make his artists perform and deliver the goods, within a limited time frame. The childless thirty-six-year-old, who grew up with not a merely dysfunctional but a nonfunctioning family, was learning a quick lesson in the challenge of managing adolescent girls—not an easy task for the most experienced and committed parents. And these girls were being unleashed from the bonds of (broken) families and schools and set loose in rock clubs, house parties, and Hollywood studios. Kim wanted to create warriors, and warriors he got.

"A thirty-six-year-old man is not prepared to be the father of five sixteen-year-old girls," Fowley says. "If I would have been older, I might have known more. If I would have been a parent, I might have known more. But I wasn't a parent so I had no idea at all of what a parent is supposed to do. I wasn't hired or I didn't hire them to hire me to be a dad. I wasn't there to be the priest or the rabbi. I was there as a coach to turn them into rock 'n' roll warriors and then produce them and publicize them and manage them."

There was little time for fun, or coddling, or drama, or hanging out. With members spread across Autopia, "it was like going on tour just to get them to rehearse," recalls Fowley. "So when these girls would show up, driving a hundred miles a day, okay, it's two o'clock; we have till eight or seven. There was no socializing, there was no gossiping; it was the marine corps, boot camp. I conducted everything from a military training point of view, which might have been construed as being mean, but it's a mean business, it's a mean world, and mean people don't want to see a bunch of schoolgirls become a part of the rock 'n' roll dream."

Mercury had been founded thirty years earlier in Chicago. Through a strong catalog of jazz, country, and classical recordings, and mergers with the Dutch company Phillips and German company Siemens, it had become a powerful label known internationally as Polygram. Mercury theoretically had the benefits of both a small, community working environment and a global distribution and marketing team. The label had several successful acts among its three main pop divisions: rock, soul, and country. Rush, the Bar-Kays, Thin Lizzy, Bachman Turner Overdrive, and Kraftwerk were part of the Mercury stable. Before the Runaways, Rosencrantz had signed the Ohio Players and the percussionist Coke Escovedo, two acts more associated with disco than rock. The label had also put out the New York Dolls' two records, though their failure to make those albums commercial successes would presage the Runaways' difficulties breaking into conservative American radio. The label would have noted success with other glam-inspired hard rock acts, including Kiss and Bon Jovi.

Mercury was not known for its female artists.

"The label was run out of Chicago by a bunch of old men who didn't understand rock 'n' roll," says Fox. "They were trying to become a hipper label, and we were a possibility."

The people who were going to sell the Runaways to the media were excited about the signing. Cliff Burnstein worked radio promotion for Mercury. (He later became a top artist manager, working with Metallica, Jimmy Page, the Red Hot Chili Peppers, and many others.)

"I knew of Kim Fowley," Burnstein says. "He was a character. He was semi-famous if you knew your music; that was kind of exciting to meet somebody who had actually done stuff like he had."

Mike Gormley was director of publicity at Mercury. Based at label headquarters in Chicago, he flew to Los Angeles to see the new band that the company was so fired up about. Fowley picked the publicist up in a chauffer-driven delivery truck. They sat in the back on a pile of tires and went promptly to a party in Beverly Hills. The publicist saw the Runaways' demographic potential in action.

"There were very worldly teenagers at this party," Gormley says. "They knew what was going on. That was the ingredient for other teenagers at the time. These L.A. kids just knew the score. The Runaways were born from this youth movement."

The thought of working with the legendary Fowley intrigued Gormley; he also knew an all-girl band would be an easy pitch to press. He says the Runaways were a priority for the label. "At the beginning stages, a lot of money was put into promoting and marketing," says Gormley. "They were important. There weren't a lot of bands at Mercury that were causing that kind of buzz."

The West Coast office of the New York–based music publishing company Peer Music was in the same building as Mercury. Somewhat coincidentally, the Runaways also signed a publishing deal with Peer. Ultimately, it would be Peer that would help deliver the Runaways' greatest moment of success, their tour of Japan. Ralph Peer Jr., whose father had founded the company, and who had recently moved to L.A., made the deal himself. The Runaways were one of his first California signings.

"It was not the normal act that you would see being promoted," Peer recalls. "I felt it had some strengths as a result of that, but not everybody did. It was not a time when the music business was taking chances, since there was such a huge market for what was already accepted, which certainly did not help the group.... Different can be either good or bad. I thought what they did they did well. It held together. It wasn't as pastiche as the Monkees, for instance. These kids knew what they were singing about."

Peer's deal with the Runaways was also set up by Fowley. It was the first but not the last time the two men worked together. The publisher—who was the kind of guy who wore a tie to the office, not cowboy boots or peach suits—acknowledges that the producer's techniques were unorthodox.

"Kim has a vocabulary that's a little different from what we were used to," says Peer. "He really felt they needed to be hardened and badass on stage, and that was how they were going to get the type of audience they wanted."

Helping the Runaways break through internationally was a personal mission for the scion of the publishing family.

"The deal was a little unusual for us," says Peer, who eventually took over his father's company. "This was a new signing to a large record label, so we paid special attention to it. Certainly I did. It was unusual for anyone to be pushing a group like this in the company."

If nothing else, men like Rosencrantz, Peer, Gormley, and Burnstein saw potential financial success in these five eager teens. Selling them to the rest of the rock biz—let alone the public—was not so easy.

12 Hot on Your Heels

When Joan Jett first met Kim Fowley, she mumbled into her cheeseburger. Her painful shyness—"extreme stage fright," she calls it—paralyzed her. When she began bringing songs to the group, she turned off the lights when she sang—"I had to sing in pitch black initially 'cause I was so nervous," she recalls. "I just had no confidence." Audiences petrified her. There was no talk of her becoming the front person because, as she would have been the first to admit, she wasn't ready for the attention.

The Runaways stimulated a metamorphosis. Jett's transformation from awkward teenager to global rock star began with her picking up an electric guitar, grew via songwriting, built to commanding the microphone, and climaxed with her becoming leader of her own band. Self-expression bred confidence bred assertion. The brutal barbs of the critics couldn't take away the support of the fans. It was a process of discovery and affirmation that all of the Runaways experienced to varying degrees, but no one more than their pimpled co-founder.

Notwithstanding his contractual pedantry, Fowley encouraged his "bitches" to create material. All the members contributed to songwriting, although Fowley usually got his name on the credits, too; he knew that publishing fees are the pension of pop. The songwriting experience was cathartic and constructive. "We're putting our lives into music," West told a reporter for London weekly *NME*.

"Our feelings," Currie agreed, "into music in a way that no thirty-year-old men could."[1]

Joan in particular emerged with a penchant for snappy riffs and to-the-point lyrics, capturing teenage heartache with songs about obsession, revenge, and ennui. She recalls those creative sessions with Kim as foundational to her development as an artist and a person. Taciturn and a good listener, she took his profanity and soliloquizing in stride, but was no dummy or wimp. No one was going to bully Joan Jett, and Fowley probably didn't even try. The sixteen-year-old child of a failing marriage found the emancipated eternal teen an oddly sympathetic ear for conversations about female adolescence. He didn't judge, he didn't preach, and he never fined her.

"Kim and I started writing together, especially once the five girls were together and Cherie was in the band; we really became a writing team," Jett says. "It was pretty much a lot of stream of consciousness, being in a room with Kim and kind of just playing whatever riffs were in my head that day, and singing melodies. If I would play something, he'd start singing, and he'd start making up words, and if it sounded like something good, we wanted to keep, I'd write it down—get a pen and paper and start scribbling furiously and make him repeat. I'm sure we had tape recorders around. I would record it on little cassette things."

The Runaways were no happy, collectivist sisterhood. As Jett began to shine as a songwriter, Kari Krome's star started to fade. Almost as soon as she had signed the publishing deal with Fowley, the lyricist had started to have misgivings. Did Kim really believe in her talent, or did he just want to get between her legs? Her insecurities gave her writers' block. As new members came into the Runaways, Krome felt pushed out, creatively and personally. She says she was increasingly only too happy to get away from Kim's toxic mix of advances and abuse.

Kari remembers riding an elevator with Jett and West, and trying to tell them that Fowley was harassing her. They asked her if she was fucking Kim.

"I was just like, No. But I was like, 'He's bothering me. What am I supposed to do?' And they did not come to my defense or anything. They just looked at me like I was an asshole. Nobody wanted to make any waves and see their gravy train leave. That was their bank ticket and they wanted to be in that band and they wanted to go somewhere. So no one was going to say anything to Kim, and say, 'Hey, this isn't cool.' God forbid.…

"I just wanted to get as far away from the Runaways as I could, and frankly, I was kind of embarrassed by some of the music they did. It really came out kind of stupid. It was not what I heard in my head."

By the time 1976 came rolling in, it was becoming clear that the Runaways were not going to be like a band version of Suzi Quatro, many of whose early songs were written by glam hit makers Nicky Chinn and Mike Chapman. Jett says that it was never her plan to be a vehicle for Kim and Kari's compositions: "My initial intention was to form a rock'n' roll band and play, and go on the road, and write songs. So I didn't intend on just doing other people's songs."

The Runaways didn't have a lot of time to celebrate their record deal (nor did their manager hand them a fat check). Signing a major-label contract brought new scrutiny and responsibilities, and the band had to deliver—fast. So much for school. Along with writing more songs, the Fabulous Five needed to learn to play together, hone a live act, and develop their look. "We were working our balls off at that time, just getting ready to be rejected," says Jett.

Rehearsing was crucial. Every day, members of the expanding Runaways support team—managers, roadies, assistants to managers, etc.—would round up the girls from their various Exopolis pockets. They would rehearse a few hours, take a break, then practice some more. Maybe, they would get some time to watch a movie together, a screening of *The Rocky Horror Picture Show*, the sci-fi musical whose gender-bent outfits influenced the Runaways' glam look. Drug use was enjoyed by most members but it was not a distraction from the jobs before them—although Fox does recall that one time, Ford showed up to rehearsal so luded out, she couldn't find the notes on the strings. And then there's the day the Runaways decided to rehearse in the buff, according to a story Lita told one reporter. But most days, the girls had to play music; they didn't have time to play games.

"We were in a massive crucible that was traveling at a thousand miles an hour, so what would normally take a year of development took three months," says Joan.

With an American tour imminent, per contract stipulation, the Runaways needed to get in some hours in front of a crowd. But they had to gig surreptitiously, away from the Hollywood spotlights, until the five had honed their act.

Their first show as a five-piece was at an infamously unpolished club in Garden Grove, a northern Orange County suburb, called Wild Sam's. It was New Year's Eve 1975. Cherie Currie did not have stage fright. For her first non-lip-synced rock 'n' roll performance, she walked straight up to the microphone, grabbed it, flipped her hip, aimed her finger at the guys in the audience, and the "Cherry Bomb" detonated. "She threw a few winks and you could see them squirming in their seats," Kari Krome wrote in an article in *Who Put the Bomp*.

The band didn't know enough songs for the multiple sets they were supposed to play, "so we stalled," Fox recalls. Ford played endless Ritchie Blackmore solos. Fowley divided the audience into boys and girls and led them in cheers. Amps fell over. Fans got rowdy. "… the rock & roll party of the year was on New Year's Eve when the Runaways played at Wildman Sam's," wrote Krome. "Garden Grove will never be the same." Thus launched the spirit of '76.[2]

Lisa Fancher caught the Fabulous Five at another obscure venue, a new teen club called Boomer's, which she described, in her *Who Put the Bomp* feature on the band, as "by the beach." The venue was packed beyond capacity on a Tuesday; a lot of the clubgoers were girls. Chunks of plaster began falling from the ceiling and the floor bounced like a trampoline from the weight of hundreds of feet jumping up and down. "Literal pandemonium" ensued: boys fighting, girls and boys tearing the bathrooms apart. The teenage Fancher was eerily prophetic in her dissection of the frenzy: "There's this very early-Who-on-the-edge feel to the Runaways that makes one wonder if they're going to continue at this pace or turn around and start punching each other out."[3]

A running refrain in histories of the Runaways is "Kim Fowley ripped them off." The assumption is that the producer lined his pockets with the vast amounts of money the band was making. Undoubtedly, no glorious payday followed signing. Then again, according to the contract, Fowley only got $5,000 up front, before delivering the first album. The band already owed him more than $8,000 for costs he had accrued since August, according to a rider to the Mercury contract.

"The families never paid for anything. I paid for the roadies, I paid for the food, I paid for everything, I fronted the money, and the families never pitched in," Fowley says often, ruefully.

Fox says that Fowley gave the group $5,000, which mostly went to costs like instruments and clothing. Just as she had once talked her father into tying money to trees, so West coaxed money for a pickup truck out of Kim, so she could haul her drums. Another five grand went to Kenny Ortega, who was hired to teach the girls to dance. The band met the choreographer through his work with spectacle rockers the Tubes; the Runaways opened for the Tubes at the Golden West Ballroom in January. In later years, Ortega became famous for directing the *High School Musical* trilogy and the Michael Jackson film *This Is It*.

"He was paid mad money but he was very gracious and he showed up and worked hard with them and they were a great act, a great live act," says Fowley. Ortega taught the athletic girls not typical girl-group moves but "synchronized movements like the backfield of a football team. They would start one song and at the end of the song they would be in another formation, so when the second song started another girl would be the centerpiece, so they had revolving people in the lead singer's place. It was ballet coordinated, athletically coordinated, so these girls constantly moved. They were better than the Beatles or the Stones live, they were better than the Move who were God live in England. They were better than any Motown band. He got them all something to do within their abilities, and it was a group movement, and it really unified the band as a performing unit."

Whether Ortega was worth a third of the Runaways' signing bonus is an open question. Some fans didn't like the band's new polished steps—generally the same fans who didn't like the new blonde singer. Lita Ford has said the choreographer helped her learn how to move on stage. But Fox says he mostly worked with Currie and did little for the band as a whole. His biggest production was the Alice Cooper–style grand guignol of the operetta "Dead End Justice," a moment of high theatrical camp during which Currie was shot on stage, falling to the floor with blood oozing from her mouth. It was so Hollywood—the blonde femme fatale always ends up dead.

Fowley was Hollywood. He spent money on frivolous things, like garment bags with the band's name on them. For their official debut at the Starwood on January 28 and 29, 1976, T-shirts were made saying "The Runaways" in felt script lettering, with each of the girls' names underneath. Their look then was still South Bay, working-class: jeans and T-shirts. The parents got shirts, too, labeled "Sandy's Mom," "Lita's Dad," etc. Ever the shrewd showman, Fowley also had one made for his friend

Robert Plant, singer for Led Zeppelin. "Robert Loves Kim," read Plant's shirt.

The Starwood was a somewhat strange choice for the Hollywood launch of the Fabulous Five, since it was mostly associated with hard rock and metal bands. But Bingenheimer had begun booking the club. Besides, the Runaways needed to prove themselves before this crowd, too, which at these shows included Plant, Zeppelin guitarist Jimmy Page, Kiss's Ace Frehley, and Patti Smith Group guitarist Lenny Kaye. In a burst of hubris, Jett acknowledged the presence of rock royalty in the room with a snippet of lyric from "Yesterday's Kids."

"We understand there are some famous rock 'n' rollers in the audience," she said. "Well we just want to let you know, we're hot on your heels."

"She threw it down," Fox recalls. "The rest of us were like, 'You did not just say that.' But it was cool."

The Starwood gig earned the Runaways their first review in the mainstream press. In a February 2 *Los Angeles Times* story, Richard Cromelin called them "the most potent and sassy girl group to emerge since the Shangri-las." While noting that the band had "ample room for musical improvement," and somewhat paternalistically offering them tips for their betterment, Cromelin also said that part of the charm of the band was their lack of polish: "The group is still in its developing stages and would be wise to see that improvements don't come at the expense of the genuine intensity and aggressiveness that already make it one of the most refreshing bands to emerge from the streets of the Los Angeles basin."[4]

The underground also stood behind its hometown heroes. Phast Phreddie praised the gig in *Back Door Man*, calling it "a landmark in L.A. rock history as it welcomed a return to street-rock that has been conspicuously absent since the days of the riots on the Sunset Strip."[5]

Live, the Runaways showed they could play. (Bands weren't propped up by backing tracks in the '70s.) Live, they bonded as a band. Live, they had fun. Live, audiences loved them. Many artists talk about the high they get performing concerts. But no one had experienced exactly what the Runaways were experiencing: Five teenage girls making sexy, strong music together, in front of screaming, frenzied fans. The Beatlemania script had been flipped.

"It's really magic going in front of a live audience and feeding off of the energy, and having it turned around and thrown back at you," says Fox. "It's this incredible love and excitement, and there really is this moment when you walk out on stage before the first note is played, there's this sense of anticipation. And it is a moment in which time just stands still, right before that first note comes out. It happens in the audience, it happens on stage; it's magic that you get to do every night."

13 Rock 'n' Roll Pigs

The day she joined the Runaways, Jackie Fox said she wanted to be a rock 'n' roll pig, the kind of savage who destroys hotel rooms, according to Fowley. Fox doesn't remember this; it could be another story the legendary prick made up. Whether he or she coined the phrase, it's an image he relishes, a metaphor for decadence, gluttony, chauvinism, and bad behavior that would resonate in the Runaways' lifetime.

"I mean, slopping around in the mud," Fowley says, digging deep into the phrase's dirt. "Just going wild like a pig rampaging through a barnyard and wallowing in the mud. Rock 'n' roll pig. A girl food fight.... That was part of the joy of the Runaways, was the food fight, farting contests, rock 'n' roll pig that's destroying the world, upsetting the apple cart, blowing minds, pissing people off—everybody who wouldn't let these bitches be assholes.... And the asshole element and the celebration of that behavior, and the justification of that behavior, was the key to the real Runaway's recordings and live shows."

In pop cultural parlance, rock 'n' roll pigs are girls going wild, hormonal hotties rutting in animal behavior. In critical theory talk, they're decadents reveling in the carnivalesque aesthetic that has been celebrated by literary scholars for its subversion via inversion. In his 1968 classic study *Rabelais and His World*, Mikhail Bakhtin wrote that vulgar language and literary bodily obsessions—the lost aesthetic of the grotesque—can be tools of social revolt. The Russian semiotician described how the French Renaissance novelist Francois Rabelais used depictions of the bawdy, rowdy carnival celebrations of peasants to, as the French would say, *épater la bourgeoisie*. "... one might say that carnival celebrated temporary liberation from the prevailing truth and from the established order; it marked the suspension of all hierarchical rank, privileges, norms, and prohibitions," Bakhtin wrote.[1]

"I want to go to the carnival," Bikini Kill sang on their 1991 debut album, a manifesto of third-wave feminism. For women, celebrating the carnivalesque—upsetting the apple cart, in Fowley's words—can be particularly liberating. No more nice girls (as another feminist group used to call themselves). Partying, pulling pranks, peddling pee popsicles (more on these in a minute): If you look at the Runaways' behavior—or at least their mythologization of their behavior—as part of their text, then rarely have a group of young women milked the power of the grotesque and the fun of the carnivalesque with as much zeal as the Runaways did. Like celebrants molested at Mardi Gras, the girls also experienced the perils of suspension of prohibitions.

Most of the Runaways moved to Hollywood or its vicinity. West stayed with her sister Teri. Jett and Ford lived with Fowley for a time, then Joan got her own apartment with Lisa Curland, across the street from the Whisky, on San Vicente, in the heart of the Sunset Strip. It was the kind of place where anyone and everyone would drop by—one night the Dead Boys' Stiv Bators, the next Darby Crash of the Germs. Their soirees were famous.

"Eventually Kim threw me out of there," Joan says. "Too much crazy partying on my side, and he didn't want me to kick the bucket in his place. And I went out and got my place... [The parties] were usually where everybody got together before we went to the shows and have a few drinks or something, and there were occasionally crazy things going on there, but for the most part it was really just a gathering place before whatever was going on at the Whisky that night, which a lot of times was really cool stuff."

"It was a party house and whenever things were too boring at the Whisky, we would just nip out to Joan's," recalls Nicole Panter.

"It was sort of a hangout, kind of homey, kind of bare," says Germs drummer Don Bolles. "The thing I remember the most is they had parties a lot. Before going to shows at the Whisky a Go Go, we'd go to Joan's and hang out. She was so funny. She would tell us about all the crazy stuff they did… She was a lot of fun to hang out with. She was like a giggle. She was fucking hilarious, really nice. A good party gal."

Jett and Curland were teenage girls living on their own. They set their own house rules and their own punishments for bad behavior. One infamous evening at 1023 San Vicente, Joan poured urine into dessert cups, stuck them in the freezer, and—like Martha Stewart gone very, very wrong—served pee popsicles.

"It was for assholes, a passive aggressive way of getting back at them in your apartment," she says. "We'd be having some refreshments, pull out some popsicles, and say, 'Hey, have some of these.'"

The Runaways and their associates were also notorious for their way with seltzer bottles. They would spray them out the windows of their vehicles, at women who had given them dirty looks, at prostitutes on the road, at people who they had stopped to ask for directions. Sometimes they were avengers, sometimes they were just mischief-makers. *Crawdaddy* magazine writer Charles M. Young was there the time they nailed a shopper at the Mayfair Market in West Hollywood. The woman had been complaining loudly about damn Jews, an offense that particularly annoyed Fox.

"I used to carry this two-liter bottle of seltzer water with a spigot on top," says Kent Smythe, the six-foot-two, twenty-three-year-old fledgling punk whom Fowley hired to be the Runaways' Boy Friday: driving them around, running their lights and sound, being their roadie. "When the woman came out, I sprayed her. Then she ran over and was hanging on the car, and we drove off."

The Fabulous Five were burgeoning rock stars, pulling merry rock-star pranks in the company of other rock stars. Disneyland was the ironic, iconic site of two instances of high jinks. Bingenheimer drove members of the Runaways and British space rockers UFO to the Happiest Place on Earth one day. They were having a good time, until they realized UFO guitarist Michael Schenker was missing. They found him "'luded out of his mind," Fox says, walking into trees and falling into hedges. They managed to get Schenker through the vast parking lot to Rodney's car, where he continued to sleep for the rest of the day and night's activities, right through the usual wee-hour frolicking in the Rainbow parking lot.

The DJ called Fox the next morning. "I don't know what to do," he said. "Michael pissed all over my car."

"Rodney, go to a car wash and have them shampoo the back of the car," Fox advised.

"But it's Michael Schenker's piss!" exclaimed Rodney, ever the groupie.

"It doesn't matter whose it is; it's going to stink!"

In 1977, Barry Levine decided to photograph the Runaways at the Magic Kingdom. But Mickey Mouse's keeper would not let the band in as they were dressed, because Jett—in all too typical '70s punk fashion—had a swastika on her jacket, says Fox. So the band changed into clothes purchased at the gift shop. For reasons of taste or perhaps perversity, they chose children's T-shirts, which looked particularly fetching on the buxom Ford. "Mickey stretched out," remarks Runaways friend Hernando Courtright.

"At one point we were marching in a line and we had put our arms around each other's shoulders," Jackie says. "They came over and said, 'You have to leave now; you can't be photographed here.' ... We got kicked out of Disneyland for 'lesbian behavior.'"

"One of the girls threatened one of our people with a homosexual act," said Bob Roth, head of Disneyland publicity, to *Rolling Stone*. "They were fondling one another or something."

"They were doing weird things with French fries," said Frank Whiteley, another Disney rep.[2]

She may not have said she wanted to be a rock 'n' roll pig, but Fox certainly has the best stories of naughty behavior. She crashed with boyfriend Randy Rhoads, Ozzy Osbourne's legendary guitar player, at his friend's house one time. When she woke up in the morning, she saw that the guitarist had pulled down the pants of another passed-out friend and written "kiss me" on his ass.

Fowley called Fox "the girl next door" type. For certain men, the key thrill to that stereotype is getting the "good girl" into bed. Jackie wanted to play along, but at sixteen, she didn't understand the game the older men around her were playing. In photos, Fox often looks easily as provocative as her bandmates, whether she's throwing her long legs across Kim's torso or holding a banana at crotch level. Bingenheimer set her up with Sweet's Brian Connolly (Fox says nothing happened). She hung out with Gene Simmons. She admits to dating Rhoads and Billy Squier (a Robert Plant look-alike who had an early '80s pop-metal hit called

"The Stroke"). In retrospect, she confesses she was looking for love in all the wrong places.

"I was sort of naïve about other people's sense and judgment and maybe their desire for experimentation or lack of involvement," she says.

Decades later, doing research for her fiction, Fox took the Myer Briggs Personality test, which described her as an idealist. The designation hit home.

"It talks about how we yearn for great romance and have a habit of projecting onto people these artistic deep temperaments where they don't exist," she says. "I would do that with these guys in rock bands. I'd go, There's going to be this heavily deep romance imbued with great meaning. And they're like, I feel like getting off. Some of that is the era. I was projecting this onto guys who are risk-taking, in-the-moment pleasure and excitement seekers. That's the type of people who usually want to go and be rock stars."

The most extreme story of Runaways tomfoolery reeks of nonsense. Allegedly the girls once—or maybe more than once—tied a man to a chair then left him, perhaps unclothed. In some versions of this story, he was a writer in San Diego who asked stupid questions, like if they could really play their instruments. (Said idiot probably did exist, but "we just threw him out the door," Jett later told *Creem*. "I think we would have killed him.") In other versions—told to this writer by both Fowley and Blue—the man was a fan in Scandinavia and they left him outside, naked. In 1976, *Crawdaddy* chronicler Young reported a similar story, only he wrote that the incident took place on New Year's Eve 1975, the night of the Fab Five's inaugural gig at Wild Man Sam's. Either the Runaways carried a lot of rope with them, or they talked a lot of crap.

Fowley brought other people, such as Smythe, into the Runaways camp to help him. Kim, better than anyone else, knew he wasn't equipped to manage five teenage girls; he just wanted to be their producer and co-songwriter. With the important exception of the late Michelle Myers, his omnipresent personal assistant, most of the Runaways' support team were men. This, of course, was typical of the music biz—and allowed

Fowley to balance out the power dynamics with his new charges. The Runaways were pretty good at taking care of themselves physically, West and Ford particularly. But sometimes, it was nice to have muscle like Smythe around to clear out the assholes. "He was there from the very beginning and he was loyal to the girls, and to me, to the record company, to everybody," Fowley says.

"Kent was a good friend of mine," says Jett. "He had this great old VW bus and would come out and pick me and Cherie up in the Valley and take us to rehearsal. He turned us onto really cool music, stuff like Roxy Music, that I probably never would have listened to if someone hadn't turned me onto it."

Kim hired a relatively inexperienced man in his mid twenties—a guy who seemed clean-cut, straightforward, and good-looking—to be the Runaways' manager. Scott Anderson handled the day-to-day business of the band and usually went on the road with them, something Fowley refused to do—unless someone paid him. "I felt that Scott Anderson should be hired because he could carry out the vision of the Runaways and not get in my way because he wasn't a producer and a publisher," Fowley says. "He's twenty-five going on fifty, he wears neckties, he's clean cut, no drugs or alcohol, all 'sir' and 'maam' … a real gentlemen. And he went on the road, and after a couple of tours he was no longer the manager … Apparently the qualities I described might not have lasted outside of the L.A. city limits."

These men were not necessarily good chaperones. Smythe and Anderson became close—very close, in certain cases—confidantes and co-conspirators of various members of the bands. They wound up earning the wrath and ire of others. Smythe was an unrepentant and sometimes cruel prankster; Anderson was a skeaze. They didn't think much of each other, either.

"His whole thing was just fucking Cherie and being fabulous," Kent says of Scott. "I didn't find him to be a good influence. He was only interested in having a sixteen-year-old blonde blow him."

These were hedonistic girls set loose in decadent times. No regrets, no apologies, no guilt, no buzz kills. The men around them walked a tightrope of indulgence and support. And at least once, in perhaps the most controversial event in a controversial story, some of them may have crossed the line into exploitation, or even worse.

In the 2010 edition of *Neon Angel*, Currie describes an incident in a motel room that she dubs "Kim Fowley's Sex Education Class." According to the account, under the guise of teaching Cherie and Sandy how to have sex, Fowley performed oral sex on a very inebriated young woman and masturbated her with the handle of a hairbrush. Anderson and a roadie whom Currie calls Stinky were in the room. Cherie says they did not stop the producer because "Marcie," as she dubs the woman, was encouraging him. Currie says she finally left in disgust, but that Sandy went back in for more.

"Kim felt he wanted to show us the right way to have sex, and that's what he did, using a young girl," Currie said in a 2010 interview with this author. "My reaction was total disgust. Still, to this day, it rattles my cage quite a bit."

Currie dates the Sex Education class to New Year's Eve 1975. This makes sense; the Runaways could well have stayed in a motel near the Wild Man Sam's shows. She states, however, that it happened before their show opening for the Tubes in Huntington Beach, which took place on January 22, so Cherie has her chronology confused.

Fowley denies the incident specifically and categorically. He says Currie's memory is damaged by drugs and that she has a vendetta against him. "I get to be her punching bag for her convenience," Kim says. "Cherie is an ignorant, uninformed, hateful hillbilly who happened to look like Greta Garbo."

Fowley furthermore says he never "had sex" with anyone in the band or with anyone who was under age during the time he worked with the Runaways. "They can talk about it until the cows come home but, in my mind, I didn't make love to anybody in the Runaways nor did they make love to me," he says.

Smythe also says the incident, or anything like it, did not happen. Anderson could not be found for comment.

Jett does not deny that this "class" might have taken place, but says she has no memory of it. "I'm not saying it didn't happen, but I just cannot remember that," she says.

Ford says she had never heard of the Sex Ed class until asked about it some twenty-six years later: "I wasn't there; I don't know anything about it."

Currie insists that the incident is true and that she has affidavits from West and another witness attesting to it. Her account is borne out in parts by at least three other people who also claim to have witnessed it.

In notes for her memoir, West wrote an account that is very similar to Cherie's. She also places the scene as happening before the Tubes show. She admits to going back into the room—but only because that's where they had left their burgers. Rather than protesting Kim's actions, Sandy tried to appear nonchalant. "…I was beginning to become desensitized to him and his shocking behavior," West wrote. "This, however, was definitely a new low, even for Kim…I figured, maybe if we all acted like it wasn't a big deal, it wouldn't happen again and maybe no one would want to leave."

Kari Krome remembers the incident with shock and horror. She also places the incident in Orange County, and says she was there, too. Krome considers Fowley's act to have been the equivalent of a rape.

The victim "was extremely intoxicated…," she says. "Kim was doing his usual thing of dancing around acting like a derelict. And everyone was just ignoring him. The air was heavy. It's like when you know there's a bad element in the air and you can feel it.

Krome says, "There was no participation involved, it wasn't like, 'Oh I was really drunk and I had sex with somebody and really regret it the next day.' There was none of that. And it was really shameful. His treatment of her body during the process, and his complete disregard for the fact that she was a human being, was what struck me."

No one interceded, Krome says. Afterwards, they acted as if nothing had happened.

"Nobody did anything. I think everyone at first was shocked, and I think some of them then didn't give a shit. A lot of the lax attitudes of the time: oh, someone's fucked up and passed out and someone's having sex with an incoherent body. That was socially acceptable at the time."

The victim, Kari says, went into shock and denial. They never talked about it. "You can see it when the wall comes down on somebody. It's shameful, it's shaming for her. She felt horrified."

The wall came down for Krome, too. "At that point, I started drinking as much as I could. What was done was done and I just wanted to be drunk to deal with it."

Denise Lisa also remembers Kim fucking a female who had passed out in front of others, including members of the Runaways.

"We all watched," Lisa says. "We were all high. It's that haze and not knowing what to do. It was all about drugs, rock 'n' roll, and sex back then."

Lisa, too, went into a state of denial. She never talked to the victim or to anyone else about what happened. But she calls Fowley "a dog. He's a gross man."

Even by the standards of the time, epitomized by the legend of members of Led Zeppelin fucking a groupie with a dead shark, the "Sex Ed Class" crosses boundaries of not just good taste and morality, but of potential psychological damage for vulnerable teenagers.

Jackie Fox says that if there was a Sex Education Class, she didn't know anything about it until years later, when Currie talked about it in *Edgeplay*. "Cherie could very well be mistaken about the details," says Fox. "Cherie conflates things."

Jackie does say that she was not always around Fowley and the other band members.

"I suspect a lot of things happened I don't know about," she says. "There was this world of things, especially where Kim was involved, that no one talked about. We just pretended this stuff wasn't happening."

So how do four different women have similar memories of this incident, if it never happened? Fowley blames the stories on a sort of collective hysteria caused by drugs. (Currie, West, Krome, and Lisa all admitted to having had serious issues with substance abuse.) "Possibly, whatever the story is, there's a thin line between role playing or being drunk," he says. "After a while you hear something, it becomes urban legend; 'I think this or that happened.'"

New Year's Eve was also allegedly the night that the Runaways tied up a male fan and left him on the street, according to Young's *Crawdaddy* piece. Were the Runaways perpetrators or victims that night? Or none of the above? Kim likes to talk about rock 'n' roll pigs. But then he admits that a lot of Runaways lore is myth and hype. "You're looking for dirt," he says, "and there's only lint."

"Everyone in the band has different memories of the events that occurred, and it is tempting to want to believe everyone's accounts," Fox wrote in a 2009 blog regarding the "sex education class." "Unfortunately, it's been almost twenty-five years since the Runaways were a band and even under the best of circumstances memory is a funny thing."

Maybe, a situation that some people saw as consensual and mutual was construed by others as gross and manipulated—and the gap between those two viewpoints has deepened with time.

Or maybe, someone is lying.

14 "The Magna Carta"

In 1976, nothing quite said a rock band had arrived like an album. Albums were tactile objects of an analog age: twelve-inch, long-playing records made out of black "vinyl" (really acetate) encased in cardboard. Or they came in the form of a palm-sized cassette, or maybe even an eight-track tape. Record stores such as Licorice Pizza and Tower provided cool places for music fans to hang out when the clubs were closed. (Cartoonist and *Simpsons* creator Matt Groening worked at a Licorice Pizza near the Whisky.) The Runaways had each had their own transformative experiences discovering an album in a bin, or rushing to the store for, say, David Bowie's new release. In late May, less than one year after Jett and West first met, the Runaways' eponymous debut hit those same shelves.

"The dream was still intact," Joan recalls. "And there was this album with us on it, and our voices, and it was really exciting to see it in the record stores. All the stores that I'd seen in Hollywood when I was a fan, I would go and shop for records, and now my record's there."

The Runaways recorded their debut in March 1976 at Fidelity Recorders in Studio City, with "additional studio insanity," according to the liner notes, at Hollywood's Criterion. Fowley "produced and directed" (again, the wording of the notes). Most bands had producers, sure. But directors?! Were the Runaways a band or a theatrical show? A musical group or a B-movie come to life?

Bingenheimer is credited with "orchestration." To be clear, besides guitars, there are no stringed instruments on *The Runaways*.

As with everything else, *The Runaways* happened very quickly—so quickly, in fact, that according to journalist Lisa Fancher, there were whispers that Fowley had already recorded the album with other musicians, then stuck the girls' voices and pictures on it. This type of rumor—that women don't really play their instruments—dogs female musicians to this day. Unfortunately, some of that sexist belief may be rooted in the actual experience of the Runaways.

Although she was a full member of the group by then, Jackie Fox did not play on *The Runaways*. He's not credited on the album, but Blondie's Nigel Harrison recorded the bass parts.

Jackie says that Kim was afraid that, as a novice bassist, she would take too much time in the studio to get the parts right—and in studios, time is money. The snub was slightly humiliating, as she says she taught Harrison some of her bass parts.

"I think Kim just wasn't sure that he'd be able to get something out of me because I was so new, and he wasn't willing to take the chance because it was not a big recording budget, and hey—every cent he spent was money he didn't get to keep," Fox says. "I don't think Kim cared about making the best possible record."

Jackie's missing from the music, and she, Joan, Lita, and Sandy are missing from the album cover. Only Cherie—the rock 'n' roll Greta Garbo—is pictured on the front of *The Runaways*. In a shot by Tom Gold, she wears a shiny sequined shirt, holds a microphone straight out in front of her, and looks down to the right from her heavily made-up eyes. Her hair is in a meta-'70's blow dry. She looks a lot like David Bowie.

Fowley says that they chose the shot of Currie not just because she looked like a blonde goddess—though there was that—but because it was the best shot out of a measly selection. Perhaps Kim was too cheap to hire a professional; Gold was simply a fan. In any case, the other members were not pleased. Resentment over Currie being presented as "the Runaways" would fester then explode two years later in, fittingly, a photo shoot.

"Cherie was happy about it," Fowley says about *The Runaways* cover. "Cherie and I never got along; we had brief moments of being civil and cordial in offices but we did not get along, so it wasn't favoritism. She just happened to look good and the cover was great, I thought. So did Mercury."

The album opened into a gatefold, a more elaborate and expensive package that demonstrated the label was at that point willing to invest money in its new signing. Except for a slightly grinning Fox, the whole band peers unsmilingly from a group photo, dressed in blue jeans and various casual shirts. They're a tough-looking gang of high school babes staring straight at the camera. With her shirt unbuttoned down to her belly button, Cherie, in the middle, looks like the gang leader—she's in a provocative butch pose femmed up by a diamond choker. All five are also pictured in separate portraits on the back, with their ages and instruments. Jett is wrongly ID'd as sixteen—already the exploitation of the Runaways' youth was turning into fabrication. You could ogle these girls for hours, playing the record over and over, and wonder what they're like, what they like, if they'd be your friend, if they'd love/kiss/fuck you.

"This album is for the young of age and the young at heart. It's for those who know it's great to be young and who enjoy their youth in the best way they know how," Jett says in a "Message to You" next to the photo.

The Runaways is Kim Fowley's favorite Runaways studio album, mostly because it's the one where he had the most control so it reflects his crude pop sensibilities. "The girls didn't understand why the first album worked," he says. "It worked because I wrote most of the songs with somebody. … Everyone's first album is always the one where they don't question authority. Rock 'n' roll was a dictatorship; Stan Ross told me that. Somebody has to say this is how we're going to do it."

Fowley wasn't just a dictator; he was a dick. Fox and Currie were his two favorite targets because they were youngest and most vulnerable. "Everyone else was the tough chicks, they'd say 'fuck you,'" Jackie recalls. "We took the brunt of his verbal abuse."

Kim made Currie sing in the dark and harangued her constantly. "He was trying to tear her down," says Fox. "His theory was that if he could make her feel ugly, she would sing more attractively to get attention."

Most of the ten songs on the debut had been in the band's repertoire for a while. But this was the first recording of "Cherry Bomb," which sets the provocative tone as the opening track. Joan and Sandy lock into the stuttering rhythmic lead for two bars. A whooshing sound announces the arrival of Cherie, and here she is, all itchy, impatient urgency: "Hello world, I'm your wild girl … I'm the fox you've been waiting for." The giddily simple song bristles. A dash of moaning makes it clear that Fowley had abandoned bubblegum aspirations for jailbait appeal. Two minutes and eighteen seconds later, Fowley and engineer Andy Morris earn their money with some echo, and the Runaways' legacy on soundtracks, TV shows, and commercials was assured. In 2012, their very first recorded track remained their biggest money-maker, according to their publisher Ralph Peer. "Cherry Bomb" has been featured in the films *Dazed and Confused* and *RV,* and covered by Miley Cyrus, Bratmobile, the Dandy Warhols, L7, and Shonen Knife. In 2012, Hollywood Records released the debut of an all-girl band named Cherri Bomb.

Jett sings the first-ever song she wrote, "You Drive Me Wild," as *The Runaways'* second track. She growls the title, introducing the world to that rasp that would become simultaneous with love of rock 'n' roll. This version has been spruced up and goosed compared to the early demo recordings, and Ford pushes it further with a serious blues-rock lead in the break. Jett credits her own guitar sound to her ignorance. "On the first album, I didn't have a distortion pedal," she says. "I didn't know what that was. My guitar sounds really clean; that's just because I didn't know totally what I was doing yet, or how I wanted to sound. I didn't know how to set up my amp properly. I was still learning. Lita knew all her gear; she knew exactly what she was doing. She was much more practiced than I was, for sure."

Fowley says Joan channeled the early Beatles for "You Drive Me Wild"; he dubs it "Liverpool revisited."

Currie's back on the drug-addled "Is It Day or Night?"; she and Jett split the vocal duties on the album. Cherie over-delivers the hard lyrics a tad. Metal was never a good fit for the singer; riffs laid the root of her rifts with Ford. "It's a total Kim song," Fox says, "about being fucked up." Fowley's take on the track: "Kim Fowley by himself knows how to write a good song."

Joan and Cherie share the vocals on "Thunder," two teenage girls dueting on a song about the awesomeness of sex. Kim credits the composition to "the genius of Kari Krome and the late Mark Anthony." Fox says "Thunder," whose rhythmic riff sounds a wee bit too close to "Cherry Bomb," was a holdover that they soon dropped from their repertoire: "We considered it a little too pop; we wanted a harder sound."

Sandy's cowbell counts the listener into the Velvets' cover "Rock & Roll." The song, with its tale of a girl discovering rock 'n' roll on the radio, then becoming a star herself, was wishful thinking, if not prophesy. Ford and Jett's tag-back leads keep the song playful, not dumbed down. And then, in the old vinyl days, side one would end with Currie's echoing "It was all right!" and you'd flip the record over.

Side two kicks off with a mostly forgotten Runaways tune, "Lovers," another song about sex, written by Fowley and Jett and sung by Joan. Fowley claimed he wrote the song by using all the words that a computer had determined the Beatles had used the most. "It was Kim's attempt to write a Beatles song by osmosis," Fox says. "Obviously it didn't work. It's not a song any of us particularly liked and we didn't play it live." The song's cheesy call-and-response isn't fully realized, but West's barreling drums offer a nice switch from the album's repetition of ch-ch-ch beats. Fowley admits it was not his finest moment. "It shouldn't have been on the album," the would-be Brian Epstein says. "It was stupid. Wrong kind of stupid."

"American Nights" had all the makings of a hit, of a rock'n'roll party anthem to be played to death on classic-rock radio—a favorite track for generations of Rock Band or Guitar Hero players. Kim's lingering sub-Beat images—"alleys of screams"—decorate Anthony's killer hooks: that great "whacka whacka whacka" wait-for-it at the end of each line. The Runaways play the song like passionate pros, locked in and on the beat, hitting those whacka's right on time every time. Maybe, Joan should have sung "American Nights," or at least split the vocals with Cherie. Currie tries to draw up rock'n'roll authority by singing deep, but the effort sounds forced, like a kind of masculine drag instead of an all-night scorcher. Jett's hoarse but direct alto might have worked better.

But even as is, "American Nights" beats the shit out of a heap of other over-played journeyman rock songs that still keep their extension-wearing one-hit wonders afloat in Viagra funds. Fowley says he "asked and begged, pleaded and cajoled" for it to be the second single, but Mercury refused to release a second single from the first album. "American Nights" could have earned the Runaways the moniker that they take on for the first time in the song's lyrics: the "Queens of Noise." Instead, their label left them stuck as "Cherry Bomb."

Jett twists and shouts the opening "aow" of "Blackmail." "Go Lita!" she screams as the blues song swings into the instrumental break, and Lita goes. The song bristles with hurt and malice—"buh-lack" the future leader of the Blackhearts pronounces. "Joan's songs were full of suspicion," Fox notes drily. Fowley takes partial credit: "Once again Kim Fowley and Joan Jett deliver the Liverpool goods."

Currie nails the vocals on "Secrets." The song's just the right mix of playful and adolescent for Cherie's more glam sensibilities; she doesn't have to pretend she's something she's not. Fox says the band had to re-write "Secrets" in order not to have to pay Steele royalties. The tune's credited to Currie, Fowley, Krome, and West. Bobby Sky plays some rather unnecessary piano; he's better on "American Nights." "It's a good album cut," Kim says. "It's all about teenage codes, what everyone knows, living a double life."

The Runaways goes out with a bang—literally. "Dead End Justice" earned the band fame and infamy. The almost seven-minute-long song is the Runaways' answer to the Shangri-La's' "Leader of the Pack" and Queen's "Bohemian Rhapsody." The rock operetta tells the story of two juvenile delinquents, played by Joan and Cherie, who break out of jail together—only Cherie doesn't make it. The song starts auspiciously, with Jett singing lines that Currie speaks her answer to and Lita punctuates with a ripping lead. Then they switch roles; Currie calls, Jett responds. "Dead end kids in the danger zone," they sing together in the chorus, in some of the band's best lyrics. The song's credited to Fowley, Jett, Currie and Anderson—his sole songwriting credit.

But then "Justice" breaks down. In a cheesy spoken segue, Currie de-scribes their JD journey to jail in sing-songy rhymes. "This is like a movie," she talk-sings—a bad B-movie. West lays down some martial beats, but the fight's already been sucked out of "Dead End Justice." The song trails out with Cherie tinkling some piano bars that sound like Ian Stewart is in the next room playing "Paint it Black." "Dead End Kids" devolves into rock 'n' roll melodrama, hard-rock kitsch—another novelty song by the maker of "Alley Oop."

The binary nature of "Dead End Justice" is apparently a direct result of its genesis. "Dead End Justice" crudely fuses together two songs: "Dead End Kids" and "Justice." "There was some sense they weren't good enough on their own, so Kim put them together as a 'girls in juvie' drama," Fox says.

"We proved we could do the whole *Tommy* opera in one song," as Fowley puts it.

People love "Dead End Justice." It's the song that made Kathleen Hanna, singer of Bikini Kill, Le Tigre, and Julie Ruin, a Runaways fan. "It reminded me of being a kid and making stuff up," she says. "The whole talking about juvie and getting in trouble and being these messed-up girls. We were those messed-up girls with feathered hair."

Hanna and the great techno-booty performance artist Peaches capture the song's camp on the ill-fated 2011 Runaways tribute album *Take It or Leave It*. Kathleen takes Cherie's parts, Peaches Joan's. As kitsch pastiche, "Dead End Justice" rocks.

"I'm proud of *The Runaways* LP," Fowley told *Melody Maker* in perhaps his most hyperbolic prose ever. "This album could win a Nobel Peace Prize. It's as important as the Magna Carta. This is a significant sociological statement. An album for teens, by teens."[1]

Alicia Velasquez remembers the Runaways' first album helping inspire her to form her own band, the Bags. "When we heard the Runaways record, it wasn't as slick or technically impressive, but it was fresh and innovative and daring," says the singer who performed under the name Alice Bag. "We could see ourselves in the Runaways. Besides, it was more fun to fumble our way through 'American Nights' than to practice scales, hoping to someday be able to play 'Bohemian Rhapsody.'"

Thousands of miles away and years later, *The Runaways* would still reach kids with its anthems of adolescence. Omid Yamini was an Iranian-American teenager stranded in Virginia when he discovered the band's music in the early '90s. "Lyrically and thematically, that first album was written by teenagers for teenagers," says Yamini, who went on to amass perhaps the largest Runaways collection in the world. "'Cherry Bomb' was a perfect anthem for kids from troubled and dysfunctional homes, who were not fitting in at home or at school, who were out partying on the streets. It has a lot of messages and depth to it. My household was a mess and we found ways to escape. They captured that musically, with an element of hope."

Making the first album was one thing. Selling it was another. The record company launched a fairly ambitious publicity campaign for SRM 1-1090 (the catalog number for *The Runaways*). "Mercury Records has the new Stooges!" announced a press release signed by Mike Bone, who was in charge of the label's National Album Promotion (and later became president of Chrysalis Records). "The buzz on the street says the Runaways are going to happen big. Think about it; sixteen-year-old beautiful girls playing hard rock. If you can't relate to it, you're dead."

Never mind that by May 1976, Jett and Ford were both seventeen.

The band biography released to the press by Mercury got the members' ages right. In nicely worded, not-too-hypey prose, the bio explains the importance of the Runaways in the first paragraph: "There are two myths that exist in rock: that neither teenagers nor females can rock. Bull!! Who do you think Chuck Berry, Brian Wilson, and Paul McCartney have been singing to all these years? Male collegians? Rock and roll exists because teenagers exist."

The bio continues in this straightforward vein, offering snippets of each member's history. Towards the end, it comes back to the teen angle: "Some people might not like the idea of five girls daring to tackle rock and roll on a gut level. The Runaways' music is not for weak bodies and hearts, just for young bodies and the young at heart."

Mercury's publicity head, Mike Gormley, found out pretty quickly that the Runaways would be an easy sell, press wise. He took a test pressing and a photograph of the band to the New York headquarters of rock magazine *Circus*. By April 27 they'd published a news piece; by that summer, a cover story. The April article makes fun of the age angle, reporting that Fowley "swears by everything holy that no member of the band is over sixteen years old. How Fowley intends to keep them that way, God only knows."[2]

"I knew right away we'd get press on them," Gormley says. "An all-girl band was so unique; they were also young and pretty sexy."

Gormley credits Fowley with drawing initial attention to the Runaways and teaching them how to handle the press. He also says the girls were just adept at interviews and press shoots; he never needed to babysit them. "By the time I was with them they had a natural thing. They were very interesting people to talk to," he says. "They were tough and they were knowledgeable and they knew how to manipulate guys. Kim was a little magic potion to the whole thing. His involvement was a definite plus. The press loved him."

Actually, the press loved and hated Kim and the Runaways. The band earned a lot of ink, but much of it—especially as a backlash to the attention the girls were getting built—expressed a venom that seemed outsized for such a young act. They were frequently trivialized and objectified—"nymphet" was a favorite term. Sometimes, they were outright demonized.

"The thing that gets lost in the aura that surrounds the Runaways now is how big a joke we were considered back in the '70s," notes Fox.

The first album garnered mostly positive reviews; the attacks came later. And the response came from a variety of media: mainstream magazines such as *People*, daily and weekly newspapers, and the often cranky music press. Influential *Creem* magazine—probably the most important taste-maker among rock heads—bought the teen beat. "The Runaways' album can easily be earmarked right alongside the first Stooges record in its expression of teenage passions, its slurring of lyrics into pouting monosyllables, and its final call to dance to the rock 'n' roll beat," Robot A. Hull wrote in a review that ran between write-ups of the Ramones' and the Modern Lovers' first albums.[3] Talk about auspicious company: In those three eponymous debuts, the first outcroppings of Yankee punk can be traced. *Creem* got it right back then, but in the years since, the Runaways' importance to an emergent American underground has been outshadowed by those East Coast male peers.

Fowley aggressively courted the press, and their reviews often echoed his pitches. Critic Ben Edmonds caught some of the earliest Runaways gigs and rehearsals and was primed for the album's release. But even he was a little circumspect in his review for *Phonograph Record*: "The group's limitations are perfectly evident halfway through the first song, but much of the album's considerable charm is that no attempt is made to mask the ground-floor level of this band's development." Except for West, whom, he concedes "could easily hold her own in any company," Edmonds describes the band's playing as "good enough." "They score their heaviest points on attitude. Their music is obviously born of suburban nights spent listening to third generation rock and roll and wishing they could do it, and then going to concerts to see an endless stream of old men do the supergroup shuffle and knowing that they could do it after all."[4]

Los Angeles Times critic Robert Hilburn also weighed in with somewhat tempered praise, calling *The Runaways* "flawed, but not nearly enough to keep the album from being a most inviting introduction to a delightfully promising female band that is firmly entrenched in the Quatro/Sweet/New York Dolls tradition."[5] The same week the album debuted at 188 on the *Cash Box* charts, that trade publication gushed: "This album contains ten of the hottest, sweatiest, nasty-est most straight-ahead rock 'n' roll songs that we've ever heard."

Scott Isler at *Crawdaddy* liked the bad-girl angle: "...*The Runaways* is good music for housewrecking."[6] But his tone was positively genteel compared to Kris Needs, whose review for *ZigZag* dripped with drool. Needs literally began his treatise by talking about masturbating to the picture of Currie—though he "cleverly" cut the word short and exchanged it for another verb: "This platter boasts one of the most fetching sleeves I've had the pleasure to mas .... ogle at." He calls the band a "delectable teen dream." Oh yeah, the music: Fortunately he liked that, too: "the music sounds as fresh and exciting as the girls look," Needs opined.[7]

One of the most astute reviews was evidently the only one written by a woman; rock criticism was very much a man's club in the '70s (and would remain so for decades). In *Circus*, Georgia Christgau wrote that *The Runaways* "is more complicated than it is great." She compared the band—unfavorably—to '60s actor Hayley Mills, who "interpreted her roles as she saw it." Apparently not impressed that band members wrote or co-wrote most of the songs, Christgau complained that the Runaways stuck to their script. "On record, the band sings everything as if by rote; there's nothing to indicate that they have asked to be seen as they see themselves."[8]

Some critics didn't get the band at all. *Rolling Stone* dismissed *The Runaways'* "muddled production" and "uninspired playing."[9] The so-called Dean of Rock Critics delivered the most negative review of the Runaways' first album. *The Village Voice's* Robert Christgau (Georgia's brother) gave *The Runaways* a C-, dismissing it as "Kim Fowley's project, which means that it is tuneless and wooden as well as exploitative."[10]

The Christgaus were New York City–based journalists, who worked at a healthy remove from—and turned a jaundiced ear toward—Fowley's machinations. The Runaways were increasingly to experience a deep American divide: the Manhattan-based publishing industry's skepticism of/distaste for/jealousy of West Coast culture. Brits such as Bonham got L.A. and the Runaways in a way the Christgaus, or the Runaways' soon-to-be nemesis Lisa Robinson, never would.

"New York press hated everybody who wasn't from New York, until somehow you became cool or you were from England," Gormley says. "Especially L.A.-based bands going into New York: You were up against a wall. Some people made it through that wall and some didn't. They had that whole teenage girl thing going against them in New York. People thought that was just an image, that Kim Fowley put them together."

Fortunately for the Runaways, much of the rock press in the '70s was based outside of Manhattan: in Detroit (*Creem*), England, and L.A. (*Back Door Man, Who Put the Bomp, Slash*). Those critics didn't necessarily take their instructions from the publishing establishment, record labels, or radio. "The press in this country at that time had much more imagination. They, at least, considered themselves hipper," says Gormley.

Gormley, who later managed the all-girl group the Bangles, admits that sex was part of the selling point for the Runaways. "It's the opposite of what I did with the Bangles. They weren't a female band, they were a rock band. We didn't push sexuality per se at all. With the Runaways, that was part of the presentation."

But he also says that when he pitched writers, he tried to get them to focus on the band as musicians. "Ask them about their music and their writing; don't just ask about the lingerie they're wearing."

Some journalists paid Gormley more heed than others. A number of prominent feature stories followed the reviews. Most of the scribes wrote with one hand down their pants.

The first major feature on the Runaways outside of the local press ran in *NME*, one of the three London music weeklies. (*Sounds* and *Melody Maker* would also soon chime in.) Chris Salewicz was a respected English music writer who came to L.A. in June and spent some time with the Runaways. It was clearly new territory for him: He compared the Topanga Canyon club, the Corral, to the John Ford Western *Stagecoach* and unwisely tried to order a white wine at the sometime biker bar.

But Salewicz respected and understood the Runaways' music in a way that became increasingly rare in the rock-crit sausage fest. He was floored when the band took the stage: "… the Runaways are drowning the audience in their utter, unrelenting beautiful arrogance," he wrote.[11] He appreciated their glam influences. And he saw past Currie's tresses to Jett's 'tude (even while getting her age wrong): "Joan…is as much the Runaways as the Runaways are Southern California…Joan would appear to have been born (all of sixteen years ago, remember) blessed with a vital understanding of the essence of rock 'n' roll."

But even Salewicz got into hot water when he asked the band if any of them were groupies. West just about throttled him. He was probably lucky Ford didn't punch him. "I hate those chicks," Currie told him. "I mean, they give us shit already."

Ditto when he asked the group if they were feminists. "We don't even think about it! We're not even part of it!" answered Jett.

Salewicz drew the loudest howls when he asked the Runaways about Patti Smith. "Hate her fucking guts," the members chorused. (They also mocked the Ramones.)

The Runaways had gone backstage at a Patti Smith concert in Huntington Beach, only to be sent away by the queen of New York punk. Such un-sisterly behavior was not unusual for Smith; she was also engaged in a rivalry with Blondie singer Deborah Harry (who supported the Runaways). But unfortunately, the Runaways took Patti's bait.

"She's really a drag," West told Salewicz.

"Watching Patti Smith is like morbid curiosity," said Currie, who also mocked the older singer's "saggy tits." "It's like the way people look at a dead dog lying in the middle of the road with its guts spilling out."

This bashing of a fellow female musician and beloved New York artist would haunt the Runaways' career.

While even Salewicz couldn't resist slipping in the occasional "come up and see me sometime" come-on, he generally wrote with his brain not his dick. The *NME* story had substance and sympathy—not qualities always to be found in even positive Runaways write-ups.

In a one-page article headlined "Runaways—Teenaged, Wild & Braless," *Circus* writer Michael Barackman bought the bad-girl pitch. By the end of the first graf he'd revealed that the braless Currie smoked and Ford was dating Ritchie Blackmore (one of her guitar heroes; he was thirty at the time). The worldly women Gormley describes had apparently not completely emerged when *Circus* caught up with them. Fox acted as the band's primary spokeswoman; she came across as more earnest than brainy. "'We want to be the next rock phenomenon,' she bubbles... 'Musically, we've developed a whole new style that's never been heard before, and our term for it is "doo-doo."'"[12]

At least Jackie didn't push herself up by putting other women down. Joan delivered the most impolite and impolitic dis of this interview: "Let's face it, you can't be big ugly things like Isis," she said.

The alternative press writers who had given the Runaways their first, sympathetic reviews were often women: DD Faye and Lisa Fancher. The band quickly ran into the tone-deaf lechery and misogyny of the traditional press. In the preface to his August story for the London-based *Sounds*, former Doors and Iggy Pop manager Danny Sugerman admitted that his interview with the band was "horrendous" and that he wanted to slag them off. As the article unfolds, one has to wonder if he was just pissed because the band didn't sleep with him. "The Runaways are your wet-dream come alive," he wrote breathlessly. "Five female nymphet rockers."[13]

Sugerman was a shitty writer and drug addict who thought he was a rock star and died married to Fawn Hall of Iran-Contra infamy. Like Needs, he spent much of his write-up jacking off to the album cover. Incredibly, he wrote that "the inside portrait shows 'em fat 'n' greasy 'stead of fun." (Thus Jett's lookism came back and bit her on the ass.) Such was the brilliance of the music press.

A writer for a female audience had a different take. A September article in 'Teen magazine described the Runaways as being the readers' possible best friends, or even being the reader: "They're aiming just for you." The un-bylined writer didn't gawk or drool or jerk off. "Teen Girls' Rock Revolution" quoted Fox talking about Greek philosophy, not "doo-doo": "Kids today have the same problem kids had way back when Socrates wrote about how uncouth youth was," Jackie said.[14]

In Runaways coverage, "doo-doo" was apparently in the eye of the beholder.

Whatever hurdles the Fabulous Five had to overcome in journalism were nothing compared to the roadblocks they would run into at radio.

For a brief time in the 1960s and early 1970s, commercial American radio provided an outlet for new music. A proliferation of FM stations benefited from and helped promulgate the soundtrack of the counterculture. But by 1976, corporate interests had increasingly taken over those stations with programmed playlists that were essentially safe surroundings for radio's real raison d'etre: commercials. Most program directors, music directors, DJs, and station managers were men, who saw rock radio's primary audience as other men, who, they believed, wanted to listen to men like themselves (or men they wished they could be). At most, there was room for one token woman on these stations. Suzi Quatro and Fanny had run into this wall already.

After the Runaways and Harvard Law School, Fox worked radio promotion for a record label. She experienced the chauvinism first hand. "I would literally call up radio stations, and they would say, 'We already have a girl artist in rotation,'" she says. One well-known DJ asked her, "Well, what are you going to do for me." This was a course she hadn't taken at Harvard—Fellatio 101.

Fox's experience makes her sympathetic to the difficulties Mercury faced—but she also thinks the label didn't try hard enough. "Our record company had no idea what to do with us," says Fox. "Forget even the difficulty of being an all-girl band; we didn't fit cleanly into what was getting played on AM radio. We were more of an FM band. But with FM, there really was hostility to the notion of an all-girl rock band. And I don't think the songs were strong enough. The ones that were best in terms of songs weren't quite hard enough for FM. They didn't really fit into the Led Zeppelin/Aerosmith vibe. I think we were just seen by the label as being a novelty act."

Cliff Burnstein was tasked with the job of pitching *The Runaways* to radio. The response was "not good," he says. The future A-list manager remembers the conservatism, not the sexism, of stations as the hurdle. He had run into the same problem trying to promote the New York Dolls.

"Radio was not terribly adventurous," he says. "Something that's a little bit off standard sound was hard to get played. People had all different reasons for not really wanting to play it. For the most part, people didn't like it; they didn't think it was good."

"Cherry Bomb" was the only single Mercury released from *The Runaways*. And "Cherry Bomb" was an unapologetically, provocatively female record, about a sexually aggressive girl. It was not gender neutral, like Heart's "Barracuda," or "American Nights." It was not cute and catchy, like such later hits as the Go-Go's' "Vacation" or the Bangles' "Manic Monday."

A few stations, in Boston and Cleveland, played "Cherry Bomb." Rodney Bingenheimer spun the Runaways as much as he could on his new show at KROQ, Rodney on the Roq. Their cover of "Rock & Roll" was his theme song. But even he ran into resistance from cranky callers.

"The only time I was offered payola was not to play the Runaways," he says. "What did I do? I played them even more."

Chuck E. Starr also played "Cherry Bomb" every night at the Sugar Shack. "That was really the summer of the Runaways," he says. "People were pogoing to Cherie's music."

Rhythm guitarist/ vocalist Joan Jett and drummer Sandy West formed the initial nucleus of the Runaways. In this 1977 photo, they sit outside SIR Rehearsal Studio in Los Angeles.
Photo by Brad Elterman

Bassist/singer Micki Steele completed the first lineup of the Runaways, with West and Jett. She found greater success with the Bangles.
Credit Getty Images

Teenage poet Kari Krome wrote lyrics for some of the Runaways' first songs and introduced Jett to Kim Fowley.
Photo by Donna Santisi

Lead guitarist Lita Ford emulated such hard-rock heroes as Ritchie Blackmore and Jimi Hendrix.
Photo by Jenny Lens

The Fabulous Five had attitude to spare. Left to right: Lita Ford, singer Cherie Currie, Jackie Fox, Sandy West, and Joan Jett.
Credit: Michael Ochs Archives/Getty Images

Kim Fowley was the Runaways' brilliant but eccentric mastermind. Jackie Fox played bass in what Fowley dubbed "the Fabulous Five."
Photo by Brad Elterman

Around the same time the Runaways inked their label deal with Mercury, they also signed to Peer Music Publishing. Left to right, front row: Jett, Fox, Ford, and Currie; back row, Ralph Peer, Fowley, manager Scott Anderson, and West.
Credit: From the collection of Ralph Peer

Years before Madonna or Katy Perry, Cherie Currie stormed the stage wearing a bustier.
Photo by Bob Gruen

More feminine and friendly, Jackie Fox was cast as the band's "girl next door."
Photo by Brad Elterman

Sandy West was the Runaways' not-so-secret weapon, a skilled musician who hit the drums hard.
Photo by Brad Elterman

Baltimore Orioles fan Joan Jett became enamored with punk music and style.
Photo by Brad Elterman

Live, Currie would spit blood from her mouth during the band's enactment of "Dead End Justice."
Photo by Bob Gruen

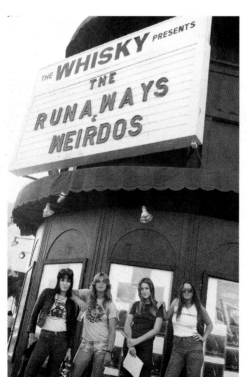

Vicki Blue joined the Runaways as bassist in the summer of 1977.
Photo by Donna Santisi

Legendary rock club the Whisky became the Runaways' home.
Photo by Brad Elterman

During their first shows without
Currie, at the Whisky in August
1977, Joan Jett and Lita Ford flexed
their new guitar-driven dynamic.
Photo by Jenny Lens

Punk pioneers Johnny Rotten and
Joan Jett hold court at the Whisky,
March 9, 1978. Lisa Curland's
reflection is caught in the mirror.
Photo by Jenny Lens

By remaining accessible and
interested, the Runaways
inspired LA musicians. At
a 1977 party for *SLASH*
magazine, Joan and Lita
talked with Rodney
Bingenheimer, while Germs
Darby Crash and Pat Smear
wrestled in the background.
Photo by Jenny Lens

John Alcock was called in to produce the Runaways' last album in secrecy.
Photo by Donna Santisi

Runaways' shows became loaded with tension. At a Nov. 13, 1977, gig at London's Hammersmith Odeon, Jett rubbed her sweaty body against Blue.
Photo: Redferns

Laurie McAllister became the Runaways' last bassist in the fall of 1978.
Photo by Donna Santisi

L.A. rock legend Rodney Bingenheimer was an early and avid Runaways supporter. They were frequent guests at his KROQ show. From left to right: West, Bingenheimer, Jett, Ford, Van Halen singer David Lee Roth, and McAllister.

Photo by Donna Santisi

When the Runaways broke up, Jett felt devastated and betrayed. She assembled a new group of women, whose drummer is pictured here, to fulfill a contractual obligation to make a film, which was never completed.

Photo by Donna Santisi

The band's final lineup was its best musically, but emotionally, they were already falling apart.

Photo by Donna Santisi

Despite tension over her appearance in the film, West showed up for the premier of Blue's documentary *Edgeplay*.

Photo: WireImage

In the film *The Runaways*, Kristen Stewart played Joan Jett and Dakota Fanning was Cherie Currie.

Photo: Getty Images

But Starr reached maybe thousands of L.A. teens. The Runaways needed hundreds of thousands of American teens.

The Runaways were in a Catch-22. They needed radio to sell records. But the only way stations would play them was if they were selling records. "If I can prove the consumer likes it a lot, I can make them play it," Burnstein says. "I couldn't do that with the Runaways."

"As time went on it became obvious that it was just a press thing," says Gormley. "The only way they were going to sell albums was to continue with the press aspect. But press didn't sell a lot of albums. I don't know if it ever does. People need to hear the album all over the country, and they were just hearing the story. And then 'Cherry Bomb' was the single, but people wouldn't play it because it said something about grabbing until they're raw."

The Runaways did break into the *Billboard* 200 at 194. "Cherry Bomb" never even charted.

15 American Nights

On April 8, 1976, the Runaways played a show at Francis Polytechnic Senior High in Sun Valley, California. They were suburban teens performing for other suburban teens—maybe their toughest audience. The student union was a somewhat unusual venue for a band that had already serenaded rock stars at the Starwood. But then the show had been booked by a longtime supporter, *Who Put the Bomp* writer, and Poly High student Lisa Fancher.

The future founder of Frontier Records penned a passionate pitch for the show in her high school newspaper, *Academy in Peril*. "They'll change your mind about the general concensus [sic] that girls can't play rock 'n' roll," Fancher wrote. "They'll make you proud to be a teenager. The Runaways will make you glad that rock 'n' roll music isn't dead."[1]

You would think bringing a hot rock band to campus, at a mere fifty cents a ticket, would have made Fancher the coolest girl in school. But the Runaways were tepidly received by the Valley girls and boys. "Everybody there was an asshole anyways, so after a girl band played they were, like, 'What is this crap?' They hated it," Fancher says.

Along with radio and press, gigging was a crucial way for a band to break big in the '70s. (Not only was there no Internet or social media, there wasn't even MTV.) From high schools to industry showcases to CBGB's, the Runaways played hard. Everywhere they went, they had to convince skeptics that they could handle their instruments. Poly High was a tough crowd; so was CB's. But slowly, city by city, state by state, country by country, the Runaways proved that they were no made-for-TV monkeys. Poly High may not have been ready for them, but the Runaways more than honored Fancher's promise, proving girls can play, validating teens, and reinvigorating rock 'n' roll.

Poly High was not the only school the Runaways played. Bingen-heimer recalls going to see them at a middle school in Fullerton. He had Roger Taylor and Brian May of the British glam-metal band Queen with him, and he was going to introduce the Runaways to the crowd. But apparently no one had cleared this with the principal. After taking five freeways to this suburb in the shadow of Disneyland, Rodney and company finally pulled into the parking lot, only to be blocked by the school's administrator. The sight of three middle-aged, long-haired men on a campus of pubescents apparently did not thrill said gentleman.

"Where are you going?" the principal asked.

"I have to introduce the Runaways," Rodney said. "I'm with Queen!"

"I don't care if you're with the king. Off limits, no trespassing."

The Runaways played their first show outside of Southern California on April 30, at the University of California, Berkeley. Fowley generated hype for the event by warning the members that militant feminists at the notoriously progressive school had sent the band death threats, god-dess knows why. (Kim liked to manufacture controversies. After Sweet wouldn't let the Runaways open for them at a Santa Monica Civic Au-ditorium show, he sent people to picket the British band as misogynists.) No protesters materialized in Berkeley, although Fox—sick with bron-chitis and wired on prescription meds—passed out at the end of the show. The city of San Francisco blacked out, too, apparently done in by a heat wave. "I was lying down by myself in this unsupervised, pitch-black hotel, puking," Fox recalls. "It was fun."

Back in L.A., they played a showcase for the annual convention hosted by *Billboard* magazine. The gig drew celebs such as the band Thin Lizzy, and the Runaways "had everyone on their feet, pleasingly amazed at the power of this all-girl group," *Teen* magazine wrote.[2]

But it was at the Starwood, just before the launch of their first tour, that Currie debuted the outfit that would simultaneously catapult the band's fame and mire them in controversy.

Cherie and Jackie liked to shop in lingerie boutiques, such as the infa-mous Frederick's of Hollywood. This wasn't unusual for denizens of the Sunset Strip, where go-go girls and groupies often set the sartorial stan-dards—glitter babies and drag kings shopped Frederick's, too. No one in the band was adverse to provocative garb. West drummed in tight pants with elaborate cutouts; Ford wore short shorts, with underwear and sometimes labia poking out of her spread crotch; Jett liked leather. They were real musicians but they were also young sexual beings. Often, it was hard for the press and fans to believe they could be both.

The designer Ciri had made custom jumpsuits for the band. But the day before the Starwood show, Currie spied a yellow bustier with black stitching and bows. (The lingerie is usually referred to as Cherie's corset, but technically it was a bustier, a modern adaptation of the Victorian belly crushers.) The beautiful undergarment matched her hair and eyeliner. What's that saying about snakes? "Black and yellow kills a fellow?" Garter belts and fishnet stockings completed the stripper outfit. Cherie looked fabulous. Fowley and Anderson loved it. The musicians had their doubts.

Since Jett sang half the band's songs, Currie had plenty of time to change costumes on stage at the Starwood; from this point on, she would change multiple times during a show, from T-shirt and jeans to jumpsuit to corset. During "You Drive Me Wild," Cherie disappeared into a dressing box set up on the stage, as if about to perform a magic trick. She reappeared to the opening chords of "Cherry Bomb," resplendent in her underwear. The sixteen-year-old did not feel objectified; she felt empowered as the packed venue went apeshit. "I moved with a vengeance, releasing all my fears," she wrote in 2010's *Neon Angel*. "I felt like a conduit of pure power from a place I didn't know."[3]

"She became Brigitte Bardot at that moment, she became a femme fatale at that moment," says Fowley.

The bustier gave Currie the rock 'n' roll authority that Fowley said she lacked. That's how she felt at least. But to many observers, especially people who had followed the band for a while, it was a gimmick. They assumed it was Fowley's idea; he and Currie both swear it was hers. "I wish she'd had more like it," Kim says drily.

"The corset was a very cheap attempt to reach the lowest common denominator," says Phast Phreddie Patterson. "DD and most writers knew that. Women definitely knew it. I believe the Runaways may have been taken more seriously if Cherie wasn't all tarted up."

"They were a good rocking band but I thought the whole corset thing was really sad," says Fancher. "It was just creepy to see a sixteen-year-old girl wearing a corset. It detracted from being a Joan Jett kind of kick ass band.... I don't even know how much Cherie was into music before then, but I don't think she liked the music that much. I think she more looked the part."

Even some of the young male fans who were presumably the target demographic for Currie's outfit were turned off by its blatant shtick. "It just to me wasn't sexy at all," says Mike Hain. "It seemed cheap. I mean wearing black leather, that was cool. That was rock and roll."

Still, lots of acolytes clearly dug the new Cherie. And Currie didn't wear the garment like a coquette; she strutted the stage more like a panther, as if she were wearing a sports bra or a "wife-beater" tank top. Cherie wasn't imitating strippers; she was dressing like her hero, Tim Curry as Frank N. Furter. She and Jett were huge fans of *The Rocky Horror Show*, which had a nine-month run at the Roxy in 1974 and was made into a movie, *The Rocky Horror Picture Show*, a year later. Currie looked and moved like a "sweet transvestite," not a jailbait fantasy. The trouble was, while she projected one image, she was not in charge of how that image was perceived.

Currie's bustier was certainly a historic breakthrough—or lowering of the bar. After her, many pop and fashion stars made underwear their outerwear: Vanity, Madonna, the Spice Girls, Pink, Katy Perry. Some of these artists highlighted their femininity and sexuality with satin and lace; others flaunted exaggerated cups like giant, ironic quotation marks. Kathleen Hanna, who sometimes performed in a bra when she sang in Bikini Kill, felt that rather than the corset sexualizing Currie, the singer desexualized the corset.

"It was so awkward and weird and draglike," Hanna says. "The way she moved was so weird, and almost mocking pornography poses. Cherie kind of looked like a little kid playing dress up, slash, a skinny boy in drag. When I watch videos of them, I'm like oh, she brings out the idea that being a woman is a role. It's like something that you can put on and take off, and if we lived in a genderless society, anybody could be a man or anybody could be a woman or whatever they want. And I feel like her performance to me, that's what it said to me more than like, oh I want to have sex with her, she's so hot."

Hanna may have sensed a Brechtian self-awareness in Currie's poses. But as the Runaways would soon find out as they set off riots in the U.K. and spawned soft-core porn spreads in Japan, lots of guys did want to have sex with Cherie in her hot outfit.

And at least one of them was at the Starwood. According to Currie's book, after the June 13 show, she had sex with an unidentified pop star after being set up with him by Fowley. Writing that afterward she felt like a whore, Cherie implies that the producer pimped her out to the older man. Fowley denies this specific accusation, though does sometimes refer to himself as having been the band's pimp. Fox also says that Cherie misrepresents the evening. The bassist says she was with the singer after the show, and that Currie willingly went home with the star, whom Jackie identifies as Rick Springfield, a handsome twenty-five-year-old Australian marketed as a teenybop star; he had a pop hit in 1981 with "Jessie's Girl."

"Cherie's characterization was that Kim pimped us out," Fox says. "It's not inaccurate, but it's not accurate either, because she paints herself as a very unwilling participant....Did money exchange hands? I doubt it. I think it was more Kim thought, If I get something going between Rick and Cherie it's publicity fodder, because he loved it when we were associated in any way with guy bands."

In mid-July the Runaways embarked on their first tour of the United States, a two-month affair that would find them honing their craft, partying madly, fighting wildly, and screwing plenty. Playing shows night after night was the ultimate grind; some members found the work more grueling than others. Relationships blossomed, fell apart, and realigned. Being a rock star was no longer a Hollywood fantasy. Now, it was a job.

The tour was booked by Howard Rose, a powerful agent whose only other clients were Crosby, Stills & Nash, Dan Fogelberg, Queen, and Elton John. Fowley did not join the band and their roadies in their motor home. Rather, Anderson was in charge. As Currie wrote, this "was a little like putting a fox in charge of the chicken coop."

The Runaways had to drive clear across the country for their first show, on July 18, at the Tomorrow Club in Youngstown, Ohio. The motor home broke down about halfway and they wound up switching to two rental cars—not a good omen. The second show of the tour was crucial. Cleveland's Agora was a fabled venue in the town often considered the birthplace of rock 'n' roll. The Fabulous Five were playing the heartland now. If they could break through to the Midwest, they were good as gold. Cleveland in particular was a key opportunity, having helped make stars out of the likes of Bruce Springsteen and David Bowie. "At that time, Cleveland had the reputation of being one of the big breakout markets of rock," says Cliff Michalski, who wrote about music for the local weekly *Scene*. "Up-and-coming bands went there to create positive buzz, get a positive reaction, and get local airplay."

And if the Agora was any indication, the Runaways were rock stars indeed. "At the Agora on July 19, they earned one of the best responses I've ever seen a group receive at the club, with some of the individual reactions literally bordering on nympholepsy," wrote Michalski in *Scene*.[4]

"It was something I'd never seen before," the writer recalls. "I'd seen a number of teen idols where young girls went crazy. This was the first show where teenage guys were going crazy over an all-girl group."

The show sold out and fans smashed or conned their way through the door. Michalski estimates that 1500 people, mostly males, packed the 1000-person venue. In *Neon Angel*, Currie describes the crowd as in a near-riotous state. The tumult surprised the Agora's booking agent, Joyce Halasa. "… we've never had so many break-in before," she wrote in an August 3 letter to Toby Mamis. "What a zoo. I AM IMPRESSED WITH ANY BAND THAT CAUSES SO MANY FOLKS TO GO THROUGH THE TROUBLE TO TRY TO BREAK OR CON THEIR WAY IN."

A bootleg of the concert captures the band in full glory, locked in and loving it. Currie sounds replete with that vaunted rock 'n' roll authority, growling, "I'm the fox you've been waiting for" like a death threat. For Ford especially, the show may have been some kind of breakthrough. On a new song, "Don't Use Me," her fingers fly like lightning over the frets.

"That was the night that Lita suddenly became a guitarist," says Fowley. "Cleveland was the night she got her spontaneous groove on."

The fans called the band back for four encores. Afterward, the Runaways were almost panting backstage, Michalski says, "a combination of tired and kind of astonished."

Unfortunately, the Agora gig may have been the exception, not the rule. Four days later, at an Elyria venue called the Joker, "a very subdued, noncommittal crowd gazed at them with their asses on their hands," Michalski wrote. The next night, at Charlotte's Web, in Rockford, Illinois, the band was already having trouble hitting their marks: "Only occasionally was there interaction between members, and then, the forced, derivative motions were disheartening," wrote Cary Baker in *Triad* magazine.[5] Still, *Triad* gave the new band five pages in its October issue.

Catching the band at the launch of their first tour, Michalski saw them as more than a novelty. "The Runaways possess at least rudimentary knowledge of their axes and stage presence, an equivalent knowledge to that of a majority of first-tour outfits, with solid indications of potential future improvement," he wrote in moderate prose. He was also concerned; some of his comments show remarkable prescience. Even at their first gigs, he could sense the pressure of the road looming over them. "One of my most vivid impressions from meeting the girls, besides their unmistakable enthusiasm and friendliness, was a sense of their awe and disbelief over what was currently happening with their lives, and an inability to absorb and understand these hundreds of things they're being bombarded with constantly," he commented. "They've lapsed into a if-this-is-Friday-it-must-be-Elyria attitude over their gigs just two weeks into the tour, trusting their management people to care for the details. Hopefully, they're deserving of that trust."

Michalski's two-page feature ends with a warning/premonition: "... the title of a New York Dolls album has also regularly emerged in my thoughts about this band. That title is *Too Much Too Soon*, and I sincerely hope it doesn't turn into the Runaways' epitaph."

"They were very upbeat at the time, maybe too optimistic," Michalski recalls decades later. "They had blind faith everything would keep coming their way."

Their bad-girl image aside, the five teenagers were in many ways innocents far from home, traveling American highways for the first time. The road was an adventure and a drag. "Before our summer tour I'd never been on a plane," Currie told *Circus*. "I'd never been more than 100 miles from L.A. in my life."[6]

"Being on the road was like taking a small child and a few of her friends to the zoo for the first time," Cherie says years later. "There was wonderment at everything we were experiencing, good or bad."

While their peers and fans were in school, the Runaways were journeying from Ohio, to Illinois, to New York, back to Illinois, to Texas, then all the way back to Boston, then the Midwest again. It was a grueling schedule. Somehow Fowley's promised tutors never materialized.

Ford graduated; Fox and Jett got their GEDs; Fox remembers helping West with her homework. Currie bragged to reporters about dropping out, unfortunately sounding more like an American rube than a rebel.

But who could bother with lessons when you were staying at Swingo's? The Cleveland hotel's reputation for revelry rivaled that of the Riot House. Fox remembers getting rowdy with Kiss's Ace Frehley in the Swingo's bar, the Keg & Quarter. An older man tried picking up the sixteen-year-old by telling her he invented the radial tire. They got thrown out of the bar for being too loud—Jackie blames Ace's "cackling." She went back to her room only to get stampeded in the hall by two guys who pushed her into her room, set up a projector they were carrying, and began screening porn on the wall.

"Who are you?" a freaked out Fox asked.

"We're the Dead Boys!" members of Cleveland's gnarliest punk band exclaimed.

Armed with seltzer bottles and bad attitudes, the Runaways got to act like rock 'n' roll pigs across this great nation, from Boston to Austin. Just imagine the truck-stop scene as these five young women rolled out of the RV or rental cars. Anderson was always on the phone, doing business or something; Fox says they used to surround the phone booth and pull their shirts up to get his attention.

In Chicago, they visited their label headquarters. The "suits" took their clients out to dinner at a business club. The Runaways wore platform boots and Frederick's pants. "People were staring at us," Fox says. "They were trying to be nice to their artists. They were clueless."

Their publicist remembers walking down a Chicago street with the Runaways when two men walked by and grabbed a girl's ass. Foolishly, the harassers stopped to see how their gesture was received. Ford "walked over and grabbed their crotches with a vengeance and said something to the effect of, 'Don't ever touch me again,'" Mike Gormley recalls. "We just kept on walking. They weren't innocent; they knew how to take care of themselves."

The road was stressful. Currie, in particular, battled homesickness. She had never been parted from her twin for so long. Plus, her mother had moved to Thailand with her new stepfather and her little brother; mother and daughter parted on bad terms. Her weight dropped from 120 to 97 pounds, according to *Circus*. One night, she slipped on the fake blood in "Dead End Justice" and was knocked unconscious. At the very start of their first tour, they canceled shows because Joan and Cherie had both lost their voices.

"To actually be in that situation, where there was no food, no clean clothes, being pushed in a van or car with no heater, going from one toilet gig to another, trying to prove to the world that you can rock and change their life, and when you come back from all of this, what type of balance, what kind of sanity, can you possibly have?" Fowley asks rhetorically.

Like so many musicians before and after them, Currie and most of the band members turned to drugs and alcohol to relieve the ennui and manage the stress—not to mention to have a good time. Joan and Lita drank; Sandy snorted; Cherie gobbled 'ludes.

Jackie says she didn't do drugs: They didn't agree with her; she didn't like the feeling of being out of control. Being straight in the Runaways was not a virtue. It exacerbated the new kid's inability to integrate. It also made her more keenly aware of the abuses to which the others had made themselves comfortably numb.

"I couldn't handle how unsupervised, how ripped off and abused we were because I didn't have drugs between me and the event," Fox says. "All of that shit that you guys talk about, I felt it first….I think it's one of the things that made me a little more delicate, which wasn't a good thing to be in the Runaways. The herd doesn't like someone who can't keep up. Even if what you can't keep up with isn't good for you."

Years later, West told her friend Jerry Venemann that management treated the Runaways like Judy Garland: one pill to get them onstage, another to put them to sleep afterwards. Fowley denies using drugs, except for those he was prescribed for the effects of polio, or distributing them. In *Neon Angel,* Cherie says that Anderson provided her pills.

The singer and the manager also started having sex.

Currie describes the affair in detail in her memoir. But she wasn't the only Runaway Anderson fucked.

Fox remembers Fowley calling the band together for a meeting, livid. When Jackie entered the room, he hollered at her: "Did you sleep with Scott, too?"

"No!" she swore.

"Well, you're the only one."

Sexual relationships between management and clients are, of course, unethical and generally not a good idea—though husband/wife manager/artist combinations are not uncommon in the music industry. In

Anderson's case, the sex was also illegal. The Runaways were still minors, after all; statutory rape was a felony in California. The freakish Fowley most often gets blamed for exploiting the Runaways, but it was Anderson, the supposed nice guy, who took sexual advantage of their youth and his power.

"We never thought of it as, 'Oh, he just slept with four teenage girls,'" says Fox. (She says the manager came on to her, too, but she wasn't interested.) "It wasn't unusual then; you have to have that context. The whole Roman Polanski thing didn't raise more eyebrows because people were sleeping with teenage girls. It wasn't that shocking then."

Perhaps Anderson's liaisons weren't shocking, but they were annoying. Lavishing attention on Currie, the manager fed her ego and sense of entitlement. Jackie remembers him taking Cherie out to dinner while the rest of the band walked around desolate city outskirts, trying to buy a cheeseburger.

Not only was Anderson an asshole; he was inept. Runaways tours became a trail of stolen cars, unpaid hotel fees, and angry venues. The problems began in Cleveland. Halasa had booked the Runaways for five shows in the region. But from the start, she had trouble getting tour support from Mercury, in the form of press kits and radio ads. "I got the distinct impression that Mercury has no grip on the goldmine that the Runaways represent," the agent wrote to Mamis. "I had to ask them to act like a record company."

The real issues lay with the guy who was banging his charges but seemed incapable of dealing with their label or anyone else. The Runaways skipped out on their very first hotel bill, at Swingo's. They skipped out the next night, too, and didn't pay for a truck rental. "I have to think that a part of Mercury's lack of action comes from their contact with the band's management, Scott Anderson," Halasa wrote.

A Mercury staffer in St. Louis, Robert Chiado, spelled out his problems with the manager in a four-page letter. The Runaways were booked to open for Spirit. But they missed their flight from New York and therefore their sound check. They were also late to perform, causing the concert to be cut short and angering the headliner. The 10,000-seat hall wasn't even half filled. To compound matters, instead of taking responsibility for the band's tardiness, Anderson "bad rapped" Chiado to others.

Such mismanagement could have made the band look like amateurs or swindlers, to their label and to their fellow musicians. Fortunately, the local agents didn't hold it against them. "The girls are great to work with," Halasa wrote. The day of in-store appearances in St. Louis was "very successful," Chiado said in his letter. "The girls were great to be with—I love them all and look very forward to being with them again."

But the effects of mismanagement would prove deadly to the Runaways. In big letters across the bottom of the otherwise typed missive to Mamis, Halasa added a note: "The saga of the Runaways should be used as a textbook case on 'How to Let a Gold-mine Slip Through Your Fingers' or '1001 Ways NOT to Break a Rock & Roll Band.'"

Throughout out all the high jinks and malfeasance, the band played like professionals. Thrust half-naked and vulnerable in front of volatile crowds, they became the angry, alienated youths that they sang about.

"We wanted to be rock stars," Fox says. "We wanted to work hard, we were willing to work hard. I mean, being a teenage girl, you do have a lot of energy. We never had time to get truly jaded about playing. We never phoned it in, not a single show, not even the bad shows that were off because somebody snorted too much coke. We were still not apathetic at all about performing, and I think that's why we were a great live band. Because we really took the attitude, if someone is willing to pay us, we are going to play our best. We were all fully present on stage every night."

"It's really easy to have 20/20 hindsight and go, 'Where's the supervision?'" Jett says. "I didn't see the girls going, 'where's our supervision?' back then. No one was concerned…We may have been kids, but we were also professionals. We wanted to play the gigs. I don't think we ever wanted to go out and play bad. I don't remember anyone ever getting ripped before shows. That's just not what we did. We would play the show and then we did what we did. It was really important to be good. We were telling people we were good, so we had to play good."

Sex and drugs were supplements to, not distractions from, rock 'n' roll. The Runaways didn't let recreational activities or off-stage drama mire their performance.

"You've got teenage girls, you're going to have drama no matter where you are," Ford says. "I just wanted to play guitar. I just wanted to tour. I took my job very seriously."

"The Runaways were professional in the studio recording," Fowley says. "The Runaways in the rehearsal room were professional; co-writing songs, professional; on-stage, professional; interviews, professional. They were professional when it counted, and the rest of the time they were horrifying."

The most important show of the tour took place August 2 at CBGB's. The long, narrow Bowery Avenue nightclub, whose name stood for Country, Bluegrass, and Blues, had become the nesting ground for the New York punk scene, helping launch the careers of Patti Smith, the Ramones, Television, Talking Heads, Blondie, and more. It was the Runaways' first New York City gig. Los Angeles was the home of the film and recording industry, but New York was still the center of the cultural universe.

For better and worse, the Runaways' hype preceded them. CB's was packed with "wall-to-wall ogling males," Lisa Robinson wrote in *Creem*.[7] Anyone who was anyone in the rock scene was there. Some observers—Robinson, in particular—came with their nails sharpened.

The bootleg *BOMB CBGB's* captures a band at least as tight as the one that rocked the Agora. Wisely, Currie did not wear her corset in front of the sophisticated crowd. Still, influential journalist Robinson mocked the band's style, particularly the Ciri-designed outfit worn by Jackie. She described it as "an American Airlines red Eydie Gorme jumpsuit directly out of *Beyond the Valley of the Dolls*" in her "Eleganza" column for *Creem*, referring to Russ Meyer's classic 1970 sexploitation flick about girls and rock 'n' roll in Hollywood. Robinson didn't try to hide her East Coast prejudices. "Only a girl from California could wear such an outfit."

Robinson admitted she had been offended by the Runaways' *NME* comments about hometown heroes Patti Smith and the Ramones. One of the few female rock scribes also seemed to have been put off by the heavy drool factor in the CBGB's crowd. "It was as if everyone had come to see a freak show, a novelty act, and it was more than a touch nauseating," Robinson wrote. The band's performance failed to win her over, but her comments revealed as much about her own gender biases as they said about the Runaways. She confessed to not knowing why "ogling" males seemed more "grotesque" than ogling females. She denied the Runaways their own agency and practically called them dykes, denouncing "this invention...this creation...A band made up of girls trying to act like boys." She preferred '60s groupie band the GTO's—

apparently that was how girls were supposed to act. Robinson said Jett's eyes looked dead.

Catty and chatty, the *Creem* writeup was not without its valid points and well-placed zingers. Mocking their choreographed poses, Robinson observed, "The Runaways do near-perfect imitations of rock stars doing imitations."

Robinson's comments, which were also published in England, stung. A year later, the Runaways would denounce her as their least-favorite critic. Years after that, Robinson would come around and praise Jett's solo work.

Reviews of the Runaways' New York debut captured the different ways men and women could respond to the band. According to *New York Times* critic Robert Palmer, it was only the women in the audience "who looked less than enthralled."[8] In his short but important review of the CBGB's show, Palmer wrote that the Runaways seemed to exist to entice males, not empower females. He noted that Fowley helped the Runaways design their act "with the idea of appealing to the fantasies of male rock fans and rock critics, and on these terms he has succeeded." In the paper of record, Palmer praised the band's playing and "their variety of street-corner femininity." He singled out Jett's "assured" performance; Currie, however, seemed "inexperienced and perhaps a bit nervous."

The Runaways got a mixed reception in oh-so-cool New York. But at the Armadillo in music-loving Austin on August 22, 1976, "the crowd cheered so loudly that they did two encores," a critic for *Records* magazine wrote. The writer saw nothing less than the rescue of rock 'n' roll in the Runaways' set, something the "trendys" in New York couldn't understand, "probably because one can't be fashionably decadent and enthusiastic at the same time."[9]

"Rock is back!" cheered *Records* magazine. "The Runaways are rock and rollers."

16 Trouble in California Paradise

It didn't help the Runaways' credibility or morale that as they trudged across America, trying to save rock 'n' roll, their supposed backers didn't have their back. In her *Eleganza* column, Robinson reported that she received a phone call from Fowley the afternoon of the CBGB's show. Kim told her that he, too, was upset with comments the band had made to the press—about him. He badmouthed the Runaways' badmouthing. "… like so many bands who were 'put together'—they resent that," the Runaways' manager told the Runaways' detractor. (Robinson refused to talk to the band members, she admitted in the writeup—so much for balanced coverage.)

The almost two months during which the Runaways were on the road was by far the longest time they had been away from the all-consuming Fowley since the nucleus of the band formed in August 1975. Liberated, the dead-end kids bolted. Like Frankenstein's monster, Kim's creation turned on him.

"I don't think Kim liked being around five snotty teenage girls, you know: arguing about things and yelling back at him," says Fox. "At some point we started getting recognition and we realized we could yell back and say, 'fuck you.'"

"They're not supposed to fight me; they're supposed to fight the enemy!" Fowley says.

How serious the split was, and whether Kim pushed or was jumped, is unclear. In his *Sounds* article, Danny Sugerman wrote that "Fowley was stripped of his 'directorship' by the cocky Runaways and 'friend' Scott Anderson" but was still under contract to produce their second album—and owned their material. *Circus* magazine reported in November, "Now he's in exile due to antagonism with Cherie, who says, 'He was very abusive and I could not tolerate it.'"[1] A September 18 article by Robert Hilburn in the *Los Angeles Times* said Fowley "had apparently broken with the group."[2] Hilburn reported that the producer, like Jimmy Page tossing aside Pamela des Barres for Lori Mattix, had started a new band with girls who were even younger than the "older" Runaways—at sixteen and seventeen, the Fabulous Five were already over the hill. Fowley gave the new group a name the Runaways had rejected: Venus and the Razorblades. Meanwhile, Hilburn noted, the Runaways sold out two gigs at the Starwood that week. The Fab Five were crying all the way to the bank.

Fowley did produce a coed group named Venus and the Razorblades, whose members would eventually include Runaways refusenik Danielle Faye, singer Steven T., drummer Nickey Beat, and singers Vicki Razor Blade and Dyan Diamond (even the latter's name smacks of Currie clonedom). The band was undoubtedly a middle-finger salute to the Runaways—though the girls would actually "borrow" a few songs from their competitors. Faye says that having seen the Runaways' success, she didn't want to miss another opportunity. She also admits that she had learned how to put up with Kim's shit.

"I had developed a harder shell, playing in Hollywood," she says. "His personality was just normal to me at that point."

The Runaways talked shit about Kim, and he talked shit about the band. He made his cruelest comments to *Crawdaddy*. Charles M. Young embedded with the group for a multi-page feature that ran in the October 1976 issue of the American music magazine. The cover photo shows the band aiming slingshots and water pistols at the reader—oh, so bad! The intrepid reporter visited them at home, watched them practice with Kenny Ortega (Fowley was banned from the rehearsal), and even recorded the members' measurements as they recited them over the phone to a seamstress (that's investigative journalism for you). Currie confessed her rape experience; Fox said she had lost her virginity two years earlier; West talked about Quaaludes; and Ford said, "I think about fucking a lot when I play my guitar."

Pissed that Young had revealed their sexual secrets, the Runaways dumped four pitchers of water on his head the next time they saw him.

Young caught the band in the midst of their fallout with Fowley. In fact, his reporting of Kim's comments about his would-be minions made matters even worse. Then again, Kim Fowley on a tirade is a journalist's wet dream. He compared an all-girl group to a band of dwarves or amputees. Typically, he reached for a golden screen comparison: "As Elia Kazan was to James Dean, I am to the Runaways." Most of his ire, he aimed viciously at his erstwhile Brigitte Bardot.

"Handling Cherie Currie's ego is like having a dog urinate in your face," he told Young. "The best thing that could happen to this band would be if Cherie hung herself from a shower rod and put herself in the tradition of Marilyn Monroe and Patty Hearst. I am a con artist who wanted to pull the ultimate scam. They are assholes who didn't understand the hustle."

In *Neon Angel*, Currie writes that she was devastated by Fowley's comments. Telling a minor she should kill herself was unconscionable, evil even.

"I came from a very loving family that didn't curse and went to church," Currie says. "It was a real culture shock for me to be around this person that was so controlling and so verbally abusive.… He didn't know how to deal with such young girls."

"Kim didn't really like Cherie," Fox says. "It was really clear that he thought she was the person in the band that he could exploit the most. She was the one that he felt he most needed. But he didn't like her. I don't know if it was because he thought he needed her, or because she wasn't rock 'n' roll enough, because she didn't fall into line, or whether it was just a personality thing."

Fowley's shit-talking about the Runaways may in part have been a gimmick, an attention-getting strategy—good, juicy press. That's what Fowley told the band. But Anderson had clearly inserted himself into the band's management—not to mention their pants—more than Kim had bargained for. By the end of the year, the Runaways realized they had jumped out of the frying pan and into the fire.

The Runaways fought plenty amongst themselves, too, verbally and physically. Ford's tempers and West's strength were legendary. Usually, they turned these traits on obnoxious outsiders. Sometimes, they turned them on each other.

One day Cherie became fed up with Kim's hectoring; she saw herself as a blossoming rock star, while he kept calling her "dog piss" and "dog cunt." She stormed out of the rehearsal room.

"The next thing I knew, I was being thrown over a Porsche 914," she remembers. "I landed clear on the other side."

Sandy—short but muscular—had grabbed the skinny singer and tossed her. The drummer bounded around the car to dust Currie's butt off.

"I'm so sorry," West said. "But we have to stop this. I can't lose this band."

It was rare for West to turn on any of the girls, particularly Cherie. Sandy usually acted as protector, not assailant. She was sweet but fearless.

"When we were on the road being humiliated by these guys and bands, she'd jump up and posture," Currie says. "I always felt so safe with Sandy. She could have this tough posturing and exterior, with this huge, beautiful smile on her face."

One time Sandy went ballistic on Fox, who had been complaining publicly about Currie's increasingly diva-like behavior. "Sandy in particular could be really aggressively protective of Cherie," Fox says. Fowley, too, came down on Jackie, banning her from attending parties for a while—until she had the opportunity to be seen in public with Sweet singer Brian Connolly. Kim wanted that kind of publicity.

Cherie and Jackie generally got along. Compared to their tough bandmates, they were "soft"—friendly, feminine, user-friendly, so to speak. But sometimes—like when she had to wait for Currie to get ready when their roadie would pick them up to take them to rehearsals—Fox would lose her patience. During performances of "Dead End Justice," Jackie and Lita would mock beat up the singer. On certain nights, the bassist would throw a little extra into that act.

Figuring out whom to room with on the road was a measure of shifting alliances. Jackie says sometimes she stayed with Currie, sometimes Ford, sometimes Jett, sometimes Kent Smythe, "because I got to the point where I didn't want to be anywhere near the band." Fox and West did not get along personally—not a good sign for a rhythm section. "She was a drug-addicted lesbian who wasn't that bright," Fox says. "What did I have in common with her?" Smythe says Jackie annoyed everyone and no one else wanted to room with her, though for a while at least, he got along with her fine. In *Edgeplay*, Ford also talks about the band not liking Jackie. The former student councilor was a know-it-all, a complainer, and a bit of a girly-girl.

One morning, Ford and Fox were sharing a hotel room. The guitarist had been out all night; the bassist needed to make a phone call. She tried to speak quietly, but Lita still woke up, screaming, "Shut the fuck up!" Ford grabbed the phone, hit Fox over the head with it, wrapped the cord around her bandmate's throat, climbed back into bed, and went to sleep.

"I stayed away from her for a couple of days and then we were fine," Jackie says. "It's her temper. But it would blow over and we'd be fine. ... I don't think Cherie could shake off Lita's tantrums as much. But to me, they were just Lita."

Fowley says that the Runaways' biggest problem was that the members did not come together organically, never liked each other, and ultimately, in some cases, came to hate each other. "I never knew them to ever go out shopping together, or have any meals together, or literally as friends go anywhere together as five girls," he says. "Never. They were hand picked to be in this group and they organically did not come together. ... They had different motives, and different agendas, and different comfort levels and insecurities ... They were so hateful toward each other, and so snippy toward each other—nobody went the extra mile for them, including them. They weren't interested enough to get along with each other."

But several members and observers of the band say that it was Fowley who drove them apart. As Krome and Foster both found, he liked to pit the girls against each other, whether for sport or for control. "I feel like he manipulated all of us not to get along with each other, because if we had ever gotten together we probably would have stood up to him a lot sooner," says Fox. "He had a divide and conquer mentality."

Over and over, Fowley says he was training warriors. But sometimes, the Runaways didn't know who was on which side.

When things would get really tense, Fowley would tell the Fabulous Five to physically attack him.

"We had a deal where anybody who wanted to burn off some energy and was annoyed with Kim Fowley—any of the Runaways, or the roadies—could bum rush me and I would fight back, and they would fight me, and they would break any bone they could find," Kim recalls. "I never was knocked off my feet. All five girls, plus two or three of the roadies—eight of them couldn't ever get me off my feet. I can really battle."

17 England's Dreaming

In September of 1976, ten months after they had formed, the Fabulous Five achieved a dream that takes many bands years: They flew across the ocean to tour Europe. For most of them, it was their first trip overseas. First stop: the United Kingdom.

"We really wanna destroy England," Joan had told Chris Salewicz that summer.

Beginning with Salewicz's controversy-provoking *NME* article, the English press honed in on the Runaways with more (tea and) sympathy than the American press ever evinced—and, arguably, with more drool. In part, this interest was a result of the fact that London housed three weekly music papers who were always hungry for new things to write about—and, at the very least, five teenage girls trying to change the world with guitars and drums made for good copy. Plus, in 1976, punk rock was exploding in London and other cities. With their garage-band sound, glam roots, and Jett's leather-biker look, the Runaways found sympathetic ears among many punk fans.

England, in general, seemed more open to new sounds and images, particularly for women. Suzi Quatro moved from Detroit to London and went to the top of the pops. She never achieved the same level of success with her music in America as she did across the pond, despite her regular appearances in the late-'70s on the '50s-nostalgia-themed sitcom *Happy Days* as Leather Tuscadero. Chrissie Hynde also moved from the Midwest (Akron, Ohio) to London in the mid-'70s, though the band she formed—the Pretenders—did break big in the States. Such female-led bands as the Slits, Raincoats, Au Pairs, Siouxsie and the Banshees, Selecter, and X-Ray Spex were integral to the London punk scene—though they did not necessarily look upon the Runaways as role models or peers.

"England was a lot kinder to us because they kind of saw us as part of the burgeoning punk movement there," says Jackie. "So we were treated a lot more kindly and audiences were more receptive to us, except that the audiences there were almost exclusively males. They were crazy because it was all guys and it was very much working class guys."

"We would play Europe and it would be a sea of leather and denim, just all dudes," Ford says.

True to Jett's wishes, the Runaways cut a swath of destruction through the U.K. At the Fab Five's first foreign gig, at the Apollo Theatre in Glasgow, Scotland, overheated male fans nearly rioted. (Yes, the Runaways were the original riot girls.) "Screaming, pleading, tearing at their clothes, the frenzied teenagers stormed the stage to get nearer their pop idols," reported top tabloid *News of the World*—admittedly, a newspaper prone to exaggeration, if not outright fabrication.[1] London's version of the *New York Post* or *National Enquirer,* the *News* said that out of 2,000 fans, three were female. Writers Andrew Drummond and Barry Powell presented the reverse Beatlemania as women's resignation not liberation. The tabloid quotes members bragging about being objects of male fantasy, not subjects of female desire. "When we get audiences just busting with fellers like that it naturally turns us on," Ford said. "We're not for Women's Lib, you know. We're just girls and it's a terrific feeling to have the audience with you panting and cheering."[2]

Other sources confirm that the Edinburgh boys indeed went wild. Objects rained down on the band, including, according to *Neon Angel,* a bowie knife. Security managed to keep the crowd somewhat under control during the show, said *NME.* Outside afterward was another matter. Like a scene from *A Hard Day's Night,* fans surrounded the Runaways' getaway cars—only the Runaways' fans were rowdy boys, not screaming girls. It took fire hoses to keep the mob away. According to *Neon Angel,* one lad got run over. About twenty men followed the band to their hotel and serenaded them with chants and cheers. Four die-hards lasted the night and were awarded with an audience with the Queens of Noise.

Describing the evening for *NME,* Mick Farren wrote that the Runaways inspired "the greatest piece of spontaneous role reversal since Jeanne D'Arc got herself up in stainless steel drag and commenced to hack and slay."[3] He went on to compare the post-gig pandemonium with the kind of mayhem that typically greeted the Bay City Rollers, a bubble-glam boy band with whom the Runaways got compared more than once. "What happened was, after the Runaways' opening concert at Glasgow's prestigious Apollo Theater, a mob of males—that's right, males—went after the band with the same mindless determination to get a limb for a keepsake as is displayed by Rollers fans rutting after their simpering Scottish love-objects."

Farren also reported that the Runaways merited this rowdy reception. They played better than the Ramones, sang better than Patti Smith, and "certainly do these things with a hundred times more animal energy than the Bay City Rollers," Farren reported. "They also work their asses off."

The *NME* critic singled Ford out for praise, perhaps spending a tad too much time admiring her physical assets—yet acknowledging the empowering image of a girl plus guitar: "There's something quite spectacular about the ongoing relationship between Lita's body and instrument," he noted. West, he wrote, was "the strongest player in the band." Cherie spent too much time in the wings, he said. Joan and Jackie didn't bother him one way or another.

Offstage, Farren found a very different band than the one that had given Salewicz and Young such juicy material. Apparently Fowley and Anderson were having second thoughts about encouraging the band's loose lips and bad-girl appeal. The *NME* writer was disappointed to find the Runaways obsessively protected by their handlers and rather reticent. He compared the touring operation to a convent. "Talking to the girls is on a strict milk and cookies level," he wrote.

Farren's article offers evidence that management had reason to worry about the girls. Currie kept falling asleep, he reported, and admitted to having lost twenty pounds in the last few months. These could have been signs of drug abuse, anorexia, depression, or exhaustion. "We can't afford to be anything but careful," Anderson tells him. "There's the responsibility to the girls' parents. Then there's possible legal troubles in the U.S., because some of them are still sixteen."

This was the one Runaways tour where a parent was also on board. For legal reasons, Fowley said a social worker had to travel with the band. "Me, the drug-free one, thought the social worker would cramp our style," says Fox. "If we met some hot guy over there, I didn't want somebody chaining me up in our room. So bizarrely I thought we'd have an easier time with our parents because they had shown themselves as rather amenable to what we wanted to do ... The two cool parents were Joan's mom and mine. My mother was a registered nurse, and we thought that might make it a little more palatable."

Mom didn't come to squash the fun. "My daughter is old enough to know what she's doing," Ronnie Fuchs told the *News of the World*. "She's in no moral danger."[4]

Farren needn't have worried too much about the Runaways not living up to their bad reputation. They would quickly get into a spot of official trouble.

From Glasgow, the band traveled to Birmingham, England. They were then supposed to head to the continent for a few shows, before returning to the U.K. to finish their tour. But they ran into a little snag when they reached customs in Dover.

Like all Runaways' legends, the story of the girls' detention at the English border has multiple versions and smacks of hyperbole at best, outright prevarication at worst. The most plausible version goes like this:

Sandy, Cherie, and Joan liked to collect hotel keys—souvenirs from the road. A nosy police officer discovered a handful of these stolen goods in a suitcase as the Runaways prepared to cross the English Channel. There may also have been a purloined blow dryer. Sandy and Cherie were still minors and therefore not imprisoned. But Jett was now eighteen. She sat in a cell by herself for nineteen hours, screaming for her bandmates.

"It was stupid!" Joan says. "I was amused for a minute, then I started getting freaked out. So I started singing 'Dead End Justice' down the hallway."

In *Neon Angel*, Currie tells a blood-racing story about the drugs the cops didn't find—or didn't bust her for. But really, it was a silly escapade. Hotel keys and a blow dryer—naughty, naughty Runaways! Mercury played the harmless stunt up for all it was worth, even circulating a press release. "Three Members of Runaways Rock Group Arrested in British Police Fiasco!" blared the headline of the release, dated October 4. Here was proof that the Runaways really were bad girls! A genuine arrest! The next thing you knew, Joan and Cherie would be busting out of juvie together.

In actuality, Jett paid a $70 fine. The detention caused "sold out appearances in Brussels and Hamburg," according to the release, to be cancelled. The release said the shows would be rescheduled to the end of the tour, but for some reason, that never happened.

Instead, the Runaways continued to search and destroy England. They landed in London—rock-star, glam-rock, and punk-rock Mecca—for two shows at the Roundhouse, opening for legendary metal band Metallica. Globally, these concerts could prove even more important than the CBGB's gigs.

Londoners are at least as sophisticated as New Yorkers and possibly even bigger snobs. Some Brit crits found the same grounds for dismissal of the Runaways as Robinson had. John Ingham, in *Sounds*, criticized the girls' appearance. Platform boots, flares, and choreographed rocker moves were "recherché to say the least."[5] He also found their musical style insufferably tired. "It's dinosaur-rock, a non-stop barrage of riffs and clichés that have been floating around for the last fifteen years." (Hear the imitation of Robinson's lamentation of rock stars imitating rock stars.)

But Ingham admitted that the girls could actually play: "They rock with the best, a tight, hard-hitting combo that don't apologise about their gender." This backward praise was becoming a tired refrain in Runaways press. How many male bands had to continually prove their instrumental capabilities?

Ingham concluded his review with the hope that the "ex-Rodney's Anglophiles" would absorb the influences of London punks the Clash and Sex Pistols, "because it would be great to see five women drag American rock into the '70s."

In fact, the girls—Joan Jett in particular—did latch onto London's vibrant music scene. The dedicated glam rocker was like a kid in a candy store on King's Road. Back in L.A., she raved about the Sex Pistols to anyone who would listen. She adorned her black-leather biker jacket with buttons, stickers, and safety-pins—just like Sid Vicious.

The Runaways played Sheffield, Bristol, Exeter. The fans again nearly rioted in Liverpool. Harry Doherty of *Melody Maker* caught "California's lusty teenage exports" there, at Eric's Place, and found—surprise!—they could actually play, even though "their main asset is most definitely their promiscuity."[6] Whatever that means. One wonders if he misunderstood Joan when she told him she would never get married; did he think she was swearing off dependence on one man in order to sleep with many? Did he realize she was rejecting heterosexist institutionalization?

The writer of *Bump N Grind* fanzine also raved about the Eric's show. "Talk about packing the punters in," he wrote. "...There wasn't even room to blink in comfort. Still, it was worth it ... When you're standing in front of Joan Jett, you start to wonder if it's all a dream."[7]

The Runaways finished their English tour in Leeds. It's unclear why they didn't continue on to Europe, as planned. What is clear is that despite all the media scrutiny, the Runaways' first album commercially had not lived up to hype and hope—it was a bit of a (cherry) bomb. A little criminal scandal provided good cover for the girls' hightailing it back home, where Fowley and parents could watch over the wayward chicks, and the band could get back to work in the studio.

18 Queens of Noise

The Runaways first declared themselves the queens of noise in "American Nights." It was a bold assertion of identity—"we're the queens of noise"—immediately followed by a submissive retraction: "The answer to your dreams." The lyric was written by Mark Anthony. Fowley loved the concept so much he asked another man, Billy Bizeau of the Quick—a new pop-punk group he was "directing"—to write a whole song about it. Bizeau's composition was slightly less ambiguous about gender roles in its aggressive sexuality: The Runaways were "not just one of your toys," the lyrics of "Queens of Noise" stated. It became the lead and title track of the Runaways' second album.

The only problem: The album with this snarling title sounded more pop than punk.

Back home, the Runaways and their families fired Anderson, but not before he'd gotten Currie pregnant. Fox flew to New York to meet with some heavy-duty rock managers. But no one wanted to work with the band unless they could cut Fowley loose; he had his claws too deep into their careers. The girls' best option was to crawl back to the man who had, after all, given them their name, their contracts, and their infamy. The "monster" who had been locked out of rehearsals was now granted the role he said he didn't want: Fowley became the Runaways' manager.

He was a slightly humbled monster. Kim admitted he was trying to amend his dog-cunt ways. And the musicians were taking a more mature, professional interest in their own business affairs. "I was pretty heavy handed in my discipline and authoritarian stance," he told Lisa Fancher on New Year's Day, 1977. "Now it's more of a collaboration and we discuss everything."[1]

It was useful for the Fab Five to have Fowley back in their corner; no one could lay on the hyperbole like him. "I think the Runaways are the most exciting band in the world right now," he told Fancher. "I'm very high on them. I come and go with them. We may fight again. At the moment we're all friends, we all work together. They're the best band in the world right now. ... If there is a next Beatles, it will be the Runaways."

At the same time that he was taking up the reins of management, Fowley was loosening the reins of production—and dropping the "director" credit. The Runaways wanted to take more time producing the second album, and to have more control. Fowley thought that was a mistake, "but I just wanted the money," he says. "I realized that life is too short to argue with a bunch of girls, so I decided to get a coproducer in."

Earle Mankey had played in the L.A. prog-pop band Sparks and was an engineer at the Beach Boys' Brothers Studio in Santa Monica. He had worked with Elton John and Helen Reddy. An avid fan of '60s girl groups, he had seen the Runaways live and tried to get Fowley to hire him to produce the first album. Instead, Kim later brought Mankey in to produce the Quick, a band that sounded not a little like Sparks. Fowley says that to audition for the job coproducing the Runaways, Earle provided a tape of the sound of rain falling on a leaf.

"You hear the plop, plop, plop, but it was so well done because he put different reverbs and echoes on it, and the rain would get harder and softer," Fowley says. "I said, 'You got the job. If you can record rain falling on a leaf, you can record a bunch of bitches.'"

Fowley seemed to hire men who could act as his foil. Mankey was a family man, "a nerd/genius/egghead/professional/nice guy," in Kim's words. Fowley could be the brilliant, charismatic, but slightly tone-deaf idea guy who would write and pick the songs; Mankey was the talented audiophile who would add layers of sound and artistry. Theirs was a classic routine: good cop/bad cop.

"Kim talked to the label and did the songwriting and berated the artists," Mankey says. "And I did the music."

Fox remembers Mankey being in over his head with five teenage girls. "Poor Earle; I don't think he realized what he was getting himself into," she says. "I don't think Kim could face the possibility of being in the studio with us for a whole album. I think his attention span was wearing thin, and we took over. And Earle was a really nice guy; he wasn't really a strong enough personality to corral everybody and say, 'You need to do this.' So there were definitely too many cooks involved."

Recording in the Beach Boys studio with a former member of Sparks, the Runaways were seriously tapping into California musical history. Dennis Wilson came around. So, of course, did Rodney Bingenheimer. Plus there was the irony of an all-female group recording in a space with such a fraternal name. Brothers was an impressive twenty-four-track studio with one fairly large main recording room, "the size of two or three living rooms," according to Mankey. Aesthetically, it provided a serene setting. A stained-glass mural depicting an endless summer sky filtered blue light on the brown walls and carpet. Grow lights shone softly on plants. Drums were set in one corner, bass in another, and amps spread out around the room. "It was a good room to smoke dope in," says Mankey, who helped build Brothers. "It was supposed to be a relaxed place for the Beach Boys to record all night long."

There was a second studio for "extra sounds," mostly guitar overdubs. Fowley recalls Brothers having a meditation room.

The Runaways may have wanted to take their time with this album, but in fact it was recorded in a mere two weeks in the fall of 1976, with some preproduction (writing and rehearsing songs) completed at SIR studios. Several songs had been in the band's repertoire for a while; some were at least partially written in the studio. They played the songs live as a group, rather than laying them down instrument by instrument. There was no electronic click track keeping the beat for the drummer, no dividers separating the sound. Mankey says that, give or take a console-wrecking incident or two, the Runaways worked like professionals. All of them, including Fox, played on the album—some more than others.

"They were a good band without being prodded," Mankey says. "I had my own idiosyncrasies about problems you run into when you record, and also girl group damage. I pushed songs in certain ways; cleaned up, clarified, pointed direction of songs to suit my own tastes. As always I had a limited amount of success manipulating a band. They did what they wanted to do in the end."

Far from the enfant terribles of Runaways legend, Mankey found the girls mostly well behaved and good at taking direction. "They were young and they had been browbeaten by Kim enough that they were just trying to follow orders," he says.

Still, "There was one heck of a fight in the control room one day," the co-producer says. Lita got mad at one of her bandmates—Mankey doesn't remember which one or why. Ford pushed the other member into the studio's brand-new twenty-four-track mixing console, knocking it off its riser and spilling a beer into it for good measure. Brothers had to close for a couple days while the console was fixed. "It was the talk of the studio," Earle remembers. "I was on the bad list for some time."

Despite her pugilism, Ford's guitar playing blew Mankey away. In fact, he used her overdubs for many of the rhythm tracks as well as the leads; her riffs drove the album. "It's just astounding how young she was and how amazingly good she played," he says. "Lita was standout. I knew lots of guys who were thirty who couldn't play like that."

But Jett was Earle's favorite. "She could sing so well, and I liked the quality of her voice, she sounded rock 'n' roll. She knew how to do it, sang in tune, and didn't sound insecure about it. Whereas with Cherie, it was, 'Okay, can you sing these notes? Okay, let's work on it a bit.' When it was all done, Cherie had a very light delivery, almost like she wasn't quite sure if she sang it right."

When Jett and Currie split vocal duties on the first album, no one seemed to care. For *Queens of Noise*, the division of labor/tracks became an issue. In articles and photos, the front person had become the focus of attention, not surprisingly. It made sense that Cherie would therefore want to take the lead in the studio. The problem was, she couldn't do it. The Manilow fan's pop sensibilities ran counter to her bandmates' hard-rock and punk tastes. They didn't agree on delivery and they didn't agree on material.

"Joan opened her mouth and had a radio voice," Fowley says. "Cherie does not have a radio voice. She has a visual look, a passable voice, but she's not one of the great singers."

At one point during the recording of "Neon Angels on the Road to Ruin," Currie was oversinging the "oohs" and "aahs." Ford asked, "What are we, in fucking church?"

It didn't help matters that Currie missed a couple of days of recording to terminate her pregnancy. Needless to say, Anderson wasn't around for the abortion. Cherie lay alone in the hospital afterwards; her sadness was "unfathomably deep," she wrote.

The rest of the band kept working in the studio. When Currie returned, she discovered that the Runaways had recorded Jett singing

"Queens of Noise." Currie threw a fit. She thought Bizeau wrote the song for her (although she was more a queen of pop than noise). The singer feared she was being edged out of the group.

Trouble was, no one shared Currie's aesthetic. At one point during the *Queens* sessions, she and Steven T., who became the Venus of Venus and the Razorblades, laid down a cover of the Beatles song "Strawberry Fields Forever." "Why would you even try to do a Beatles song?" Fox wonders. "But they did, and it was very pop, and had the same breathiness in the vocal. We were all trying to be more rock 'n' roll, and it created quite a problem, because you have one singer who's trying to be melodic and breathy, and everybody else is trying to do rock. So we like the girl who's singing the rock vocals better. And that's how you end up with nobody being in the singer's corner. And that's how you end up with a band that is coming apart at the seams."

While the bassist admits that "we all liked Joan's vocal better," she also says that, strategically, the band should have let Currie sing "Queens of Noise." "This was one of the things that I think was a huge mistake in the band. Whatever we thought of particular vocals, we should have stood up and said, 'Cherie is the lead singer; Joan, you only get to sing two songs on the album,' because Joan was pushing Cherie aside."

One year later, after she'd quit the band, Currie admitted that her sensibilites were straying from her bandmates': "I was always into making a hit single and they didn't feel like they needed one," she told *The Wasteland* fanzine. "I like rock 'n' roll, but not trashrock, like 'Hollywood' or 'Johnny Guitar.'"[2]

Sometimes, Cherie was right. She loved the song "Midnight Music," a slow, heartfelt anthem about being on the road, which she'd written with Fowley and Steven T. No one else liked it. "That one seemed really sappy to me," says Mankey. "It was a battle to get that one to work on a rock 'n' roll record."

Thirty years later, "Midnight Music" adds a reflective, mournful tone to *Queens of Noise*. When Cherie ends the song with a wistful, "Everything feels like it's just 'bout to break," the prophesy reverberates with irony. The track's a million times better than, say, "Johnny Guitar," Ford's George Thorogood–wannabe blues rocker that closes the album.

Fox also missed *Queens* sessions thanks to a bout of pneumonia. When she came back, the band had recorded "C'mon" without her. Jackie rerecorded her part but couldn't keep up with the uneven rhythm of the others' playing. "I don't know if it was because I wasn't there, or just because it was a bad day, or therefore they thought, 'Oh, goody two shoes isn't around, so let's snort a bunch of coke,'" she says. "I thought it was so bad, I said I'd quit the band if you put this on the album." "C'mon" did not make it onto *Queens of Noise*. (It is on the outtakes compilation *Flaming Schoolgirls*, along with "Strawberry Fields.")

It was Fowley's job to manage the egos and try to make everyone happy. So he gave Currie her "Midnight Music," Ford her "Johnny Guitar," Jett her "I Love Playing With Fire." "He would often tell me he was trying to play politics to keep everyone happy," Mankey says. "He didn't just manipulate everything. He would say, 'We're doing these girls a great disservice. They're just little girls, barely out of school; we're putting them through this rock 'n' roll hell. Their parents are allowing this; they don't know what's in store for these girls.' He was feeling bad."

Neon Angel plays up the drama of the recording sessions. But at the end of the day, getting to make an album in the Beach Boys' personal studio was still more fun than going to high school. Fox recalls having a blast writing and recording the song that became "Hollywood." The tune started as an old Runaways song, "Go for It." There was a spoken-word routine in the middle that she and Ford went out to the street to record, for a little cinéma vérité. Kent Smythe was supposed to come up and cruise them, but instead two drunks wandered by and got on tape. The cut became "Hollywood Cruising," and then just "Hollywood," a song about making it to and in Tinseltown that was partially, at least, autobiographical.

Queens of Noise sounds cleaner and more polished than *The Runaways*; that's its appeal and its failure. For Fowley, the album was "compromise city." "It was a necessary step for them to make a competent record that showed that they could do more than be a dirty joke," he says.

The album lays down its gauntlet with the title track's dare to "Come and get it boys." (But what about the girls?) Bizeau wrote "Queens" in the studio. He walked slowly into the room, sat in the corner by the tape recorder, and played. Mankey says he assumed the song had already been written, but found out later that Bizeau was tripping on acid and "just made it up as he was over there."

Jett also sings the second track, her song "Take It or Leave It." It is, as Fox would say, another dark love song. Its tightly snarled hook then gets swallowed by Currie's power ballad, "Midnight Music"—ladies and gentlemen, light your lighters. "I sang four or five part harmony on this," Currie said in the *Queens of Noise* press kit. "It turned out more fantastic than I thought it would."

"Bruce Springsteen would be very receptive lyrically to the sentiment," Fowley said then. "The guitar work here is reminiscent of Roy Wood's work with the Move." Three decades later, he says of "Midnight Music": "That's what Taylor Swift does now in country rock: teenage diary confessional statement."

Fox is more forgiving: "It turned out to be this really lovely song, but I didn't like it at the time."

The second album's fourth song was one of the Runaways' oldest tunes, "Born to Be Bad." Mankey dug the rap about her mom that Jett laid down on the bridge; its rebel sass had an aura of authenticity. "I just loved the way Joan sang it," he says. In the press kit, Jett called the blues tune "a slow ballad about someone who is a born loser."

Side one ends with Cherie singing the song that provided the title of her memoir, "Neon Angels on the Road to Ruin." The song's lyrics about "cobra kings," "battered boys," and "shattered girls" are pure Fowley (Ford and Fox also get songwriting credit). "This is what was going on and we put it down," Kim says. "I was a war correspondent."

"Neon Angels" was another meta song, rock 'n' roll about rock 'n' roll. "It's all about people in the audience who are really destroying themselves in a very charismatic and religious way," Fowley said at the time.

"Lita and Sandy and I had a hell of a lot of fun playing it," Fox says. "We liked good hard rock."

Jett again kicks off side two, with one of her best songs, written at Brothers for the album. "I Love Playing with Fire" is a driving rocker about passion and desire, in which Joan calls her lover "my little dark dynamite." (Could she have been singing to the Cherry Bomb?) Fowley described the tune in the press kit as "Joan singing about getting ripped off and almost destroyed by superficial love." In a sort of role reversal, men hanging out in the studio—including Bingenheimer and Gormley—got to contribute handclaps.

"California Paradise" was one of the few songs that survived the Kari Krome era, though by the time it made it to vinyl, Fowley, Jett, and West had also gotten their name on the tune. Currie sang, hissing the chorus's "you're sssso nice-sss." On tour, the Runaways would usually start their set with this geographical introduction. Back then, Fowley called it "the answer to 'California Girls' by the Beach Boys, although musically it resembles a Gary Glitter record."

"It establishes the mythology," says Kim. "It's a great album cut for rock critics and masturbating youth."

Another tune of regional boosterism followed, this one extolling the virtues of the town that brought the Runaways together: "Hollywood." "It's a fun song about a girl wanting to become a star knowing that you can become one," said Jett, who wrote the track with Kim and Jackie and sang it.

In "Heartbeat," two rock stars spend the night together then separate for their lonely tours. In the *Queens* press kit, Currie said she and Fowley wrote it, but Fox tells a different story. She had penned a love song for Joey Ramone with Ford. "I come back into the studio one day and my song has been rewritten, and now it's Cherie's love song to David Bowie and there are five writers on it," Jackie says.

"Heartbeat" was supposed to be the album's hit single. Fowley says it got airplay in Nashville, where people thought it was the new record by the Seattle sister-fronted band Heart, but Mercury failed to push it.

Queens ends with "Johnny Guitar," a song written by Ford and Fowley to show off Lita's guitar skills; Jett sings it. The lyrics stumble through overwrought sexual metaphors—"I'm a hunter he's my gun"—and the guitar playing is showoffy. "I'm sorry; teenage girls from the suburbs playing the blues—just no," Fox says. "It's just an awful song."

If you take the needle off after track nine, *Queens* is a solid, great-sounding rock record: memorable melodies, strong hooks and riffs, lots of attitude.

"I'm really proud of this album," Jett said in the press kit. "It really is a lot more listenable than the first. It still has the ballsy rock and roll thing of the first LP, but it's got some slow songs, too."

Maybe *Queens* was a bit too shiny. The Runaways were increasingly caught between a (punk) rock and a hard place. Did they want to fit in on FM radio with the bloated hard rock of such bands as Boston and Rush, with whom they played shows? Or did they want to be leaders of the new wave in L.A., bringing home the styles and sounds they heard while in New York and London? More and more, the band itself would divide on this question. *Queens of Noise* was betwixt and between. It did chart slightly better than its predecessor, making it to 172 on *Billboard*'s albums chart.

"When the album came out everyone said it's great, so much better than the first album," Fowley says. "It was great because it was complicated and artistic and interesting and layered and textured... But I wanted vaginal teeth in the second album. I wanted guns in their hands. I wanted them to blow up the world and piss on rainbows and set fires. I wasn't interested in doing a layered record for a bunch of assholes who are going to still dislike them and still doubt them."

Mankey worked on a few albums with Fowley after the Runaways, including Helen Reddy's *Ear Candy*. He says the producer was always honorable, if unconventional. "Kim has never done bad by me. Lots of guys in bands owe their start to him.

"It wasn't just Kim taking these innocent girls from the soda shop; they wanted to do it too," Mankey continues. "Almost all successful rock 'n' roll people I know have given up something of their normal life to do it. A few made money off of it, but many didn't."

The Fabulous Five ended their first year together where the trio had begun: The Whisky. Since they last played there, the club had temporarily become a home for musical theater, but now it was booking rock bands again—and emerging as the epicenter of L.A.'s growing punk scene. On New Year's Eve, 1976, and New Year's Day, 1977, the Fab Five played with the Quick. Five hundred fans were turned away at the door the first night, Lisa Fancher reported in *Street Life* magazine. The Runaways' audience was expanding beyond the usual leering rockers; they played to a more gender and ethnically diverse crowd than ever. This was the face of the first wave of Angeleno punk: inclusive of women, queers, Mexicans, African-Americans.

The Runaways were an inspiration for this rising generation of music fans, arguably the most important L.A.-based band of the time. They had jump-started the city's moribund rock scene, Fowley told *Los Angeles Times* critic Robert Hilburn.

"When the Runaways started, there were no local bands who were considered punk-rock," he said. "Now we have fifteen bands who are heavy-metal or punk-rock or street rock."[3]

The Motels, Van Halen, Pop, the Ratz, the Dogs, etc.: All these insurgent acts were making L.A. the new Liverpool, Fowley asserted and Hilburn agreed. Soon, there would be a slew of bands inspired by punk, many of them fans of the Runaways and friends with Jett, in particular: The Germs, the Bags, X, the Blasters, the Go-Go's, the Minutemen. In the summer of '77, Fowley started a punk rock series at the Whisky; the Germs, Screamers, Dils, and Weirdos played the first show.

Hilburn made the Runaways and their New Year's Eve performance the center of a January 4, 1977, *Los Angeles Times* story called "Homegrown Punk-Rock Blossoming." "… the stars of the evening and the local punk rock scene are the Runaways," the powerful critic pronounced.[4]

Jett sensed the burgeoning movement, too. "'77 is the year for L.A. rock!" the queen of noise shouted from the Whisky stage as the New Year came in.

At those Whisky shows, the Runaways introduced several songs from *Queens*. Fancher noted the band's changing dynamics: "Joan Jett seems to be usurping Cherie Currie's role as lead singer. Joan sang at least half of the songs while Cherie was in the dressing room making a costume change…The same holds true of the LP, too; Joan sings half the songs. Maybe Cherie was off changing her clothes again."[5]

Longtime fan Fancher was of two minds about the concert; in fact, she wrote both a pro and a con review. Her heart seemed to be in the latter. "… what I saw was a very rehearsed, meticulously staged rock band go through their moves; the actual musical ability was about adequate for what they were representing and the songs were a mélange of nirvana-inducing monotony," she commented. "Not only are the Runaways as good as any male band now, they are just as mediocre."

And so the backlash began.

19 Living the Dream

Mercury released *Queens of Noise* early in 1977. The cover showed all five musicians, dressed in black and hanging onto poles like, well, strippers. The cheesy image—shot by a professional photographer this time, Barry Levine—looked like Renaissance art compared to the advertising that ran in some newspapers and magazines. Five thumbnail photos of the members descend the left side of the ad, like a printout from a photo booth. The photos reveal body parts. Cherie is pictured from the neck to the navel in her bustier; Jackie is shot from the navel to the upper thighs, with her legs spread; Ford tilts her ass; Sandy's hips are shown from the side wearing what looks like bondage wear; and Joan sits on a ball and chain, legs also spread (at least she's wearing pants). Under the photos are the players' names, ages, and instruments; evidently, the girls had somehow not aged in the eight months since the debut. For the textual sales pitch, Mercury must have sought the most offensive quote they could find in Runaways press (admittedly a, er, stiff competition): "... these five California nymphets brought the house down with some hot, hard, bitching rock 'n' roll, and the fact that they are young and extremely horny teenage females was a bonus. And what a bonus!" quipped clever Tony Parsons in *NME*.

For an album on which the girls were trying to be taken more seriously as artists, this was Mercury's grand marketing plan: women without heads or faces, just fetishized body parts, like croppings from a bondage mag. Hot, hard, bitching, and horny.

The press release for *Queens* wasn't offensive but it was distinctly lackluster: "Their second album, *Queens of Noise*, shows obvious maturity—they're seventeen now, you know," it explained.

The press can be wolves, sensing when a prey is injured, weak, or unprotected. The pack pounced on *Queens of Noise*.

"These bitches suck… [d]espite what the West Coast Blow Job Coordinator might say," pronounced one of the most infamous Runaways reviews, written by Rick Johnson for *Creem*. Johnson proceeded to enumerate the ways he hated the Runaways, including calling Jett and Currie "[b]allerinas trying to be weightlifters," dubbing West "the worst drummer in the history of rim shots," calling Fowley the band's "guiding vapor," and complaining about the album's slowness. Johnson's idea of a kicker also revealed his Neanderthal hand: "The whole hype reeks of that age-ole rock 'n' roll maxim—girls are just sissies after all."[1]

Once their calling card, Fowley was turning into the Runaways' albatross. Writing in *NME* and completely ignoring the contribution of Earle Mankey, Mick Farren blamed Kim for the album sounding "dated … overblown, over-produced and ponderous."[2] In fact, Fowley agreed, eventually at least, with much of Farren's critique: He, too, thought the album should have tried to capture the band's raw power, rather than tweak it. Like Johnson, Farren critiqued the album's pace. He was condescending in his assessment of the musicians' abilities to play ("raw, half-foamed talent") and to control their own sound. Blaming Fowley was another way of denying the women their own role in their music's success or failure.

The *Village Voice*'s Robert Christgau again panned the band, this time giving the Runaways a C and calling them "bimbos." His admittedly funny review read in its entirety: "I'll tell you what kind of street rock and roll these bimbos make—when the title cut came on I thought I was hearing *Evita* twice in a row. Only I couldn't figure out why the singer wasn't in tune."[3] (Christgau apparently didn't notice there were two singers.)

The fact that the press resorted to rather childish, extremely sexist name calling—bitches, sissies, bimbos—tells you as much about the critical establishment as it does about *Queens of Noise*. Rock critics were allegedly steeped in the counterculture tradition of New Journalism, but it seems that the Runaways provided them with an opportunity to unleash their pornographic and misogynistic ids.

Mercury's interest in the band whose members were no longer children and who were beginning to assert themselves in adult ways was clearly waning. Outside of that offensive S&M-inspired ad, the label did little to promote *Queens of Noise*. The album sold even more poorly than its predecessor.

"I totally hoped it would be the next big hit, but they never were," says Earle Mankey. "Don't forget it was released by Mercury, and they didn't really stand by it. Mercury was not a powerhouse. Denny always believed in it enough, but I wondered if it was just a business connection with him. ... I don't really think that the label was on fire about the Runaways' album."

The Runaways could only do so much to promote themselves to radio and press. But they could take their music directly to the people. The Runaways spent the next year playing hard across the U.S., crossing the Pacific to conquer Japan, then flying the opposite direction for their first full European tour. From Saginaw to Tokyo to Stockholm, the musicians continued to prove their prowess live.

"The one upside to how competitive we felt to each other was we felt we had to be more dynamic and interesting on stage than the next person," says Fox. "Instead of a bunch of people playing their instruments, every single one of us performed and was interesting. We had these personas. They weren't intentional personas. They were the personas that worked."

The Runaways started the tour on a low note: opening for Rush in Saginaw and at Detroit's famed Cobo Hall. There's a scene in *The Runaways* movie where a male group disses the musicians and Jett pisses on their guitar for revenge. The scene is based on the band's experiences with Rush. No urine was actually involved, but the girls probably wish they had thought of it.

Rush, who were also on Mercury, were a paradigmatic classic-rock band of the '70s. Geddy Lee sang in a high falsetto that, if Currie had tried it, Fowley would probably have told her she lacked rock 'n' roll authority. The trio played lumbering, complicated songs about pretentious subjects. Rush was very successful. And, apparently, they were assholes. At Cobo Hall, they denied their labelmates a sound check. When Currie tripped on stage, they laughed.

"Rush was one of the most dreadful bands ever," says Smythe. "We were treated like shit."

"The audience for Rush's music was not the audience for us," Fox says. "They were the least receptive audience we ever played to. People were booing."

"They stood on the side of the stage and laughed at us during the show," Jett recalls. "Man, what's that about? That's crazy. It's obvious you feel threatened. We all took it as an affront and took it as a message that we had to buckle down and prove ourselves. Every day we ran into something; if it wasn't a name band, it was somebody belittling us or laughing, not taking it seriously. We were always challenged, every day, sometimes all day."

The Runaways were not just struggling to earn R-E-S-P-E-C-T; they were struggling to stay on the road. Mercury did not provide tour support this time. Instead, the band relied on performance fees to cover their expenses. They didn't.

"Whatever money was picked up at the box office was spent on food and drugs and parties," says Bruce Patron, who was one of the tour roadies. Actually, after a few weeks, he became the only roadie and the driver of whatever vehicle they had rented/stolen that day.

"What happened was the roadies all quit after the first week or two," Patron recalls. "They had a lot of experience, and I had never done it before. Nobody was getting paid; there was a lot of bullshit; there was no money. I wound up having the time of my life."

Anderson was gone and Fowley still wouldn't travel. Smythe was the road manager and Carlos Bernal managed the tour, "dealing with hotels and doing lots of drugs," says Patron. High jinks, pranks, escapades, and drama defined the tour. "Kent is a wonderful human being," says Patron, who, like Smythe, went on to work with the Go-Go's. "He's genius but he's got an evil streak. Not like evil killing people, but pranks and practical jokes."

The Runaways toured like outlaws: They snuck out of hotels at night to avoid paying bills, borrowed cars from Mercury for three days then kept them the whole tour, and abandoned rented U-Hauls. To Patron, it was fun; for the Runaways, it was stress. "There was drama about money and people not getting paid," he says. "There was a lot of drama with the band."

Fowley tells a story about the band borrowing a car from the label in Milwaukee and the vehicle showing up a month later, burnt, with no tires, in Harlem. "Mercury Records said, 'Well guess what: That car has now been added to the money you owe us from royalties,'" he recalls. "At one point, they had this big list of damaged hotel rooms, and torched cars, and damaged everything."

In Pennsylvania, Bruce Patron rented a truck from U-Haul. They were supposed to return it in Pittsburgh, but instead they used it for the remainder of the tour, all the way to L.A. There, they put it into neutral and sent it coasting down a hill, across Hollywood Boulevard, all the way to Sunset.

At least once, the cops got called. The Runaways had gotten locked out of their room at some cheap Midwestern hotel. They took the screens off the windows, reached in, opened the window, and crawled inside. The hotel notified the police. To keep their freedom, the band had to pay for the bent screens.

Sometimes, the band needed protecting from assholes. At one "shitty little club," in Smythe's words, the man who ran the venue decided that his office would be the band's dressing room. "He stood behind his desk, expecting the band to change in front of him," Kent remembers. "We corrected his thinking."

Being roadie for five musicians kept Patron busy. Smythe set up Ford's guitar because she was so demanding. "I was afraid of her," Bruce says. "She would throw things around and I would duck." Currie was also hard to deal with. "Cherie seemed entitled: 'I'm a star and I'm entitled and I'm Bowie.'" Patron didn't want to have anything to do with Fox because everyone knew she was uncool: "She was more prissy, a Valley Girl type." He mostly hung around with the easygoing West. "She was just a cool drummer kid."

Out of all the Runaways, Jett impressed Patron, who still works in the concert industry, the most. "There was this thing about Joan," he says. "It always seemed like there was a part of her that was getting off on this: 'I can't believe this is happening to me, that I'm really up here on stage in a jumpsuit, like a badass rock star, but I'm just really me, just a kid.' There was always this sense about her, like, 'I'm living the dream.' Any celebrity that can communicate that, it's really appealing."

Smythe has somewhat different takes on the members' personalities than Patron. At the time, he got along with them, though by the bitter end, even he and his good friend Joan were split. "I liked Lita," he says. "She had a short fuse. She was honest with herself, she wouldn't bullshit you. You had to tread lightly."

Far from being a difficult diva, "Cherie was easily pushed musically," Kent says. "She was open to what any of the girls would come up with. She was just a singer; she did what she was told to do. She was an easygoing girl who wanted to have fun and happened into this crap."

He often wound up rooming with Jackie. None of the others wanted to, "because she was annoying, like she knew everything." Sandy was nice. Mostly he hung out with Joan—until she caught him fucking her girlfriend.

During the *Queens* tour, Smythe says Joan and Cherie had "this whole little lesbo fling. They used to refer to themselves as Salt and Pepper."

All in all, the *Queens of Noise* tour could have been the basis for *Spinal Tap*. "They all wanted to play really loud," Smythe says. "The sound they wanted, you had to play at ten."

The Runaways again had a crazy touring schedule: from Michigan to Texas, back to Ohio and Boston, back to Texas, back to the Northeast. They were supposed to fly but couldn't afford to so mostly drove. On March 5 they played Detroit again, this time at the Royal Oak Music Theatre, and they were the headliners. Their opening acts were Cheap Trick and Tom Petty and the Heartbreakers. While this would seem like a golden moment in the band's career, it was far from perfect. Petty went overtime and as the last act, the Runaways only got to play half an hour before the venue's curfew. (Now they knew how Spirit felt in St. Louis.) Still, the show helped cement their friendship with the Rockford, Illinois, band Cheap Trick, who were also struggling to get America to listen to their melodic take on hard music.

Cheap Trick drummer Bun E. Carlos had met the Runaways in Beloit, Wisconsin, on their previous tour; they all signed his copy of *The Runaways* suggestively, except for the down-to-earth West. A year later, the band seemed hardened and demoralized. They were driving a rental car that they had failed to return and were "living on nothing, on peanuts and stuff," he says. "The gild was off the lily for the band.... We knew they were being taken advantage of... They were out there paying their dues and suffering. Their attitude was, 'We're getting fucked over by our manager but we're out there.'"

The Runaways returned to the Agora. Michalski says most of the members had the same optimism as before, but Fox seemed more "realistic." "She was by far the nicest, the most intelligent, the most personal," he says. "You could see the direction she was headed; she had a more general impression of what was going on. She seemed to be operating on another level than the other four." The differences worked for and against her. "She was also not as good of a player."

The Runaways tour was not one long, drug-addled orgy, as *The Runaways* movie can make it seem. "They didn't have any money for drugs," Carlos says. "We'd smoke a joint after the show. Nobody had the dough to get any hard drugs or pills. You got some beer in the rider; you were eating pizza."

By the second tour, Currie had developed an attitude, Carlos noticed. "There was really the band, and Cherie," he says. "It was the singer, and then the rest of the band. There was that thing going on."

In Boston, the Runaways played the Rat, a legendary rock dive. It was a hot night, figuratively and literally. In the crowd were Iggy Pop and David Bowie. "I went strictly to see them; I thought it was important to see their work," Pop recalls. He was most impressed by Jett, who he called "a real competitor....None of the other girls put a foot wrong, but she was the one."

It was only spring, but Fox recalls the packed venue being unbearably hot—so much so, that during "Heartbeat," she ripped off her sweater and proceeded to play in her push-up bra. "Heartbeat," of course, was the Fox song Currie had rewritten and made about Bowie. Jackie was in one of her frequent spats with Cherie; the undressing was also a sort of fuck-you-I-can-show-even-more-flesh gesture.

Live, the Runaways got to connect directly with their fans. But the grind was tearing them apart. "Their life on the road was much harder than it needed to be," says Cliff Burnstein. "I think that took quite a toll on them, and if they had arguments, it's probably because they were touring under such shitty conditions."

Back home, the Runaways played a triumphal return gig April 1 at the Santa Monica Civic Auditorium. They asked their new friends Cheap Trick to open for them. At month's end, they played a four-night stand at the Whisky. Then they flew to New York for two nights at CB-GB's. A tour of Australia, where they were getting airplay, never materialized, but that was okay: The Runaways were about to make their biggest journey of all.

20 Big in Japan

As any animé lover knows, the Japanese take their pop culture seriously. Reverence of woman-child superheroes with wide eyes and long legs has become a trope of manga comics, Miyazaki movies, and Murakami artwork. The spending power of the eternally adolescent female Japanese consumer went global with Hello Kitty. The Runaways strode into this burgeoning market like childish but hypersexualized action figures come to loud life. Schoolgirls loved them, the camera caressed them, and for one glorious month, the Runaways got a taste of what Beatlemania was like.

Other artists cleared the flight path for the Runaways. By the mid 1970s, many American and European rockers had realized that the Asian nation provided a devout fan base and lucrative market, even, sometimes, for artists who had little success elsewhere. There was a phrase for the phenomenon, used in magazines and eventually song titles and even a band name: Big in Japan.

Elvis Presley was big in Japan. The Beatles were big in Japan. Suzi Quatro was big in Japan. And in 1977, while they were still trying to make a ripple in American air waves and get taken seriously by the British press, the Runaways became big in Japan.

"For the Japanese, there was a novelty value in a Western girl group going over there," says Ralph Peer. "I never viewed them as a novelty act, as in a freak show, but clearly they were different. Being different was appealing to the Japanese."

Peer credits his publishing company, Peer Music, with facilitating what became the Runaways' most triumphal—and troubled—moment. The Runaways' publisher had worked with the Tokyo Music Festival in

the past. The promoter of the prestigious and deep-pocketed event contacted Peer regarding this new all-girl band. "Neon Angels on the Road
to Ruin" had already been a hit there; "the Japanese people in their neon
paradise really took to that," says Fowley. A tour of Japan was booked by
Japan's top agency, Udo Artists, part of the mighty music empire helmed
by Tats Nagashima, the man who brought the Beatles to Budokan. The
festival covered the band's costs in Japan—meaning, for the first time,
the Runaways had their own hotel rooms. By the time the Runaways
landed in Japan for their June shows, "Cherry Bomb" was number one
and they were already stars. The Runaways would have three hit singles
and three charting albums in Japan.

"We were delighted," Peer says. "We had not earned back our advance in the U.S. It looked like a bad deal had been made, then we had
this situation where the records became popular in Japan. It really made
a difference to us."

From the moment the Runaways touched down in Tokyo, they were
a sensation. A phalanx of fans—1,500, according to a Mercury press release—met them at the airport. "We get off the plane and there are photographers and reporters and flashbulbs in our face, and we don't have to
go through customs, we are just waved through, and there are people
there screaming for our autographs and they're being held back, and we
were like, 'Whoah,'" recalls Fox.

The frenzy frightened some band members. But unlike the loutish
lads in England, the Runaways' Japanese fans were mainly excited but
polite young women.

"When we got there, there were thousands of Japanese schoolgirls
screaming at the airport," says Smythe, who was the band's tour and road
manager in Japan. "It was scary at first. We'd seen Beatlemania stuff. We
figured they would knock you down and rip your clothes off. But they
were respectful. 'Sign, please.' I approached things assuming the worse. It
ended up being better than I expected."

The paparazzi and the devotees followed the Runaways throughout
Japan. The band played four gigs in Tokyo, as well as shows in Osaka and
Nagoya. They also appeared on Japanese TV, thanks in part to Peer's
connections with the Tokyo Broadcasting Corporation. A forty-eight-
minute extended music video—originally released on VHS in Japan, and
now available only as a grainy YouTube video—captures them in concert
and playing live in TV studios. They joke in front of a room full of re-

porters ("I'm Sandy West," Currie says), get out of their cars outside a venue wearing kimonos (Cherie rocks hers like it's a Mary Quant mini dress), and drive a jeep around an empty lot, smoking cigarettes. There are lots of schoolgirls in uniform black jumpers and a theater full of cheering fans—except for a group of insolent male teens who lounge, unimpressed. *The Runaways—Live in Japan* also intersperses Runaways shots with footage of cars driving through tunnels and Japanese bikers in trick formations. The Runaways equaled movement, speed, daring.

In this vintage video, as well as in clips from their TV shows, and of course in *The Runaways: Live in Japan* CD, the Runaways look and sound confident, excited, bemused, impudent, bored, amused, empowered. This is their moment and they own it.

The Fab Five weren't the only American rocker chicks conquering the East at that time. Suzi Quatro makes a cameo in the *Live in Japan* video. "They had in Japan and around the world completely accepted me in 1973," Quatro says in an email interview. "I became the blueprint for strong women, and it must be said, the first female rocker to break on through to the other side. Therefore when the Runaways toured there ... the blueprint was already in place and it wasn't such an unusual thing anymore. I had already done it, so the journey was a little easier, which makes me feel very happy about breaking the rules in the first place."

In her memoir *Unzipped*, Quatro talks about her love for Japan, and visa versa. She also describes her horror at witnessing a demonstration of the traditional cultural deference of women to men. A customer repeatedly slapped a waitress who had spilled a drop of tea. Suzi moved to intervene, but her husband restrained her, saying she would be offending Japan's cultural traditions.

Noting that females dominated her audience in Japan, the singer and bassist wonders if they embraced her as a sort of anti-geisha, a futuristic role model for a rapidly modernizing nation.

"Maybe, I represented the 'tough' female in every woman in Japan and around the world," Quatro says. "I had loads of screaming women in front, more than guys in a way. They were 'rebelling' through me."

The Runaways also attracted a largely female audience in Japan. "Japan was still a society that represses women," says Jackie. "In the '70s it was really bad. And the Japanese sexuality was very in your face, which I never use to describe the Runaways, but they liked Cherie's corset, which here is a little shocking. But the Japanese have always been more forward thinking when it came to theatricality: American rock bands, the wilder the better. To this day, Japanese girls who go to school in uniforms want something they can't have. There was just this obsession with Western rock. It was something so totally different, and they could be unabashed about screaming for a girl band, because it wasn't sexual."

Japan mattered so much to Leather Tuscadero, she went there for a second, ceremonial marriage to her bandmate, Len Tucker, in June 1977. The Runaways attended the nuptials. It must have been a thrill for Joan to spend time with her idol (though she was perhaps a wee disappointed to see Suzi tying the knot). Quatro says that every night in Japan, Jett would come to her show and "stand on the side of the stage and take in every single thing I did. She studied me, in detail. I must say … taking inspiration is one thing, but copying a stage show is another. I, of course, not realising what she was doing, would put on my best show possible, 'show off' even. My ego was flying that there was this young girl so intent on me."

In the Japan footage, Jett sports the same haircut as Quatro, only dyed black. But she also clearly cuts a figure that's all her own: popping gum, puffing a cigarette, sneering while singing, just generally oozing tough cool. She looks as much like Sid Vicious as Suzi Quatro. She is all Joan Jett.

"It must be pointed out that she imitated the original Suzi look," says Quatro, "and took it more to a punk place. I was a little more rounded. Joan only saw the 'tough' part of me. And now I am happy to say that we are very different types of performers. I am proud of how well Joan has done, and proud that I was a part of her journey, and very happy that she found this healthy outlet."

The so-called Queen of Rock 'n' Roll certainly paved the way for the Queens of Noise, beginning in the 1960s with her youthful all-girl band the Pleasure Seekers. But the Runaways deserve credit for taking girl-powered rock to the next level, or at least trying to.

"Timing is everything," says Peer. "In business that's absolutely true. It's really tough to be a first of a breed. No deference to Suzi, but she was a solo artist; it's a little different presentation with a little different hill to climb. These folks were going out there with an in-your-face image. The question was whether they were going to be taken as seriously or not. Kim really wanted them to be taken seriously. I think most of the band did, too. In Japan, since they were there as a novelty act, compared to the norm of Japan, they got taken seriously once they did their thing. I don't think that could have happened if they hadn't had this long prelude."

In the Japan footage and recordings, the Runaways come across as a band that has found its groove. This was what they did—no matter what drama was occurring off stage, on stage, they delivered. And in Japan, the drama off stage was tsunami-sized.

The first problem was the magazines. When the Runaways arrived in Japan, they found their photos already splattered across the music and celebrity journals—as well as on the cover of *Goro* and *Big Goro*. *Goro* was a publication that, speaking generously, could be considered Japan's prequel to the American men's magazine *Maxim*. *Big Goro* was a special issue of *Goro* (designed to make its readers feel big?); its nearest American contemporary at the time was *Playboy*. But *Goro* and *Big Goro* didn't feature the whole band on their covers. Currie alone stares out from both with her black-rimmed eyes and hair-sprayed feathered wings. (Decades later, John Cameron Mitchell would adopt this hairstyle for his German transgendered character Hedwig.) On *Goro*, she's clothed in a gold, satin, sleeveless, V-necked shirt. On *Big Goro*, she wears her corset, panties, and fishnets. She sits with her legs open, a black piece of fabric strategically stretched over her genitals. She's pouting, like a pissed-off teenager who just wants to sit comfortably but has been told to stay in this pose. Inside *Big Goro*, she lounges petulantly and provocatively, or crawls on all fours (enacting Fowley's jeers about "dog-cunt"). In other shots, the camera hones in on her face, eyes closed; on her fishnet-encased leg; on her crotch. Currie doesn't look happy. That unease is part of the images' sadistic appeal. The Runaways had always pushed buttons visually and played with their jailbait image, but this "spread" crossed a line. It's soft-core kiddie-porn, clichéd cheesecake, not at all rock 'n' roll.

Unaware that she had done the photo shoot without the rest of the band, and incensed that she had reduced the Runaways to a masturbatory tool for fetishistic pedophiles, her bandmates deemed Currie persona non grata in Japan.

"We were furious," says Fox. "Five days went by and Lita and I wouldn't talk to her, and neither would Joan. I think the gall of it really pissed us off."

Look closely at the videos from Japan, and you can see the freeze-out. Cherie's generally by herself. No one talks to her. In one candid moment, the camera captures the singer looking overwhelmed, and all alone.

Currie herself felt exploited by the shots. She was a girl, the daughter of a starlet, who grew up in a city obsessed with beauty. For all her rebellion, she wanted to participate in that glamour. She hadn't found in punk, as Joan had, an at least partial escape from looksist pressures. Cherie was hardly the first or last person to be the victim of a photo shoot. The interplay between photographer and subject is always a sort of seduction and courtship. When the subject is a young girl and a mature man operates the camera, the photographer usually wins. Critical theorists talk about the dominance of "the male gaze" in Western visual culture. One of the amazing things about the Runaways was the way they stared back at the camera, simultaneously capturing and defying that gaze. Jett always says that the group owned their sexuality. In the *Big Goro* shots, Currie gives it away.

In *Neon Angel*, Currie says that Fowley told her that all of the band members were posing for individual shots. The singer had reason to believe him; Fowley pal Brad Elterman did visit each of the Runaways in their homes—but those portraits are elegant photojournalism compared to these girlie-mag images. Cherie remembers feeling uncomfortable as the Japanese shutterbug told her how to pose. Then her grandmother saw what was happening—her granddaughter on all fours in fetish wear in front of a camera. Grandma chased the photographer off with a cane.

Who really holds the blame for these tasteless shots: the minor or the adults who set her up? "A photographer took a child who did not have … the best childhood … and she's at a photo shoot, and she doesn't have a real strong sense of self," says Kathleen Hanna. "And there's a male photographer telling her what to do … I'm forty-three, and I sometimes have a hard time asserting myself in photo shoots now. When I was thirty-seven, I started crying in a photo shoot because they were trying to get me to do shit I didn't want to do, and I was having a really hard time expressing it, because you really want to please people."

Big Goro was not the only Japanese magazine out to sexploit the Runaways. In a formal culture like Japan, the repression of daily sexual expression bubbles up in unusual and sometimes cruel ways. Of course, this happens in post-Puritan America also, but the peccadilloes across the Pacific Rim can be especially kinky. There are sex cults built around love for anime characters, or for schoolgirls, or for women—or men— dressed as anime characters or schoolgirls.

In *Neon Angel* and *The Runaways* movie, the *Big Goro* incident is depicted as an eventual catalyst for Currie's departure from the group. Ford in particular blows up at her. In an interview that fall with *NME*'s Julie Burchill, Jett also called the magazine "the final thing." But Lita says the singer has exaggerated her reaction to the shots.

"I don't know why she made such a big fucking deal about that," Ford says. "I don't remember being that mad at her. I think it's just something dramatic that they had to put in the movie."

It seems unlikely that the guitarist was shocked by the explicit nature of the photos. Lita, known by the guys in the biz as "the one with the body," has never been afraid to display and exploit her physical assets. There are ample shots in Japanese magazines of the guitarist wearing hot pants with barely covered—or partially uncovered—private parts. In one image inside that same issue of *Big Goro*, she stands in a pool wearing a white, see-through top. All the band members, even Jett, wore black bikinis and boots in another shoot.

It may not have been *how* the photos depicted Currie, but the fact that the magazine *featured* Cherie, that rankled Ford and the rest of the Runaways. Since that first album cover and *Bomp* magazine cover, Currie had become the focal point of the Runaways. But the Runaways wanted to be like the Beatles, or the Who, or the Rolling Stones—a gang of equals. This was a collective identity that seemed generally denied to girl groups: Diana Ross became the supreme Supreme, even though she was not the primary or best singer; Labelle took Patti Labelle's name, though surely Nona Hendryx and Sarah Dash were crucial partners; Suzi Quatro left her sisters to be a solo star. Fanny and Isis were societies of equals—but they also never made it big, not even in Japan. The press kept shoving Currie out in front, and in the Japan footage, her performances merit the star treatment. But the band kept pulling her back. No wonder she got fucked up.

"The Japanese were pro Cherie; being blonde was an influence," says Peer.

Mike Gormley says it was normal for the media to focus on the front person. They are, after all, in front. "Writers always want to talk to the lead singer, male or female," the publicist says. "Sometimes you have to convince them someone else in the band is more interesting, or as interesting. Focusing on Cherie: to me that was natural. She's the lead singer and she was beautiful and sexy. Of course they're going to. I would convince TV producers and directors to not just focus on her, because the band was an interesting band. It wasn't just a backup band to Cherie. They were all attractive in whatever way."

"There is always a 'face' of the group, and she was it, which was helped by the outfits she wore," says Quatro.

You can see the male gaze in action in the footage from Japan. The camera keeps stopping at Currie's crotch, or at Ford's butt in her hot pants. The drool factor is so obvious, it makes you laugh.

There's a moment in the *Live in Japan* video that's at once cheesy and chilling. The band plays "Wild Thing." Perhaps because West sang the song and she didn't have much else to do, Currie goes into this weird pantomime at the end. It's the classic, clichéd box routine: Cherie is stuck inside a box, or a small room, made evident by the way she places her hands on imaginary walls all around her, then pounds on the walls, in time to the beat, in step with Sandy's pounding on the drums. Her movements get increasingly frenzied, like Marcel Marceau on speed, as she tries to beat her way out. At the end of the song, she collapses.

Ultimately, the irresolvable rift that split open in Japan was not the one between Currie and Ford, but the one between Fox and everyone else.

For the brainy, friendly, drug-free bassist, the mismanagement, endless stress, and sense of working so hard for so little were becoming intolerable. In fact, on one of the rare nights that they shared a hotel room, while on tour in America, she told Jett that she wanted to quit. "She got down on her knees and was crying," Jackie says. "It was really such an outpouring of emotion that I hadn't expected from her, so I stayed."

If Jackie was tired of the Runaways, the Runaways were getting tired of Jackie. She whined. She didn't party. She was a know-it-all. She didn't fit in. "Sometimes, being in the Runaways was a little like taking the wildest school trip ever with some of the baddest girls in high school," Currie writes in *Neon Angel*. "Unfortunately, Jackie's presence was like having the world's most uptight teacher along for the ride."[1]

The different attitudes of the Runaways are evident in the way they talk about Japan. In *Neon Angel*, Currie describes being showered with gifts and attention. The tour renewed the band; she didn't want to leave. "The Japanese really understood us, they got us," she wrote.[2]

Lita loved the tour, too. "Japan was nuts, it was great," says Ford.

Fox remembers the experience differently. "It was a bad month," she says. "It was kind of overwhelming. It was a nonstop day. There were photographers following us around. And we were never out of anyone's sight. We spent long hours in rehearsal rooms and TV studios and sound check."

Far from being feted and petted, Jackie says the band was over protected and tightly controlled by Smythe, the jack of all trades in Japan. "My take on Kent was he was the straight guy who was around these hot little girls, and none of them gave him the time of day, and they treated him like a servant. One in particular, who will not be named," recalls Jackie. "So he was really resentful, and when we get to Japan we're big stars, and I think it just all—the combination of drugs and instant celebrity, but at the same time we weren't let out of our hotels. So we were on this very tight leash, but no one was really holding the leash."

There were still good times. Prankster Smythe had a tape recorder, on which he would secretly record the girls, then embarrass them with playbacks. *Playboy* magazine hosted a banquet for the band. "There was still fun stuff going on, but at the same time, there was still a huge amount of anger and resentment towards Cherie," Fox says.

One day the Runaways appeared on a popular talk show, the Japanese equivalent of *The Tonight Show*. They made their live entrance down a flight of stairs. Lita and Sandy had reached the bottom when all of a sudden, smoke from dry ice appeared. Jackie stopped. Cherie, right behind her, said, "Move, bitch," then shoved the bassist. Jackie slid to the bottom of the stairs in front of a live audience.[3]

And then there came the incident that Fox calls "the last straw." A rare 1966 Gibson Thunderbird bass was Fox's pride and joy. It was a heavy instrument that needed strong, stable support. During rehearsal for a show, she placed the Thunderbird on a stand, and it wobbled. She told Kent she needed a better bass stand for the show; "no problem," he answered. The concert went fine. But when she came back for her encore, Smythe handed Jackie a substitute bass and told her the Thunderbird had gone out of tune. It would be hours before anyone would tell her what had really happened: The wobbly stand had never been replaced, someone had tripped over it, the bass had fallen off it, and Jackie's prized instrument snapped.

Something snapped in Jackie, too.

"When my bass broke, I was so upset about it, and I was as much upset that no one would tell me—it took hours," she says. "And then I realized there was no one looking out for us, I have no allies in the band. This sucks; get me out of here."

Eighteen months of giving up everything to be a Runaway had led to this: jack-off photos and a busted bass. The destruction of her beloved instrument was a personal wound, but it was also symbolic of the way the band was disrespected as musicians. She hadn't even been allowed to play on the first album. Here she was, robbed of an instrument again. Back in her hotel room, Fox felt angry, hurt, betrayed, and abused. Still, no one came to talk to her. She called her friend Randy Rhoads for comfort. Then Smythe yelled at her about the phone bill.

"I did not just freak out and leave," she says. "What I had was an anxiety attack. I was teenage and alone.…I had room service and I had this full-blown panic attack. I got really angry that I had no one to talk to and no one looking out for me. I had ordered a coke, and I picked up the bottle and I threw it against the wall, and it was a satisfying smash. But it wasn't enough.

"I knew I couldn't afford to wreck the hotel; I was already on this tight financial leash, and I was so angry," Fox continues. "And then I got angry at myself because I was being a pussy and was scared to leave. Then I saw this piece of a broken bottle, and I was not trying to kill myself, and I was not doing it consciously, but I was angry and I wanted to hurt something. So I picked this up and cut myself on the arm, on the inside. I still have the scar; it's pretty big."

Mental health professionals and feminist scholars have become increasingly aware of the incidence of self-injury among teenage girls. Slicing one's arm in a gesture that imitates suicide but is not suicidal is perhaps the most common form of such injuries. Girls who partake in this behavior repeatedly are called "cutters" or "delicate cutters" (the latter was the name of a song written by Kristin Hersh for the 1980s group Throwing Muses—Hersh was describing herself). Often, such acts are ways of making inner pain external. Depression is anger turned inward; Fox wanted to hurt someone, but nice girls next door didn't do that, so she hurt herself. That lonely night in a Tokyo hotel, Jackie was not trying to kill herself or be dramatic; she was externally manifesting inner pain. It was the proverbial call for help.

Finally, someone heard her. Cherie, the other "soft" Runaway, the one with whom Fox shopped at Frederick's—the one dealing with her own drama in Japan—knocked on Fox's door. "She has this really great heart, and I think she knew that I would be upset that my bass broke," Jackie says.

In *Neon Angel*, Currie writes a dramatic scene where she wrestles the glass out of Jackie's hands. Fox says that, in fact, she had put down the makeshift knife a half-hour before the singer knocked. Either way, it was Cherie who did, finally, show up and get Jackie to an emergency room. The doctor bandaged the bass player's arm, gave her a sedative, and sent her back to her hotel. "The drama was over," Fox says. "It was a private drama."

The next day the Runaways taped a TV show. No one said anything to Fox about what had happened. "It was really weird," she says. "What made it tolerable was the fans in Japan are so great."

It wasn't tolerable for long. Fox had another panic attack. This time, she decided to quit. She called her mom. Ronnie Fuchs called Kim Fowley. Fowley called Smythe. Smythe spent 700 yen on a bus ticket and left it at the hotel's front desk in an envelope labeled "Jackie Fox."

"When Jackie quit the band, she called me up all angry: 'When's my limo going to pick me up'," Smythe says. "I went down to the front desk, bought a bus ticket, put it in an envelope with her name on it. I watched her pick up the envelope very quietly, get on the bus, and leave."

In the liner notes for the live album, which was produced by Smythe and the band, there's a cryptic inside joke: "We thank ourselves for spending the 700 yen."

Fox flew home alone, her rock 'n' roll dreams shattered like that Coke bottle, or her beloved Thunderbird. But she was also relieved; now, she was safe. In liner notes for Cherry Red's CD-version of the live album, Fowley calls it "Jackie's flight to freedom."

"No one said goodbye," Fox says.

It was a horrible denouement for the seventeen-year-old girl next door, the overachiever that outsiders, at least, found to be the most approachable Runaway. But within the band, Fox had become her own worst enemy. Jett had talked her out of leaving once. She wasn't going to do it again. In fact, in an interview shortly after Fox quit, Joan accused Jackie of using self-injury as a way out of the group.

"In Tokyo, she wanted to go home and we said, 'no, you can't,'" the guitarist told *Bump N Grind* fanzine. "She had obligations to fulfill. She had to finish the fuckin' tour. But she didn't want to, she said, 'I wanna go home,' so she did the most outrageous thing she could think of to get attention."[4]

Joan had a T-shirt with the Fabulous Five's picture on it. When Jackie left, she took a cigarette and burned a hole through the ex-member's face.

"That stuff's going to happen when you're in a band: misunderstandings, hurt feelings, this and that," Jett says. "But when you make what you consider a war move and you quit, it's like come on, okay, you quit. You're out. Don't play games; this is serious, this is my life."

Currie, on the other hand, expressed sympathy toward her sometime comrade. "Joan, Sandy, and Lita are like one fist, and me and Jackie were just staying there waiting for one of us to get knocked up," she told *NME*. "Me, I was never afraid. But they were just very, very vicious and in Japan Jackie couldn't take it any longer. I don't blame her at all, because they pushed her and pushed her. She tried to hang on but just couldn't."[5]

Hernando Courtright knew Jackie before she joined the Runaways. He called her his little sister. "Jackie's problem is she has a high IQ," he says. "To some degree she's too smart for her own good, to be in a rock band. When you're too smart, you over-analyze things. She was more intellectual than she was creative. It's hard because you have to put up with a lot of stupidity."

After she left the Runaways, Jackie never played in another band.

Fox left her bandmates high and dry in Japan, with the Tokyo Music Festival—their primary gig—still ahead. Joan played bass for the prestigious show, Lita covered rhythm and lead. Fortunately the tracks for *Live in Japan* had been recorded already.

Fox wonders what would have happened if she had stayed.

"We had one thing in common: We did have each other," she says. "Even if we didn't all get along, we were all in the same boat. We were also teenagers, and this was before boy bands, and teenagers weren't rock stars, and none of us, whatever the musical disparity in the beginning, no one in the band, the Runaways, was a musical genius. And nobody sucked either. It took me a month to make the transition in my head from lead instrument to rhythm instrument. But once I got there, it's not like everyone's musicianship was so finely honed that there was this big difference. By the time you get to *Live in Japan*, I don't think anyone listens to it and says, 'You know, everyone is pretty good except for the bass player.' We were a pretty cohesive band at that point, and I think if we had stayed together, I think we would have been pretty good."

Live in Japan, released by Phonogram in Japan in September, is the Runaways' best record. The group was always tightest, most ferocious, and most fun when they were alone together on a stage, rather than locked in a studio with Kim. The Runaways also got to co-produce *Live*, working with Smythe, who was more of a peer than a dictator, meaning they got to determine their own sound. There are no cheesy keyboards or moans. Whatever divisions were occurring offstage, on stage and on the record, the Fab Five sing and play in unison. West anchors and drives the band—gone is the sluggish pace of the studio recordings. Currie sounds powerful, not tortured.

The Runaways were able to skim the best songs from their first two records: "Queens of Noise," "California Paradise," "Rock & Roll," "You Drive Me Wild," "Neon Angels on the Road to Ruin," "Cherry Bomb," and "American Nights." They also included a few they hadn't released before. Fowley lifted "All Right You Guys" from Venus and the Razorblades. Written by Danielle Faye and Bob Willingham, it's a ridiculously simple ditty, to the point of inanity, as the throwaway title indicates. But the Runaways make the mindless pop mean and muscular. Fox says they played it because they needed more songs for Currie to sing. This was the song they performed at the Tokyo Music Festival, with Jett on bass. "I've never liked this song," Jackie says. "I can't get over lyrics that don't make a lot of sense."

West finally gets her moment in the spotlight on "Wild Thing," a live staple since the Runaways' early days. "Wild Thing," like its three-chord cousin "Louie Louie," is rock at its most primitive: emotive, sexy, barely spoken, all played between the lines. West had a decent voice, but there's nothing fancy in her delivery. Live though, as captured in the Japanese videos, she was a bit of a showman. The instruments stop on the verses and West raises one of those long, sinewy arms diagonally into the air, drumstick pointing to the rafters: "Wild thing, I think I love you." Then she smashes the sticks down for two beats. "I want to know for sure."

She's pointing at the audience. "C'mon on and hold me tight." Her hand is in the sky now, twirling the stick. "You move me." The song was West's signature, one she carried with her to her post-Runaways ventures. The title "Wild Thing" adorns a page in her mother's scrapbook of Sandy. "Wild Thing" was Sandy West.

On "Gettin' Hot," Ford smokes. She and West play the Deep Purple–worthy metal riff in exact sync—locked in. Even Currie pulls out her inner hard rocker for some respectable wailing. "Lita and Sandy had written this opening they didn't know what to do with," Fox says. "They took lyrics I'd written, added a chorus and chord changes. Everyone was happy: Cherie got to sing it, and it was a hard rock song that showed off Lita's guitar playing better than anything we'd ever done."

Fowley's take on "Gettin' Hot": "Jackie can cook as a songwriter. It was a good song, it wasn't great, but it was fun if you were throwing up beer somewhere."

Fowley wrote "I Wanna Be Where the Boys Are" with Ronnie Lee, guitarist for Venus and the Razorblades. On *Live in Japan*, the song follows Ford and West's chugging outro to "Neon Angels," a piece of powerful playing that, like "Gettin' Hot," was built on one of the Runaways' pillars—the drummer and the lead guitarist's twinned metal chops. After a corny intro about "you boys in the audience," the band plows hard and fast into "Boys"; now the hard rockers are creating the blueprint for hardcore punk. Jett growls and snarls the tough-chick manifesta: "I wanna fight how the boys fight/ I wanna love like the boys love… I'm the bitch with the hot guitar/ I am the L.A. sonic star." And she was.

"It was a great song to showcase her voice and attitude," says Fox. "The rest of us liked it, it was pretty rock 'n' roll."

On *Live*, Currie follows Jett's anthem with her own, "Cherry Bomb." This wasn't a competition: This was a double-barreled shotgun. On "American Nights," they come together, Currie nailing the should-have-been hit like she didn't on record, Jett shouting raspy exhortations to the audience.

The crowd is going wild. "You're beautiful," Currie tells them. "Arigatou"—thanks in Japanese. *Live in Japan* ends with "C'mon," the song Fox booted from *Queens of Noise*. Jett wrote it—another taut song about desire—but Currie sings the lascivious lines: "Your eyes are wild, your body's shaking."

The Runaways had finally made a great album from start to finish. Sandy Robertson gave *Live in Japan* five stars in *Sounds*, writing, "The good news is that this lavishly packaged Japanese import reveals the Runaways to be one of the best hard rock 'n' roll bands onstage/on the planet, regardless of age and/or sex."

The album jacket was also their best. The gatefold featured the Runaways standing in a row in their Ciri jumpsuits, their guitars standing in front of them, unsmilingly defiant and assured. The lavish package Robertson refers to included glossy photos of each of the members and a souvenir obi (sash).

There were two major problems with the live album: One, Mercury refused to release it in the States. Fowley says he begged them to, but they said no. One year later, another American band demonstrated the marketing potential of a live Japanese album; the Runaways' friends Cheap Trick finally broke through to an American audience when their disc *Cheap Trick at Budokan* hit the top 10 and went triple platinum.

Secondly, *Live in Japan* captures a band in full glory, but the Fab Five were no more.

21 Another One Bites the Dust

When they returned from Japan, the Runaways were supposed to tour with Alice Cooper. The smart pairing could have finally broken the band in America. Like the Runaways, Cooper's glam boogie didn't take itself more seriously than it was meant. Main man Vincent Furnier played with gender stereotypes by naming himself after a woman and wearing dresses and makeup on stage. Unlike the Runaways, he had had a number one album, 1973's *Billion Dollar Babies*, and Top 10 hits, such as "School's Out." But with no bass player, the Runaways had to bow out of the tour.

Thanks in part to the Runaways' success, female teenage bassists were at least a little more plentiful in 1977 than they had been in 1975. Reportedly thirty-seven women auditioned for the part.[1] "I think a lot of girls in Southern California were very inspired by them," says Danielle Faye. "The punk movement was just starting, and I think they inspired that, the do-it-yourself type thing. ... There were a lot of killer girl musicians in L.A."

Faye once again almost became a Runaway. "I got called to join the Runaways by Kim to replace Jackie," she says. "He said, 'We got to get you fitted for a jumpsuit! Meet me at LAX!'"

But again, Faye had cold feet. "At that point, I was hearing the things that went on behind the scenes with the Runaways," she says. "There was a lot of acrimony and a lot of drama. I had already heard stories, like he was really rough on them, and no one was getting any money; he had stranded them out on the tour, and the girls were all fighting."

The Runaways tried to hire future Go-Go Charlotte Caffey, "but she said no," Fowley says. His next choice was a precocious seventeen-year-old from the tony OC seaside town of Newport Beach. "I said, 'Why should we let this girl in?' And they said, 'Because she looks like Lita, they look like sisters. And she can learn the bass parts.' So, okay."

Victory Tischler was, in her words, "an Orange County kid," a golden girl from the Golden Coast. Her family lived in one beach community and had a summer house on the opposite coast, in the Hamptons. Vicki—or Tory, as some people called her—didn't like school, so she had private tutors. She got a high-school diploma at age fifteen-and-a-half. "I had a different upbringing from the other girls," she says.

Her whole life, Vicki has loved horses. She was privileged enough to be able to afford to ride them as a young girl. And she was unlucky enough to get thrown at age ten, when her horse spooked. She bumped her head; maybe she had a concussion. No big deal, she thought at the time. But a few days later, she started feeling disoriented. Next thing she knew, she was staring at the ceiling tiles in the school nurse's office. She had had a seizure. She would have several more over the next decade.

Tischler was smart and ambitious. With her brains, looks, and riches, she probably could have pursued any career. But she wanted to be a rock star. She knew about the Runaways. In fact, she was one of the many Exopolis kids whom they inspired to pick up a guitar. She saw the Fabulous Five open for the Tubes. "These girls came on stage," she remembers. "I really wanted to be a part of it. It's what I wanted to do, the minute I saw them. Prior to that, I wanted to be a photographer or a director."

The first Runaways album made her jealous and desirous. "You're sixteen years old. You want to be a rock star. You see a gatefold album that has this all-girl band. Not only was it an all-girl band, they were the same age as I was. I put the record on the stereo. You see the Mercury label spin around; it represented legitimacy. It was a real deal. I just could not fathom how that happened, how that opportunity came their way."

Tischler was already a music fan, mostly of the blues. "I wanted to play like Bonnie Raitt," she says. At sixteen, she tried forming her own all-girl band, Juice. She played guitar. The band needed gear. In the legendary spirit of the Sex Pistols nicking equipment from David Bowie, they broke into the rehearsal room of a Pasadena outfit called Van Halen. Right before they were scheduled to play a battle of the bands at the Whisky, Juice booted Vicki. Then the band got written up in the *Los*

Angeles Times. The betrayal sent her "careening out of control," Vicki says.

Hurt and pissed, Tischler wanted revenge. She stole the singer's phone book; in it was Kim Fowley's number. Tischler knew Fox had left the band. One day she was at a mall when a girl came up to her and said, "Aren't you in the Runaways?" Vicki's friend Marci Blaustein answered, "No, but she's going to be."

The guitar player called Kim and lied. "I said I'd been playing bass for two to three years," Tischler says. "'Bass is my life; I like Suzi Quatro, that's why I play bass.'"

Invited to audition, Vicki now had a problem: She needed a bass. She called up a guy in Santa Ana who had placed a classified ad. She said she would buy his instrument if he would teach her how to play. "This Mexican guy taught me all the songs on the Runaways' albums," she says. "My fingers bled, but I learned how to play those songs."

Tischler met Fowley and Jett at Larrabee Studios. She played them a few songs. They invited her back two days later to play with the band at SIR studios. "I was really scared. I had no self-confidence—a lot of balls, but not really. I walked in there and Lita looks at me and says, 'Oh my god, you do look like me.' Cherie says, 'Come on in.' We hung out for a little bit, jammed. It went fine."

The Runaways asked Vicki to leave the room. A short, tense time later, they invited her back in. "Welcome to the band," they said. On July 5, 1977, Tory Tischler became Vicki Blue.

Joan came up with Vicki's stage name. They were sitting on a couch, which was the only piece of furniture, in Kim's West Hollywood apartment. Stacks of clothes leaned against the walls; dishes moldered in the sink. Fowley sat on the floor in his dirty underwear eating scrambled eggs. A new name was like donning an alter ego. "'Blue' was something to stand out with," Vicki says. "It heightened my confidence."

Kent Smythe, who would become the new member's nemesis, remembers her introduction to the band differently. Fowley picked her and named her, he says—only the manager said her last name with a sly, knowing chuckle, as if it were not spelled B-l-u-e.

Like all the Runaways except Ford, Vicki came from a family in crisis. Her father had died the year before. Because of their wealth, her mother insisted she become legally emancipated before she joined the

Runaways; Mom had a smart sense of the band's managerial disarray. "My family was afraid people could come to them for any money owed," Blue says. So at age seventeen, Vicki was on her own, traveling Europe with a rock band. It was a dream, when it wasn't a nightmare.

Before she could be revealed to the public, Blue had to lose ten or fifteen pounds—Fowley's rule. As Lita told *Melody Maker*, unintentionally stating the rockist double standard, "No one wants to see a female version of Randy Bachman." Girls who weighed 130 pounds were not skinny enough for rock 'n' roll, apparently, or at least for Kim's Hollywood notion of rock 'n' roll. A humiliating forced diet probably didn't help the shy, inexperienced teenager feel at ease with the world-weary rock stars around her.

Victory Tischler-Blue, as she now calls herself, has an agenda. She has made one film about the Runaways, *Edgeplay*, and she would like to publish a book of her photographs of the band. Having been pushed and abused when she was in the group, she has learned to play offense, to try to control the narrative about the band like it's a chess game. At different times, she will present that narrative differently. Or maybe, her feelings about the band change, based on her ongoing personal, professional, and legal wranglings with various members. In a 2010 interview, she says, "Nobody was mean." Two years later, she says, "It was such an oppressive environment. I hated every minute of it. They were mean to me. With the exception of Cherie, initially they wouldn't give me an inch. It was not fun. Back then it was a lot of posturing."

She does consistently say that it was hard to fit into a band that had already spat out three bass players. "I was the new kid," she says. "I was like the red-headed stepkid for a while. I was really shy. It's always tough when you walk into a ready-made situation."

This is how incohesive and alienated the new lineup was: Blue never revealed that she was really a guitarist; the band never asked. "We never hung out together," she says. "We never jammed. They never knew that I could barely hold my own as a bass player. As a guitar player, I could blow Joan out of the water."

Lita and Vicki did eventually get along; decades later, they remain friends. Years after the band's breakup, Blue become close with Sandy, too. In the beginning though, only Cherie was nice to her. But Cherie wasn't around for long.

Cherie Currie was always late. It drove the rest of the band crazy. Fox remembers sitting in the car outside her house, waiting endlessly for the singer to put on her makeup so they could rehearse. Blue had only been in the band a few weeks, but she was already getting tired of the singer's tardiness. "She's always late," she says. "We were all sick and tired of it. Then she would leave early."

One day—presumably once Blue had slimmed down—Barry Levine was photographing the new lineup. In the *Neon Angel* version of the story, Currie was on time but had to leave a few hours later, to return the car she shared with her sister Marie; she says it was Lita who was late. In everyone else's version, Cherie was late, again.

"From what I hear, she was mad that I was late for a photo session, and I was mad because she was late for a photo session," says Ford, who has not read Currie's book. "My memory of it, she was always late for everything. She was having an affair with the manager; he would always cover her for it. It pissed me off—as it would any real musician, you know. I was sitting here for two fucking hours, and I'm sick of it. When they do it on a regular basis, it gets to be boring for a while. She was two hours late, and I just yelled at her. I never hit any of those girls. I don't remember kicking down any doors either."

There had never been any love lost between Ford and Currie. The metalhead mocked the pop fan's singing. She resented the way Cherie hogged the publicity. She had no tolerance for diva behavior. She hated Barry Manilow. On that July day in that photo studio, "Lita had had enough," Blue says.

The notoriously hot-headed Ford laid into Currie. About being late. About not being professional. About putting family before the band. Cherie retreated to the dressing room. Ford may not remember doing it, but Blue and Currie both say that the guitarist followed the singer and kicked the door down.

Lita gave Cherie a choice: band or family.

Around the same time that Currie first joined the Runaways, her mother announced that she and her new husband were moving to Indonesia. Marie Harmon assumed that her younger children would join her. But Cherie chose to stay in L.A. and with the Runaways. The decision caused a long and deep rift between mother and child. The singer frequently said that the Runaways filled in for her broken home.

"We were a family," she asserts. "We protected each other. We spent years together protecting each other, making each other better performers, making each other who we are today. The five of us together were exceptional, magical. We cared about each other a lot."

But less than two years later, when Ford again asked her to make this admittedly untenuous version of Sophie's choice, Cherie had changed her mind. Maybe, it was never the Runaways that she wanted but a career, and by 1977, she saw that a successful career might lie outside the band. Or maybe, after years of separation from her mother and her father's illness, Currie had changed her mind. "Cherie comes from family that loves each other and stays together," says Blue.

"Family," Currie said to Ford.

Cherie walked out of the studio and out of the Runaways.

"It was very intense," Blue recalls. "Horrible."

Currie's fate with the Runaways may have been sealed from the moment of her tryout, when she suggested singing a Barry Manilow song. After she left, the band ruthlessly mocked her tastes. "She wasn't into rock 'n' roll, she likes mellow songs," Jett told Sandy Robertson at *Sounds*. "She'd make me change lyrics of songs that I wrote … [mimics] 'I'm not gonna sing that. That's DIRTY!!!'"[2]

Part of the problem may have been that, perhaps because of their increased intimacy, Currie started to change Jett—to civilize her. "I wasn't acting my normal self," Joan told *Bump N Grind*. "I was becoming another Cherie, I guess, and the band came in and finally gave me a buncha shit saying, 'What the fuck are you doing, Joan. Why are you like this?' Like I wasn't being rowdy anymore, and within one week after that, I was back to my normal self, destroying hotels, and fire extinguishers in the halls, and things like that."[3]

To Julie Burchill, Jett was more charitable about her bandmate's influence on her. "Cherie made me much more … sophisticated, I think," she told the *NME* writer.[4]

Cherie lobbed her own media bombs back at her ex-bandmates. She accused the Runaways of being petty and constantly bickering. "I lost respect for them, and when you lose respect for your band members, you've lost everything," she told *The Wasteland* fanzine. "There was just so much going on, and I thought, 'Why put up with it?'"[5]

Her bandmates were jealous of the attention she received, she said. "They hated my guts, the stupid bitches ... they were afraid that if I was out of the band they wouldn't know how to survive," she told *NME*. But she also admitted that she wasn't really the "wild girl" she pretended to be. "That's just a character I portrayed. I'm just a normal everyday teenager. I like flowers and horses. I like the country and stuff."[6]

The Runaways conceded they were sick of being a side act to the Cherie Currie Show. "If she had her way the four of us would be sitting here with masks over our faces so you couldn't tell who the fuck we were," Jett said to Robertson.

Every Runaway had a healthy ego—they had to, to survive Fowley and hecklers and labels and critics. But what really irritated Currie's bandmates was the way she seemed to think they were beneath her. "No one else got the feeling that well, we're better than anyone else," Jett told *Bump N Grind*. "We are the same as everyone else in this fuckin' laundromat."[7]

In *Neon Angel*, Currie writes that she neither courted nor desired the focus of the press, as proved by one incident: Shortly before she left the band, *Rolling Stone* wanted to run a feature on the group—with a solo shot of Currie on the cover. Cherie refused to do the shoot, and the Runaways lost the cover.

The center of attention also bore the brunt of abuse. More than the rest of the band, Currie had to deal with the pervs and the critics—and the pervs who were critics. There was something about the Runaways that brought out the worst in even the best of men. Legendary music scribe Lester Bangs wrote a stunning piece of stream-of-consciousness porn for *Back Door Man* about the bodily acts he wanted to perform upon the teenage vocalist. Bangs conceded that the Runaways' music "sucks syphilitic rodents," but he desired their singer anyways, because she was a "child ... which is why I wanted to defile you in the first place." The article, which reads like a deranged rant from a Mansonite stalker, understandably disturbed Currie. No one was penning fantasies about biting the "pathetically teeny titties" of Joan, or Sandy, or Lita (of course, Ford's breasts weren't teeny).[8]

As with Fox, Currie was never able to penetrate the bond that Jett, West and Ford had formed before she joined the Runaways. Resentments mounted. Release brought relief.

"After leaving I felt like a ton had been lifted off my shoulders," Cherie told *NME*.[9]

Losing Fox was hard, but bassists are replaceable. Currie, however, was, for better or worse, the face of the band. She was the namesake of the Runaways' biggest song. Where would they be without their Cherry Bomb?

"Here in the States people in the music business think the Runaways have had it, especially as I've now quit the band," she humbly told *NME*. "They could have stuck together without Jackie, but not without me."

Amazingly, as with Jackie, no one tried to talk Cherie out of leaving. Fowley, who was neither in Japan nor at the shoot, did not try to later mediate a resolution. After all, there was certainly no love lost between him and Currie.

"'So I guess Joan's the front girl now.' That was my response, not call up Cherie and say why don't we kiss and make up, or call up Jackie and kiss and make up," Kim says. "I was so exhausted by the constant, 'Fuck you Kim Fowley, you're a piece of shit, you're an asshole, anybody could have produced us, anybody could have cowritten these fucking songs— we're the fucking bitches everybody loves, you're lucky, we hate you, go fuck yourself.' I mean that's all you're hearing by then, you're not going to sit down and say well wait a minute, let's kiss and makeup. And maybe Jackie stands there and says that was a cry for help, and I wasn't mature enough. And they certainly weren't either. We just let her go and went looking for another bass player, and when Cherie was drummed out, I should have called up and said, 'Nope, you can't quit. Let's put this back together again, this is too big.' … If you think about how many times various Beatles members quit or various Who members quit, or of course the Rolling Stones fighting amongst themselves, it was so gigantic that they put it back together again and continued on for a few more records for a few more years. But in the case of the Runaways, I was so exhausted from the constant fuck-you-I-hate-you-shit that, okay she's gone. One less thing to worry about."

According to Fox, her departure threw off the balance of the pentagram, and the Runaways never recovered. "When I left, these delicate threads that held these five things together just broke," she says. "The band was very unbalanced because Sandy and Lita wanted the band to be much harder. And Sandy and Lita and Joan had managed to get even harder as time went on. I was still Cherie's friend in the band, and I was a little calmer. She lost a potential ally in some things, and it just fucked up the chemistry."

Jett agrees that the Runaways were never the same after Fox and Currie left. "We all had dark stuff going on toward the end of the band, after Cherie left," she says. "I think we all knew that was the lineup. I just sensed it was going to slowly die. I can't explain it. I knew the public wouldn't really accept me as the lead singer. I was too, whatever—not the taste of what people wanted to see. But we were still out there trying. I think you can see it. Look at any picture of us as a four-piece; you won't find one picture of us smiling ever. We were depressed."

For Blue, Currie's departure was shocking. Her one ally was gone. She must have wondered what she got herself into. Plus, she was a fan of Cherie's and of the mix of personalities in the quintet. "I think the contrast between Cherie and Joan was incredible," Vicki says. "When I was in the band and we were a five-piece, I loved the dynamic between the two of them."

Blue compares the quartet lineup to Abba. "The light/dark top/bottom dynamic, that wasn't there now," she recalls. "We had the butch top flanked by the two clones. It was like Lita and I were the girls, Joan and Sandy were the guys."

Jett took her Fabulous Five T-shirt and burned another hole, this time through Currie's face.

"I was pissed and I was eighteen, and my view was, you guys just bailed on the project," she recalls. "Things get tough and you just bail. Jackie's situation was different than Cherie's, but I was hurt by both of them. Personally, as friends, I just felt betrayed, I suppose. So that was my way to get back at them."

Years later, Joan came to understand her bandmates' decision.

"I think some of the girls got very homesick when we were on the road, and that definitely factored into people wanting to not—you know, it's hard work and major sacrifice to do that kind of stuff that you love. You pretty much give everything else up, and everybody else. They really weren't willing to give up their whole life for this, and I really get that, I really do. And I can't begrudge people that."

22 Waitin' for the Night

Currie was right: the Runaways couldn't replace her. But her departure did not mean their demise. It provided the catalyst for what the band probably should have done two years earlier: Make Jett the front person.

By Japan Joan's metamorphosis was complete, her shy chrysalis a tattered relic. She had long ago become the band's lead songwriter. The former Miss Larkin had developed a stage persona that also became her off-stage identity: the tough tomboy in black leather and black eyeliner. Punk provided a sympathetic context and community, and Jett made punk look cool. Inspired, perhaps, by her new friend Johnny Rotten, she had also worked up a distinctive vocal style: a keening rasp punctuated by yelps, growls, snarls, and screams. It was the kind of voice a person could sing or shout along to, invested with emotion but not unattainably virtuosic.

There was apparently little debate about the transition. Joan already sang half the songs, after all. The band had no regrets about getting rid of the corset shtick. There were some tunes Jett didn't feel like she could sing. Those were probably the ones the band didn't like anyways, like "Midnight Music."

"I remember the discussion Joan had where she had to become the lead singer," Blue says. "'It's all on your shoulders.'"

The Runaways rehearsed the new lineup and began learning material for the next album. On July 21, they tried out a cover of a song that Jett had heard in England, by the Arrows, a group popular across the pond but not in America. It was a ridiculously simple, catchy song whose sentiment Jett related to. Fowley says that the rest of the band didn't feel the same way. Toby Mamis says Fowley wouldn't let them cover it because he couldn't get a piece of the publishing. Whatever the case, "I Love Rock 'n' Roll" never made it out of the Runaways' rehearsal room.

After, once again, playing in the 'burbs to test out the new lineup, the Runaways performed their first Hollywood show, back at the Whisky, on August 27. The line stretched down the block. The quartet played a few of Jett's new songs: "Wasted" and "You're Too Possessive." They also unveiled outfits that displayed their cheeky sense of humor and solidarity against a common enemy: T-shirts with a corset painted on.

By ditching and dumping on Currie's bustier, the Runaways symbolically and literally purged their past. They wanted to be appreciated as players, not playthings. "Playing in this band is what I do for a living," Ford told *Melody Maker*. "This is my vocation. It upset me when I used to read what a novelty we were or that it would be over in six months. When the fan mail started coming in, it felt really good. We got thank-you cards from all over the world. People gave me extra incentive to move forward."[1]

The Whisky garment must not have sat well with one audience member. Cherie Currie, there with her sister Marie, lunged ashtrays at her old bandmates.

"I really wanted them to be good," the singer told Steve Clarke at *NME*. "I've no grudges against them. I'm doing my own album. I wish them the best of luck. But they were so unprofessional. They were like a bunch of whining little babies up there, and for them to do something like that was so immature and unprofessional..."[2]

The reviewer for the *Los Angeles Times* was more impressed with the Whisky show than Currie. "While the Runaways' presentation was slightly tentative, the lineup changes should have no major bearing on the group's future," Richard Cromelin wrote. Joan did not bowl him over as a front person: "... Jett seemed preoccupied with holding things together and overly intent on striking tough attitudes, all of which contributed to a slightly stiff, unconvincing posture." Perhaps, the critic preferred his sheroes a little more buxom: "In contrast, lead guitarist Lita Ford is emerging as a marvelous performer."[3]

English critic Sylvie Simmons caught the late-night Whisky show and pronounced the Runaways "more confident than ever." Blue, who didn't even rate a mention in the *Times*, "played competently." Despite losing her voice, "Joan Jett looked and performed like she'd been waiting to take over the starring role from the word go," Simmons wrote.[4]

But there was also a disturbing reaction from part of the crowd at the Whisky, Simmons reported. A few male fans heckled the band, shouting, "Get 'em off" and "Come here and I'll take all four of you on." No one ever treated Led Zeppelin like strippers or wrestlers, even when Robert Plant would take his shirt off.

The Runaways wasted no time recording their third studio album. *Waitin' for the Night* was whipped out in two weeks in August, at Larrabee Sound Studios in West Hollywood. The band had to work fast; an A studio like this wasn't cheap. Pros at recording by this point, the band went into Larrabee prepared.

"I think it was called rehearsing," Fowley says. "There was no partying going on or playback parties. The record company would come once and see how it's going."

As on the first album, the Runaways' newest member was kept off the record. Almost all if not all of the bass parts on *Waitin'* were contributed by Sal Maida, who played in a band called Milk 'N Cookies, as well as with Roxy Music. Blue says she played on one song, but is unsure which one. Apparently, the band did know that Blue couldn't hold her own on the bass. She says she didn't really care.

"I wasn't that attached to it," Vicki says. "I was there every day for the whole session. It was fun."

Mercury released *Waitin' for the Night* in November, making it their second studio album that year, their third album of 1977 counting *Live in Japan*. That's a prodigious pace for any band, let alone one wracked by internal upheaval. The disc captures the Runaways as a lean, mean machine driven hard by Jett. She wrote or co-wrote eight songs and sings them all. Ford wrote two tracks by herself. It's probably the band's best-sounding record, not too raw but not too pop. Few effects augment the tight playing, not even reverb—there are no keyboards, or strings. Uptempo and driving, *Waitin'* could be a lost Ramones record (except for the one Lita Ford wankout).

The Runaways were more anxious to be taken seriously than ever, and they worked hard in the studio. Jett and Ford showed up for every mixing session. Fowley associate Harvey Kubernik was there, too. "For the first time things in the studio went down well," he wrote in an article for *Melody Maker*.[5] "Kim gave us a lot of control, and I think it's our best album yet," Joan told Harvey.

The jacket featured another Levine shot. All of the Runaways wear the signature Jett look: jeans and black jackets. There's no sexual tease here. They're standing behind a razor-wire fence. Jett and Blue grip it, sending blood (or, as *NME* critic Julie Burchill wrote, "lip-smacking tomato ketchup") running down their hands.

Waitin' kicks off with the bristling "Little Sister," a song Jett wrote with Inger Asten, apparently someone's pseudonym. The wisened adult offers some world-weary generational advice to a younger girl. The attitude is hardened but not without hope: "This mean world can be yours so don't hesitate." Jett may have already been sensing her leadership position. "Little Sister" was the first of many anthems of empowerment she would come to write, sing, or produce.

Mercury released the second track, "Wasted," as a single in the U.K.; it was another could-have-been, should-have-been hit. The three-minute rocker by Jett and Fowley gets cranking with one of Lita's gnarliest riffs, the kind that makes you want to scrunch your face up and play air guitar. Sandy gets to bash the (imaginary) arena walls. Joan sings the anti-drug lyrics like a taunt—could she have been singing about Cherie? Fowley has one word for the track: "God."

"Gotta Get Out Tonight" rocks with a great Chinn-Chapman bubble-glam girl-group vibe; Fowley buddies Rodney Bingenheimer and Harvey Kubernik add handclaps to the verse. The lusty Jett tune could have been one Currie was too prudish to sing: "I'm getting oh so wet," Joan talk-sings. It's a classic song about a favorite teen-girl activity: slipping out of the house at night. Fowley describes it as "Joan being suburban but herself." (Miley Cyrus should cover this song.)

Perhaps sensing the need to slow things down a bit—even Led Zeppelin had their "Stairway to Heaven," Nazareth their "Love Hurts"—Jett emotes "Wait for Me," a plea to a lover. Listen to the way the guitars and drums tumble in perfect sync on the riff—"It's a bond that can never be broken," Joan sings, her voice thick with want. The song ends in an eruption of howls, Ford's guitar echoing out. Kim didn't like it: "Joan being needy doesn't work in leather."

Lita gets to flaunt her fancy fretwork on her Black Sabbath–style psych-out "Fantasies." Dripping with erotic innuendo, the song demonstrates that girls have wet dreams too. After Jett's tight riffs, the track feels overwrought; West's addition of "cow tree bell" and gong complete the *Spinal Tap* vibe. You can hear the uneasy alliance between the glam-punk Jett and the hard rockers starting to fray.

Side two gets back to briskness with "School Days," the B-side of "Wasted." The Jett/Fowley tune is the Runaways' answer to Alice Cooper's "School's Out," another great garage-rock anthem.

Ford's second contribution to *Waitin'* fits much more snugly into Jett's amped drive. "Trash Can Murders" is based on a true story. Creeps like Charles Manson and the Hillside Strangler cast a dark spell over the City of Angels in the '70s. The song's perspective changes in the third verse, from second person to first: Jett/Ford becomes the avenging "night prowler ... night howler." It's maybe the rockingest song ever written about a mass murderer, and it should have been a hit, too.

Fowley, however, didn't want "Murders" on the album. He had brought Fleetwood Mac singer Stevie Nicks to the studio one day, and she offered the band a song she had written, "Gold Dust Woman." They turned it down because, they said, Nicks didn't need the money. "It should have been, 'Thank God Stevie Nicks walked in here 'cause now we're going to have a hit,'" Kim says.

"Gold Dust Woman" would have been a better sub for the next tune, the throwaway "Don't Go Away." Jett sings about getting wet again, albeit with sweat, this time.

Time to bring the lighters out for the title track, a song that must have been hanging around in the Runaways' drawers for a while, given the Krome co-songwriting credit. It's a slow song about the vampire life, bogged down by typically Fowleyian lyrics such as "Shades of gray don't fade away/ They're waitin' for the night." Long and laborious, "Waitin' for the Night" feels like an elegy. Kim agrees it was a mistake. "The ultimate love-me-I'm-lonely song," he says. "Who cares. They want their asses kicked, they don't want to sit there and cry with you. But again, Joan needed to do that the same way the rest of them and Joan needed to do the Earle Mankey stuff. And that was the problem; there wasn't enough teenage dog shit in there."

The album snaps back to life with the great freedom anthem "You're Too Possessive." "Get outa my life/ Get off my back, I ain't your wife," Jett roars. Years earlier, she'd told a reporter she would never get married, and she meant it.

"I thought the first album was God, I thought the second one was Compromise City, and I thought *Waitin' for the Night* was imitating the Sex Pistols and having vaginas do it," Fowley says.

The change in lineup didn't faze the critics. Sandy Robertson still gave them five stars in *Sounds*. "The amazing thing about this album is the way the Runaways and Kim have made an art statement that says (I think) 'Here's the reality behind the dream we sold you' while still maintaining enough pop content to keep their original fans interested," the Runaways' stalwart opined.[6]

Writing for *NME*, Julie Burchill congratulated the Runaways on dumping "the bass-playing sugar-plum" and "sparrow with Jayne Mansfield aspirations." She wrote, "Joan Jett was always the magnet to whom eyes flocked like iron-fillings." And yet she saw Fowley's role in the band as still oppressive and crude—"he can only contaminate them with his own cynicism." Burchill, a maverick cultural critic who cut her teeth in the music press, sensed the Runaways' feminist promise: "Veteran blondies guitarist Lita Ford and drummer Sandy West prove that anything boys can do, we can do better." But she didn't buy the constant sexual shtick: "They come across as acting not like teenage girls, but as how dirty old men would like teenage girls to act. I'm sure that the Runaways like sex, but if they did it as much as they would have you believe they wouldn't have had time to cut one single, let alone three albums."[7]

The Runaways were even beginning to sway the *Village Voice*'s Robert Christgau into believing that they were not just Fowley's playthings. He admitted that the "band surprised me live, nowhere near as willing to pander sexually as its publicity suggests," he wrote in his review of the third album. He raised their grade a whole third, to C+: "I guess if somebody has to strike macho guitar poses I'd just as soon it were girls." In the end, though, Jett's "shrieks" left him still unconvinced.[8]

Rolling Stone still considered the Runaways a novelty, but, by now, also saw them as "an anachronism." Reviewer Wesley Strick had little use for Ford's songs, but praised Jett's. He criticized Fowley for putting "ersatz teen sentiment" in the "babes'" mouths.[9] In fact, Fowley only cowrote three songs on the third album. But the old credit from the first album was back: "Produced and Directed by Kim Fowley."

That must have been wishful thinking. By the time *Waitin' for the Night* was released in November 1977, Fowley had lost his grip on the Runaways.

23 Take It Or Leave It

The Runaways were sick of Kim Fowley—and visa versa. Once a selling point for the band, by 1977, the Giant Peach had become a burden. The biggest issue was not so much his verbal abuse of the girls—sure, he could be annoying, but Jett, West, and Ford had gotten used to him. They were rarely the targets of his invective precisely because they were not the type to be intimidated or bullied.

"If Kim said something to me I didn't like, I would say, 'Don't talk to me like that,'" says Joan.

"I wasn't one who got called names, at least not to my face," Lita says. "I stayed to myself a lot in the Runaways. I was just really interested in playing the music. I just wanted to play; that I did and that I did well. For that I never got picked on."

West's opinion of Fowley may have changed over time. In *Edgeplay*, the drummer speaks harshly of the Runaways' sometimes producer/director. That tone fits in with the film's narrative: Fowley is set up as the bad guy, who screwed with the band's heads and screwed them out of their riches. Sandy was also the first Runaway to try to sue Kim, for money owed, in a case filed in Los Angeles in 1983. (He tried to countersue; both cases were dropped. "It was Dodge City," Fowley says. "One day she barked. I barked back. And then, after I barked back, the barking stopped.") But Joan says that during the Runaways' existence, Sandy and Kim were fine with each other. "Sandy always got along with Kim," Jett says. "If Kim gave her any shit, we gave it right back. Kim didn't push Sandy around....Kim Fowley did not want to get punched by Sandy. She could bend him and break him in half."

Blue made Fowley seem like an evil creep in *Edgeplay*. Every film needs a villain. But the bassist credits the Svengali with changing her life. "I liked him," she says. "I thought he was really weird. He did something I had never seen anyone do before: Out of his mouth would come these incredible phrasings and rants and thought connectivity. The girls would always bitch about him. I found him intoxicating. To this day, we have a good relationship. He let me demonize him and villainize him in *Edgeplay*. I learned how to make something out of nothing with Kim. It was the most valuable gift anyone could give me."

Jett liked the guy, too. They shared an apartment together for a time. They wrote songs together. "We were friends," she says. "I felt pretty close to Kim, like I could tell him almost anything....A lot of our songs center around partying and having sex and falling in love and out of love, so it was pretty frank discussions we would have. He was a lot of fun, and funny."

The Runaways' own feelings did not drive them from their idiosyncratic manager. It was other people's perception of Fowley's role in their music that was dragging the group down. He was an outsized man with an outsized personality. That was colorful when the Runaways themselves were naïfs figuring out how to navigate the media. By the end of 1977, he was sucking all the air from the room.

"A lot of people don't like Kim," Jett told *Sounds*. "A lot of press people, record companies. Lots of people I talk to say they hate him and they think he's an asshole, and that's one way that he's maybe harmed us a bit, because people won't take us seriously, they think we're just a Kim Fowley product. In other ways, it's pretty good because he's gotten us press."[1]

Egomaniacal gestures like the "produced and directed" credit didn't lessen the perception that Fowley had the Runaways on strings. To this day, Fowley—in a particularly foul mood—will say that he invented the Runaways. That bothered—and bothers—Jett.

"They just think that because of past things that Kim has done—they just think, 'Oh, well, they're just another Kim Fowley hype and he directs everything they do,' which is completely untrue," Joan said to *Bump 'n' Grind*. "He got us our recording contract, y'know, he helped finance the band, which any stupid manager should do, right? But he didn't tell us what to sing, or how to dress or how to talk—we do everything that we want."[2]

Then there was the issue of money. The Runaways never had any. They worked constantly: rehearsing, gigging, recording—repeat. They had signed a major-label record deal. They were forever doing interviews and photo shoots for magazines. But they had little to show for it: forget about mansions, Rolls Royces, designer couture, diamond jewelry. Even though the band sometimes acted like they were living the high life, that was just part of the show. Sure, they might show up at a record signing in a limousine: Fowley had hired the car two blocks away, just for appearances.

An eye-opening document titled "Runaways U.S. Tour Notes," rescued from an old management file, indicates the dire nature of the Runaways' financial straits, as they set off to tour in 1978. Vicki needed a bass. Sandy "needs money to pay her rent and car payments for January and February." Joan's "pressing need would be for rent for Jan & Feb." Lita "probably" needed rent money, too, but what she wanted was a Marshall stack.

In his filthy apartment and dirty underwear, Fowley wasn't exactly living the high life himself. But, surely, the Runaways must have been making some kind of income.

"It was hard for me," says Ford. "I wanted to know where the money went, what it was being spent on. Nobody was telling me anything. I would get pissed off; the girls in the band wouldn't know why I was pissed off. They'd look at me like I was a fucking idiot. Who wouldn't want to know? It sure wasn't in my pocket. That was a problem."

This is perhaps the most common perception of the Runaways: That Fowley took their money. It's a charge the band leveled in many interviews in the following decades. Fowley's thievery is a running theme in *Edgeplay*. In the 1990s, Jett, Ford, West, and Currie united in a lawsuit against Mercury and Kim, wresting control of the band's name and rights, and winning back royalties—money owed.

Kim Fowley adamantly denies that he cheated the Runaways out of money. On the contrary: He says that he never saw a return on the time and money he invested in the group from the very beginning. By the time Mercury signed the Runaways, Fowley had given up his dog palace and was living at a friend's house. He says he had less than $10 left in his bank account.

Mercury did not give Fowley and the Runaways a giant record advance. The money they did pay was recoupable, which means that the label deducted their own costs—for tour support, marketing, studio time, burnt rental cars—from any and all money earned. Mercury got paid before Fowley got paid. Fowley and Anderson got paid, for their expenses and their percentage, before the Runaways got paid. The Runaways did not get paid.

"There was never any royalties for any records sold because you had to go tour and tour and tour," says Fowley. "And sometimes you have to show up and play for free or for discounted money. And the record company would give an advance for future income to get these girls to these places, so it was very frustrating that they're getting popular, but there was never any money, because all the money to go on the road went to the record company.... The Runaways were so busy being self-destructive that they didn't last long enough to start recouping past the advances and the cost of being a band."

The costs of being a band could be high. Another management document enumerates the "Accounting for JAPAN TOUR." The expenses, including items like hotel, rehearsal fees, and truck rental, total $22,539.14. The biggest costs indicate that someone was making money off the Runaways: $5,400 for manager commissions and $3,600 for agency commissions. There's also a mysterious $6,000 for "cash picked up in Tokyo." There's no indication how that was spent, but presumably, it was not on the band's daily expenses, such as food. They were given a "per diem" for those, whose total cost was $1,350. Divided among five members for thirty days: That's $9 a day. Meanwhile, Fowley—who didn't even go to Japan—apparently made $5,400, or $180 a day. There's no indication in the accounting of how much Smythe was paid. The document does not list any income from the live and TV shows played. But presumably, the manager should only have received commissions as a percentage of monies paid to the band—a high rate would have been twenty percent. If the Runaways made $27,000 in Japan, then, after expenses, they netted less than $5,000—$1,000 each (if Fox were to get paid in full). That's actually not a bad investment, considering the effect their visit had on sales in the country. But twelve grand a year wasn't much of a rock-star salary, even by 1977 standards.

The biggest problem was the fact that all the money went through Fowley. He owned and controlled everything: The Runaways' name, their songs, the masters of their recordings, their contracts. Once Anderson was fired, there was no one keeping an eye on Fowley—there was no accountability to the band. He should have provided them with regular financial statements. His failure to do so was not at all unusual for artist management at that time, especially for a new group.

"The business was really crude and terrible for the artist," says Cliff Burnstein. "The deal Mercury made was with Kim Fowley. Money would go to Kim; how he wound up divvying it up, only he would know."

If the Runaways were work for hire, as Fowley claimed they were contractually, then they should have been paid minimum salary requirements, per California law. Fox, the lawyer, says they were not.

Fowley probably did not pay the Runaways every dime they were owed. But the idea that he was getting rich off of the band is unlikely. The Runaways got a lot of press; they toured the world; they made history. But the Runaways did not sell records. Their albums were released in multiple countries, and they went gold in Japan and Australia. But overseas money dribbles in slowly, and usually at reduced royalty rates. The only Runaways song that has continued to produce publishing income is "Cherry Bomb." Jett and Fowley are the only two songwriters making money on that track. For some reason, Fowley did little merchandising for the band. The Runaways' primary source of income was from shows—and touring could be as expensive as it was lucrative.

For all the virulent Kim-haters—and there are many—several people who worked with him say that he was an honorable businessman. "I never had a dishonest dealing with Kim," says Ralph Peer. "He's seen as being flakey, but I've had a lot flakier dealings in the music business."

"He's never, ever done bad by me," says Earle Mankey. "Lots of guys in bands owe their start to Kim.... He considered himself a scam artist and was very proud of it. He could have been selling toothpaste but he liked music. He took it very seriously. He's not bad; he's just a scam artist. That is the music business, after all."

In hindsight, even members of the Runaways admit that Fowley didn't use them as some sort of cash cow. "He's a straight shooter," says Blue. "He formed this idea out of a weird notion. He worked it and manipulated it and saw it all the way through. He believed his own press with it. It was Kim's idea. Most of the band, like followers, fell into it."

There is no doubt that by the time the Runaways had burned through three lineups in as many months, the band's relationship with Fowley had also soured. Fowley was turning the fame the Runaways had brought to his moribund career into a springboard for personal rebirth: producing Helen Reddy, promoting punk nights at the Whisky, managing the Quick and Venus and the Razorblades. He was never well equipped to be a manager, and now his attentions were divided multiple times.

Choosing quantity of projects over quality, Kim suffered from dilettantism. He had ADD before it was an acronym; at age seventy-two, he was still handing journalists piles of his latest CDs, DVDs, and even a book. "My crime would be recording too many marginal people instead of working with quality rock artists," he says. "Maybe I'll go to heaven because I recorded a lot of people nobody else would record."

Fowley cut his teeth on pop ephemera, on stick-in-your-craw ditties by throwaway artists. He might not have really understood the FM rock aesthetic of the '70s. "When he was on familiar ground, pop, he probably could do okay," says Burnstein. "But the Runaways weren't a pop band, they were a rock band. I think that he was possibly out of his element there. … Maybe it was doomed really right from the start. It looked so promising on paper, but in fact Kim wasn't the right guy for the kind of music they were meant to be doing and the climate that they were in. He really was not a manager, not at all."

Kim liked to make hits out of nothing, to turn street kids into glitter stars. But he knew nothing about artist development, about nurturing and protecting and building a career for the long haul. He used to tell the Runaways that the band would end when the last member turned twenty-one. "I'm really bad at intimacy and personal relationships," he says. "What I'm really good at is working on projects with people if we have a common goal, whether it's writing a song together or making a movie together. Or we band together for X amount of time, and you have friends in a foxhole fighting the enemy. But when the war is over and the album is due, everybody scatters."

Besides, selling the Runaways was like flogging a dead horse. Mercury had barely promoted *Queens of Noise*. Fowley must have known that the label had no interest in a band without a lead blonde. "He had given up on them because without Cherie, he didn't feel he had any chance of commercial success," says Mamis. "I don't think he lacked belief in Joan's ability, I think he just lacked belief in the industry's willingness to accept it."

The constant drama of teenage girls was wearing even Fowley, a total drama queen, down. "After the fuck-yous started, I just did the minimum," he recalls. "I lost interest when chaos ensued on the road, and the parents and I had no control over it....I had a rock 'n' roll idea that turned into a slumber party on steroids, and I wasn't interested in continuing it anymore."

A new man had already come a courting: Toby Mamis. The former Quatro publicist began negotiating a takeover in association with Peter Leeds, Blondie's manager. At first, the split between Fowley and the band seemed amicable. In interviews that fall of '77, they made it sound like the decision to part was mutual. "We're in the process of splitting now," Jett told Julie Burchill. "Kim's had offers from people like Sinatra. He wants to be where the money is, and I respect him for it."[3]

"It wasn't all bad," West told one reporter. "He did some good for us, it's not such a sad story."[4]

One contemporaneous article says the divorce went into effect October 12.[5] But according to Mamis, as well as to letters and legal documents from that time, the separation, in fact, dragged out in messy fashion. Fowley had his claws deep into the band, legally and emotionally, and he wasn't going to just let them walk away.

Kim wanted Toby to buy him out. "He wanted to be reimbursed for everything he was owed," Mamis says. "He was still unrecouped in his investment in the Runaways."

According to Mamis, he was willing to pay for the Runaways. But then Fowley started getting mean. He said the Runaways could not perform because he owned the name. That meant he was denying the band their primary form of income. Fowley threatened to sue the girls. "Over the course of that time, as Kim can do, as people tend to do sometimes, he said and did some things that just upset the girls even more than they already were," Toby says. "Finally, they said, screw it: Let's just tell him the contract is invalid, and let's just move on."

Documents from that time reveal just how nasty Kim could get. As of January 3, 1978, Fowley was still claiming to be the Runaways' manager—well, really, their owner. In a letter from Fowley's lawyer,

Walter E. Hurst, to the law firm Rudich & Wideman, Hurst threatened legal action if Toby Mamis did not "stop interfering in contractual relations between Kim Fowley and the four (4) entertainers authorized to perform under the trademark registered name 'THE RUNAWAYS.'"

In August of 1978, Hurst wrote a letter to something called the Hollywood Call Board stating that Kim owned the name the Runaways and all merchandising rights associated with it, as well as the fictitious names of each of its members. In other words, he owned "Joan Jett" and "Sandy West" and "Vicki Blue." The letter must have been an attempt to suppress a merchandising effort—though according to one court document, the Call Board was a prostitution ring.

A memo dated Oct. 26, 1978, and presumably written by either Fowley or Hurst, orders that a memo be placed in each song file of every Runaways album, stating that according to their contracts, all of the songs belong to Kim—even the ones he didn't write, or that they recorded after their split from him. The memo promised that Fowley would pay the songwriters their 50 percent share of any proceeds.

Perhaps this is why one of the first songs Jett recorded on her own was a cover of Lesley Gore's hit "You Don't Own Me."

The Runaways scattered once and for all at the start of 1978. They dropped a "Dear Kim" letter in the post on their way to tour America. They had shown their contract with Fowley to an entertainment lawyer, who had deemed it "a joke … unenforceable," Mamis says. "They sent him a termination letter that said your contract is invalid, and we're no longer abiding by it."

Mamis says that Fowley freaked out, that he threatened the new manager publicly—physically and legally. Toby admits to being worried, but nothing every happened: "He's all fluster and no brawn."

Fowley says he didn't contest his firing. "I called my lawyer and said, 'Well at least that problem's over with.' And he said, 'Yeah, do something else with your professional life.'"

A press release from FTM Public Relations ("Famous Toby Mamis'"s company) announced the Runaways' new relationship with American Entertainment Management, Leeds's company, on March 1, 1978. "With four albums and three overseas tours already behind them, they have far more experience than most musicians their age," Blondie's manager is quoted as saying. The management is "in collaboration" with

FTM, the release states. But, as with so many things connected with the Runaways, the relationship between Leeds and Mamis eventually fell apart. For all practical purposes, Toby—Joan's old friend—became the Runaways' new manager.

Even Fowley's staunchest champions would probably concede that he was a Svengali: a manager or producer who exerts inordinate control over his acts. Yet that common showbiz term is itself problematic, a stereotype that needs dissecting and perhaps dismissing.

The word Svengali comes from the George DuMaurier novel *Trilby*, a bestseller in 1894. The villain Svengali uses hypnotism (not unlike Fowley making women faint) to make his client submit to him, professionally and sexually. But scholars have pointed out that the descriptions of Svengali as a dark, coarse man with a big nose are laden with anti-Semitism. For centuries Western civilizations have deflected guilt about bloody capitalism by turning its agents into dirty money-changers—dark Jews, not good Christians. Pop fans are no exception. Music historian Gayle Wald has noted that by demonizing Svengalis, artists and consumers deny their own role in the star-making machine.

"Svengalis are useful in crafting modern pop mythologies," Wald writes. "Where money is concerned, they deflect agency away from pop stars—who, notwithstanding the degree of commercialism of their music or the loudness of their boasts, are still not supposed to want wealth more than making art or pleasing their fans...."[6]

Wald doesn't specifically write about Fowley. But her essay expresses the way characters like him become scapegoats—the easy bad guy:

"Ultimately, the figure of the Svengali is a means of containing and deflecting expressions of desire in pop music. Through him, we can personify the larger predations of the music industry, its constant hunger for product and profit. By vilifying the powerful headmaster of the Motown 'charm school' or the evil father figure behind the Jackson 5, for example, we can turn our attention away from our own complicity in the objectifying dynamic."[7]

In making Kim Fowley the bogeyman of the Runaways narrative, journalists, filmmakers, historians, and authors have picked an easy target—and absolved their own guilt.

It's a simplistic storyline that one crucial character has long opposed. Joan Jett was the first Runaway to meet Fowley. She adamantly rejects the idea the Runaways were his victims.

"The whole abuse thing is maddening to me actually," she says. "It's kind of implying that we just stood there and took it. You don't like it, you leave. I think in hindsight people have to create monsters and look at why things didn't work out. And look at their own shit and responsibility in not making it happen."

Fowley was loud, rude, crude, manipulative, coarse, bullying, mean spirited, vulgar. He made enemies like a corpse makes maggots.

"He was an arrogant, asshole, misogynist idiot," says photographer Jenny Lens. "He, like Malcolm McLaren, had two bands that could have gone far, and they both manipulated their bands and fucked it up. The Runaways could have, should have, would have…They had everything going for themselves, except his ego had to go in there and pit the members against each other and screw around with them and screw them over."

There's no doubt Kim behaved inappropriately for a grown man around teenage girls. He's the first to admit it: "My wiring isn't complete. I had the elements of something better and something bigger and it didn't happen because in the end, it didn't happen …"

He may have conceived of the Runaways, found them, named them, financed them, signed them, and trained them. But he did not own them. Smart as he is, Fowley somehow forgot that the Emancipation Proclamation abolished slavery in 1863.

Still, Fowley deserves credit where credit is due. "For good or bad, he's the reason the Runaways came together," says Kathleen Hanna. "He started Joan's career, and I'll forever be indebted to him for that."

"Kim gave us such an incredible opportunity and tools, and they were totally unorthodox," says Blue. "He'd say, 'Hey dogbreath, come over here and suck my cock.' What he was saying was, 'Come over here and learn from me.' If you look at him, he does stuff—he moves forward every day."

"It was a magic time for them, and they couldn't have done it without Kim," says Mamis. "Despite the negative things about him, which are true, he was an essential part of that puzzle, too."

Fowley exploited the Runaways, no doubt. "It's the price of admission to the party," says Mamis. "You make lousy deals with people you probably shouldn't have made deals with to get into the game. You get into the game and you try to move on. That's what they did. Did he turn out to be a worse guy than anybody thought? Yes. It happens. Had he done to me what he did to them, I would not make peace with him."

And yet, the Runaways floundered without their founder. "It was not the same when they dumped him," says Smythe. "They lost an important part of the whole thing. Of all the people I've worked for in the music business, he's the only one who hasn't been an asshole."

Decades after his charges dropped him, Fowley is alternately angry, sanguine, sentimental, and sad about the Runaways. He admits his lack of emotional maturity made him a poor manager, let alone a substitute father figure. "Looking back on it, I should possibly have not been a teenager along with them," he says. "I should have been more of an adult, but I wasn't one. I was a thirty-six-year-old who looked twentysomething, and I was thinking as a sixteen-year-old girl helping write these songs. I knew how to get things done, but I had no parental skills. I was certainly not qualified to deal with their discipline issues."

"He was ill equipped to handle teenage girls," agrees Fox. "I think anybody would have been ill equipped to handle these five teenage girls, but Kim in particular. I mean, he was this thirty-five-year-old guy. He was coming on to teenage girls; he had no idea how to talk to them."

Fowley refuses to be the fall guy for the Runaways' failings, disintegration, and demise. "I think I should be given a medal as opposed to a firing squad for dealing with all of it. The music and the PR and the conceptualizing were tremendous rock 'n' roll fun. Being parental or an authority figure was way beyond my pay grade."

Fowley never wanted to be the Runaways' manager. That's why he hired Anderson. He didn't want to and never did go on the road with the band. He wanted to be creative, not an administrator. "I was supposed to be the producer," he says. "I was supposed to produce, publish, cowrite, publicity, creative, and then some guy who is stable like Scott, with a girlfriend, was going to take them out on the road, and be the big brother, the young uncle, and I was going to be free to think of things and mastermind it from back home."

Kim was a soccer coach on steroids with Tourette's. But somewhere beneath all the beatnik jive and hustler shtick lay a real love for this crazy project. The legendary prick believed in the Runaways. The hardest part about being Kim Fowley must be knowing that he fucked his own dream.

"Everything involving the Runaways is just weird," says Fox. "It's left a weird mark on everybody. Nobody ever thinks about Kim, because they think that Kim's the one who left the weird mark on everybody else. But I think it left a weird mark on him as well, and I'm not sure exactly why. I think it's a very emotional thing with him, and not just because it's what he will always be known for. Like it or not, Kim, we're your Big Thing—maybe not the one that sold the most records, but the one that made your name. So I don't know if he resents us for that, or there's a guilt thing."

"It was not a pleasure cruise," Kim Fowley says. "It was not very much fun. But I always thought I was on a crusade."

24 Gotta Get Out

On October 25, 1977, the Runaways performed on *The Old Grey Whistle Test*, a prestigious BBC music show. They played "School Days," which had been released as a single in England, and "Wasted," its B-side, two of Jett's better new compositions. In many ways, the Runaways were an entirely new band. With Currie no longer center stage, the dynamic had changed. Jett and Ford were now twin focal points, blonde and brunette pillars of sexy cool confidence. It was hard to take your eyes off either of them. There was no doubting their professionalism—their experience and their expertise. Jett snarled and spat her lyrics with the world-weary snottiness of Western youth: "There's a lot I've seen at eighteen." The tight, high sound of her rhythm guitar set the pace for the deep, muscled leads that Ford tossed off like she was throwing coins in a wishing well. Lita rippled in her black silver-studded skintight jumpsuit; Joan looked all Ramones-y, slouching oh so louche in her black leather jacket, white Runaways T-shirt, and blue jeans. They were a great rock 'n' roll duo. Behind them, Sandy's biceps bulged beneath the blow-dried ends of her long blonde hair as she pounded those skins. Then she'd twirl her sticks or peel off a drumroll, and you'd realize ah, there's another force to be reckoned with. Blue hugged the backdrop in a blue jean jacket, keeping it together (just barely). None of them needed a bustier to exude stone-cold foxiness. The Five were fabulous, but the Four kicked ass.

The *OGWT* performances don't capture what had unfortunately become a regular feature of Runaways shows: crude catcalls from over-heated male fans.

The Runaways had lost their maker but they didn't skip a beat. After all, on the road, they had learned how to function just fine with a decent road crew and without Kim. There was no time for them to stop and collect themselves: They had to get out there and play the new songs. Although they were sounding better than ever, and although many critics and fans embraced the lineup changes, the Runaways' record label had given up on its signing. Mercury could have used the new personnel as a sales pitch—"the new and improved Runaways," or maybe "the leaner and meaner Runaways." The mutiny against Fowley would have been a great press angle: "Teen girls emancipate themselves!" But Mercury apparently wasn't interested in liberation, only titillation. It's a wonder they even released *Waitin' for the Night*. Maybe, it was a tax write-off.

"They didn't really have a lot of interest in the band without Cherie," says Mamis.

"They're not gonna do anything to push it, nothin'," Jett told *Sounds* reporter Sandy Robertson. "No ad, nothing. They're just gonna throw it out and hope it hits. They want us to be pop, something against everything we believe."[1]

The fall '77 itinerary included the Runaways' first European shows outside England, with concerts in Zurich, Paris, Stockholm, Hamburg, Amsterdam, and Brussels. Robertson followed them from their *OGWT* appearance in London up to Belfast. Conflict still raged between the Catholics and the Protestants in Northern Ireland. The hotel in which the Runaways were booked had been bombed a short time before they were to check in, and was under repair. Soldiers stopped them and searched their bags as they headed to their gig. "I've never been in a war zone before," Ford said to the reporter. Well, not that kind of a war zone at least.

After all, even gigs—the one place where the Queens of Noise traditionally reigned supreme—were becoming pitched battles. In Belfast, the band's "Godhead rock 'n' roll" (in Robertson's words) silenced the routine Neanderthal jeers to "Get 'em off." The chant "Bring on the nubiles!" had apparently crossed a continent and an ocean, from the Whisky to the band's November 7 show at Sheffield. At a sparsely attended show at Newcastle City Hall, "a cluster of hardline safety pin freaks," according to *Sounds* reporter Phil Sutcliffe, shouted for the headliners to take the stage: "Fuck off, cockteasers! We want 999!"[2] Women with guitars couldn't be cock-rockers; they were deemed cockteasers.

Insults and antagonisms weren't the only things that rained down on the Runaways. Fans spit on them in England, during their fall tour and again on their summer of 1978 European tour. And they got spit on that winter in the U.S., as they performed across the country with the Ramones. Even if saliva was hurled as a sign of affection ("gobbing"), coupled with the catcalls, it felt like disrespect—or even pure hatred. "The thing I remember most about that tour was being covered in spit," Vicki says of the American leg. "It was gross."

Julie Burchill interpreted the taunts as emotionally shut down louts' way of expressing themselves: "devaluation is employed in place of awe, ridicule for adoration."[3] In a review the next summer of the band's last show in Europe, at London's Lyceum, Burchill wrote that Jett had become transcendently impervious to the abuse: "... she's the first one, she's the only one, to go out on that stage with a bunch of non-boys behind her and draw strength from the heckles rather than get eaten away by them."[4]

Sutcliffe had an interesting psychoanalytic reading of the verbal attacks. "Heavy music pulls blokes," he wrote. "When the musicians are, as usual, male, they are a macho mirror to their fans who worship them like a corporate Narcissus ogling himself. But when the musicians are female, it's no mirror, it's the real thing, the challenge of a relationship rather than a solo jerk-off—so the Runaways don't get any shadow boxing, they are in for the championship every time they go on stage."

Male punk bands got spit on, too. Punk unleashed pent-up fury and resentments. But old-fashioned misogyny got wound into the rebel yells at Runaways' concerts. Mostly, the violence was just verbal.

"'Dyke. Whore. Slut.' That's all anyone focused on," Jett recalls.

Sometimes, the violence became physical, carrying disturbing echoes of the Rolling Stones' infamous Altamont concert: crazed fans and biker bodyguards. At a show in Malmo, Sweden, on June 9, 1978, a man tried climbing on stage. The Chevy-driving Swedish version of Hell's Angels who were hired to be security "wouldn't do shit," Smythe says, so Kent pushed the guy back down. The enraged concert-goer—who may have been one of the Chevy-gang thugs—started screaming and pulling himself up again. "I knew he was going to kick my ass," Smythe says. "I pretended he was a football and kicked him in the head as hard as I could. His eyes rolled up in his head and he collapsed into the audience."

The show grew uglier. People started throwing things; hundreds of fans rushed the stage. Smythe hightailed it out of there. Blue remembers him later dying his hair black as a disguise to escape town: "One of them was going to kill Kent." The Runaways had to be carried out of the venue. "The unrest came to the hotel; we had to get out of there, too," Vicki recalls.

Such mayhem may seem outsized in retrospect, perhaps part of the exaggerated Runaways lore. But the Runaways were a sensation in such countries as Sweden and Germany. In the '70s, poorly controlled crowds all too often combined with heavy alcohol and drug use to create sometimes deadly situations at rock shows. At the Riverfront Stadium in Cincinnati, in 1979, eleven Who fans were crushed to death in a race for unassigned seats. Tens of thousands of rock fans rioted at an anti-disco rally in Chicago's Comiskey Park that year. Patti Smith faced mob scenes in Italy that disturbed her so much, they helped drive her from performing live for many years.

For the Runaways, there was tension on stage, too. Blue was having trouble fitting in. Again, a Runaways bassist was the odd woman out. Like Fox, Vicki didn't take drugs—her epilepsy needed to be managed. And by the winter of '77/'78, the rest of the Runaways were partying as hard as they were working.

"The drugs were intense," Vicki says. "One of the reasons we didn't hang out together was everybody was getting high. Everyone was scattered and nobody would talk."

Stage fright paralyzed Vicki. You can see it on *The Old Grey Whistle Test*. She stands practically frozen in place, except for her left hand moving up and down the frets and her right hand picking the strings. When her face manages to break into a warm smile for a moment, the whole mood lightens. Blue explains that she was an amateur trying to keep up with pros: "They had been choreographed. I didn't have any of this training."

Smythe used to throw objects at Blue while she was on stage, to make her mobile. The irreverent joker probably thought he was being funny. Blue was not amused.

"She would just stand there, literally," Kent says. "She didn't know how to move."

The bass player remembers a general atmosphere of hostility and oppression, led by Kent. "I was really alone," she says. "I felt so disconnected from everybody. I felt out of place in the Runaways, in the world.... There was a lot of damage in that band. That wasn't unique; it was going on in the world. We just happened to be doing it in front of everyone."

At one London show, Jett and Blue were fighting. Vicki didn't sweat much on stage (perhaps because she didn't move), but Joan did. The guitarist came up to the bass player, leaned back, and rubbed her wet, salty body all over her bandmate.

"It really pissed me off," Vicki says. "It made me crazy. It was really a doggy thing to do. It hit me in such a bad place, I was going to take the bass and bash her with it."

Blue used to call photographer Donna Santisi from Europe. "She felt like she didn't fit in," Santisi says. "She really had a hard time. She felt they were making fun of her and they didn't want her in the band."

Perhaps because of the stress of the strange, new, fraught situation, Blue started having seizures again. She says she didn't even know she was having them until many years later, when West told her. The Runaways world was crazy like that—unreal, chaotic, disturbed.

Blue says that Smythe made her time in the band miserable. "I had Kent up my ass 24/7," she says. "He would not leave me alone." She cites a litany of abuses: He left her luggage behind. At a show in Texas, he flicked the lights on and off at her as she performed, causing a strobe effect that can trigger seizures in epileptics. At 3:00 one morning in Sweden, he pushed her into her hotel room saying, "It's bondage time for Vicki." She punched him and threatened to quit the band. From that point on, for the rest of that last tour of Europe in the summer of '78, a line of white tape divided the stage. Smythe was not allowed to cross it into Blue's territory. "I said, 'It's him or me,'" she says. "I felt smashed down because of Kent. He was like the cloud that hung over the band, a real sick fuck."

The roadie turned road manager denies most of the bassist's accusations. No tape divided the stage—"I went wherever I had to go." He says he never used a strobe and only changed the light colors as one would normally in a rock show. He didn't threaten to tie her up in Sweden, he says; instead, she cold-cocked him after she saw him talking to some female fans, for reasons he still doesn't understand.

Smythe doesn't remember the bassist ever suffering a fit while in the band and confesses that he and others in the Runaways' entourage may not have taken her condition seriously. "There was a feeling among some people that her seizures were a way of wanting attention. I don't know we ever believed them, as cold as that may sound."

Smythe admits there was no love lost between him and Vicki. Blue's introduction into the group allowed him to play top dog for once. "She hated me, because she found out quickly that I was higher up in the food chain than she was," he says. "She thought she could order me around. I just laughed at her."

According to Kent, Fowley forced Blue on the band and the Runaways never liked her. "No one wanted her to hang out," he says. "All she did was put her beautiful face on the album covers."

The Runaways played a string of four shows at the Whisky at the end of December. They needed money: These were the gigs that were supposed to pay their winter rent and buy Vicki's bass and Lita's amp. The shows sold out, but while the Runaways still had a strong fan base back home, "… they're finding it hard to get a following in this country," Robert Hilburn noted in the *Los Angeles Times*.[5]

On January 7, 1978, the Runaways embarked on a North American tour with the Ramones—"three months of heaven," Joan called it.[6] It was a genius pairing: two of America's premiere bare-bones rock quartets—one from each coast—barreling through clubs and theaters, bringing punk rock to the hinterlands, from El Macombo in Toronto to the Gusman in Miami, New York's Palladium to the Santa Monica Civic Auditorium. The bands alternated the headlining spot each night. They were supposed to get co-billing, although, even in the Runaways' hometown, it was clear the New York band was the main draw. They traveled through Canada, the northeast and the Midwest in the dead of winter, "the coldest winter in the history of the universe," Blue says. The car would hit patches of black ice and skid off the freeways. They'd get back on the road and keep driving.

The tour launched at the Palladium. On the Ramones' home turf, in front of a few thousand fans, the Runaways almost swept the Ramones off the stage. Jett and Ford had the flu, but "… the band still all but stole the show from the Ramones," *Billboard* reported. "The lyrics of some of the songs are interesting as they come from women under twenty years old who have grown up with and have internalized the philosophy of women's lib… Watching them it was obvious that if they go out and play everywhere they can, every time they can, they have the charisma and the basic talent to be the next Kiss in two years."[7]

If only.

The Runaways were bursting with energy, never stopping as they played ten songs in forty-five minutes, plus an encore. "They literally bound across the stage, jumping back and forth in unison as a team, totally in control of what they are doing ... the dynamic foursome has swept across the Palladium stage and left their mark for all time on New York audiences," *Rock* magazine reported.[8]

In the *New York Times*, Robert Palmer wrote that the band had "come a long way in a short time ... the music has become both tougher and more personal ... increasingly they are writing lyrics with real feeling and bite. The Runaways may have begun as a hype, but at this point they are no joke."[9]

The tour made it all the way across the country in the first month, landing at the Santa Monica Civic Auditorium January 27 for a show presented by Rodney Bingenheimer. Despite being the hometown faves, the Runaways opened for the Ramones, to a partially filled theater. "Nonetheless, fine, solid playing brought the audience trickling back in to listen and leer," wrote Sylvie Simmons in *Sounds*.[10]

"[T]hese young women are capable of furious music," opined a critic for *Westways*. "If nothing else, they represent the emancipation of the electric guitar."[11]

Away from their home bases, both pioneering bands discovered that America was not exactly taking this new wave of music to heart. Ford remembers the audiences being more hostile to the Ramones' dumb-punk act than to the Runaways. "The Ramones were very before their time," she says. "The Ramones would put chicken wire up on stage. People used to throw handfuls of change at the Ramones. We never had to use the chicken wire."

Fewer than 400 people showed up for a show at Orlando's Great Southern Music Hall. The Runaways impressed the critic from the *St. Petersburg Times* more than their brother act. "Seriously, the band plays straight-ahead, high-energy rock well worth hearing and seeing live," Bob Ross wrote.[12]

Don Bolles caught the tour at Dooley's in Phoenix. The turnout was underwhelming; "they were both bands that nobody gave a shit about at the time, except for a few people." A punk fan and musician, he had the Runaways' first album. "They were good!" he recalls. "I was disappointed that they didn't have the hot chick in the fucking corset. But this other girl is great. I thought Joan sang it better."

Bolles, who would soon after this show move to L.A. and join the Germs (Jett would produce the definitive SoCal punk band's sole studio album), wasn't normally a fan of hard rock, but the Runaways impressed him. "I thought those girls held their own," he says. "They didn't look like a bunch of trained ponies up there… They were definitely treading on man's soil. And they were doing a good job! There were a lot of guys whose cock rock was not as good as their cock rock."

The pairing with the Ramones made apparent an inherent and growing problem for the band: Were they punk rock or weren't they? Most of the members considered themselves rock or hard rock. "I'm not into punk rock," Blue told a Canadian magazine. "I can't stand three-chord punk, it gives me a headache."[13]

Even the Sex Pistols–loving Jett resisted the labels punk and new wave: "It's more a media term, the punk label, than anything else," she told the *St. Paul Dispatch*. "Because a lot of young bands are springing up, someone hung a label on them."[14] The Runaways were scarcely alone in trying to avoid the taxonomy/hype; many artists who are considered the ultimate punks—from Iggy Pop to the Slits' Ari-Up—rejected the term. But the Runaways' identity crisis reflected a growing divide among the members.

By the time they had hit the road with the Ramones, the Runaways were homeless. Mercury had dropped them. Mamis was shopping for a new label. In the meantime, with the concept of tour support a distant memory, the Runaways were truly living from gig to gig. According to contracts for the shows, they were paid between $500 and $2,500 a night. Booking agents Magna, the band's management, and roadies all had to be paid. Still, at the end of the day, touring probably wasn't making the Runaways rich, but it was paying their bills.

For the first time in three years, the Runaways took time off in April and May, perhaps because of the ongoing legal battle with Fowley. "I didn't do a fucking thing, man, absolutely nothing—I avoided interviews, photo sessions, anything I could—I was just so burned out from touring, I needed that time off," Joan told a reporter.[15]

A June 2 gig at the Whisky grossed the Runaways a handsome $7,560. Elvis Costello and Nick Lowe were there, along with members of the Tom Robinson Band and the show *Beatlemania*. Then, the Runaways headed back to Europe, playing much bigger gigs than they had across America, in countries where they were considered rock stars: Sweden, Norway, Germany, Switzerland, Holland, France, Belgium, England. They drew impressive paychecks: $3,000 to $6,000 a show. From June 9 to July 16, they probably grossed 100 grand. But the cost of bringing band and crew across the ocean was also higher than stateside. "We flew everywhere, had crews, and stayed in hotel rooms," Blue says. "If we made five to eight grand one night, we had to buy ten hotel rooms."

Many European countries had music magazines that were basically photo books. The Runaways were stars of these magazines. And unlike in Japan, where Currie was always featured, the Germans and Scandinavians were as likely to put Lita, or Joan, or even Sandy, on the cover. "Even before you go to Europe it's like, we're in all the pop magazines," Jett told one interviewer. "All the magazines over there are like *Teen Parade* and stuff here...we're presented as already being huge rock stars."[16]

There were good times. Clowning around at a Holiday Inn in London, Joan pushed a fully clothed Sandy into the pool. (West reportedly wound up with pneumonia.) In London they hung out with Thin Lizzy singer Phil Lynott. Jett was spotted clubbing with Gaye Advert of English punk band the Adverts (ah, to be a fly on that wall!). There were always fans around, wanting to party—or whatever. "A lot of people wanted to come back to the hotel with us," Blue says. "Sometimes they did; sometimes they didn't. We had lots of groupies. Joan and Sandy got all the girls. Lita and I got all the guys."

But the fissures in the group were becoming apparent even to the reviewers. "Throughout, there seemed to be a battle going on between the basic heavy metal sound laid down by guitarist Lita Ford and pop overtones spearheaded by Joan Jett, trashy yet invaluable," wrote Kelly Pike in *Record Mirror*, in a review of the tour's final show, at the Lyceum in London.[17]

In her *NME* review of the same show, Jett partisan Julie Burchill admitted that "the Runaways surely can't last much longer." For her, the band was all about Joan: "Joan Jett is the best thing ever to savage a stage and you're a moron if you can't see beyond her X chromosome...she is IT, she's what you've been waiting for."[18]

Also writing for *NME*, Burchill pal and cowriter Tony Parsons (they scribed the amphetamine-fueled punk rant *The Boy Looked at Johnny* together) managed to get Jett to talk about the band's increasing musical differences. (Parsons would later write a trashy novel about the music industry, *Platinum Logic*, that includes a band inspired by the Runaways.) "She [Lita] says my songs are too easy to play, and she don't like it when I write slow melodic songs like 'Wait for Me' or 'Waiting for the Night' …and she don't like punk!" Joan told the reporters. "How can she not like punk? Me, I hate all those guitar solos…"[19]

In the midst of the spit, the management turmoil, the heckles, the on-stage tension, and the ever-present drugs, there was one brilliant bright spot during the spring of '78. The Rock 'n' Roll Sports Classic captured a moment of glorious '70s cheese. An impressive collection of has-been and wanna-be pop stars gathered at the University of California's Irvine campus in March for a sort of glorified track meet. The Jacksons (including Michael), Earth Wind and Fire, Barbi Benton, Kristy McNichol, Leif Garrett, Anne Murray, Sha Na Na, Boston, Gladys Knight and the Pips, and the Runaways were among the rock, soul, pop, and country acts who competed in running, swimming, jumping, and bicycling events. All four members of the Runaways participated; at some events, they comprised almost the entire team for the West. Joan won a cycling race and came in second and third in two sprints.

"Sandy and I were so into it," Jett recalls. "We were the jocks, we were so aggressive. That was fun."

The recurring champion—indeed, the biggest winner of the entire televised faux Olympics—was Sandy West.

First, the lifelong tomboy took the women's 100-yard dash, besting Murray, Jett and Ford. Joan tackled Sandy at the finish line, a spontaneous demonstration of pure joy. Then West won the 60-yard dash; Jett placed second. For the 50-yard swim, the sometime surfer competed against men and women. She quickly moved out in front, "once again the focal point of competition," noted the commentator, Susan Anton. Anton poured on the praise as the Runaway clearly took the lead: "Sandy West is definitely the news in this competition. Playing the drums up there for the Runaways has certainly given her a lot of strength and stamina." Sandy came in a strong stroke ahead of forgotten pop tart Bobby Alessi and Boston singer Fran Sheehan. What did she do to prepare for this? Anton asked her as she stood poolside, dripping and smiling. "Nothing!" a slightly winded but exuberant West shrugged.

In front of 20,000 cheering spectators and a national televised audience, the girl who insisted on playing drums, the teen who dreamed of a band like a football team, the young adult who defended her bandmates like family, the woman who would lose her life amid drugs and violence, beamed like a champion. Never underestimate the strength of a Runaway, the show telegraphed to thousands of viewers, many of whom had probably never heard of the band. Put these women on a level playing field—or in a pool—and they will kick ass.

25 And Now... The End

Imagine you're a teenage girl, going through the usual shit teenage girls go through—fake friends, heartache, changing bodies, warring parents, school daze. You meet a few other girls with whom you share a common interest—and then for the next three years, you're together almost every day. You travel to all sorts of foreign countries, which is cool. But everyday, you also put up with a ton of crap. Add drugs, and alcohol, and shitty road food, and arid airports, and cheap hotel rooms to the mix. Now get out in front of people every night, and watch your personal business get splattered across the pages of magazines. The harder you work, the more you fail—there's no money, and then half of you quit, and then there's no record company. You're falling without a safety net, and you're still a teenager. How long would you last?

The Runaways needed a label. And they needed an album for that label to release. Their poor sales in the U.S. scarcely provided an incentive for investment. Elsewhere, the story was slightly better—the Runaways had gold records in Japan and Australia. An executive at Phonogram's Netherlands headquarters believed in the band. But, understandably given the turmoil that surrounded the group, Phonogram International needed a record to sell before they would commit.

In a sense, the Runaways were in a position that hundreds of American artists—particularly jazz musicians—had faced before them: Revered abroad, dismissed at home. Suzi Quatro had to move to London to become a star; Patti Smith was mobbed in Italy, ignored in Iowa.

Mamis negotiated a complicated deal with Phil Wainman, an English producer and songwriter who'd had success with pop and glam bands including Sweet and the Bay City Rollers. Wainman had worked with the famous hitmaking duo Chinn and Chapman, of Quatro fame. But now he had his own label, Utopia, through Phonogram. In exchange for producing their album, the creator of "Fox on the Run" would have the rights to release the Runaways' records in the U.K. And the rest of the world would have a new Runaways album.

In August, Ford, Jett, and West flew to London. Blue did not go. The official explanation was that she had had a seizure, hit her head, suffered a concussion, and wasn't fit to travel. In fact, Vicki's days with the Runaways were numbered. "I didn't want to go to Europe again," she says. "I was constantly on the road, constantly on planes. I woke up one day and said, 'I don't want to do it anymore.'"

The band had no intention of having Vicki play on their fourth studio album. But for some reason, everyone maintained a public face of unity. "As you know, we are not using our bass player on this LP," Mamis wrote in a letter to Wainman. "This is a matter which requires utmost secrecy. The fact is, this will result in a better album, and the other three girls are in complete agreement."

The Runaways stayed in a houseboat on the Thames. Mamis stayed in L.A. Leeds was in Europe at the time, but the girls did not have a good relationship with their totem manager. For three years, the Runaways had earned a reputation for being wild girls—but they hadn't let their partying mar their professional career. That summer on a river in the middle of London, unsupervised and falling apart at the seams, the Runaways blew it.

Just as Joan's apartment had become rock 'n' roll party central in L.A., so, too, did that houseboat. Members of the Sex Pistols, Siouxsie and the Banshees, the Who, Thin Lizzy, and the Slits all came to visit, hang out, party, get drunk, get high.

"We spent a night with them in a houseboat in Chelsea that they were staying in," Slits bassist Viv Albertine recalled. "They were just such cool girls, Joan Jett especially: There was no rivalry, and I was very pleased for her that she got her own thing together and it was so successful. Sandy was a lovely girl, the first girl I ever met who I could fancy, she was so centered without being boring."[1]

"London at that time was party central," producer John Alcock says. "There was a small circle of clubs and bars. Once you were in the door, you met everybody. The Runaways did like to party."

The boat housed another infamous incident in Runaways lore. West was heading to a pub. Sid Vicious was on the boat with Jett. "Sid said, 'I'm going to carry Joan down the stairs so she can go to sleep,'" Sandy later recalled in an interview with the Electric Ballroom radio show. "I said, 'No, you're not going to. I'm going to take care of what's going on around here,' because he was a mess. I picked him up over my shoulders and I carried him out to the bow of the boat and the tide was out, and I threw him overboard. He landed in the mud."

There's a similar story about Rat Scabies of the Damned: Joan and Sandy were backstage at a Damned show at the Starwood in the spring of '77. Scabies kept hassling Jett, until West physically intervened. The Runaways may or may not have been thrown out of the dressing room. The Rat told people he'd made it with Joan. "I turned him down several times which destroyed his ego, so he had to say he fucked me, which he didn't," Jett told Sandy Robertson.[2]

Asked decades later about both incidents, Joan couldn't remember either.

Whatever was happening on that boat, it didn't look good. On the first day of recording, the Pistols showed up with the Runaways at Wainman's studio and passed out on the floor. Jett either joined them or merely vomited. Fresh off working with teenyboppers the Rollers, the producer was not amused. He called Mamis and cancelled the deal. "He abandoned the project on the spot," says Mamis.

The next year, Wainman produced Generation X and the Boomtown Rats, creating a classic operetta with the latter's hit single "I Don't Like Mondays." Then he left the music business.

Mamis went back to the drawing board. He tried to hire Kenny Laguna, another bubblegumish pop-rock producer/songwriter in the vein of Chinn and Chapman. But Kenny blew him off. So Toby headed in a very different direction.

England-born, L.A.-based producer John Alcock was most famous for having worked with hard boogie band Thin Lizzy; he knobbed the FM staple "The Boys Are Back in Town." He had also recorded Who bassist John Entwistle. With his classic rock training, Alcock immediately fit in with Ford and West. Joan was a different story.

"I got brought in because I had done Thin Lizzy," Alcock says. "They wanted somebody who could give them that hard sound."

The Runaways had retreated to the City of Angels to lick their wounds. The producer met them there, at Hamburger Hamlet, in West Hollywood. He conversed individually with each member, at separate tables.

"They were kind of reticent," Alcock says. "You could see it on their faces; 'why are we meeting with this guy?' We spent some time talking. I asked each of them individually what they wanted out of this record, how they wanted to develop. They said, 'Focus more on the music and less on the image.' So I said, okay, let's do it."

Even before they began recording, Jett was withdrawing from the dominant role she had played on *Waitin' for the Night*. In July, she told reporters they were going to have Blue try her hand at singing. West also wanted to do more vocals. Meanwhile, Joan's creative well was running dry. Say what you will about Fowley: The Runaways' primary songwriter wrote more with him around than without him.

"We're going to be more open to doing other people's songs," Jett told Brenda K. "I mean, if somebody submits a really good song, why not do it?... 'Cause I really don't have any songs, I've got like two songs that I'm ready to submit to the band, that I think are worth doing, y'know, and everything else I've written are pieces of shit."[3]

Meanwhile, West had definite ideas about the album, and her own increased presence on it. "We want a really full sound—like, clean, but still raw," West told K. "I don't think the drums have ever been up enough, except on the live album, so I'm looking for a more powerful drum sound. And I wanna, maybe, sing a little bit."

The Runaways recorded *And Now ... the Runaways* at Hollywood's Rusk Sound Studio in September, in an atmosphere of great secrecy. "I was sworn that nobody must know that someone was doing an album with the Runaways," Alcock recalls. "The contractual situation was unresolved. No one was allowed to know we were doing this thing."

"When John was brought in, I don't know what was going on," Blue says. "Everybody was cordoned off separately. Paranoia started happening."

Alcock says he never even met Blue—"I didn't know who she was; I was told she was sick." Vicki says she was at preproduction meetings. "I didn't like him. He was really different. He brought this whole other vibe to the band." Ford played bass on *And Now*.

The producer went into the album with the goal of taking the band more seriously as musicians. "On previous Runaways albums, they'd been directed to say this, do that, don't think, do what I tell you," Alcock says. "I tried to give them much more say. I tried to treat them like a band rather than a media phenomenon."

After Fowley's trash shtick and Mankey's pop polish, this should have been just the respect the Runaways were looking for. The band had a manager who believed in them. They had a producer who treated them as musicians. Nineteen and twenty years old now, the packaged teenagers were on the cusp of adult autonomy. Faced with the daunting task of moving forward against incredible odds, in desperate need of the artistic and professional drive that had always united them, worn down and strung out, the Runaways turned on each other.

The first hurdle was the dearth of material. Despite the months off in the spring, despite the urgency of recording a new album, despite the faith of her friend who was now her manager, Jett still brought only two songs to the console, the rather forgettable "My Buddy and Me" and "Takeover." Ford brought an equal number, "I'm a Million" and "Little Lost Girls." For the first time, West brought her own solo composition: "Right Now." The rest was filler.

Some was better filler than others: Sex Pistol Steve Jones and Paul Cook gave the Runaways a decent anthem, "Black Leather." Bowie guitarist Earl Slick and oddball rocker Tonio K contributed the hooky if trite "Saturday Nite Special." But why a band—any band—would record versions of the Beatles' "Eight Days a Week" and Slade's "Mama Weer All Crazee Now" is anyone's guess. Sure, the Runaways had covered songs before—but never had an album led off with three tracks not at least co-written by one of them. It was an atrocious start.

There had always been an uneasy alliance of musical tastes in the Runaways. That's probably true of every single band that has ever banged two instruments together. Each member brought different influences and ideas to the table. This gave the Runaways' albums variety and depth. But by 1978, the differences were dividing even the core members. Joan, the glam fan, was finding herself in the anarchic simplicity of punk. Lita and Sandy were more and more banging their heads to metal. Alcock may have intended his individual conferences to allow each member equal say. Instead, the hard rock veteran provided a sympathetic ear for Ford and West's growing alliance.

"John Alcock had done a lot of heavier bands, harder rock and stuff," Jett says. "He and Sandy and Lita really hit it off. Their musical interests stem from a harder place than mine. Even though I love the bands they love, they grew up listening to certain things. I came from a different place. I was also getting into the whole glitter stuff. Sandy and Lita weren't into that as much as me. In the studio I could just feel a pulling away, of the producer and Sandy and Lita into this world that didn't seem to have room for me."

For the first time ever, Jett felt outnumbered and disempowered in the group she had helped form. Worse than that: Joan felt betrayed.

"I got the sense that I was being pushed out," Jett says. "I thought to myself, 'I'm not getting fired from the band I started.'"

Mamis also blames Alcock for rending the Runaways. The producer lured the players with promises of forming a new, heavy band; Alcock confirms he, Ford, and West played together after the Runaways' breakup. "He drove a wedge between them because he favored Sandy and Lita's heavy metal over Joan's punk pop," the manager says. "That is what really hastened the demise of the band.... He really clearly was trying to split the band up."

Not surprisingly, Alcock recalls this period rather differently. He emphatically denies that he drove the Runaways apart. He says that the band was happy with *And Now* at the time it came out. "They looked upon it as a step forward," he says.

The supposed musical differences between the band members have been exaggerated, Alcock points out. Jett quickly entered regular rotation on classic rock radio, and as recently as 2011, Ford was pledging her allegiance to punk.

"If you look at what Joan did immediately after the Runaways, and what Lita did and Sandy tried to do, it was all pretty much in the same direction," Alcock says. "This bit about musical difference is the old story everybody latches on to when a band breaks up. Those musical differences were kind of slight. Joan didn't go on to be the Sex Pistols or the Damned. She wanted to do rock stuff with a basic punk tinge. Lita and Sandy also wanted to go in a rock direction. The reason the Runaways broke up has much more to do with the business stuff surrounding the whole affair."

There's no question that the Runaways recorded a lousy last record. *And Now ... The Runaways* captures a band no longer comfortable in its own skin. You can see it in the album art—Barry Levine, the most clichéd of all the Runaways photographers, at work again. What the hell are the Runaways doing in tuxedos on the cover? In the airbrushed back image, the band doesn't even touch each other; it looks like four separate shots stitched together. They're wearing way too much makeup and hideous clothes. And what kind of a title is *And Now … the Runaways*? Some lame tip of the hat to show-biz clichés? A non-sequitur nod to Monty Python? There was nothing at all different about this lifeless, ersatz, MOR rock fade-away.

Lead track "Saturday Nite Special" opens with a gargle of doodling guitar that makes one wonder if Alcock was simply indulging Ford's worst habits. Jett talk-sings the verse like a petulant child, wondering why she's recording this shit. The song's got a nice boogie riff, very Thin Lizzy or BTO-ish, but the lyrics offer a litany of clichés about a ravenous femme fatale: "I'm looking for action, I'm hungry at heart." Foreigner themselves might have been embarrassed to record a tune this tepid-blooded.

The Runaways play "Eight Days a Week" like they're shuffling in slow motion—nothing like belaboring a lousy choice. Duane Hitchings's keyboards lend an awful chintzy new wave vibe, almost as dated as Lita and Vicki's tiger-striped shirts.

The pace blessedly picks up for "Mama Weer All Crazee Now." Still, the choice of another cover, and the song's dependence on Hitchings's stride piano, indicate just how artistically bankrupt the Runaways had become. Jett does transcend, sounding confident and full-throated in a way she hadn't yet emerged on *Waitin' for the Night*.

Joan especially sounds good compared to Ford's first lead vocal appearance on a recording. The beat slows again for "I'm a Million," in which Lita and Sandy do a decent Deep Purple impression—for six ponderous minutes. Ford's thin voice can't hold the emotional weight of the tale of a girl on the make, and Jett is inaudible.

West makes her second career appearance as lead singer, her first on a song she wrote, with "Right Now." The power-pop ditty takes a 180-degree turn away from Ford's air-guitar anthem, an indication that Alcock was right: West wasn't all about metal any more than Jett was all about punk. The throwaway but fun girl-group-style confection was as far from hard rock as the Runaways got. Given the success another all-girl L.A. band, the Go-Go's, would have with a similar new wave sound, West might have been leading the band in a smart direction. But they didn't follow.

Finally, six songs into the album, Jett charges in with the rather silly "Takeover," a Ramones-ish rocker that bizarrely indulges in anachronistic red-baiting. Communist infiltrators in New York and L.A.; was she kidding or just, as the song says, dumb? The astute progressive political sense Jett was to cultivate as an adult had apparently not emerged yet.

Joan goes for a double with "My Buddy and Me," a me-and-you-against-the-world anthem that still resonates. It could be a rallying cry for gay pride, or just a song for anyone who doesn't fit in. "Leave us alone," Joan cries emotively; Ford's guitar rather anemically responds to the call. But she's not just speaking for herself; she's speaking for the listener, too, and for future generations of listeners: "We won't get down on our knees and neither should you," chants the original Rebel Girl.

Dispiriting as the title sounds, "Little Lost Girls" is the one track where the band finally comes together. Jett wails Ford's plaintive cry—"I want to run, run, run, run away from here"—and Lita doesn't overplay. It's catchy, evocative, smart. Even the synthesizers almost work. And its story of would-be rebels turned waifs rings hauntingly true.

And Now closes with "Black Leather," a metal song written by Jett's punk pals. Joan snarls and Lita wanks hard but they don't quite get it together. Sandy sounds locked into a click-track. Thankfully, Hitchings sat this one out.

In a sense *And Now* was the Runaways' most democratic album, with Ford, Jett, and West almost contributing equally to the artistic conversation. But rather than writing together, they were each staking out solo positions. There was no sense of unity—Jett added little to nothing to the others' songs, and visa versa. This was a three-legged stool with no seat. At least on the covers, they all agreed to be equally mediocre.

This is how bad *And Now* was: Phonogram in the U.S., England, and Japan turned it down. It was only released at the time by Phonogram Europe. In England, a fledgling punk label named Cherry Red picked it up. They pressed it on four different colored vinyls and released "Right Now" as a single. The label's investment was slight, so when *And Now* sold "quite a few thousand copies, that worked for us," says Iain McNay, the label's founder and owner.

Mamis tried to rally the troops. "For the first time, the Runaways' sound on record matches their onstage sound," announced a FTM press release in October. The publicity promised "an extensive promotion and merchandising campaign." In reality, *And Now* sank quickly and mercifully into oblivion, mostly unremarked. Even diehard Runaways chronicler Sandy Robertson, singling out Sandy's "bubbly, tough" contribution, struggled to find something nice to say in his *Sounds* review. "Well, producer John Alcock has managed to whip up a strong studio sound, but he still can't save much of the material from being exposed as downright lame," he wrote.[4] Thankfully, Robert Christgau didn't bother to review the non-release—one cringes to think what the *Village Voice* critic might have said.

On October 3, the Runaways performed one of the oddest shows in their strange career. The soiree at the Plaza Four Club in Century City marked the L.A. opening of the Broadway musical *Annie* and was a benefit for the Park Century School in Santa Monica. Hosted by writer Harold Robbins and his wife, the charity gala drew the likes of the Gabor sisters, Phyllis Diller, Hugh Hefner, Angie Dickinson, Henry Mancini, and Jacqueline Bisset. Photographs capture the Runaways standing with leggy blonde actress Suzanne Somers and Sex Pistol Steve Jones. Jones joined the band for their performance of his song "Black Leather." It was Blue's last show with the Runaways.

"Ironically, I felt I found my rhythm finally at the last gig," Vicki says. "I was so comfortable and free on stage."

Did Vicki jump or was she pushed? Tough bitches though they pretended to be, the Runaways had trouble firing anyone. Passive-aggressively, they preferred to drive people away. Like Jackie and Cherie, Blue was the one who called it quits. One day she walked into Mamis's office.

"I don't want to do this anymore," Vicki said.

"I'm not surprised," Toby answered. "When do you want to leave?"

"Right now. I'm out of here."

Blue never said goodbye to Sandy, Lita, and Joan.

"I left the band because the drug use was so intense," Vicki says. "There was no communicating with anybody anymore. Joan was so hooked into punk; Lita and Sandy were hooked into heavy metal; I was hooked into blues. Nobody was talking. We all hated each other. God, man, it was horrible."

Although Blue never had a music career after the Runaways, she still treasures the experience and its influence on her as a filmmaker and photographer.

"I love that I was in the Runaways. It's such a sacred, special thing in my life. It benefitted me every way imaginable: confidence, career. It was the foundation of a lot of things for me," Vicki says.

The next and final Runaways bassist was from Eugene, Oregon. Laurie Hoyt was also a tomboy rebel. At age eight, she begged her parents to let her get a Mohawk. At eighteen, she moved to L.A. to be a rock star. At twenty, she took the stage name Laurie McAllister and became a Runaway. "She fit the Runaways perfectly," says her sister, Susan Hoyt. "I used to say it was so cool that the punk rock movement came around to explain Laurie."

McAllister was a beautiful woman, but not the kind of bottle blonde that Fowley kept hiring. She was lean and lanky, with long, brown hair and bangs that covered her eyes. And she could really play the bass. In a video of the band performing "Weer All Crazee Now," she exudes confident, funky fun, shaking her head and body and slapping her instrument with a zeal that seems almost spastic after the comatose Blue. Laurie may have been the bass player the Runaways had been looking for all these years. They found her too late.

"At that point they just weren't gelling," says Donna Santisi. "I don't think anyone could have come in and fit in."

The Runaways were in free fall. They had split into two camps: West and Ford on one side, with Alcock as support, and Jett and Mamis on the other. In John, Lita and Sandy found someone who not only appreciated their musical talent but appreciated their taste. They were anxious to be taken seriously, and he did. Joan and Toby were heading in a different direction. They wanted to make a movie starring the band—a sort of distaff *A Hard Day's Night,* called *We're All Crazy Now.* The script was a mess of cowboy clichés and B-movie inanity. The rest of the band didn't get it at all.

"The others didn't want to be in a Runaways movie," Alcock says. "They figured they'd grown up now. Sandy and Lita wanted to be taken more seriously and be in a band rather than trading off the Runaways idea."

More than anything, failure killed the Runaways. Everything they went through might have been worth it, if they had a hit, or even a record label that stood by them. But grinding against a resistant and even hostile music machine took its toll. "When you've got a band of musicians who don't have a lot of money, the stresses and strains of that are enough to break them up," says Alcock.

It was no secret that Mamis favored Jett; he would continue as her manager after the band's breakup. That alliance may have helped push the others away. Maybe Ford was jealous the way she had been with Currie—although Mamis has nothing but praise for Ford's talent. "She's blessed," he says. "She's a great guitar player and a beautiful girl."

It had been more than three years since Sandy and Joan first jammed together in that Surfurbian rec room. During all the band had been through, all the lineup and management and label changes, the two original members had always remained close friends. Jett and Ford had also always been copacetic with each other. Suddenly Joan found herself alone.

"There's a part of me that says to myself everybody bailed," Jett says. "At the end they were not into doing the Runaways thing, it was so apparent. I could be totally wrong, but my gut isn't usually wrong. They were feeling their oats, whatever it was, let's get rid of it.... I tried to make it happen up until the end. By the very end it was painfully obvious nothing was going to happen."

The Runaways played a string of shows around California in December, including a couple at the Whisky. On New Year's Eve, they appeared at the Cow Palace in Daly City, just outside of San Francisco. It was their last show.

The official announcement of the Runaways' breakup did not come until April. In fact, for many months, the members pretended the band was still together. After all, *And Now* had just been released; it would be stillborn if people knew its creators had called it quits. Finally, a letter from Joan went out to members of the Runaways fan club.

"Sandy, Lita, Laurie, and I have talked it over and we have decided to try our own things for a while," the missive said. "With five albums and two world tours and what seems like a lifetime of experiences behind us, we felt it was time to get out there and try a few things that we could not do as a group. ... We're still great friends and we hope you'll join us in wishing each other the best and brightest roads ahead."

If only.

26 Girls on Film

A crush of fans and a phalanx of photographers mill outside the ArcLight Cinema on Los Angeles's Sunset Boulevard. They're straining for shots of the quiet, dark-haired girl and the pale blonde one. Both teenagers teeter in heels and mini dresses as they pose for the crowd. This Hollywood street scene is familiar territory for the Runaways, the rock band whose name is emblazoned on the marquee.

Except it's March 11, 2010, and the women aren't musicians, they're actresses. In fact, they're two of the most popular teen stars of the moment: Kristen Stewart, who has developed a fanatical following for her role as Bella in the vampire *Twilight* films, and Dakota Fanning, already a red-carpet veteran at sweet sixteen.

Nearby are the actual women Stewart and Fanning portray in *The Runaways*, the biopic that's celebrating its Hollywood premiere on this night of leather and glitter. More than three decades after Cherie Currie stormed out of a photo session, she and Joan Jett are on stage together again. Before the film rolls, they suck in one more round of applause, alongside their thespian simulacra—like wizened artists posing beside wax models of their younger selves. It's a somewhat surreal moment of hard-earned and long-sought acclaim for women who were once dismissed as pop strumpets.

But there's something wrong. The Runaways were a girl gang of at first five, and then four. Only two Runaways are here tonight, for this triumphal return to the spotlight. And though the title implies the movie is about the whole band, Fanning as Currie and Stewart as Jett suck up most of the screen time. It's a cruel irony: *The Runaways* depicts a band struggling to be taken seriously as a collective of equal musicians while exploitative, slobbering hangers-on threaten to tear them apart. And yet the film, directed by music-video maker Floria Sigismondi in her feature debut, divides the contentious entity perhaps more definitively than any previous filmic or written history. Sandy West, the band's co-founder, is reduced to a stoned sidekick. Pioneering powerhouse Lita Ford is a bitchy irritant. Jackie Fox and Vicki Blue are replaced by a completely fictionalized, mostly silent composite character named Robin. *The Runaways* is the thing it hates.

From their first rehearsal at West's house to the last show at the Cow Palace, the Runaways were together for fewer than three years and five months. Their legacy has far exceeded their time as a band and their success during that time, in part because of their ongoing resurrection on screen, in part because of the faith of their fanbase, and in part because of the extraordinary subsequent success of a couple of the band's members. The story of the Runaways after 1978 is also a twisted tale of friendships, fallouts, failed reconciliations, recriminations, threats, drugs, lawsuits, tragedy, and death. Much of the saga has played out on and through film.

The first to continue to flog the dead horse of the Runaways was Toby Mamis. Jett's manager was still trying to get *We're All Crazy Now* made. He'd gotten money from investors, had promised a soundtrack. Jett felt obligated to her friend and supporter. In August of 1979, she agreed to shoot the movie with unknowns filling in for the other Runaways (talk about betrayal). Kenny Laguna, who had turned down producing the Runaways, had finally met Jett and was hooked. "I'm in love with Joan," he remembers thinking. "She reminded me of Darlene Love—the reckless abandon, the ability of a woman to let it all hang out."

Laguna and musical collaborator Ritchie Cordell helped with the *Crazy* soundtrack. The filmmakers shot in the heat of summer, in the desert. They were shitty conditions for someone in good health. And Joan Jett was a mess.

"I got very upset with Joan's drug use," says Mamis. "It was never good. But it was getting worse. She appeared to always be on some kind of depressants. It was just not good, and I talked to her about it. But what can you do, you know? People are headstrong....There was nothing good going on in her life, she was just bummed and depressed."

"She's really somebody who's all about loyalty, and her band is her family," says Kathleen Hanna. "I mean the Runaways was her family, and all she wanted to do was play music."

Jett's drug and alcohol use were becoming deadly. In photos taken that last year of the band, she looks bloated and blurred. She hides her body under unbecoming overalls and puffy red blouses.

Joan's friends worried that she would commit suicide. Photographer Donna Santisi stuck by her through this difficult period. "I was sort of protective of her," says the older woman. "She was always wasted. And there were a lot of fans hanging out. I was around a lot just to help her out."

In September 1979, Jett was hospitalized with a heart infection—an ailment frequently caused by dirty hypodermic needles. Heroin was certainly a drug of choice among many of her musician friends and heroes. Smythe remembers seeing her shoot up once, but couldn't swear what was in the needle. "The Runaways were not into smack," he says.

Four years in the fast lane had taken its toll, physically and emotionally, on Joan. She had hit bottom. "She was going to die," says Santisi, one of the few friends who visited the musician during the six weeks she spent in the hospital. A couple times, she took Joan out for fresh air and Mexican or Indian food. On October 24 the hospital released Jett. Not long thereafter, Laguna—who within a year would become her manager—flew her to New York, where he lived and she restarted her life. Mamis never got his movie.

The next to exploit the Runaways post-mortem was another of their former managers. Claiming to own the band's name, Fowley led his 1980 compilation *Hollywood Confidential* with a song, "On Suburban Lawns," credited to the Runaways. McAllister was the only previous band member who played on this track. Kim licensed outtakes from *Queens of Noise* and *Live in Japan* to Cherry Red and other labels internationally as a 1980 compilation called *Flaming Schoolgirls*. The cover advertises "The Runaways with Cherie Currie" and features a large image of the singer overshadowing tiny shots of the rest of the band. Fowley and the labels were probably trying to capitalize on Currie's star turn in the movie

Foxes, even though her solo music career had gone nowhere fast. Ironically, the following year, Joan Jett was to become an international icon with the mega-success of "I Love Rock 'n' Roll." Rhino Records quickly tried to catch that wave by releasing the Runaways' last album, in a different order and retitled *Little Lost Girls*. In 1991, when Jett was again drawing attention with her involvement in grunge and Riot Grrrl bands, the original trio's demos made it to vinyl and CD as the album *Born To Be Bad*, released by the French label Marilyn. Michael Steele complained publicly that Fowley had illegally released the tracks without her permission. To this day, the producer professes ignorance of *Born To Be Bad*. The industry shunned the Runaways when they were active, but plenty of necrophiliacs wanted a piece of their corpse.

The most heinous offense committed in the name of the Runaways was the 1987 album *Young and Fast*, a collection of unlistenable dreck from an amorphous group of women fronted by youngster Gayle Welch from New Zealand and produced by—wait for it—Kim Fowley. Fowley claimed to still own the rights to the band's name. Apparently, he thought the Runaways were another Menudo, and any group of females would do. Or maybe he was just desperate to revive his flagging career by exploiting the act for which he had become, to his chagrin, the most famous. All that *Young and Fast* proved was that however much the Runaways may have benefitted from Kim Fowley, Fowley needed the Runaways a hundred times more than they needed him.

More understandably, actual members of the Runaways tried, at various points, to keep the band's flame burning. Currie and West played together off and on, perhaps most memorably nailing "American Nights," among other songs, at a Squeezebox party at Don Hill's in New York, in May 2001. The singer's voice had grown into the song; the second-generation glam punk audience didn't know what hit them.

"We kept that alive, whatever part of the Runaways, what it meant to us," Cherie says. "On that stage, she and I played off each other all the time. Her dynamic performances made me a better performer. I'll never forget looking over my shoulder to see that smiling face."

Both women went through harrowing periods where they were addicted to freebasing cocaine. Just as the drummer defended the singer in the band's early days, so is Cherie fiercely protective of Sandy's memory. "I always felt so safe with Sandy," Currie says. "She could have this tough posturing and exterior, with this huge, beautiful smile on her face …

There was no one better than this woman. ... There's no woman I've seen with that kind of power and stage presence. She was a mountain of talent."

Fox joined West and Currie for a couple shows in 1994, in L.A. and San Francisco. But the bassist turned Columbia Records attorney was put off by the drummer's condition. "She was so high that I went and sat in the other band's dressing room to get away from her," Jackie says. "I'm really sensitive to people's energy, and it was all over the place, and it was awful. She couldn't sit still, or stop talking; it was in your face."

There have been a few attempts to reunite the whole band. At one point, the Gibson Guitar Center in Los Angeles wanted to bring the Runaways together to have their handprints memorialized in concrete at Hollywood's Rock Walk. A promoter also offered money for a reunion tour. But both times Ford balked. The mother of two young sons, she, too, was put off by West's condition. "I didn't want to bring that into my family," Lita says. "It scared me. I didn't want it around two little kids."

She was also unwilling to bury the hatchet, not so much with Jett, but with Jett's manager, Kenny Laguna, whom she didn't like. "We all got on the phone together," she recalls. "It didn't go so well. So that was it. If we can't stay on the phone together for more than one minute, how are we going to stay in a room together."

In 2012, Ford had a change of heart. "Timing was really a thing with me. It just didn't seem like the right time," she says. "Now we would be dead on ... It's now or never. We're all getting older. We all still look good. If it's not now, it ain't going to be ten years from now. Because then it's going to be a joke."

For the first time in decades, Ford broke bread with Jett in late 2011, at a restaurant in New York. "It was weird," Lita says. "When I saw her, it was like seeing Joan. Same old. She looked great. We always got along."

"It was really great seeing her," Jett says of the reunion with Ford. "It was great to give her a big hug. We went through so much, and I think we really changed things, and I think hopefully now she can see that a little bit."

Joan put Lita in touch with Cherie. They dined in L.A. As fast as you can hit "Post," a gushing update about the reconciliation spread via social media. "Before I could even digest my dinner, she put it all over Facebook," Ford says. "Everyone started automatically thinking there is going to be a Runaways reunion, which would be great. Now's a perfect time. I'm all for it. I just need Joan's okay. If she's going to do it, she needs to let me know."

Jett has not responded to Ford's public calls for a reunion, or private messages. "At least we can establish our friendship again," Lita says. "You have to crawl before you run. All I'm trying to do is be friends."

Joan has never embraced the idea of a reunion. She made her view clear in a 2002 interview with the radio show Electric Ballroom: "I don't see the value in doing it personally, for my own self and just for the whole history of the band....Fans who were around at the time got to see what the Runaways were meant to be.... You can't always go back and see what was and what made a magic time. You can't recapture something...Trying to recapture that can be very sad, when it doesn't come together the way people always expect things to do. I'd rather leave it the way it was."

Then Jett added a tantalizing equivocation: "Never say never."

The Runaways didn't even come together to take back what their record company and management had stolen from them. In 1994, West, Jett, Ford, and Currie sued Mercury and Fowley for $70,000 in back royalties. Laguna had put the ex-members together with Artists Rights Enforcement Corporation, a company helmed by Chuck Rubin that seeks to collect monies owed to musicians—for 50 percent of the take, in perpetuity. Rubin has represented "Louie Louie" composer Richard Berry and the estate of Frankie Lymon. To some artists, royalty rescue ops like AREC are saviors. To others, they're bottom feeders.

Fox was not part of the 1994 legal action. "We had to eliminate the opportunity of helping Jackie Fox, because she had created her own arrangement with the record companies," says Rubin.

Fox says she did not want to be part of the suit because she did not think it was a good financial arrangement. "I knew this wasn't a good suit," she says. "The real cause of action was against Kim, and I don't want to give up 50% of everything to this company."

Jackie had already learned from a friend at Mercury that the Runaways had long ago earned back their advance and were owed royalties. "Sometimes you can get what you want by calling up and saying please, rather than suing somebody," she says. "So I use please first. They go straight to lawsuit."

Laguna says Blue was not a party in the action because she was never legally a Runaway, only a side player. "Vicki Blue had nothing to do with the major recordings at all," Rubin says. Vicki disputes this. There has been a series of lawsuits and legal threats back and forth between, on the one side, Laguna and the two Runaways he manages, Jett and Currie, and Fox and Blue on the other (although always as separate parties). Kenny admits he likes to sue. The charges and countercharges of these cases are tiresome and depressing. Even Fox, the lawyer, complains about the legal battles: "You never want to be in a lawsuit if you don't have to. It's horrible."

The suit against Mercury and Fowley was settled out of court in '96, under a confidentiality agreement. "We were able to uncomplicate the complications that the Runaways had when we met them," Rubin says, rather complicatedly. An undisclosed financial lump sum was paid ("they did very well," Rubin says), and the litigants now get regular royalty checks—minus AREC's half.

If nothing else, Rubin's company released Fowley's hold once and for all on the Runaways. "We basically litigated him out," says Rubin. "He had to make a compensation to them for certain things we felt he was obligated to, and he did, and he was out. I don't think it would be appropriate or right for him to receive added benefits from the investigation that we conducted."

Laguna admits great riches were not released—"it was coffee money for Joan." But for West, it was sometimes all she had. Fox says she also gets royalties from Mercury. Before the suit, she got them from Fowley—if she received them at all.

Mostly, the Runaways lived on—and fought on—in movies.

After she left the Runaways, Blue turned to making still and moving images. For her first full-length documentary, she chose a subject she knew well: the band she played in as a teen. Directing *Edgeplay: A Film about the Runaways* gave Vicki a chance to come to terms with this period that lasted not much more than a year but left her, like the others, profoundly changed—both damaged and transformed. "Let's talk about celebrating the spirit of a sixteen-year-old girl!" she says. "We realized our ambition at a very young age because we were so true to our passion."

The film also provided its maker a forum for airing grievances and settling scores. "Doing the movie was important to me," she says. "I had to shift that power."

Krome, Currie (prior to working with Laguna), Ford, Fox, and West all opened themselves up to Victory Tischler-Blue. They revealed dirty deeds in the Runaways history, in sometimes painful and shocking detail. Their frankness was a result of both the filmmaker's personal knowledge of events and the deep friendships she had forged with almost all of the Runaways. Jackie didn't know her replacement before Vicki began working on the documentary (they met once before, at Cherie's wedding to actor Robert Hays). In the course of making the film, the bassists became fast friends. Jackie helped produce *Edgeplay* (because of legal actions by Laguna et al, her name was left off the credits) and acted as Blue's attorney.

"We instantly bonded," Vicki says. "We had a different skew on the Runaways than others do. I love Jackie. We fight all the time. I love fighting with her. We have hot fights."

Mostly the bassists were battling others to get Blue's movie made. "Every day there was a new fucking lawsuit," Vicki says. "Jackie is the best entertainment attorney I have ever worked with in my life."

Due to this alliance of the two members left out of the royalty settlement, Laguna and others have called *Edgeplay* "the revenge of the bassists." It's a bit of a puzzling description, as while the movie is searing and sobering in its depiction of what the members went through, Blue also presents the subjects as brave if difficult heroes and pioneers. *Edgeplay* only violates the Runaways' legacy if a viewer expects some hagiographic treatment through a rose-colored lens. Incomplete and sometimes maddening, the film still makes you want to learn more about the group.

Jett and Laguna vehemently dislike *Edgeplay*—"girls whining," Laguna calls it. They refused to participate in it because, they say, they knew it would be sensationalistic. That knowledge was partially informed by West and Currie, who came to them after their interviews with Tischler-Blue, upset that they had said things they did not want to make public. *Edgeplay* marked the end of Currie's friendships with Blue and Fox. The film also upset Jeri Williams, who was interviewed—in tears—with her daughter Sandy West. She calls *Edgeplay* "in poor taste." She asked the filmmaker not to use the footage of her, despite having signed a release. "The reason I allowed her to do that was I wanted to let young girls know that there are downfalls in your life," Sandy's mom says, explaining why she agreed to be interviewed.

Jett refused to be interviewed. "I didn't want to be part of something that was like a Jerry Springer who did this, who did that," Jett says. "I wanted to talk about the music, I wanted it to be about what we did, about something important. If you film any band about the things that went on offstage, bands are like families and they're dysfunctional. There's good stuff and there's bad stuff. To focus on that is such a waste to me."

Not having the cooperation of the most iconic member of the band presented a major hurdle. Even more problematic were the rights to the Runaways' catalog. After seeing a rough cut, Peer Music had agreed to let Blue use Runaways songs. Under pressure from Jett and Laguna, the publisher rescinded that permission. *Edgeplay* is a Runaways movie with scant actual Runaways footage or music, and only glimpses of Joan Jett. That it succeeds as well as it does is a testament to both the power of the subject and Blue's filmmaking.

Blue's plan was not to unearth skeletons and dish Runaways dirt, she says. She swears that she originally put together a film that was a tribute to the band—"a beautiful movie about girls who had stars in their eyes." This was the cut that Peer saw and approved. She did not provide this author with a requested copy or viewing of that cut.

Edgeplay upset Currie, Williams, and West. In fact, agony over her on-screen confessions may have sent the drummer over the edge.

Blue tells a disturbing story about an incident around the year 2000 that marked an ugly, and potentially lethal, nadir in intra-Runaways relationships. Vicki was at her home in the Hollywood Hills, when someone started pounding on her door, loudly, even violently. At first, the filmmaker was relieved to see that it was Sandy. Then she got a good look at her.

"She has this look in her eyes," Blue recalls. "She's high like I've never seen her high before. Tries to push her way in. She says, 'Joan wants the footage. I'm here to get it.' The violence, that side of her."

West had a thuggish friend with her as well as a gun. "She was so fucked up," Vicki says. "I thought she was going to kill me. It was an out-of-body experience."

Blue called 911. The operator put her on hold. She called Jackie; Jackie called 911 and got through. The LAPD sent officers and helicopters. They nabbed Sandy. But Vicki declined to press charges against her friend and former bandmate, because she knew the jailbird was on probation. "Do I want to send her back to prison?" she asked herself.

Blue maintains that Laguna and Jett—or "JoanandKenny," as she refers to the pair—manipulated Sandy into threatening her. "They got to her. Sandy's very easily led," Vicki says, slipping into the present tense, as if West were still alive. "She's a follower."

Laguna says he and Jett did not direct Sandy to get the footage. "I believe that Sandy did that because she and Cherie were really upset after they did their interviews," Laguna says. "They felt they had been taken advantage of. Sandy was upset and she was capable of trying to scare her and say Joan did it."

The experience caused Blue to flee Los Angeles for the desert and shelf the movie on which she had been toiling away.

One day, many months later, Vicki pulled out the footage. She started seeing a different film than the bio-pic she had originally edited. With no Runaways music, except for covers of songs written by others, Blue had to reedit her film anyway. What emerged, as Vicki went back to the drawing board, was a very different movie—the kind of movie Jett and Laguna feared.

"I was able to make a movie about child abuse instead of a movie about a rock band," she says. "It was healing for me and for Jackie. Sandy got to tell her story. Cherie got to tell her story. Lita got to tell her story. Each one of us got to rewrite our history a little bit, not to change it, but to skew it."

This is the film *Edgeplay* became. Vicki got her former bandmates to talk on camera about some of the most sensationalistic and traumatic things that happened to them during and after the band. Disconcertingly, the director leaves the film rolling after subjects break down, ask her to stop, and sometimes seem to think the shoot is over. Blue says she did this on purpose, as she knew the film would be controversial and she would be accused of editing quotes out of context. This unfinished quality—including sequences that seem to be shot over the ends of tape, are overexposed, or are scratched—gives *Edgeplay* a raw, cinéma vérité feel.

This technique matches the subject. *Edgeplay* deepens the lore of the Runaways' career by exposing lurid chapters, from Fox's cutting incident in Japan, to the sex education class, to Currie's sexual relationships with Jett and West.

Most disturbing is the footage of West. Jackie picked up Sandy from jail on the day of her release and took her to a remote location to be interviewed. At this vulnerable moment, the drummer confessed in a husky but still strong voice to having committed ugly acts of violence as a drug runner and enforcer. It's riveting footage, a VH1 *Behind the Music*–style interview turned tragic testimonial.

On a comic note, Blue had a harder time getting footage from Fowley. After much wrangling back and forth, Kim showed up for his interview with a guitarist. He delivered his quotes with musical accompaniment. Then, when it was over, he told the filmmaker each answer was a song that she would have to license—i.e., pay for. Vicki got the last laugh: She instead acquired footage VH1 had shot of Fowley.

Edgeplay offers a case study in how stardom at a young age can mar lives, and in how rampant sexism and sexual abuse were (and still are) in the music industry. But in a sense, it fails where all media have long failed the Runaways: It's about the players' personal lives, not their music. Tischler-Blue admits as much, saying, "*Edgeplay* is a movie about child abuse disguised as a rock documentary."

Blue's Sacred Dogs Entertainment released *Edgeplay* in 2004. The Lifetime channel put it in rotation for two years. Blue says the film cost $100,000 to make and has earned much more. It has also provided nice royalties for Ford and Suzi Quatro, who filled in the musical gaps left where Runaways songs should have been.

West showed up at the premiere at the Beverly Hills Film Festival. She and Blue reconciled and remained close up until Sandy's death. According to West's friend Pam Apostolou, the drummer liked *Edgeplay*. The movie made her feel validated, a star again.

Edgeplay is one of the many sore spots that, thirty years later, still divide the Runaways from each other. The members were filmed separately from each other, on the beach (Ford), by desert boulders (Currie), in an abandoned building (West). They are all still these striking blondes, at once proud and defensive—and alone.

However much Jett and Laguna may dislike it, *Edgeplay* paved the way for *The Runaways*. (And *The Runaways* in turn generated interest in, and revenue for, *Edgeplay*.) The documentary raised general awareness of a band that had previously had a devoted following but a low public profile. Many in the community of Runaways fans and commentators believe that Jett and Laguna sought to have a film made in reaction and as a rejoinder to *Edgeplay*. Sigismondi has admitted that the documentary influenced her own script.

Joan Jett initially did not want a Runaways movie made. She thought the past should stay in the past. "I was always pretty resistant to it, both a Runaways reunion, or just any sort of movie situation, just the whole thing," she says. "I was, I guess, afraid that the only thing that can happen is things can go wrong. Maybe it was a way to protect it for myself, because the Runaways is so special to me and meant so much."

It was Laguna who pushed the idea of a movie: "I always said someday we'll do a story about the Runaways."

In the first decade of the twenty-first century, Kenny began working with Currie. The manager tried to get *Neon Angel* republished in a revised edition that targeted an adult audience. He discovered that the path to publishers lay in getting the book produced as a film or TV show. Art and John Linson, a father and son team who had produced *Lords of Dogtown*, signed on as producers. Then River Road Entertainment, the studio behind *Into the Wild* and *Brokeback Mountain*, came on board.

The producers brought in Floria Sigismondi. The daughter of opera singers, Sigismondi had made a cult name for herself with her fantastical, goth photographs and music videos for acts including Sigur Ros, the White Stripes, and David Bowie. She had been looking for a feature film to produce when she was given *Neon Angel*. "I just fell in love with Cherie's story," Sigismondi says. "It's quite an arc for a character. She went through so much, and I really think of her as a hero."

Jett says that the quality of the team that was put together convinced her that it was time to let the Runaways' story be told—or, at least, her and Currie's version of that story. The movie was based on Cherie's book. Jett and Laguna executive produced. Before she died, West sold the producers her life rights. So three of the fabulous five were on board.

The producers and distributor offered to buy Ford's and Fox's life rights, but both former Runaways initially turned them down. Ford has said that the sum offered was insultingly small. Fox says she was offered between one and two thosand dollars for her life rights—chump change. Nonetheless, "we were willing to make a deal with them," she says. "Their behavior in dealing with us was less than honest and forthright."

By the time the lead guitarist and bassist agreed to participate, they were too late. The filmmakers had figured out how to make the film without them: by eliminating Jackie's character and minimizing Lita's.

They had also figured out how to preemptively block the lawyer: Laguna and Jett sued Fox in August 2009 in New York, seeking to prevent her from interfering with production of the film. The case was dropped in February 2010 for lack of jurisdiction. Fox says it was a nuisance suit.

Laguna says Ford and Fox made a huge mistake by not participating in *The Runaways*. But unless the musicians had been given the kind of artistic control Jett had as executive producer, or Currie had as writer, they probably would have surrendered their life stories for not only little money, but for minimal glory. The filmmakers did acquire West's rights before she died and still largely left her out of the movie about the band she co-founded (admittedly, not an atypical fate for drummers, who often languish in the background). At the end of *The Runaways*, the closing credits say what happened to Jett, Currie, and Fowley (for whom the filmmakers also acquired life rights) in their subsequent lives. There's nothing about West, Ford, or Fox. The movie is about *The Runaways* in title only. It should be called *Neon Angel*, the name of the book on which it's based—or maybe *The Joan and Cherie Show*.

The Runaways demonstrates the difficulties of making a film about real people who are still living. Sigismondi says she would have liked to have made a movie about the entire band, "just because they were really five completely different girls." But it was tough enough to negotiate the needs and concerns of three people with considerable egos. By honing in on Cherie's and Joan's story, Sigismondi avoided some of the mess that still surrounds *Edgeplay*. "It just would have been out of control," Sigismondi says. "Maybe it would never have been finished."

The filmmaker says she was very aware of Currie's and Jett's concerns as she was writing and shooting *The Runaways*. "What I realized, talking to them, was that this very short period of time held a big place in them. It was a very delicate thing; it wasn't like it was all heartfelt. There was anger. There was resentment. There was sorrow."

Jett was a regular on the film set. The actors have said her presence was inspiring—Joan famously told interviewers that she coached Stewart to play her guitar like she's fucking it. But it must also have been intimidating. The film's depiction of her as a tough, iconoclastic pioneer is certainly flattering. It's also revelatory. The rocker has always been tight-lipped about her sexual orientation, but in the film, she's clearly portrayed as a bisexual heartthrob. Sigismondi says Jett raised no objections to the steamy scenes with Currie. Joan agrees she was fine with them

Not surprisingly, the tryst between two female teenage celebrities made the marketers and media go nuts. A Google search for "Kristen Stewart Dakota Fanning kiss" finds more than half a million citations, from the *New York Daily News* to the Huffington Post to MTV to scores of Twi-fan blogs. It's just the sort of prurient fixation Jett spent decades trying to avoid.

The Runaways is ultimately about two girls coming of age—one lost, one purposeful—with the hilarious but dubious guidance of an unlikely father figure. Sigismondi uses Currie's character to show what can happen when a young woman puts her sexuality up for display. The singer wants to celebrate her blossoming body by wearing a corset. But the outfit sets the pedophiles and the detractors aflame. Currie gets little help from a home life in shambles and the Scott Anderson character, who feeds her pills. To survive the band, she has to quit. Sigismondi makes the singer's departure an act of assertion and will. She also makes it seem like Currie's quitting marked the end of the band, when of course, the Runaways recorded two albums and toured the world twice after Cherie left. This is just one of the liberties the film takes with the truth. Fanning captures Currie's bruised beauty but not her rock-diva volcanic force.

"I said to Dakota Fanning, you got off easy; you played her as a martyr because that's how Cherie wrote her book and that's how it was adapted to the screen, but you should have played her as Courtney Love," says Fowley. "Courtney Love on steroids."

Chewing up the scenery with his dandyesque outfits and outrageous one-liners, Michael Shannon as Fowley in many ways steals the show. Sigismondi and Shannon humorously capture the Sunset Strip Svengali's charismatic complexity. He is *The Runaways'* deliciously evil villain and witty court jester.

Stewart as Jett beams rock 'n' roll energy. The famously taciturn actress turns the hangdog moodiness of her Bella persona into a statement of quiet riot power. The guitarist is all dark, Elvisesque sensuality mixed with a fierce, feminist determination. She has a clear understanding that the Runaways are exploring uncharted terrain and a vision of their victory. Currie's departure shatters that vision. It hurts her more than the bottles thrown at the band, male musicians' chauvinism, or Fowley's vulgar admonishments.

This is all pretty true to Jett's story, and the musician has nothing but praise for the actor. "I found Kristen to be just through and through, first of all, totally professional, and just great to be around. And I found us to be really, scarily similar, just in our physicality, the way we move through space," Joan says.

Still, Stewart isn't Jett. She's a movie star playing a rock star. The difference was evident the weekend of January 22 to 25, when *The Runaways* made its world premiere at the Sundance Film Festival. On Saturday night, Jett and her band the Blackhearts performed a sold-out show at the club Harry O's. Holding her guitar low across her hips, winking at audience members with her big eyes, looking like a gymnast with her lithe, yoga-sculpted body poured into a black catsuit, singing hit after hit in her sexy rasp, Jett was an electric presence, a pop-cultural survivor, a rock 'n' roll legend whose originality can't be replicated in two dimensions, no matter how well Stewart pouts and poses.

At one point, Currie joined Jett on stage. So did the younger thespian versions of the musicians, Stewart and Fanning. This was it: Were the real Runaways going to play on stage together again? Were the teen queens going to make like rock stars, too? All the Jettheads and Twi-fans in the packed Park City venue held their breaths. Cherie looked like she was itching to grab the mic. But this was Joan's moment, and she wasn't going to share it. She introduced the other ladies on the stage, then turned back to the boys in the band and rocked out.

There's a power women wield behind an instrument that's different from the one used in front of a camera. This was what Fowley never understood. He tried to direct the Runaways as if they were in a movie, but a rock band generates its own locomotive force. Stella Maeve, a young actress who portrays West in *The Runaways* and knows how to pound skins, says one of the best parts of making the movie was when the actors actually played music in the live sequences. "It was so much fun," she says. "They wanted to pad my drums. I had to put up a big fight: Listen, I can't have padding on my drums."

The filmmakers certainly scored by nabbing stars with the wattage of Stewart and Fanning. The coup garnered *The Runaways* a heap of publicity that a flick about a thirty-year-old band by a novice filmmaker would never have gotten on its own. And yet, that attention may well have backfired on the movie, creating outsized expectations about an indie production that's purposely raw. After a Monday morning screening at Sundance, the first question Sigismondi fielded from the audience was what was she going to do about all the *Twilight* fans who can't go see a film rated R? "I didn't make my movie for *Twilight* fans," Sigismondi answered, to much applause.

But River Road and distributor Apparition certainly marketed the movie to Twi-fans, releasing still after still and trailer after trailer featuring Stewart and Fanning. There was a great deal of fanfare around the Sundance screenings—lines stretched for blocks—and around the film's initial rollout in major cities on March 19, 2010. But the Twi-fans, either unable or unwilling to, didn't come. Meanwhile, *The Runaways* was not well pitched to the art-house crowd who might appreciate it as a vintage period piece and female buddy movie. Many Runaways fans, particularly partisans of Ford, Fox, and West, were turned off by the film's reinvention of history. The April 9 general release was scaled down. The Runaways flopped at the box office. The ten-million-dollar film did eventually find a second life in DVD sales. But like the band it depicts, *The Runaways* generated press heat, but froze when it came to making bank.

There's a deep irony here: Hollywood was so busy trying to exploit *The Runaways'* teenage girl stars that it ignored the important musical document in its hands. History repeats itself as farce.

"Some of the stuff that the movie depicts is timeless, like, if you're a young woman in the public eye, how do you display your sexuality?" Jett says. "Is it in a way that's going to be powerful, or in a way that's going to be used against you? Those are absolutely still issues. It's funny how little has changed since the Runaways started. Maybe the movie can start a conversation about that, too. Not just in music, not just about rock 'n' roll and girls in rock 'n' roll, but across the board about how women are looked at and how, if they try to be sexual or use sexuality in a powerful way, how they're judged much differently than men."

Behind the scenes at Sundance, Jett and Laguna were almost as unhappy with the way the Linsons, River Road, and Apparition were handling *The Runaways* as were the members who were left out of the film. They knew the Stewart-Fanning sex scene was being exploited—that the Runaways' trailblazing music was being reduced to a lesbian canoodle. They were also upset that the film was not dedicated to West. Sigismondi said she wanted a tribute to the late drummer added to the credits. But for mysterious reasons, the producers refused to allow this basic honor, which might have placated Runaways fans who were uneasy about the film's poetic license with historical events. Not to mention, commemorating Sandy was the right thing to do.

For Currie, *The Runaways* provided a chance to be center stage again. But she too was nervous and hesitant. "The script; it was really hard," she says. "It seemed like all the negative things were in there and no positive stuff. There were so many great times we had that weren't in the film at all...I have mixed emotions."

Currie says West would have just rolled with the film: "I think Sandy would think of this movie the way she thought about life. She just appreciated anything in any form. She would have enjoyed the moment."

Sigismondi's movie gets some essentials exactly right. *The Runaways* offers an important, moving, and all-too-rare portrait of female musicians. From the opening shot of drops of menstrual blood, Sigismondi vividly paints the intense, hormonal rush of puberty in all its raw, awkward power, with no teen-spirit romantic blush. With lush sets and period costumes, she re-creates the glory days of Los Angeles glam. She writes a sharp, sensual coming-of-age narrative driven by a killer soundtrack—not just the Runaways, but also Suzi Quatro, David Bowie, and the Sex Pistols—setting an erotically charged scene of girl love to the Stooges' "I Wanna Be Your Dog." The filmmaker neither glamorizes nor sensationalizes the ever-present drug use of a chemically charged era.

And perhaps most significantly, Sigismondi nails the central theme of the Runaways story: Five teenage girls coming together during the years after second-wave feminism, in the permissive environment of 1970s California, found personal agency and freedom by doing what boys had done for years—expressing themselves through loud, sexy rock 'n' roll. But they also ran hard into the walls of exploitation, chauvinism, inequality, and misogyny that the women's lib movement had spotlighted and denounced but scarcely toppled. The Runaways sought to "own their sexuality," as Jett likes to say, but as soon as they put their sexuality out there, it became a battlefield, as others in the male-dominated music industry and media—not to mention their own fans—sought to take possession of it, or at least rent/consume it. "It's not about women's liberation," Shannon as Kim Fowley says in *The Runaways*. "It's about women's libido."

The Runaways were a Hollywood band, formed and made famous on the Sunset Strip: It was inevitable they became a movie. Sigismondi's film was not the band's first interaction with cinema, and it probably won't be the last. Sex, drugs, and rock and roll: All the classic ingredients of a biopic are there for the taking in the band's short but notorious history.

But there's also something much deeper, a feminist narrative that Sigismondi's historically inaccurate picture gets emotionally right on: The Runaways is the story of young female artists fighting ferociously, painfully, proudly, and almost fatally to be subjects, not objects, of their own story. Sigismondi uses her skills as a music video director to make the songs drive the action, thus giving such Runaways tunes as "Hollywood" and "I Wanna Be Where the Boys Are" a potency they've rarely been afforded. *The Runaways* ranks with *Velvet Goldmine* and *Christiane F: A True Story* as a vivid portrait of the eminently colorful glam-punk scene. And it adds to a thin but rich tradition of movies about female rockers: *Ladies and Gentlemen, the Fabulous Stains*; *The Rose*; *All Over Me*; *Truth or Dare*; *Edgeplay*; and *What's Love Got to Do With It*. It's *Dreamgirls* with balls.

27 Bad Reputation

They came. They saw. They fought and fucked and played and hustled and sang their hearts out. They didn't conquer, but they weren't defeated. The various women who founded and passed through the Runaways, and the man who brought them together, continued on a strange variety of life paths—not destinies, but not necessarily choices. Willpower was exerted, yes, but luck, or lack thereof, also played its mischief-maker role. An imponderable number of factors, including unwavering hostility to their deviance from defined gender roles, continued to confound and complicate the former Runaways' wishes. A few found a way to rise above the haters. Others struggled. At least one foundered.

Laurie Hoyt McAllister joined the all-girl group the Orchids, orchestrated by—sigh—Kim Fowley. Denny Rosencrantz (here we go again) signed the band to MCA, but the album was buried, either, depending on whom you believe, because the label realized singer Sindy Collins was too young contractually, or, as McAllister wrote in a YouTube post in 2008, because Collins refused to fuck Fowley.[1] Laurie hooked up with Dutch artist and musician Herman Brood. She moved with him to Amsterdam, where they had a crazy, junky relationship—the Sid and Nancy of the Netherlands. She eventually moved back home to Oregon, where she died of an asthma attack on August 25, 2012.

"I would like to say playing with Joan, Lita, and Sandy was one of the most incredible experiences of my life," McAllister wrote in a YouTube comment in 2008. "I hold a place in my heart, for each of the girls, who were kind enough to let me share the stage with them."

Blue returned to her first love: still and moving images. She has directed music videos, worked on TV pilots, acted in *Spinal Tap*, and, of course, made *Edgeplay*. She's also an accomplished landscape and portrait photographer. She still rides horses, out in the desert, and has a pet wolf.

After her Runaways misadventures, Jackie Fox went to college and to law school, at Harvard, no less, alongside Barack Obama. "I went back to college ultimately because I felt incomplete, and I had a great time in college, but I don't think I would have appreciated it as much had I gone straight through," she says. She did record some demos along the way, but aside from her few gigs with Cherie and Sandy, she never returned seriously to music. She wound up back in L.A. practicing entertainment law—learning everything the Runaways had done wrong. Battling sometimes debilitating fibromyalgia, she took some time off to write a historical novel. In 2012 Fox returned to an office job, reporting on the law for an L.A. newspaper. She lives in the Hollywood Hills with her cats.

Cherie Currie continued to make music and also became an actress. For her 1978 album *Beauty Is Only Skin Deep*, produced by Kim Fowley and David Carr, she finally got to indulge her pop instincts. Unfortunately, it sank as quickly as a Runaways record. Her 1979 album with her twin Marie, *Messin' with the Boys*, featured members of Toto (Marie married Steve Lukather) and was not a bad pop-rock album. Free of Fowley at last, and singing alongside her sister, Cherie actually sounds like she's having fun. Too bad this album also tanked.

Currie did find some success as an actress. She was tough and vulnerable in Adrian Lyne's first feature film, *Foxes*. The 1980 release, which also starred Jodie Foster and Scott Baio, chronicles the listless wanderings of a group of latchkey L.A. kids seeking comfort and strength in each other as their parents are mostly absent—but without guitars and drums as outlets. (The soundtrack is more disco than glam; Donna Summer's "On the Radio" is a recurring theme.) *Foxes* is *Lords of Dogtown* but with girls, not boys, and with fewer skateboards. Currie convincingly portrays Annie, a teenage girl in deep trouble. She was largely playing herself, to chilling effect. She later starred in *Parasite* with Demi Moore, *Wavelength* with David Carradine, and *Twilight Zone: The Movie* and had parts on the TV series *Matlock* and *Murder, She Wrote*.

In 1990, Cherie married actor Robert Hays, star of the *Airplane* movies, among other films and TV shows. They had one child, Jake, who became a guitarist, and divorced in 1997. In 1989, Price Stern Sloan published the first, young-adult version of *Neon Angel: The Cherie Currie Story*; It Books republished the book in a steamier, adult version in 2010.

In her memoir, the author revealed her addiction to drugs. She also told a horrific story about being abducted, tortured, and raped, barely escaping with her life. On the cover of the 2010 edition, a photo shows the entire Fabulous Five, a sort of flipping of the script of Cherie's solo photo on the cover of the first Runaways album.

"The book means everything to me," she says. "It's not fun going down memory lane all the time...There were stories I couldn't tell in the young adult version. I hadn't addressed a lot of things that I have had to wade through now in later life. We have to come to grips with why things happen the way they did.... We have to take responsibility for our actions."

Currie continues to periodically play music. As of 2013, an album featuring Smashing Pumpkin Billy Corgan and Guns N' Roses' Slash and Duff McKagan, and produced by Guns N' Roses drummer Matt Sorum, had been in the works for a few years. In 2010, she performed at the Orange County Fair, opening for Joan Jett; Sorum and her son Jake played in her band. She had urged her Facebook friends to wear red, white, and blue to the show; it was a bit of a surreal, flag-waving non-Runaways reunion. (They shared the bill but the two bandmates never appeared on stage together.) Around this time, Currie got a reputation for her extreme right-wing Facebook posts. The singer also took up Wendy O. Williams's instrument of choice, a chainsaw. She carved a gold-hued statue of Sandy West as a guitar-playing mermaid that stands outside Kenny's Music Store in Dana Point, California, gathering flowers and other tributes.

Lita Ford has continued to blaze a singular path for lead guitarists. Her musical collaboration with West and Alcock quickly fell apart, so Ford struck out on her own, assembling a power trio.

"What I did when the Runaways broke up, I put together a band: bass player, drummer, and myself on guitar," she says. "I was the only guitar player and lead singer, a la Jimi Hendrix. I said, 'If they don't take me serious as a three-piece with a girl lead singer and girl lead guitarist, they're never going to take anyone seriously.' I just shoved it in their face. It worked: got me a record deal, and things accelerated from there."

Ford only sang lead on one Runaways song, and she did not do that well. But, with the help of some vocal coaching, she developed a competently husky style, the sound of someone just waking up or having smoked too many cigarettes. Lita's music wasn't about her vocals; it was about her guitar playing, which just kept getting better.

The Runaways' label, Mercury, released Ford's first two solo albums, and did about as poorly with them as they had with the Runaways. Part of the problem was the fact that Lita's melodic metal was ahead of its time. It wasn't until the boys who followed her around L.A. took over MTV with their hair metal that Ford's musical and stylistic leads were acknowledged and accepted. It didn't hurt that by the late '80s, she was being managed by the legendary Sharon Osbourne (Ozzy's wife). Mercury had dropped her, which was a blessing: The guitarist switched to RCA for 1988's *Lita*, which hit number 29 on the *Billboard* albums chart. Mike Chapman, of the Chapman and Chinn songwriting and producing team that had made Quatro and Blondie stars, produced. The album yielded two singles: the lightweight lighter-waving anthem "Kiss Me Deadly" (which hit number twelve) and the number eight Ozzy Osbourne duet "Close My Eyes Forever."

It's ironic that *The Runaways* depicts Ford as being upset over Currie's Japanese soft-core shoot, since Lita became famous for her provocative garb. On her debut solo album *Out for Blood*, she wore a low-cut black latex Teddy with black fishnet stockings. In the video for "Kiss Me Deadly," she writhes like a metal Madonna or a typical video vixen, miming power-yoga copulation poses with her guitar but not actually rocking out until the last twenty seconds of the power-pop ditty—then fading away. Well into her forties, she could show up for a gig in ass-less chaps and still make people notice her guitar playing.

Ford also made the news with her rock-star romances. She lived with Mötley Crüe's Nikki Sixx, was engaged to Black Sabbath guitarist Tony Iommi, and married and divorced W.A.S.P. guitarist Chris Holmes.

In 1994 she married Nitro singer Jim Gillette. After 9/11, they moved to a Caribbean island. Ford says that Gillette was controlling and abusive; she has compared the nightmare of her marriage to Ike Turner's horrific relationship with Tina Turner.

"When I got to that island, things went from bad to worse," she says. "Then I couldn't get off. There was literally no way to get off. There was no airport. You needed a private jet."

All her experiences in the music business, from Kim Fowley to the drug-crazed Ozzy Osbourne, had not prepared her for Gillette.

"I have been around slime and snakes," she says. "I've been around con artists my entire life in the music industry. I thought I'd seen the best of them. Little did I know."

It's tragic to picture the Runaway who never brooked any nonsense, who was quick with the retorts and the fists, as a battered spouse. She did escape—the Runaway found out for real what it was to run away. She was unable to bring her sons with her; they continue to live with Gillette. "I just want my kids to be okay," she says. "They're the loves of my life."

On her 2012 album *Living Like a Runaway*, Ford wrestles with the demon of Jim Gillette—and remembers the glory days of her youth. That summer, she opened for Poison and Quiet Riot on the Rock of Ages tour of America. She looked and sounded amazing, a rock 'n' roll survivor, a real-life guitar hero.

Kim Fowley parlayed his Runaways failure/fame into a string of similarly mixed successes: Venus and the Razorblades, the Orchids, Helen Reddy's *Ear Candy* album. He never stopped being an extremely industrious street hustler. Members of 1990s bands Bratmobile and Bikini Kill both recall receiving "I want to produce/manage/direct/whatever you" letters from Fowley early in their careers. In 2012, he remained a veritable cottage industry of DVDs, CDs, and even poetry. His modus operandi remained to throw everything you can against the wall and see what sticks.

But nothing really stuck. In 1982 he helmed a forgettable top 20 hit by Steel Breeze. (Who? Exactly.) He wrote songs with the talented Detroit rocker Wendy Case of the Paybacks and recorded a spoken word album, *Kings of Saturday Night*, with Ben Vaughn. But nothing came close to how close the Runaways came to making it.

Fowley and Currie publicly mended fences in 2008, after running into each other at a party at the Houdini mansion. Kim cooperated with *The Runaways*, but afterwards he said he was disappointed with the movie and its portrayal of him. He blamed Cherie and Sigismondi for demonizing him.

"The Runaways movies and the Runaways books are diaries of teenage girls, but they're not a rock 'n' roll passion play," he says.

As a bizarre rejoinder to the film, Fowley created Black Room Doom, an unruly and amorphous "female" band (including one drag queen) and experimental movie project. *BRD* has an impenetrable plot about Miley

Cyrus becoming president and a band forming for one day, recording an album, then breaking up. Like any porn movie, the lame storyline is mostly an excuse for transitions between the money shots—or in BRD's case, the musical numbers. The septuagenarian managed to get several interesting and at least moderately talented young women to express themselves, mostly sexually, for his camera. *BRD* is like a Fassbinder farce, a Girls Going Wildly Wrong D-movie. Its personnel has fallen apart at a recurring rate that makes the Runaways look like a stable marriage—though, in an early cut at least, it did feature at least one truly great song, "Hollywood Burning."

"Black Room Doom: It's a food fight, it's a female *Spinal Tap* and a lady *Jackass*. The Runaways were flaming schoolgirls. Black Room Doom are leather ladies, latex, lust, and love," says Fowley. "Forget rock 'n' roll pigs in 1975; this is hogwild female vulva uterus explosion and confrontation of all that's decent, logical, and in good taste in the twenty-first century."

Fowley hosts a four-hour show on Sirius Radio's Underground Garage. In 2009, he was diagnosed with bladder cancer. Regular hospital treatments keep the disease in remission. He milks his illness for all its publicity value by posting videos of himself at St. Vincents hospital—where he was born—on his Facebook page. "I merchandise my disease," he says.

In his seventies, Kim has found a community, and identity, of sorts in L.A.'s sexual underground. He performs regularly at clubs in full face paint alongside dominatrices dressed as nurses. "Fetish is the new gay," he says.

The loss of the band she had founded and the friends she had traveled the world with cut Joan Jett deeply. The breakup almost killed her. And yet she was also the Runaway who was offered the most immediate opportunities and who ultimately achieved the rock-star dream.

Her bandmates may have in part turned against her because she'd gone punk; in turn punks embraced and anointed Joan. In the spring of 1979, she recorded with the Sex Pistols' Steve Jones and Paul Cook in London's Chappell Studio. They cut three songs, released as an EP in Holland only: a cover of the Lesley Gore song "You Don't Own Me," Jett's composition "Don't Abuse Me," and a cover of the Arrows' "I Love Rock 'n' Roll."

Back in L.A., a brilliantly abysmal group named the Germs had emerged as the Local Punks Most Likely To Succeed or OD. Singer Darby Crash (also known as Bobby Pyn) and drummer Pat Smear were fans and friends of Joan's; you could often find them at her pad, up to no good. They asked her to produce their debut album for the seminal L.A. punk label Slash. How much she contributed to *G.I.* is a matter of some debate. The recording happened during the worst period of Jett's drug use, and the Germs weren't exactly clean and sober. At one point on the album, Crash jokes about Jett nodding off.

"At that time in her life she was not in a good place," says Nicole Panter, who managed the Germs. "Joan was in no shape to really…she wasn't present. She was there but she was not present."

Germs drummer Don Bolles says the rumors of Jett's stupefication during the *G.I.* sessions are exaggerated. "She did pass out on the couch once or twice, but I mean who doesn't when you're having a marathon recording situation," he says. "She totally did her job."

Bolles concedes that engineer Pat Burnett was a "genius" who was responsible for capturing the band's sound. But Jett also played a key role, he says. "She was really great to work with. She would tell us when we were out of tune, or when one track had better energy than another, or when one was a keeper. She did everything a producer does."

By 1980, Jett was through with the Runaways and through with L.A. The city had helped her start her rock 'n' roll dream, but now, it was just bad news for her, a tar pit of drug buddies and con men. "I think she had to leave L.A. to make it," says Mamis. "She had to get a fresh start somewhere else." What Toby didn't realize was that leaving L.A. also meant leaving him.

Jett went back to London to record her debut album with Laguna and Cordell. The Who let her record at their Ramport Studios for free. Along the way, Laguna became her manager. Jett moved back East, to Long Beach, New York, to live with him and his wife, Meryl.

Many people speak ill of the way Laguna has controlled Jett's career. They accuse him of separating her from her old bandmates, friends, even family. Vicki Blue went to see Joan once in concert. Backstage, they started running to each other for a hug—until Kenny shouted, "No touching!" Joan stopped. "She just went dead," Blue says. "It was such an extreme maneuver."

"It's weird that I can get anybody on the phone, or an email from anybody, but it's hard to get through to Joan," says Ford.

And then there are people who think Kenny saved Joan's life. He met her when she was in her worst state and still saw her potential. It isn't unusual for people who are ending addictions to sever all ties—even those to people whom they love—in order to start over. Joan was not Kim Fowley's victim, and she's not Kenny Laguna's either.

Jett and Laguna do have an unusual relationship. She lived with him and his family for years; she acts as aunt to his daughter Carrie, who now runs the label Joan and Kenny founded, Blackheart. Laguna is rarely far from Jett's side. To talk to Joan, you have to go through Kenny. He's an old-school Italian American records man, comb-over and all. She's a toned vegan punk, tattoos and all. Together, the manager and the singer bicker and banter like an old married couple. Each one gives as well as they get.

One thing is sure: Kenny Laguna believed in Joan Jett at a time when she had stopped believing in herself. He wrangled her the booking at Ramport; he and Cordell recorded a great debut album for her, full of such crunchy rock hits as "You Don't Know What You've Got" and "Bad Reputation," maybe the greatest girl-power anthem of all time. Laguna shopped the record to twenty-three labels; twenty-three labels turned them down. Nobody wanted an old Runaway.

So he and Joan formed Blackheart and released it themselves. They sold it out of the back of his Cadillac as they toured the country. Eventually, they sold enough copies that they attracted the interest of Casablanca Records, a company owned by Neil Bogart and best known for disco. Casablanca signed Jett and rereleased her eponymous debut as *Bad Reputation*.

Jett needed a band. And this time, she did NOT want to play with other women. "After the Runaways broke up, I was the one that actively was looking to play with guys instead of women because of the shit that I dealt with in the Runaways—the fact that nobody could focus on the music because it was music being done by girls," she says. "So it was like, well, I can't change that I'm a girl, but I can change that the rest of the band is a girl, and if I can just try to take the focus—if I form another all-girl band, on the heels of the Runaways, I just will never be paid attention to."

Joan Jett and the Blackhearts titled their first album after a song whose potential she had been pushing for years. And finally, the world answered that Joan was right. *I Love Rock 'n' Roll* went to number two on *Billboard*'s album chart. The title track spent seven weeks at number one on the *Bill-board* Hot 100 in 1982. The global anthem was gloriously simple in its sentiment and melody, a feel-good novelty number when sung by a bunch of guys. But in the mouth of a woman, "I Love Rock 'n' Roll" became an affirmation of everything its singer had been fighting for for years: that women have as much right to rock and roll as the next guy.

Jett churned out a series of songs in the '80s that either charted or became classics: "Everyday People" (a cover of the Sly and the Family Stone song), "Little Liar," "I Hate Myself for Loving You," "Light of Day," "Dirty Deeds," and "(Do You Wanna) Touch." She also starred alongside Michael J. Fox in the 1987 Paul Schrader movie *Light of Day*. In the 2000 Broadway revival of *The Rocky Horror Show*, Joan played Columbine. It's a sex-kitten role that would have been more suited to Currie; Jett, the dark androgyne, would have been much better as the Transylvanian transvestite himself.

There are stars, and there are icons. Joan Jett has been revered, wor-shipped, and emulated worldwide, across generations. She has played for the U.S. troops on remote bases in Afghanistan, and was one of the first American rock stars to cross the Iron Curtain. She has toured with young punks on the Warped Tour and played in front of tens of thou-sands of Brazilian and Argentinean rock fans alongside Dave Grohl and the Foo Fighters. She and the Blackhearts have twice been nominated to the Rock and Roll Hall of Fame—and twice passed over. Then again, as of 2011, only one out of ten inductees to that institution had double X chromosomes. "Rock 'n' roll probably allows me to be myself the most, but it's still not completely freeing at all," says Jett.

Like Iggy Pop, and Chrissie Hynde, and maybe a handful of other rock icons, Jett has always defined herself as the kind of person who you could meet in a bar and share a beer with—not a diamond-wearing, mansion-residing, screw-loose other. She has also remained cutting-edge, from producing the Germs to recording with Fugazi to signing Girl in a Coma to Blackheart. "The thing that was interesting about Joan and the Runaways is that nobody looked at her like a star," says Jenny Lens. "She was just like everybody else."

Nicole Panter recalls how empowering it was for L.A. musicians to see Jett hanging out in the clubs as well as on stage. "My sense about Joan always is that she has a generous spirit," the writer says. "She's the one that really walked the walk and has done so until her middle age and will do so until she dies. And that's admirable. She's been a role model and a groundbreaker and she has continued on full force with a great deal of integrity. I mean she's a real rocker…she can't live any other way."

Jett has particularly been an inspiration to generations of females. In the early '90s, she was one of the few established musicians to embrace third wave feminism in general and the Riot Grrrl movement in particular. She produced Bikini Kill's seminal "Rebel Girl" single and became close friends with and mentor to singer Kathleen Hanna.

"It was huge, absolutely huge," says Hanna. "Life changing. Because we had a peer. Because our whole mission was to reach out to other women. And to see someone of her stature—came from the Runaways, has this huge solo career, and then even gives a shit about independent music: loved Lungfish, loved Fugazi, the whole thing. Like she didn't forget where she came from at all."

The Olympia/Washington, D.C., band Bratmobile paid homage to their foremothers by covering "Cherry Bomb." Jett returned the favor by coming to their shows and acting as a big sister to guitarist Erin Smith. Joan was at the band's infamous concert at Threadwaxing Space in New York, when members of the audience interrupted the show and the trio wound up calling it quits.

"When we were breaking up on stage, she was grabbing us and shaking us and telling us don't let this happen, don't let these people who are threatening everyone break you apart," recalls Bratmobile singer Allison Wolfe. "At that moment she was the biggest support and help. …. I think I could have taken more of a lesson from Joan Jett's book and been more of a survivor and said fuck you."

When Mia Zapata, the singer for the Seattle band the Gits, was brutally raped and murdered, Joan joined the forces rallying to honor her memory, find her killer, and raise awareness of violence against women. She contributed to the benefit album *The Art of Self-Defense*. And she recorded an album with the remaining members of the Gits, called *Evil Stig* (Live Gits spelled backwards).

"I think it's always just really important to feel like there was this real connection over the generations from the '70s to '80s to '90s," says Wolfe.

"You feel like the torch is being passed," says Bratmobile's Smith. "She was into all kinds of cool stuff that people still don't get. The fact that she took us under her wing, she didn't have to but she wanted to. She treated us as people. It's very meaningful."

Many female rockers have been reluctant to identify themselves with feminism. At the same time Jett was producing Bikini Kill, artists such as Chrissie Hynde and PJ Harvey mocked Riot Grrrls. The Runaways also repeatedly differentiated themselves from the civil rights movement that had helped girls like them win their sense of entitlement. "Shit, man, how many teenage girls really care about women's rights? Not too many," West once told a journalist.[2] But, by 1991, Jett had experienced enough sexual harassment, misogyny, discrimination, and abuse to reach out and support a younger generation.

"In my early career, I'd say in the Runaways and early Blackhearts, it was pretty clear cut what a feminist meant," she says. "A feminist was a strong woman that—actually, I'm not really sure what it was that they were trying to get across then, but to me, when I was asked the question, 'Are you a feminist?', it didn't seem like it was a huge positive to say yes... It just didn't seem to encompass what I wanted to get across, and I always answered the question saying, 'I want women to feel strong but I would much rather be called a humanist.' ... The press image of what a feminist is...was in a separatist, militant women situation...So, I think what we need to do is redefine feminist, redefine it and say, 'Goddam right I'm a feminist, and I'm proud of it.' But my view of feminism is not extreme and separatist. My view of feminism is all encompassing and empowering. My view of feminism means that you can go in there with the boys and you are just as powerful and you command respect, not that you have to separate from them to get your respect. Cause then they don't see it. If you're away from them, they have no way to learn anything."

In the aughts, a meme spread across T-shirts and bumper stickers, a play on the religious slogan, "What Would Jesus Do?"; the phrase even became the title of a 2008 song by a Norwegian band called the Launderettes: "What Would Joan Jett Do?" The former Runaway had become a catchphrase for righteous integrity and girl power, a signpost by which a new generation measured their actions and words.

28 Wild Thing

Sandy West was the solid base upon which the Runaways was built. There from the band's conception to the bitter end, she was the steadfast ballast of the group, always protecting and nurturing this risky endeavor that meant the world to her. Along with Ford, she was the most accomplished and skilled musician in the band.

"She was the hardest rocking female drummer of that era," says Cheap Trick drummer Bun E. Carlos. "Part of the reason was because there weren't any. And because she was. She always sat up straight on that kit. She had a big cymbal and she wasn't just tapping the drums, she was whacking them."

Key words and phrases come up over and over again in friends', family members', and colleagues' recollections of Sandy, like hooks or refrains of songs: "Big heart," "good heart," "loyal," "strong." And then there's "the dark side." In the decades after the Runaways' breakup, West went through harrowing struggles with chemical addiction and criminal behavior. While two of her former bandmates climbed the charts and made the record books, the Runaways' anchor spiraled downward, dangerously.

Immediately after the Runaways' breakup, West was optimistic, happy. She planned to start a new, coed band with Ford, working with Alcock. She was spending a lot of time with the producer. In *Edgeplay*, West says the older man had the hots for her. He admits there was a "flirtation." Whatever they were doing together, no group materialized. Ford moved on. Sandy did not. She began to realize the enormity of what she had lost—not just her family and her musical outlet, but her only source of income. Drugs filled the hole in her heart, and drugs began paying her bills.

"They were all pretty much flat broke," says Alcock. "When you're living on the edge you get kind of desperate: 'What am I going to do?'"

Several of Sandy's friends blame Alcock for introducing her to "the dark side." "Alcock brought her into his world, and his world was pretty insane," says Mamis. "He was clearly a trigger for all that. That's where it started." The Runaways' former manager admits that the relationship was a sword that cut both ways; Alcock, too, was damaged by what Fowley and others call "the Runaways' curse." "He never really worked again," Mamis says. "The Runaways had that effect on people. They were very extreme."

Alcock concedes that West's drug use increased in the year after the Runaways' breakup, but he denies culpability. "She started doing some fairly heavy partying with people I didn't know somewhere down in the beach communities," he says. "There were some people there that she used to hang out with all the time. Those were not great people. I got the feeling that they enjoyed hanging out with her because they were getting her messed up. But at that time it wasn't that serious. It was more than just casual partying, but it hadn't yet gone into the depths of Sandy doing stuff that was illegal."

West and Alcock parted ways. He says they "started arguing about things going on in her life." Narcotic use was becoming an issue. "Because Sandy's life didn't move forward as well as the others, it was easier for her to fall back on drinking and drugs," the producer says.

Her brush with stardom, and maybe her affair with cocaine—the ego drug—made West crave the spotlight. She started her own group, the Sandy West Band. They gigged and made demos. The music was all right. But if labels thought the Runaways were dead without Currie, they certainly weren't interested in a band fronted by a drummer. Laguna says he tried to help West, but had a hard enough time selling Jett.

"She had a very healthy ego," says Ellen Pesavento, Sandy's sister. "She became delusional about how great she was. She had visions of being a really big star getting an enormous amount of attention. Meanwhile, there was the deterioration of the addiction, all that going downward."

Sandy compartmentalized her life, hiding her drug use from people that wouldn't approve. She could be a tremendous amount of fun and a dear friend. Pam Apostolou met West in 1980, when the drummer was bartending. They became like sisters almost immediately. Apostolou remembers Sandy as a woman bursting with energy, a free spirit who liked to waterski.

"The girl never wore a top," the Hollywood-based graphic designer says. "When she would stay over here, we'd have a few friends over, a fire pit in the backyard, and play music. The next morning we'd all get up, and there's Sandy in the kitchen, wearing boxers, no top, making pancakes for all of us."

West lived off and on with Jerry Venemann, a drummer and fan who was eight years younger than she. Their relationship was Platonic, but Sandy was a physical, outgoing, affectionate person. "We would kiss and hold hands," Venemann says. "She was always so playful. We'd go into Wal-Mart and she'd grab my hand and say, 'Let's skip through the aisle.'"

Family remained important to Sandy. But she didn't see her parents and sisters that often. She seemed to feel alienated by how different her life had become from theirs. Instead, people like Apostolou and Venemann filled in as surrogate siblings; she would bring them with her to family gatherings.

"Sandy was amazing in the way she drew people to her and created her own whole family," says Ellen. "She was closer to her family of choice. She felt such shame with her biological family. We didn't see her very much. That was tough."

"I don't think Sandy felt that people really understood her, other than her very close friends," says Apostolou. "She just wanted to be loved."

Often, West turned to fans for friendships. Some of those people—Venemann, Lauren Varga (a Jersey girl who formed a band, Blue Fox, with West), New York writer Kathleen Warnock, Bay Area social worker Shelley Clarke, Blackheart employees Mara Fox (who became her and Currie's manager) and Danna Taylor—were vital links in her support network.

"She was a wonderful person, very personable, very welcoming to everybody, regardless of who they were," says Clarke. "She had a presence about her. When she walked into a room, it was definitely noticed."

But there were also hangers-on who took advantage of her, who just wanted to party with a rock star. She would disappear with these people, into black holes of drug-fueled behavior.

West was known as a hard-partying girl. Thommy Price, who drummed for Mink DeVille during the Runaways' heyday and later joined Joan Jett's Blackhearts, used to run into her at music-industry conventions. They became fast friends after she burst into a quiet party he was throwing and took it over. "She was very intense," he says. "She lived a hard life, like most of us drummers do or did. I don't think she was surrounded by the best people later on. That has a lot to do with why she's not around today. She lived life to the fullest."

Casual partying turned into a search for the ever-greater high. During the '80s, new kinds of drugs and ways of consuming them were taking the life out of nightlife. Freebasing and crystal meth offered intense sensations. They also destroyed people, physically and psychologically.

"She came over to the house and she was freebasing cocaine, which I tried desperately to get her to stop," says Currie. "That's what almost took my life. It was extremely difficult to watch her do it. Having been in her position, I knew all the begging in the world wouldn't stop her. It's one of the toughest things to quit."

Family and friends staged interventions; West went into rehab a few times. But she always fell off the wagon.

A girlfriend reportedly introduced West to what Ellen calls "the evil drug. The thing that was destroying her was crystal meth. One time I drove her home. I just remember trying to relate to her. I looked at her and saw her teeth getting black. I saw the tremors. She was disconnected, couldn't have a coherent conversation."

The beautiful California girl looked old beyond her years. "It was heartbreaking," says her oldest sister.

Sometimes, when West disappeared from friends' and family members' lives, it was because she was in jail. Her arrest record starts in 1988, when she was picked up in Orange Country for driving under the influence. There were at least six arrests after that, in multiple counties: more DUIs, possession of controlled substances, possession of illegal substances, driving with a suspended license. She was able to serve some of her sentences concurrently. Friends say she took her jail time in stride, that in some ways, it was easier for her to be institutionalized, because she was being taken care of—just like she had been in the Runaways.

"She told me that in some ways being in prison reminded her of being in a band," Varga says. "She said, 'I was living in such a bad way that when I went away, that was the only stability I had for a year. When I got back out it was back into the chaos.'"

In a sense West was lucky, getting put away for minor charges, when she had been involved in much worse things. At some point, probably in the early or mid 1980s, the champion of the Rock 'n' Roll Sports Classic became involved in serious crime. She was a drug runner and enforcer for a mafia-style organization. She carried a gun. She used it to collect debts. She worked for bad guys in ugly situations. The Runaways had pretended to be delinquents on "Dead End Justice." This was the real deal.

Guilt over the things she did—things she whispered to only her closest friends—laid its heavy cloth over Sandy West.

That day when Vicki Blue picked her up from prison, Sandy talked about "the dangerous adventures of me." Her raw confessions provide the most moving scenes in *Edgeplay*: "Maybe that was the self-destructive side of me. Maybe I was out to push it. I was fearless. You go down and break somebody's door down. They've got guns all over you, you've got guns all over them. You don't know who's going to get killed. ... I had to break somebody's arm once. I had to shove a gun down somebody's throat once and watch them shit their pants. And you look around and say, I just wanted to be a drummer in a rock band."

There were details of West's activities that Blue did not include in the movie. "Sandy got involved with mob-type figures," says the filmmaker. "Because Sandy had this all-American girl look, people wouldn't red-flag her. She started running drugs into the recording studios. Sandy loved coke. That was this turn that took her down a very different road. That road led to the underbelly of the Hollywood music scene. At that time there were some really bad characters moving around. Heavy-duty drug people. Gunrunning people."

"The people she surrounded herself with at the end of the Runaways were really bad people," Varga says. "She was around when things were being shot."

Based on information that West provided to only a few people, she may have worked for Eddie Nash. Nash owned the Starwood and other clubs and restaurants. He was also a notorious drug kingpin who was thrice prosecuted for having masterminded the Wonderland murders, the bloody 1981 crime in which four people were bludgeoned to death in Laurel Canyon. In fact, West led some confidants to believe that she was somehow involved in that horrific mass murder, for which porn star John Holmes was charged. But Tom Lange, the detective who led the

Wonderland investigation for the Los Angeles Police Department, doesn't believe West could have been there. He spent years on the case and never heard of her.

Still, Lange acknowledges that the road to Wonderland stopped at several rock stars' doors. "The '70s and early '80s was cocaine, cocaine, and more cocaine," he says. "Everyone was dealing or addicted. Everybody was into that particular scene."

Dawn Schiller was Holmes's girlfriend at the time. She too has never heard of West, despite having written a white-knuckled memoir about that time and place. "She wasn't there," she says. "There wasn't even room for her in the car."

Whatever West did and didn't do, there's no doubt that hard drugs and big money were making Hollywood mean. And Sandy had a growing rage, with no fear.

It's unfair to West's strength to paint her as a victim. There were definitely people who did not help West in her life, and may have hurt her a lot: Fowley, Alcock, the friends and fans who pressed her into drugs and crimes. But she was fiercely, stubbornly independent. She carried a gun and ran drugs because she wanted to prove that she could be as tough as the guys around her. Varga says that at the end of her life, West accepted responsibility for her own actions. "She didn't try to blame anybody. She made her own choices. Unfortunately they were the wrong ones."

The one thing that definitely bothered Sandy was the breakup of the Runaways. She is angry and sad about it in *Edgeplay*. "I don't know why we broke up," she says, her tough face streaking with tears. She never got over being a part of the band, and more than anything, she wanted to play with her "sisters" again.

"The Runaways reunion is the most important thing that could ever happen right now," she said on the Electric Ballroom radio show in 2000. "It's a dream come true for me. These are my sisters. These are the girls that I grew up with… There's no reason why the most famous all-girl band in the world can't get back together for one more time."

Sandy didn't live to see that dream come true.

By the first decade of the twenty-first century, West was living in a mobile home in San Dimas. There's evidence she was getting her life together. She was living with Jan Miller, a quiet widow nine years older than West with an adult son. Miller cared for Sandy, providing her a ready-made family of choice. They became legal domestic partners.

West had formed a band with musicians out east, which they jokingly called Blue Fox, after the Runaways' bassists. A four-song self-released solo EP called *The Beat Is Back* captures her multiple talents: singer, songwriter, guitarist, pianist, drummer. The sound quality isn't great, but the songs are powerful in their autobiographical ambition and sadness—and respectable melodic sequels to "Right Now." One track is about the girls who come to Hollywood looking to be models, actresses, or rock stars—and wind up junkies, whores, and corpses. To the surfergirl who had once chosen the Rainbow over Pirates of the Caribbean, Hollywood had long stopped feeling so good. West had a new name for all of the wannabes, the old Neon Angels and Queens of Noise: "Sunset Girls."

She was working different jobs—handyman, vet's assistant, drum instructor. She had a dog, CJ, that was her child. She loved animals. "She said, 'I just want to settle down and have a family,'" Miller says.

But then she got arrested again, for possession of drugs and paraphernalia. In the era of three strikes you're out, this was one offense too many. This time, West was sentenced to state prison in Chowchilla, not county jail, for eighteen months. The environment was much more intense, as the former rock star found herself surrounded by hardcore criminals.

Before she went in, she did rehab one more time. Former Runaway Peggy Foster had connections with a Malibu facility specifically for musicians and helped West get in for free. "She was a good girl with a really big heart," Foster says. "People who are addicts can't help being addicts."

Friends say this stint may have succeeded better than others. "She really was a different person," says Varga. "She said, 'It's taken me almost thirty years to get over this band. I really just have to let it go'."

West didn't have time to find out if she was cleaned up for good. Not long after arriving at Chowchilla, the lifelong smoker developed a bad cough. It was small cell lung cancer. The deadly, aggressive kind.

West petitioned for compassionate release but was denied. Her sister Teri Miranti says she got excellent treatment in prison. Still, it must have been awful to undergo chemotherapy and radiation, then go back to a cell. She returned to Miller's loving care when she was released; they moved to a house in West Covina. By this point, West's family was back in her life, helping take care of her. She was surrounded by her six sisters, parents, and family of choice. Currie and Blue were there often. Jett saw her when she was on tour in Pomona. Sandy and Ford talked on the phone.

West's last months were full of pain, as the cancer, which moved to her brain, ate away at her. She lost some of the things that defined her: her golden hair and the strength to drum. She gained religion and a determination to do good. When she recovered, she said, she planned to speak to young people about the perils of drug use. "Through her suffering, and she really did suffer a lot, she became closer to her faith and wrote quite a few songs that were spiritual," Jeri Williams says.

Sandy moved to a hospice. On October 21, 2006, Ellen had the feeling she had to get there right away, so she drove like crazy from San Francisco to San Dimas. A half-hour after her sister's arrival, Sandy "West" Pesavento died.

"It was one of the most peaceful moments that I have ever witnessed in my life," says Miranti. "There were most of us surrounding her bed. I was on one side, Lori on the other. I had been holding her hand and Lori had been holding her hand. Before she took her last breath she started raising her arms straight up over her head. She had pretty much not moved nor talked in days. We all looked at each other; we didn't know what was going on. The nurse said just hold her hands. She raised her arms up like she was reaching up. It was one of the most amazing experiences."

One last time, Sandy West raised her drumsticks to the sky.

Sandy West is buried in Forest Lawn cemetery in Cypress, next to her father. No, Jeri corrects me: Sandy's body is buried; "she's in heaven." Currie, Blue, and Laguna were at the funeral. Cherie helped Mara Fox and Danna Taylor organize a memorial for her former bandmate. Currie played the sold-out concert at Hollywood's Knitting Factory on December 9, along with the Bangles, the Donnas, White Flag, the Sandy West Band, and others.

West cofounded the Runaways just after her sixteenth birthday. The next three-and-a-half years of her life were so full, she spent the following twenty-seven years trying to regain her equilibrium. "It's such a Greek tragedy," Ellen Pesavento says. "The disappointment for her was so beyond what I can imagine. She was an extremely sensitive person.

Her skin was thin. She came from a deep feeling nature, not a deep mental nature. Everything affected her emotionally. Trying to deal with painful emotions was where the medication came in. Maybe when she was younger, if drugs and alcohol hadn't been so prevalent in her life-style, she would have had a fighting chance. I think the deck was stacked against her. She needed another big win and never got that in her life. That's a hard one: to fall off a high peak and try to climb back up."

Maybe West was too powerful for a world that doesn't like powerful women. She had a habit of referring to herself as a man or a gentleman. Blue says they talked about her being a candidate for gender reassignment. But others think Sandy was comfortable in her skin, even if the world wasn't always comfortable with her. "She wasn't a boy or a girl," Venemann says. "She was wild thing."

The family donates its share of West's royalties to the hospice that cared for Sandy in her final days and to a scholarship fund at the Rock 'n' roll Camp for Girls in Portland, Oregon. So Sandy is not only still inspiring other women to rock, she's helping pay for them.

29 Midnight Music

Whether they starve on the prairie or fall apart in the studio, pioneers tend to have short lives. They die of hunger, exposure, neglect. Later settlers build on their foundations. As *Back Door Man* Don Waller says: "Pioneers always pay the price. It's better to get there second."

"Everything could have happened except at that time in history, it wasn't possible because the society was too misogynist," says Kenny Laguna. "Joan always says the Runaways owned their own sexuality. That's why they ran into walls."

Outside of a few countries and American cities, the Runaways were not honored in their own time. Rather, they were abused, misused, and eviscerated. "The reviews were vicious and they were vicious in a way you didn't get about guy bands like the New York Dolls," says Fox. "They were really quite sexist."

It wasn't just asshole critics who dismissed the Runaways. Other women, especially musicians coming up behind them in the punk world, disparaged their act as retrograde and regressive.

"Joan Jett has a lot to offer, but the Runaways did nothing to advance the status of women performers," Exene Cervenka of the L.A. punk band X told the *Los Angeles Times*.[1]

In some ways, the Runaways reinforced and propagated stereotypes of women in rock. They got their moniker and shtick from a male music hustler, and they peddled low-grade, retro, soft-porn images.

"I was pleased to see them emerge," Viv Albertine of the Slits told *The Independent*. "But they didn't come very much as a new thing. It was like an old man's fantasy."[2]

The volatility of the Runaways' lineup sent negative messages about the limits of girl love. The movies *Edgeplay* and *The Runaways* reinforce this sexist cliché: Get a bunch of females together, especially during the hormonal explosion of adolescence, and you're doomed to estrogen drama. The women's ongoing inability to get along has prolonged this stereotype. Jett reached out to a younger generation of female musicians, but to former bandmates such as Fox and Blue, she has extended lawsuits. The endless fighting over the rights to the band's name, legacy, and royalties has alienated friends and fans. In 2011 Jett and Currie even sued Lauren Varga when she assembled a Runaways tribute album; the legal action also cited the record company that released *Take It or Leave It*. The two discs featured such esteemed acts as Kathleen Hanna, Peaches, the Donnas, and David Johansen and were intended as a memorial to Sandy West; part of the proceeds were to go to charity. But the lawsuit quashed the release.

"The girls have never moved on," says sometimes sixth Runaway Hernando Courtright. "They stayed stuck in this situation, in the different factions. They should just enjoy what it was and move on with their lives."

Then again, plenty of male musicians are known to detest their bandmates: Mick and Keith, John and Paul, the Who. The only actual rocker catfight this author has ever witnessed was backstage at a Redd Kross show in the late '80s, when brothers Steve and Jeff McDonald set off a maelstrom of long hair and flying limbs. Expecting a group of musicians to be models of sisterhood is like expecting every black artist to uphold the race—it's a form of double standard.

"As women we don't always have to get along," says Hanna. "I guess that's part of it, for me; I'm fine with the legacy of women in bands hating each other after the band, because that's how life is."

Call it the feminist-punk answer to transactional analysis: I'm a bitch, you're a bitch.

The Runaways' story is a complicated dance of two steps forward, one step back. They were misunderstood in part because they were ahead of their time, and in part, because they were not. Musically, they were stuck between punk rock and a hard rock. Jett's songs in particular were a welcome counterpoint to the plodding prog of such peers as Rush, Boston, Kansas, and Styx.

"The Runaways saved rock and opened the door for new wave," says Chuck E. Starr. "I wonder if we would've ever had new wave music if it weren't for the Runaways. They really opened up the door for that kind of rock bebop sound. ... 'Cherry Bomb' was kind of rock 'n' roll punky, a turn towards a new type of music. They certainly didn't sound like that crappy group Journey, or Kiss—some of the other garbage that was out. Rock was lost, it was just horrible."

Meanwhile, the Runaways—Lita's guitar playing and songs especially—simultaneously created the template for the hair metal that would sweep the Sunset Strip with spandex and power ballads in the next decade. Just as the Beatles popularized the sounds created by girl groups and Motown bands, so Mötley Crüe and Poison were practically Runaways tribute bands. It was okay—what the fuck, it was insanely profitable—for guys to look like girls and sing in falsettos. It wasn't so okay for girls to play like guys—those bitches sucked.

"The Runaways were before their time," says Ford. "If we were to come out now, in 2009, we would have had a lot more chance of survival than in '75."

Since the Runaways showed it could be done, women rock bands have proliferated: The Go-Go's, the Bangles, Girlschool, Frightwig, Lunachicks, L7, Babes in Toyland, Bratmobile, the Donnas, Sleater-Kinney, etc. Many of those musicians explicitly cite the Runaways as inspirations.

"I was a fan when I first heard them when I was a teenager and found out they were teenagers and all girls and were that tight and awesome," says Theo Kogan, singer for the '90s all-girl group the Lunachicks. "They were inspirational."

"They went out on a mission to prove that girls could have fun and play music and own their sexuality and not be judged," says Phanie Diaz, drummer for the phenomenal twenty-first-century Texas trio Girl in a Coma (who record for Blackheart Records).

The Runaways kicked down doors not just for musicians, but for all kinds of artists and outsiders. They forged and flexed a way of being in the world that was not just about their relationship to other people—daughter, girlfriend, wife, mom—but about their relationship to their own desires and creative powers.

"The Runaways were hugely influential to many many women who wanted to get up on stage, whether it was an all girl band, or on their own," says photographer Jenny Lens. "The fact that yes it was a launching pad for Joan and she's done so much and influenced so many younger musicians and artists, and Joan's importance in the history of rock and roll, cannot be underestimated. For her to be on *Oprah* with Stevie Nicks was absolutely accurate because she's worked hard and she hasn't had it easy. She's focused very much on her work and had great instinct on music and songs and whatnot, and when you consider what they went through with Kim, and at the time to be a woman in a band it was very hard, let alone an all-woman band. And the fact that Joan was accessible to X and the Screamers and the Germs and everybody else in L.A. You'd be standing next to somebody in the audience one night, and the next night, they're on stage. ... There's all these bands out there but to actually know someone who you hang out with, you drink with, you party with, who's down to earth, and you see them on stage, and you read that they have a huge fan base in Japan, and not too shabby in L.A.—all things considered, the Runaways were incredibly influential and thank god for them...."

"The punk scene gave me life. It gave me an identity, a purpose. I could have become a pretty, frumpy housewife. This is the alternative. Which is more damaging?" Lens says.

Three decades later, the top teen stars of Hollywood vied to portray the Queens of Noise. "Sandy knew what she wanted and she went after it," says Stella Maeve, who plays West in *The Runaways*. "They wanted to be in an all-girl rock band and they made it happen."

Why the Runaways never broke through to the American rock audience, while bands they inspired did, remains a bit of a mystery. Maybe, they just needed a pure pop hit, like "Our Lips Are Sealed" or "Manic Monday." That's certainly what Mercury wanted from them, while ignoring rockers like "American Nights."

"A big hit overcomes everything, and the Runaways didn't have that," says Cliff Burnstein. "The Bangles had a nice new wavey image, which kind of works, it's poppier. The Runaways were competing in a much more macho kind of era in terms of the bands, all the hard rocking bands."

The Runaways also did not have MTV. Just a year after the group broke up, the music-video cable channel launched, and the cock-rockracy's grip on pop music was broken. MTV promoted and popularized girl bands, new wave, and pop metal. Once American households were able to see Joan swaggering, "Put another dime in the jukebox, baby," and Lita enticing, "Kiss me once, kiss me twice!" the ex-Runaways went straight up the charts.

"To see tough, supposedly bad girls playing rock 'n' roll should have set the world on fire," Jett says. "But it didn't; people were too threatened by it. Guys wanted to fuck us and girls didn't know what to make of us."

What the Runaways did have were lots of roadblocks. And most of those roadblocks were ones their male colleagues didn't have to surmount. The misogyny of the rock media and audience can't be underestimated.

"The Runaways play like boys—mean boys!" read one particularly appalling, but not atypical, article. "But they look like girls, and this is a big plus in their favor; the only all-girl group that has made it that doesn't give the impression that they are dykes or women's libbers...No lezzies here, kids, but real girls—the kind you've wanted to get your hot sticky hands on since you turned 12."[3]

This is what the Runaways were up against: boors who thought "real girls" weren't dykes or lezzies. The Runaways walked a ridiculously seismic line between not wanting to appear feminist/dykey, and not wanting to be pop/feminine/girlie.

Obviously, there was an element of machismo in the way Sandy bashed those drums and Joan and Lita wielded their guitars. As Fowley points out, "This was an all girl band that never wore skirts."

"Girls got balls! They're just a little higher up is all," Joan told Tony Parsons.[4]

The Runaways could mime phallic power, but they had to be sly about standing up for the sisterhood. "...we are something new—something all-girl bands have never been before," Sandy told one interviewer, right after denouncing women's lib. "We're the first girl band to play rock 'n' roll."[5]

"It's great being in an all-girl band. I'm having the best time. I don't think I could do anything else and have a better time. This is what I do best and is what I like to do. We have as much power as any guy. Maybe other bands have just done it longer, that's all. It's just like being in an all-guy band. It's tight, there's no feminist thing; the point isn't just to be all girls as to be just a hot band," Ford said in another interview.[6]

They didn't espouse feminism, yet the Runaways very clearly sought equal rights and girl power. They wanted to prove they could do what boys did. They wanted to own their sexuality, not be owned. They wanted to make their points while surrounded by other like-minded females—a united show of solidarity. And they wanted to empower other women.

"We're physical teenage kids," Joan said. "I think if people listen to it it'll give 'em a chance to open up, especially a lot of girls who might feel suppressed about sexual things; they think the guy has to make the first move. In a lot of songs it's the girl who makes the first move—why not?"[7]

Ford had some practical advice for the girls in the audience: "Be sure to take birth control pills!"[8]

The members of the Runaways paid a heavy personal price for breaking new ground. For even the ones who saw the greatest success, their songs come laden with rage, guilt and anguish. Over and over their music and art, collectively and individually, conflates desire with violence, love with hate. "Kiss Me Deadly," Ford sings. "I Hate Myself for Loving You" answers Jett. Both Joan and Lita have recorded albums with S/M themes, *Fetish* and *Wicked Wonderland*, respectively. *Edgeplay* gets its name from a word for extreme sexual acts. Toward the end of *The Runaways* movie, there's a scene where Stewart as Jett sits in a bathtub, cutting herself, singing her song "Love Is Pain." The headline of a feature in Japan's *Playboy* made explicit the potential connection between the expression of sexual desire and violence: "Fuck Me, Kill Me: The Runaways."

The most tragic aspect of the Runaways' saga is how much emotion it evokes for the members thirty years later: sorrow, anger, love, joy, regret. Sandy never got over it. Those were the best years of her life and she didn't recover from their conclusion. Jett's voice, which minutes before had broken into sobs remembering West, still pitches with hurt as she talks about the band's end. All the members are wary, suspicious, and defensive—aggressively so. Bumping into Currie in the Arclight bathroom at *The Runaways* premiere, I thought she was going to push me in the toilet as she began questioning my interest in Sandy. Within their divided factions, the Runaways are deeply loyal.

Watch videos of them in Japan, or on the *Old Grey Whistle Test*, or running a race at the Rock 'n' roll Sports Classic, and you'll see teenage girls living their rock 'n' roll dream. "How could you not love their spirit and their attitude," says Mamis. "They were rock 'n' roll kids. I thought they were the real deal."

No gold records or Rock and Roll Hall of Fame anointed the Runaways. But one thing still unites them: They treasure their brief but formative years in the Runaways.

"Every day was so full for those three and a half years the Runaways were together," says Joan. "Certainly those first eighteen months, there was really something cool going on almost every day, even if it turned out not to be fun....It was a family. I felt we had a mission. I don't believe it was a coincidence; some energy was making it happen. It was the universe, potential....It was an amazing time, probably the best time of my life."

Notes

Chapter 2 California Girls

1. The definition of zygote at Dictionary.com seems apropos here: "The cell produced by the union of two gametes, before it undergoes cleavage."

2. Anderson, Kelli, "Nine for IX," *Sports Illustrated*, May 7, 2012, 49.

3. Chad Greene, "From 'Iowa by the Sea' to International City," *Long Beach Business Journal*, January 17, 2006.

4. Jan Miller. Personal interview. January 22, 2010.

5. "Tomboy," *Oxford English Dictionary*, http://www.oed.com/view/Entry/203097?redirectedFrom=tomboy#eid

6. Judith Halberstam, *Female Masculinity* (Durham: Duke University Press, 1998), 188.

7. Halberstam, 5.

Chapter 3 The Roads to Ruin

1. "Queens of Noise," *Bump 'n' Grind*, number 1.

2. Reyner Banham, *Los Angeles: The Architecture of Four Ecologies* (Berkeley: University of California Press, 2001), 218.

3. Peter Plagens, "Los Angeles: The Ecology of Evil," *Artforum*, December 1972.

4. *Reyner Banham Loves Los Angeles*, BBC, 1972, http://www.youtube.com/watch?v=WlZ0NbC-YDo&feature=gv

5. That same year, "School's Out," a song by American glam rocker Alice Cooper, celebrated this idea of "no principals," punning on the two spellings and meanings of the word. In 1977, the Runaways may have flubbed their chance for a stateside breakthrough when they canceled a tour as Cooper's opening act, after Fox quit the group in Japan.

6. Joan Didion, *Slouching Towards Bethlehem* (New York: Farrar, Straus and Giroux, 2008), 172.

7. Didion, *Where I Was From* (New York: Alfred A. Knopf, 2003), 106.

8. Banham, 143.

9. Banham, 19.

10. Banham, 21.

11. "Los Angeles & The Runaways," *RAM*, March 11, 1977.

12. Banham, 79.

13. Edward W.Soja, *Thirdspace* (Cambridge: Blackwell, 1996), 239.

14. Soja, 274.

15. Fancher, Lisa. "Are You Young and Rebellious Enough to Love the Runaways?" *Who Put the Bomp*, April 30, 1976.

16. Farber, Jim. "Our Music Is All Crunch," *The Music Gig*, September 1976, 13.

Chapter 4 Hollywood

1. Sandy might instead have traveled east from the 405.

2. Contrary to popular belief, Los Angeles did have a public transit system, one that actually played a recurring role in the Runaways' story.

3. Banham, 17.

4. Hoskyns, Barney, *Waiting for the Sun* (New York: Saint Martin's Griffin, 1996), 93.

5. Chris Salewicz, "The Runaways: And I Wonder…I Wah Wah Wah Wah Wonder," *NME*, July 24, 1976.

6. Julie Burchill, "Gender and Other Trivia," *NME*, Nov. 19, 1977.

7. Marc Spitz and Brendan Mullen, *We Got the Neutron Bomb: The Untold Story of L.A. Punk: An Oral History Featuring the Go-Go's, the Runaways, the Germs, X, Black Flag, and Beyond* (New York: Three Rivers Press, 2001), 14.

8. Barney Hoskyns, "Boulevard of Broken Dreams: A Trip Down the Sunset Strip," *Mojo*, January 1994.

9. Phast Phreddie Patterson, "Phast Freddie's Hollywood (Circa 1973-1983)," *Rock's Backpages*, October 1996, www.rocksbackpages.com.

Chapter 5 Legendary Prick

1. Roeser, Steve, "Kim Fowley: Living and Dying in LA," *Goldmine*, Nov. 26, 1993.

2. Roeser.

3. Alice Bag, *Violence Girl* (Port Townsend, WA: Feral Girl, 2011), 164.

4. John Scanlan, *Van Halen: Exuberant California, Zen Rock'n'roll* (London: Reaktion, 2012), 41.

5. Howard Parker and Chris Rowley, "My Style of Cock: Being an Interview with Kim Fowley, in the Company of Jeff Beck," *International Times*, 1972.

6. Kim Fowley, "The Thoughts of Chairman Kim," *Rock's Backpages*, 1999, www.rocksbackpage.com.

Chapter 6 Yesterday's Kids

1. Phast Phreddie Patterson, "Local Action," *Back Door Man*, December 1975.

2. George Du Maurier, *Trilby* (Oxford: Oxford University Press, 2009), 13.

3. Timothy Green Beckley, "Young, Hot, and Ready to Rock," *Rock*, May 1978, 92.

4. Patterson, "The Runaways—Face Shifting." *Back Door Man*, November/December 1977.

Chapter 7 Secrets

1. Isabella died of breast cancer in 1990, Henry of brain cancer in '98. Their tombstone reads, "My best friends, my companions, my parents."
2. Patterson, "Face Shifting."
3. Robert Duncan, *The Noise: Notes from a Rock 'n' Roll Era* (New York: Ticknor and Fields, 1984), 93.
4. Jon Savage, "We Have Lift Off!" *Mojo*, September 2011, 54.

Chapter 8 Blood and Guts

1. Patterson, "Phast Freddie's Hollywood (Circa 1973-1983)."
2. D.D. Faye, "Rock Returns to the Whisky (For A While At Least...)," *Back Door Man*, December 1975.
3. D.D. Faye, "The Stars and The Runaways at the Whisky-a-Go-Go," *Back Door Man*, December 1975.
4. Spitz and Mullen, 48.
5. Spitz and Mullen, 48.

Chapter 9 Cherry Bomb

1. Davis's and Rosencrantz's words are recalled by Fowley.
2. Cherie Currie and Tony O'Neill, *Neon Angel: A Memoir of a Runaway* (New York: It Books, 2010), 59.
3. Currie and O'Neill, 20.
4. Salewicz.
5. Peter Cowan, "The Runaways: Trash Rock Gets Younger Every day," *Oakland Tribune*, 1976.
6. Jim Jerome, "Teeny Queens of Rock," *People*, August 30, 1976, 32-33.

Chapter 10 The Fabulous Five

1. "An Evening with Joan Jett," *Bump N Grind*, 1977, issue 2.
2. Stephen Fuchs, "Runaways Reflect Mercury West Coast Strength," *Cash Box*, June 5, 1976.

Chapter 11 Signed, Sealed, and Delivered

1. Aaron Cohen, "James Brown's Musicians Reflect On His Legacy," Downbeat.com, http://www.downbeat.com/jamesbrown.asp.

Chapter 12 Hot on Your Heels

1. Salewicz.
2. Krome, "The Runaways' New Years Eve Party," *Who Put the Bomp*, April 30, 1976.
3. Fancher, "Are You Young and Rebellious Enough to Love the Runaways," *Who Put the Bomp*, April 30, 1976.
4. Richard Cromelin, "At the Starwood: Runaways Catch New Rock Wave," *Los Angeles Times*, Feb. 2, 1976, E16.
5. Patterson, "Local Action," *Back Door Man*, April 1976.

Chapter 13 Rock 'n' Roll Pigs

1. Mikhail Mikhailovich Bakhtin, *Rabelais and His World* (Indiana University Press, 1985), 10. Retrieved from Google Books, http://books.google.com/books/about/Rabelais_and_His_World.html?id=SkswFyhqRIMC, Aug. 24, 2012.
2. "Random Notes," *Rolling Stone*, July 14, 1977.

Chapter 14 "The Magna Carta"

1. Harvey Kubernik, "Runaway Girls," *Melody Maker*, July 17, 1976.
2. Eliot Sekuler, "Runaways: Hot on Zep's Heels," *Circus*, April 27, 1976.
3. Robot A. Hull, "The Runaways," *Creem*, August 1976, 66.
4. Ben Edmonds, "The Runaways: *The Runaways*," *Phonograph Record*, May 1976.
5. Robert Hilburn, "Runaways: Young, Female, Fun," *Los Angeles Times*, May 22, 1976, B9.
6. Scott Isler. "L.A. Jets/The Runaways," *Crawdaddy*, 1976.
7. Kris Needs, "The Runaways: *The Runaways*," *ZigZag*, September 1976.
8. Georgia Christgau, "The Runaways," *Circus*, Sept. 13, 1976, 14.
9. David McGee, "The Runaways," *Rolling Stone*, July 29, 1976, 47.
10. Robert Christgau, "The Runaways: Consumer Guide Review," originally published in *The Village Voice*, accessed at www.robertchristgau.com.
11. Salewicz.
12. Michael Barackman, "Runaways—Teenaged, Wild & Braless, *Circus*, August 10, 1976.
13. Danny Sugerman, "The Runaways," *Sounds*, August 7, 1976, 10.
14. "The Runaways: Teen Girls' Rock Revolution," *Teen*, September 1976.

Chapter 15 American Nights

1. Fancher, Lisa. "The Runaways." *Academy in Peril*, March-April 1977.
2. "The Runaways: Teen Girls' Rock Revolution."
3. Currie and O'Neill, 112.
4. Cliff Michalski, "The Runaways: 16, and Savaged," *Scene*, August 5, 1976.
5. Cary Baker, "Sixteen But Not Sweet," *Triad Magazine*, October 1976, 15-19.

6. "Runaways Life Begins at 16," *Circus Magazine,* November 25, 1976. 30.

7. Lisa Robinson, "The Runaways: Naughty Nymphets Leave Lisa Cold," *Creem,* November 1976, 46-47.

8. Robert Palmer, "Teenage Runaways Play to Fantasies," *New York Times,* August 4, 1976, 15.

9. "Runaways Concert, Armadillo Texas," *Records Magazine,* September 1976.

Chapter 16   Trouble in California Paradise

1. "Runaways Life Begins at 16," 30.

2. Robert Hilburn, "Skynyrd Album Live and Well," *Los Angeles Times,* September 18, 1976, A8.

Chapter 17   England's Dreaming

1. Andrew Drummond and Barry Powell, "Oh Boy! The Girl Rockers Turn the Guys On," *News of the World,* Oct. 3, 1976.

2. Drummond and Powell.

3. Mick Farren, "From Jailbait to Jes' Plain Bait," *New Musical Express,* October 2, 1976, 55.

4. Drummond and Powell.

5. John Ingham, "Runaways (gasp): At Last An (groan) Objective (pant) View." *Sounds,* October 9, 1976. Accessed on June 23, 2011, www.rocksbackpages.com.

6. Harry Doherty, "You Sexy Things!" *Melody Maker,* October 16, 1976. Accessed on June 23, 2011. www.rocksbackpages.com.

7. "Queens of Noise." *Bump n' Grind,* No. 1.

Chapter 18   Queens of Noise

1. Fancher, "Kim Fowley Tells All," *Street Life,* Jan. 1, 1977.

2. Schizophrenia Rubberox, "Runaways Runaway," *The Wasteland,* November 1977, 1.

3. Robert Hilburn, "Homegrown Punk-Rock Blossoming." *Los Angeles Times,* January 4, 1977, F1.

4. Hilburn, "Homegrown."

5. Lisa Fancher, "New Year's Eve with Runaways & the Quick," *Street Life,* January 1, 1977.

Chapter 19   Living the Dream

1. Rick Johnson, "Runaways: *Queens of Noise* (Mercury)," *Creem,* April 1977, 62.

2. Mick Farren, "The Runaways *Queens of Noise* (Mercury)." *NME,* January 29, 1977.

3. Robert Christgau.

Chapter 20   Big in Japan

1. Currie and O'Neill, 211.

2. Currie and O'Neill, 213.
3. Burchill, "Gender and Other Trivia," *NME*, Nov. 19, 1977.
4. "An Evening with Joan Jett," *Bump N Grind*, 1977, issue 2.
5. Steve Clarke, "The Lovely Cherie Tells Thrills about the Runaways," *NME*, Sept. 10, 1977.

Chapter 21 Another One Bites the Dust

1. "Kim Fowley: The Wasteland Interview Part 2," *The Wasteland*, Volume 1, November 1977.
2. Sandy Robertson, "The Rock's Backpages Flashback: The Runaways (Interview with Joan Jett)," *Yahoo Blogs*, Mar 24, 2010, http://new.music.yahoo.com/blogs/rocks-backpages/13918/the-rocks-backpages-flashback-the-runaways/. Originally published in *Sounds* Nov. 12, 1977.
3. "An Evening with Joan Jett."
4. Burchill, "Gender and Other Trivia."
5. Rubberox, 1.
6. Clarke.
7. "An Evening with Joan Jett."
8. Lester Bangs, "Back Door Men and Women in Bondage" in *Mainlines, Blood Feasts, and Bad Taste: A Lester Bangs Reader*, John Morthland, ed., (New York: Anchor, 2003).
9. Clarke.

Chapter 22 Waitin' for the Night

1. Harvey Kubernik, "Catching the Runaways," *Melody Maker*, November 3, 1977, 35.
2. Clarke.
3. Richard Cromelin, "Jett, Ford Grab Runaways' Reins," *Los Angeles Times*, Aug. 29, 1977.
4. Sylvie Simmons, "Bring on the Nubiles."
5. Kubernik, "Catching the Runaways." *Sounds*, February 18, 1978.
6. Sandy Robertson, "The Runaways: Waitin' For the Night." *Sounds*, November 19, 1977.
7. Julie Burchill, "The Runaways Waitin' for the Night (Mercury)," *NME*, 1977, 45.
8. Robert Christgau.
9. Wesley Strick, "Waitin' for the Night," *Rolling Stone*, March 9, 1978, 61 and 63.

Chapter 23 Take It or Leave It

1. Robertson, "Interview with Joan Jett."
2. *Bump N Grind*, 2.
3. Julie Burchill, "Gender and Other Trivia."

4. Rosalind Russell, "In at the Deep End with the Runaways," *Record Mirror*, July 22, 1978.

5. "Kim Fowley: The Wasteland Interview, Part Two," *The Wasteland*, November 1977, 6.

6. Gayle Wald, "How Svengali Lost His Jewish Accent," *Sounding Out*, September 26, 1011, http://soundstudiesblog.com/2011/09/26/how-svengali-lost-his-jewish-accent/.

7. Wald.

Chapter 24 Gotta Get Out

1. Robertson, "Interview with Joan Jett."

2. Phil Sutcliffe, "The Runaways: Newcastle City Hall." *Sounds*, November 19, 1977. Accessed on June 23, 2011. www.rocksbackpages.com.

3. Burchill, "Gender and Other Trivia."

4. Burchill, "Jett in Sex Test Drama," *New Musical Express*, July 1977, 49.

5. Robert Hilburn, "Under the Rock, an Exciting Crop of Newcomers," *Los Angeles Times*, November 27, 1977, P93.

6. Russell.

7. "Runaways," *Billboard*, January 28, 1978.

8. Timothy Green Beckley, "Young, Hot and Ready to Rock," *Rock*, May 1978.

9. Robert Palmer, "Rock," *The New York Times*, January 9, 1978.

10. Simmons.

11. "Alive in L.A.," *Westways*, April 1978.

12. Bob Ross, "Ramones, Runaways, Root Boy Are Punky But Fun," *St. Petersburg Times*, March 4, 1978.

13. Ralph Alfonso, "An Encounter with rrrrrrrrunawayssssss," *Shades: New Wave in Toronto*, No. 2, 30.

14. Charley Hallman, "Runaways off in New Directions," *St. Paul Dispatch*, Jan. 19, 1978.

15. Brenda K., "The Runaways: A Lot More Than Horny Hype," *New Wave Rock*, February 1978, 36.

16. Brenda K, 32.

17. Kelly Pike, "Keep on Running," *Record Mirror*, July 22, 1978, 41.

18. Burchill, "Jett in Sex Test Drama."

19. Tony Parsons, "Flight from the Fleshpots," *New Musical Express*, July 29, 1978.

Chapter 25 And Now . . . the End

1. Chris Salewicz, "Sex Sells: The Girl Band That Changed Pop Forever," *The Independent*, March 19, 2010, http://www.independent.co.uk/arts-entertainment/music/features/sex-sells-the-girl-band-that-changed-pop-forever-1923481.html. Accessed Dec. 15, 2012.

2. Salewicz, "Interview with Joan Jett."

3. Brenda K., 36.

4. Sandy Robertson, "The Runaways: And Now the Runaways," *Sounds*, December 16, 1978.

Chapter 27 Bad Reputation

1. The Runaways, "All Right You Guys," https://www.youtube.com/watch?v=Yjnhi WmjnO4, accessed Dec. 9, 2012.

2. Salewicz, "And I Wonder."

Chapter 29 Midnight Music

1. Kristine McKenna, "Female Rockers—A New Breed," *Los Angeles Times*, June 18, 1978.

2. Salewicz, "Sex Sells."

3. Green Beckley.

4. Parsons, "Flight from the Fleshpots."

5. Farber.

6. Rosenberg, Ronnie Nina. "Daughters of Elvis." *The Aquarian*, August 1976, 27.

7. Rosenberg, 29.

8. Green Beckley.

Bibliography

All quotes are from the author's interviews unless otherwise indicated. Subjects interviewed include:

John Alcock	Bob Gruen	Ellen Pesavento
Pam Apostolou	Mike Hain	Lori Pesavento
Alice Bag	Kathleen Hanna	Ralph Peer
Rodney Bingenheimer	Gary Hoey	Iggy Pop
Don Bolles	Lavonne Hoyt	Thommy Price
Genevieve Broome	Susan Hoyt	Suzi Quatro
Julie Burchill	Joan Jett	Chuck Rubin
Cliff Burnstein	Theo Kogan	Donna Santisi
Bun E. Carlos	Mickey Kravitz	Dawn Schiller
Torry Castellano	Kari Krome	Floria Sigismondi
Shelley Clarke	Kenny Laguna	Erin Smith
Hernando Courtright	Jenny Lens	Kent Smythe
Cherie Currie	Denise Lisa	Chuck E. Starr
Darcy Diamond	Stella Maeve	Victory Tischler-Blue
Phanie Diaz	Toby Mamis	Lauren Varga
Brad Elterman	Earle Mankey	Jerry Venemann
Lisa Fancher	Dan McAllister	Don Waller
DD Faye	Iain McNay	Kathleen Warnock
Danielle Faye	Cliff Michalski	Dick Williams
Lita Ford	Jan Miller	Jeri Williams
Peggy Foster	Teri Miranti	Allison Wolfe
Kim Fowley	Nicole Panter	Omid Yamini
Jackie Fox	Bruce Patron	Ritchie Yorke
Mike Gormley	Phast Phreddie Patterson	

Some of these quotes have appeared in earlier articles by the author, including:

"Joan Jett." *Rolling Stone*, November 13, 1997.
"Queen of Noise: Joan Jett Headlines Vans Warped Tour This Weekend." *The Miami Herald*, June 23, 2006.
"Wild Thing: How the Runaways' Sandy West Was Lost." *L.A. Weekly*, March 19-25, 2010.

"Joan Jett." *Interview*, March 2010.
"Runaways Bassist Laurie McAllister dies." LATimes.com, September 2, 2011.
"Kim Fowley: Impresario, Svengali, Saint, Devil," *Los Angeles Times*, April 1, 2012.
"An Ex-Runaway Makes a Return," *Los Angeles Times*, June 16, 2012.

Other sources:

Agar, Gordie, Rodney Bingenheimer, and Cil Wilson. "Cherie Currie Interview." *JettSet*, January 1980.
Alfonso, Ralph. "An Encounter with rrrrrrunwayssssss." *Shades: New Wave in Toronto*, No. 2.
Allen, Jim. "QA: Joan Jett on Her Big Hits and Runaways Drama." *Rolling Stone*, December 17, 2008. Accessed on June 14, 2011. http://www.rollingstone.com/music/news/q-a-joan-jett-on-her-big-hits-and-runaways-drama-20081217.
Altman, Billy. "I Knew Kim Fowley and Lived: Confessions of a High Flying Jett." *Creem*, February 1981.
Anderson, Kelli. "Nine for IX." *Sports Illustrated*, May 7, 2012.
Atkinson, Terry. "Joan Jett: 3-Man Band at Whisky." *Los Angeles Times*, March 2, 1981.
Auslander, Philip. *Performing Glam Rock: Gender and Theatricality in Popular Music*. Ann Arbor: University of Michigan Press, 2006.
Bag, Alice. *Violence Girl*. Port Townsend, Washington: Feral Girl, 2011.
Baker, Cary. "Sixteen But Not Sweet." *Triad Magazine*, October 1976.
Bakhtin, Mikhail Mikhailovich. *Rabelais and His World*. Indiana University Press, 1985. Retrieved from Google Books, http://books.google.com/books/about/Rabelais_and_His_World.html?id=SkswFyhqRIMC, Aug. 24, 2012.
Bangs, Lester. *Mainlines, Blood Feasts, and Bad Taste: A Lester Bangs Reader*, John Morthland, ed., New York: Anchor, 2003.
Banham, Reyner, *Los Angeles: The Architecture of Four Ecologies*. Berkeley: University of California Press, 2001.
Banham, Reyner, *Reyner Banham Loves Los Angeles*, BBC, 1972.
Basham, Tim. "The Runaways Review (movie)." *Paste Magazine*, March 18, 2010. Accessed on June 14, 2011. http://www.pastemagazine.com/articles/2010/03/the-runaways-review.html.
Basher, Jack. "Catch a Wave? No, West Coast New Wave!" *Creem*, December 1977.
Barackman, Michael. "Runaways—Teenaged, Wild, and Braless." *Circus*, August 10, 1976.
Baudrillard, Jean. *America*. New York: New Left Books, 1990. 4th Edition.
Belloni, Matt. "The Secret Legal Battle Behind the Runaways." *Hollywood Reporter*, December 21, 2010. Accessed on November 16, 2011. http://www.hollywoodreporter.com/blogs/thr-esq/secret-legal-battle-runaways-63735.
Bingenheimer, Rodney. "Cherie Curie Interview." *JettSet*, July 1977.
Borzillo, Carrie. "Ex-Runaways Sue P'gram, Manager Fowley." *Billboard Magazine*, December 3, 1994.
Braunstein, Peter. "Hell Bent for Leather." March 2001.
Burchill, Julie. "Jett in Sex Test Drama." *NME*, July 1977.
Burchill, Julie. "Gender and Other Trivia." *NME*, November 19, 1978.
Burchill, Julie. "The Runaways Waitin' for the Night (Mercury)." *NME*, 1977.

Burchill, Julie, and Tony Parsons. *The Boy Looked at Johnny: The Obituary of Rock and Roll*. Boston: Faber and Faber, 1987.

Christgau, Georgia. "The Runaways." *Circus*, Sept. 13, 1976.

Christgau, Robert. "Untitled." *Playboy*, December 1993. Accessed June 28, 2011. Robertchristgau.com/xg/play/1993-12.php.

Christgau, Robert. "The Runaways: Consumer Guide Reviews."http://www.robertchrist-gau.com/get_artist.php?name=The+Runaways. Accessed March 11, 2013.

Christman, Ed. "Music Publisher Played Key Role in Launching Runaways." ABC News, May 3, 2010.

Clarke, Steve. "The Lovely Cherie Tells Thrills About the Runaways." *NME*, September 10, 1977.

Cohen, Aaron. "James Brown's Musicians Reflect On His Legacy". Downbeat.com, http://www.downbeat.com/jamesbrown.asp.

Connelly, Christopher. "Joan Jett Has the Last Laugh." *Rolling Stone*, April 29, 1982.

Cowan, Peter. "The Runaways: Trash Rock Gets Younger Every Day." *Oakland Tribune*, 1976.

Cromelin, Richard. "For the Jett Sett." *Los Angeles Times*, June 26, 1983.

Cromelin, Richard. "Jett, Ford Grab Runaways' Reins." *Los Angeles Times*, August 29, 1977.

Cromelin, Richard. "At The Starwood: Runaways Catch New Rock Wave." *Los Angeles Times*. Feb. 2,1976.

Currie, Cherie with Tony O'Neill. *Neon Angel: A Memoir of a Runaway*. New York: It Books, 2010.

Currie, Cherie and Neal Shusterman. *Neon Angel: The Cherie Currie Story*. Los Angeles: Price Stern Sloan, 1989.

Devenish, Colin. "The Runaways' Sad Song." *Rolling Stone*, July 29, 2004. http://www.rollingstone.com/music/news/the-runaways-sad-song-20040729.

Diamond, Darcy. "Cherie Currie?" *New York Rocker*, vol. 1, no. 10 November-December.

Didion, Joan. *Slouching Towards Bethlehem*. New York: Farrar, Straus and Giroux, 2008

Didion, Joan. *Where I'm Calling From*. New York: Alfred A. Knopf, 2003.

Ditlea, Steve. "Runaways Are First Girl Punk Rockers." *Playgirl*.

Doherty, Harry. "You Sexy Things!" *Melody Maker*, October 16, 1976.

Draw, Quick. "Cherie Currie: Her Last Interview as a Runaway." *Raw Power*, 1977.

Drummond, Andrew and Barry Powell. "Oh Boy! The Girl Rockers Turn the Guys on." *News of the World*, October 3, 1976.

Du Maurier, George. *Trilby*. Oxford: Oxford University Press, 2009.

Duncan, Robert. *The Noise: Notes from a Rock 'n' Roll Era*. New York: Ticknor and Fields, 1984.

Edmonds, Ben. "The Runaways: The Runaways." *Phonograph Record*, May 1976. Accessed on June 23, 2011. www.rocksbackpages.com.

Edmonds, Ben. "Fowley's Angels." *Mojo*, May 2000.

Epstein, Andrew. "Pop Movies: Runaway Hit to Movie Miss." *Los Angeles Times*, January 27, 1980.

Fancher, Lisa. "The Runaways." *Academy in Peril*, March-April 1977.

Fancher, Lisa. "Kim Fowley Tells All: Sex Death and the Pressure of Being God." *Street Life*, January 1, 1977.

Fancher, Lisa. "New Year's Eve with the Runaways & the Quick." *Street Life*, January 1, 1977.

Fancher, Lisa. "Are You Young and Rebellious Enough to Love the Runaways?" *Who Put the Bomp*, Spring 1976.

Farber, Jim. "Our Music Is All Crunch." *The Music Gig*, September 1976.

Ferren, Mick. "From Jailbait to Jes' Plain Bait." *NME*, October 2, 1976.

Farren, Mick. "The Runaways Queens of Noise (Mercury)." *NME*, January 29, 1977.

Farren, Mick. "Jailbait Behind Bars." *New Musical Express*, October 2, 1976.

Faye, D.D. "Rock Returns to the Whisky (For A While At Least…)". *Back Door Man*, December 1975.

Faye, D.D. "The Stars and The Runaways at the Whisky-a-Go-Go". *Back Door Man*, December 1975.

Fein, Art. "Runaways: The Only Hope for Rock n' Roll?" *The Los Angeles Free Press*, March 5-11, 1976.

Fortnam, Ian. "The Runaways/Queens of Noise/Live in Japan/Waitin' for the Night." *Classic Rock*, 2003. www.rocksbackpages.com.

Fowley, Kim. "The Thoughts of Chairman Kim." *Rock's Backpages*, 1999. www.rocksback pages.com.

Fowley, Kim. *Lord of Garbage*. New York: Kick Books, 2012.

Fuchs, Stephen. "Runaways Reflect Mercury West Coast Strength." *Cashbox*, June 5, 1976.

Gaitskill, Mary. "Joan Jett." *Interview*, August 2006.

Garr, Gillian G. *She's a Rebel: The History of Women in Rock & Roll*. New York: Seal Press, 1992.

Gold, Gary Pig. "Who Put The Bomp? Greg Shaw Of Course!" *Torpedopop*, October 2004. Accessed on June 23, 2011. www.rocksbackpages.com.

Goldstein, Patrick. "Lissome Lolitas or Teenage Trash?" *Creem*, 1977.

Green Beckley, Timothy. "Young, Hot and Ready to Rock." *Rock Magazine*, May 1978.

Greene, Chad. "From Iowa by the Sea to International City." *Long Beach Business Journal*. January 17, 2006.

Halberstam, Judith. *Female Masculinity*. Durham and London: Duke University Press, 1998.

Hallman, Charley. "Runaways Off in New Directions." *St. Paul Dispatch*, January 19, 1978.

Harrigan, Brian. "Hotline for Rock Safety." *Sound Check*, July 17, 1976.

Hay, Carla. "Runaways Tell Their Story in 'Edgeplay' Doc." *Billboard*, September 11, 2004.

Hepworth, David. "Falling Foul of Fowley?" 1976.

Hilburn, Robert. "Runaways: Young, Female, Fun." *Los Angeles Times*, May 22, 1976.

Hilburn, Robert. "Homegrown Punk-Rock Blossoming." *Los Angeles Times*, January 4, 1977.

Hilburn, Robert. "Under the Rock, an Exciting Crop of Newcomers." *Los Angeles Times*, Nov. 27, 1977.

Hilburn, Robert. "Joan Jett: Running Away from a Bad Reputation." *Los Angeles Times*, August 19, 1984.

Hilburn, Robert. "Runaways Showcase." *Los Angeles Times*, June 1, 1976.

Hilburn, Robert. "Pop Music 'The Menace and Charm of Punk Rock.'" *Los Angeles Times*, August 1, 1976.

Hilburn, Robert. "Jett's L.A Homecoming a Bittersweet One." *Los Angeles Times*, May 13, 1982.

Hilburn, Robert. "Skynyrd Album Live and Well." *Los Angeles Times*, September 18, 1976.

Hilburn, Robert. "Muddy Waters at High Tide Again." *Los Angeles Times*, March 1, 1977.

Hirshey, Gerri. *We Gotta Get Out of This Place: The True, Tough Story of Women in Rock.* New York: Atlantic Monthly Press, 2001.

Hoskyns, Barney. "Boulevard of Broken Dreams: A Trip Down the Sunset Strip." *Mojo*. January 1994.

Hoskyns, Barney. *Hotel California.* New Jersey: John Wiley & Sons, Inc., 2004

Hoskyns, Barney. *Waiting for the Sun.* New York: St. Martin's Press, 1996.

Hull, Robert A. "The Runaways: The Runaways." *Creem*. August 1976.

Ingham, Jonh. "Runaways (gasp): At Last An (groan) Objective (pant) View." *Sounds*, October 9, 1976. Accessed on June 23, 2011. www.Rocksbackpages.com/article. html?ArticleID=8336.

Isler, Scott. "L.A. Jets/The Runaways." *Crawdaddy*, 1976.

Jerome, Jim. "Teeny Queens of Rock: The Runaways." *People*, August 30, 1976.

Johnson, Connie. "Jett's 'Youth': Swagger and Self Doubt." *Los Angeles*, October 28, 1984.

Johnson, Derek. "Would You Let Your Brother Go Out With The Runaways?!?" *RAM*, November 5. no 44.

Johnson, Rick. "Runaways: Queens of Noise (Mercury)." *Creem*, April 1977.

K., Brenda. "The Runaways: A Lot More Than Horny Hype." *New Wave Rock*, February 1978.

Kent, Nick. *The Dark Stuff.* London: Penguin, 1994.

Krome, Kari. "The Runaways' New Years Eve Party." *Who Put the Bomp*, April 30, 1976.

Kubernik, Harvey. "Catching the Runaways." *Melody Maker*, November 5, 1977.

Kubernik, Harvey. "Runaway Girls." *Melody Maker*, July 17, 1976.

Kubernik, Harvey. "The Runaways' Bad Reputation." *Goldmine*, May 7, 2010. Accessed on June 23, 2011. http://www.goldminemag.com/features/the-runaways-bad-reputation.

Kubernik, Harvey. "Writing The Runaways' Stop." *Goldmine*, May 7, 2010.

Kubernik, Harvey. "The Queens of Noise." *Spin*, November 2001.118-122.

Kubernik, Harvey. "Kim Fowley: The Man Behind The Runaways." *Goldmine*, May 7, 2010. 36, 10.

Lababedi, Iman. "Joan: The Public's Vindication of an Ex-Runaway." *Creem*, June 1982.

Lababedi, Iman. "Lita Ford's Got Blood If You Want It." *Creem*, August 1983.

Lappen, John. "Joan Jett: The Original Riot Grrrl Re-enters the Rock Wars with Warner Debut." *Music Connection*, June 6-19, 1994.

Lee, Chris. "Now They're Vamping as the 'Runaways'." *Los Angeles Times*, January 17, 2010.

Lens, Jenny. *Punk Pioneers; When Punk Was Fun.* New York: Universe Publishing, 2008.

Lindblad, Peter. "The Runaways' 'Cherry Bomb' Gets a Chainsaw." *Goldmine*, April 9, 2010.

Lindsay, Christy. "Sandy West, 47." *Billboard*, November 4, 2006.

Longworth, Karina. "Sex, Drugs, and Feminist Thought." *The Village Voice*, March 17–March 23, 2010.

Luther, Marylou. "Shock Chic: The Punk Persuasion." *Los Angeles Times*, July 13 1977.

Lyne, Adrian, Dir. *Foxes*. Casablanca, 1980.

Manning, Kara. "You Can't Always Get What You Want." *American Theater*, February, 2001.

McGee, David. "The Runaways," *Rolling Stone*, July 29, 1976.

McKenna, Kristine. "Female Rockers—A New Breed." *Los Angeles Times*, June 18, 1978.

Merrill, Kevin. "A Day in the Life of Kim Fowley." *Billboard Magazine*, 1977

Michalski, Cliff. "The Runaways: 16 and Savaged." *Scene Magazine*, July 1976.

Morgan, A.J. "An Evening with the Queens of Noise." *The Marquee*, January 1977.

Needs, Kris. "The Runaways: The Runaways." *ZigZag*, September 1976.

O'Brien, Lucy. *Shebop*. New York: Penguin Books, 1995

O'Dair, Barbara. *Trouble Girls: The Rolling Stone Book of Women in Rock*. New York: Random House Press, 1997.

Palmer, Robert. "Teenage Runaways Play to Fantasies." *The New York Times*, August 4, 1976. 15.

Palmer, Robert. "Rock." *The New York Times*, January 28, 1978.

Patterson, Phast Phreddie. "Phast Freddie's Hollywood (Circa 1973-1983)," *Rock's Backpages*, October 1996. www.rocksbackpages.com.

Parker, Howard and Chris Rowley. "My Style of Cock: Being an Interview with Kim Fowley, in the Company of Jeff Beck." *International Times*, 1972.

Parsons, Tony. "Been a Broad Lately?" *NME*, 1977.

Parsons, Tony. "Flight from the Fleshpots." *NME*, July 29, 1978.

Patterson, Phast Phreddie. "Local Action," *Back Door Man*, December 1975.

Patterson, Phast Phreddie. "The Runaways—Face Shifting," *Back Door Man*, December 1977.

Patterson, Phast Phreddie. "Phast Freddie's Hollywood (Circa 1973–1983)." *Rock's Backpages*, October 1996.

Patterson, Phast Phreddie. "Local Action," *Back Door Man*, April 1976.

Paul, Scott. "Runaways Ready to Go." *The Enterprise Sun and News*, Wednesday, May 31, 1978.

Plagens, Peter. "Ecology of Evil." *Artforum*, December 1972.

Pierce, Justin. "Cherie Drops Bomb on Runaways." *Sounds*, August 20, 1977.

Pike, Kelly. "Keep on Running." *Record Mirror*, July 22, 1978.

Prato, Greg. "Lita Ford Returns With Sexual LP, Explains Runaways Movie Rift." *Rolling Stone*, July 8, 2009.

Pond, Steve. "Ford's Soft Spot for Hard Rock." *Los Angeles*, July 24, 1984.

Pond, Steve. "A Runaway Returns." *Los Angeles Times*. June 9, 1985.

Quatro, Suzi. *Unzipped*. London: Hodder & Soughton, 2007.

Ralph, Alfonso. "An Encounter with rrrrrrrrrrrunawaysssssss." *Shades: New Wave in Toronto*, March 1978.

Riley, Tim. *Fever: How Rock 'n' Roll Transformed Gender in America*. New York: St. Martin's Press, 2004.

Robertson, Sandy. "The Rock's Backpages Flashback: The Runaways." March 24, 1977. www.rocksbackpages.com.

Robertson, Sandy. "Kim Fowley; The Dorian Gray of Rock 'n' Roll." *Sounds*, August 6, 1977. Accessed on June 23, 2011. www.rocksbackpages.com.

Robertson, Sandy. "The Runaways: Waitin' For the Night." *Sounds*, November 19, 1977.

Robertson, Sandy. "Runaways: A Primer for The New Runaways." *Sounds*, September 10, 1977.

Robertson, Sandy. "No Record Company, No Producer—But The Runaways Will Rise Again." *Sounds*, July 1, 1978.

Robertson, Sandy. "The Runaways: And Now The Runaways." *Sounds*, December 16, 1978.

Robertson, Sandy. "Cherie and Marie Currie: Messin' With The Boys (Capitol)." *Sounds*, February 2, 1980. Accessed on June 23, 2011. www.rocksbackpages.com.

Robertson, Sandy. "The Runaways: The Best of (Mercury)." *Sounds*, October 2, 1982. Accessed on June 23, 2011. www.rocksbackpages.com.

Robertson, Sandy. "The Runaways: Live in Japan." *Sounds*, 1977. Accessed on June 23, 2011. www.rocksbackpages.com.

Robinson, Lisa. "The Runaways: Naughty Nymphets Leave Lisa Cold." *Creem*, November 1976.

Robinson, Lisa. "Girls Will Be Boys." *NME*, August 14, 1976.

Roeser, Steve. "Kim Fowley: Living and Dying in LA". *Goldmine*, November 26, 1993.

Rosenberg, Ronnie Nina. "Daughters of Elvis." *The Aquarian*, August 1976.

Ross, Bob. "Ramones, Runaways, Root Boy Are Punky but Fun." *St. Petersburg Florida Times*, March 4, 1978.

Rubberox, Schizophrenia. "Runaways Runaway," *The Wasteland*, November 1977.

Russell, Rosalind. "In at the Deep End With the Runaways." *The Record Mirror*, July 22, 1978.

Salewicz, Chris. "The Runaways: And I Wonder...I Wah Wah Wah Wah Wonder." *NME*, July 24, 1976.

Salewicz, Chris. "Sex Sells: The Girl Band that Changed Pop Forever." *The Independent*, March 19 2010.

Savage, Jon "We Have Lift Off!" *Mojo*, September 2011.

Scanlan, John. *Van Halen: Exuberant California, Zen Rock 'n' Roll*. London: Reaktion Books Ltd., 2012

Schulman, Bruce, J. *The Seventies: The Great Shift in American Culture, Society, and Politics*. New York: The Free Press, 2001

Sekuler, Eliot. "Runaways: Hot on Zep's Heels." *Circus*, April 27, 1976.

Sigismondi, Floria, Dir. *The Runaways*. River Road Entertainment, 2010.

Simmons, Sylvie. "Bring on the Nubiles: The Ramones/The Runaways: Santa Monica Civic, Los Angeles." *Sounds*, February 18, 1978.

Soja, Edward J. *Thirdspace*. Cambridge: Blackwell, 1996.

Spitz, Mark and Brendan Mullen. *We Got the Neutron Bomb*. New York: Three Rivers Press, 2001.

Stick, Wesley. "Waitin' for the Night." *Rolling Stone*. March 9, 1978.

Sugerman, Danny. "The Runaways." *Sounds*, August 7, 1976.

Sutcliffe, Phil. "The Runaways: Newcastle City Hall." *Sounds*, November 19, 1977. Accessed on June 23, 2011. www.rocksbackpages.com.

Thompson, Dave. *Bad Reputation: The Unauthorized Biography of Joan Jett.* Milwaukee: Backbeat Books, 2011.

Thornhill, Sherri. "Breaking News: Joan Jett Lawsuit Against Jackie Fox Dismissed." Examiner.com, February 16, 2010. Accessed on April 24, 2010. www.examiner.com/blog/printexaminerarticles.cfm?section.

Thorson, Susan. "Lita Ford Rocks at Rock The Bayou Former Site of Astro World." *All Access Magazine*, September 18, 2008. Accessed on June 24, 2011. http://www.allaccessmagazine.com/vol6/issue15/lita_ford.html.

Tischler-Blue, Victory, Dir. *Edgeplay: A Film About the Runaways.* Sacred Dogs, 2004.

Travers, Peter. "The Runaways." *Rolling Stone Magazine*, March 18, 2010.

Uhelszki, Jaan. "Punk Mama." *Guitar World*, June 2006.

Uhelszki, Jaan. "Fowley's Angels." *Mojo*.

Vineyard, Jennifer. "Hookups, Meltdowns, & Punk Rock: The Runaways' True Tale." *Rolling Stone*, April 6, 2010.

Wald, Gayle. "How Svengali Lost His Jewish Accent," *Sounding Out*, September 26, 2011. http://soundstudiesblog.com/2011/09/26/how-svengali-lost-his-jewish-accent/.

Weber, Theon. "The Runaways-Dead End Justice." *Stylus Magazine*, September 5, 2007. Accessed on June 14, 2011. http://www.stylusmagazine.com/articles/seconds/the-runaways-dead-end-justice.htm

Young, Doug. "Move Over Blondie, Here Come The Runaways!" *Rocket Magazine*, July 1978.

Young, Charles M. "Run-run-run-run-runaways." *Crawdaddy*, October 1976.

Zachary, Donna. "I Want To Be a Rock 'n' Roll Star." *Pair*, April 1977.

"Queens of Noise," *Bump N Grind*, number 1.

"Random Notes," *Rolling Stone*, July 14, 1977.

"Kim Fowley: The Wasteland Interview, Part Two." *The Wasteland*, November 1977.

"Runaways," *Billboard*, Jan. 28, 1978.

"The Gymslip Rockers," 1976.

"Runaways Concert, Armadillo Texas." *Records Magazine*, September 1976.

"The Runaways: Teen Girls' Rock Revolution." *Young n' Loving Teen*, September 1976.

"Runaways Life Begins at 16." *Circus Magazine*, November 25, 1976.

"An Evening with Joan Jett." *Bump N Grind*, 1977, issue 2.

"Los Angeles & The Runaways." *RAM*, March 11, 1977.

"Au Revoir, Cherie." July 1977.

"Alive in L.A." *Westways*, April 1978.

"Joan Jett: At 21, a Survivor." *Los Angeles Times*, May 10, 1980.

"Confessions of a Teenage Runaway." *Melody Maker*, June 12, 1982.

"Lita Ford Returns With "Sexual" LP, Explains Runaways Movie Rift." *Rolling Stone*. Accessed on June 14, 2011. www.Rollingstone.com/music/news/lita-ford-returns-with-sexual-lp-explans-runaways-movie-rift-20090708?print=true.

"The Runaways' Sad Song." *Rolling Stone*. Acessed on June 14, 2011. www.Rollingstone.com/music/news/the-runaways-sad-song-20040729?print=true.

Acknowledgments

For a long time, it seemed like I would never get this book done—like the Runaways curse was going to take me down, too. I wouldn't have made it without a formidable support team.

Sarah Lazin has been my faithful agent for going on two decades now, helping me achieve a respectable shelf-full of books, including this one. Ben Schafer waited patiently for the manuscript then made it better.

My colleagues at Loyola Marymount University supported me, emotionally and financially, as I struggled to write while simultaneously figuring out teaching. Thanks to Dean Paul Zeleza for the research grants, chairs Paul Harris and David Killoran for the flexibility and travel support, and Jeffrey Wilson and the sisters of the Immaculate Heart Center—the queens of tranquility—for the simultaneously fruitful and nourishing retreats (though I always felt conspicuous cranking the tunes).

This book began as a thesis on Sandy West while I was a mid-career Master's student at the University of Southern California's Annenberg School of Communication and Journalism. Thanks to professors Tim Page, Josh Kun, and Karen Tongson, my "committee," and to Sasha Anawalt, arts journalism goddess. Geneva Overholser, Michael Parks, and Roberto Suro also helped guide me through my nine-month return to classroom learning; David E. James shrugged his shoulders at me handing in "Girls on Film" as a final paper. Salut, Captain Freckles.

The *L.A. Weekly* published a shortened version of that thesis, "Wild Thing." Thanks to Randall Roberts for the gig and to Tom Christie for seeing it through. The *Los Angeles Times* has also supported me in this reportorial journey, publishing parts of my interviews with Lita Ford and Kim Fowley and my obituary of Laurie McAllister; thanks to editor Lorraine Ali. *Interview, Rolling Stone,* and the *Miami Herald* all published earlier interviews of mine with Joan Jett, excerpts of which appear in these pages.

I'm immensely grateful to everyone I interviewed for their time and memories. Despite our mutual initial misgivings, Kim Fowley became a great hype man and irrepressible fountain of quotes. Jackie Fox was also extremely generous with her time and memories. Kari Krome was an excellent tour guide. Kenny Laguna was particularly helpful with my initial Sandy West research and making connections. Geri and Dick Williams cracked open old photo books featuring their daughter Sandy, which I'm sure was not easy. Lori, Ellen, and Teri also helped me piece together their sister's brave but tragic life.

Several fans and friends of the Runaways opened up their hearts and their archives. Thanks to Omid Yamini (who compiled the discography), Lauren Varga, Jerry Venemann, Danna Taylor, Shane Greentree, Ute Beginn, and the keepers of the flame at California Paradise.

A string of research assistants retrieved old articles and transcribed hours of interviews: Thanks Hala Murphy, Sara Seltzer, Talia Avakian, and Donald Dilliplane for the heavy lifting. Thanks also to LMU's William Hannon Library and Rock's Back Pages for helping me sort through the past.

Marco Pavia guided the manuscript into the book you now hold in your hand. Matt Auerbach made it clearer.

The Fabulous Fictionaires remain my ultimate writing team: Thanks Vivien for all the great copy-editing catches, and Jana for the love. Jeanne Fury always makes me laugh and feel like my work may not be a total waste of time. Both gifts are priceless.

My husband Bud and son Cole put up with numerous weekends and late nights of me working instead of canoodling as well as with interminable answering machine messages pronouncing, "This is Kim Fowley …" Karlie and Kenda reminded me just what it's like to be a young woman, making noise.

I want to thank my cats and dog. Is that wrong?

And of course, thanks to the Queens of Noise for the ball busting, barrier breaking, and head banging. As Don Waller says, pioneers always pay the price. I hope this book provides you some reward.

The Runaways: Select Worldwide Discography 1976–1981

By Omid Yamini

The Albums

The Runaways
Mercury Records — 1976
Tracks: Cherry Bomb, You Drive Me Wild, Is It Day or Night?, Thunder, Rock & Roll, Lovers, American Nights, Blackmail, Secrets, Dead End Justice
Released in: U.S., Canada, U.K., Japan, France, Spain, Australia, New Zealand, Brazil, Korea

Queens of Noise
Mercury Records — 1977
Tracks: Queens of Noise, Take It or Leave It, Midnight Music, Born To Be Bad, Neon Angels on the Road to Ruin, I Love Playin' with Fire, California Paradise, Hollywood, Heartbeat, Johnny Guitar
Released in: U.S., Canada, U.K., Japan, Germany, Holland, France, Norway, Australia, Brazil, China, Turkey

Live in Japan
Mercury Records — 1977
Tracks: Queens of Noise, California Paradise, All Right You Guys, Wild Thing, Gettin' Hot, Rock & Roll, You Drive Me Wild, Neon Angels on the Road to Ruin, I Wanna Be Where the Boys Are, Cherry Bomb, American Nights
Released in: Japan, Canada, Holland, France, Norway, Italy, Australia (retitled Live!)

Waitin' for the Night
Mercury Records — 1977
Tracks: Little Sister, Wasted, Gotta Get Out Tonight, Wait for Me, Fantasies, School Days, Trash Can Murders, Don't Go Away, Waitin' for the Night, You're Too Possessive
Released in: U.S., Canada, U.K., Japan, Germany, Holland, France, Norway, Australia, New Zealand

And Now... The Runaways
Mercury Records — 1978
Tracks: Saturday Night Special, Eight Days a Week, Mama Weer All Crazee Now, I'm a
    Million, Right Now, Takeover, My Buddy and Me, Little Lost Girls, Black Leather
Released in: U.K., Canada, Japan, Germany, Holland, Norway, New Zealand, Italy (later
    reissue)

Little Lost Girls
Year: 1981
Rhino Records — 1981
Tracks: Right Now, Mama Weer All Crazee Now, Saturday Night Special, Takeover,
    Black Leather, My Buddy and Me, Little Lost Girls, I'm a Million
Released in: U.S.
Note: This is the U.S. reissue of "And Now...The Runaways" with different track listing
    and order.

Flaming Schoolgirls
Mercury — 1980
Tracks: Intro, Strawberry Fields, C'Mon, Hollywood Cruisin', Blackmail, Is It Day Or
    Night?, Here Comes The Sun, Hollywood Dream, Don't Abuse Me, I Love Playin'
    with Fire, Secrets
Released in: U.K., Canada, Germany, Portugal, Greece, Sweden

The Singles

"Cherry Bomb"/"American Nights" b/w blank
Mercury Records — 1976
Released in: U.S.
Note: This was a promo one-sided test pressing sent out with the first press kit to intro-
    duce the band, probably the very first Runaways vinyl produced!

"Cherry Bomb" b/w "Cherry Bomb"
Mercury Records — 1976
Released in: U.S.
Note: promo single

"Cherry Bomb" b/w "Blackmail"
Mercury Records — 1976
Released in: U.S., U.K., Japan, Germany, Brazil, New Zealand

"Cherry Bomb" b/w "Is It Day or Night?"
Mercury Records — 1976
Released in: France, Spain
"Blackmail"/"Cherry Bomb" b/w "American Nights"/"Secrets"
Mercury Records — 1976
Released in: Germany

"Secrets" b/w "Rock & Roll"
Mercury Records — 1976
Released in: Japan

"Queens of Noise" b/w "Born To Be Bad"
Mercury Records — 1977
Released in: U.K.

"Heartbeat" b/w "Neon Angels on the Road to Ruin"
Mercury Records — 1977
Released in: U.S., Australia

"I Love Playin' with Fire" b/w "Neon Angels on the Road to Ruin"
Mercury Records — 1977
Released in: Australia

"I Love Playin' with Fire" b/w "Queens of Noise"
Mercury Records — 1977
Released in: France

"Midnight Music" b/w "Neon Angels on the Road to Ruin"
Mercury Records — 1977
Released in: Germany

"Neon Angels on the Road to Ruin" b/w "Queens of Noise"
Mercury Records — 1977
Released in: Japan

"Neon Angels on the Road to Ruin" b/w "Take It or Leave It"
Mercury Records — 1977
Released in: Austria

"All Right You Guys" (live) b/w "Blackmail" (live)
Mercury Records — 1977
Released in: Japan

"You Drive Me Wild" (live) b/w "Rock & Roll" (live)
Mercury Records — 1977
Released in: France

"Queens of Noise" (live) b/w "Queens of Noise" (live)
Mercury Records — 1977
Released in: Italy

"School Days" b/w "Wasted"
Mercury Records — 1977
Released in: U.K., Germany, Australia

"Little Sister" b/w "School Days"
Mercury Records — 1977
Released in: Japan

"Trash Can Murders"/"School Days"/"Don't Go Away" b/w "You're Too Possessive"/
"Waitin' for the Night"
Mercury Records — 1977
Released in: Germany
Notes: A special five-song EP released by a record club.

"Mama Weer All Crazee Now" b/w "My Buddy and Me"
Mercury Records — 1978
Released in: Holland

"Mama Weer All Crazee Now" b/w "Right Now"
Mercury Records — 1978
Released in: France

"American Nights" b/w "Secrets"
Mercury Records — 1978
Released in: Brazil

"Mama Weer All Crazee Now" b/w "Eight Days a Week"
Overseas Records — 1979
Released in: Japan

"Right Now" b/w "Black Leather"
Cherry Red Records — 1979
Released in: U.K.

Note from discographer (Omid Yamini):

This is a select discography of the main Runaways albums and singles released world-wide between 1976–1981. I've been collecting everything I could find on the Runaways for close to twenty years now, and have listed all the countries from which I've found pressings of these records—but there could be more. Every time I think I've seen and know about all the variations and pressings of these records, another one surfaces—which just goes to show how far their reach was! The fact that they were getting their music released in countries like Turkey and China in the '70s is pretty amazing.

It's also interesting to note what singles were released in different countries by the labels. In the U.S., Mercury only released one single off each of the first two LPs, and didn't even bother releasing one off the third LP. In Japan they released no less than six different singles for the band in a three-year period! Though their main "parent" record company was Mercury Worldwide, some of these records were licensed by subsidiaries like Philips. If you want more specific information on the different pressings, please look it up online; there's a ton of information out there.

Credits

Index